This book is dedicated to:
God the Father, the Lord Jesus Christ, and the Holy Spirit;
the Holy God who saved this wretched sinner, It has been such
an amazing priviledge for me to write this book...
and
to my lovely wife Bev, thank you for standing by me, without
you this book would have been impossible.

Table of Contents

The Spirit of Prophecy

Second Edition

**A Ground-Breaking Analysis of the Bible's End Times
Prophecies**

by Daniel Knezacek

The Spirit of Prophecy - Second Edition, by Daniel G.K. Knezacek. ISBN 978-1-60264-885-2 (softcover); 978-1-60264-886-9.

Published 2011 by Virtualbookworm.com Publishing Inc., P.O. Box 9949, College Station, TX 77842, US.

All illustrations by Dan Knezacek ©2010.

All Quotations are from the Authorized Version of the Holy Bible, unless otherwise noted.

The author's website: www.thespiritofprophecy.ca

Printed in the United States of America.

And I fell at his feet to worship him. And he said unto me, See thou do it not: I am thy fellowservant, and of thy brethren that have the testimony of Jesus: worship God: for the testimony of Jesus is the spirit of prophecy.

Revelation 19:10

Introduction

My introduction to the subject of prophecy came while I was a teenager, in the nineteen seventies. My parents were Evangelical Christians of the Baptist persuasion, and so I was exposed to writers and speakers who were generally Biblical literalists or Dispensational Premillennialists. Over the years since, this interest has been a constant companion, sometimes taking up more, and other times less time, but always present.

This work will be somewhat complicated at times. I ask you to bear with me. The Author of the Bible is none other than the Author of DNA, the most densely compact, and complicated, information system known to man. Our scientists, though they have been able to observe some facts about DNA, have yet to figure out how it works to any great depth. God is far more intelligent than all of our scientists combined!

That same Mind is the one who has given us the many prophecies in the bible. He has put His Word together in such a way that some prophecies are impossible to understand, unless you are led to the truth by the Holy Spirit. The gospel itself is very simple, but there are layers, or depths, to the Word of God. If we reject the simple things He will block the more complex things from our understanding, and even when we accept the gospel, in all its simplicity, He will not reveal anything unless it is His timing. I believe that He has revealed some things to me, for that very reason, because He wants this information to come to light...now!

A word about the Bible; You can't see it unless you believe it! If you do not approach the Word of God with an attitude of faith, you will not see what He has for you. In order to understand the things of God you need to make a decision to believe it, first. Some people believe some things that the Bible says, but stumble at certain points. God can only lead you as far as you are willing to follow. Before we go on I urge you to decide to believe the whole Word of God, even if it does not appear to make sense. Belief comes first, and understanding will follow, though you may never understand everything about Him. He will always leave some mystery for you.

I have found that when following leads in the Bible, you can be led in several directions at once. One passage may be linked to three, five, or eight different verses in the same, or other books. Like the branches of a tree, the leads can diverge over and over again, yet still remain connected to the trunk. Rather than be like a concordance, which merely tells you where the links are, I felt the need to explain why, and how, these links are important to the study of Eschatology.

Sometimes the links do not even seem to be present, initially, until you dig a little deeper. Some passages were puzzled over for well over thirty years, such as the phrase *"the desire of women"* found in Daniel 11:37. No, I did not think of it continuously for thirty years, but every time I was confronted with it, I found the explanations given rang hollow. There was something just not right. Ultimately, I found that the common interpretations of this phrase, as found in many modern Bible paraphrase versions, are incorrect. God meant something else entirely!

Daniel's statement that *"the people of the prince that shall come shall destroy the city and the sanctuary"* in Daniel 9:26, has led many to the conclusion that the Antichrist shall come from Rome. Everyone knows that it was the Roman armies that destroyed Jerusalem and the Temple, in 70 AD. My first question was, *"which nations were represented in the Roman army that destroyed Jerusalem?"* The book of Acts (22:28) tells us that there were soldiers in the Roman armies, who had origins somewhere other than Rome. It is a well known fact that Rome was not large enough to control the entire empire without help. I found that Josephus corroborates this idea, and, as an eye witness, has some surprising observations of the destruction of Jerusalem, which are very relevant to the study of this prophecy.

If the Antichrist does not come from Rome, does this mean that the Church of Rome is a true Christian Church, or is let off the hook? Who, or what, is the Harlot of Revelation 17, and 18? Why are there two chapters dedicated to the one Harlot? Could there actually be two Harlot cities? These are other questions we need to take a look at.

When Jesus spoke of *"Wars and rumours of wars"* as a sign of the end, was He just referring to a general condition of warfare, as is commonly thought, or was He referring to specifically prophesied wars? When He said *"Let no man deceive you"*, was He only referring to those who claim to be Christ, or was he also referring to the signs of the times? Is it possible that the *"signs of the times"* could be misunderstood? Is it possible that someone could say *"We are in the Tribulation period, and it began on such-and-such a day"*, when in reality it has not? How do we know?

Israel has been involved in several wars since her rebirth as a nation in 1948. How do we know which, if any, are prophetically significant?

Is it possible that someone will point to a powerful world leader, who fits many of the common ideas of the Antichrist, and say, *"this is the Antichrist"*, when in fact he is not? At the time many thought Hitler was the Antichrist, and Napoleon Bonaparte, and today many still believe Nero was the man in question. So, why couldn't it happen again?

Regarding the ten nations of Nebuchadnezzar's dream in Daniel chapter 2, also referred to in Daniel chapter 8, and the book of Revelation; How do we know which ten nations are being referred to? What if there is more than one ten nation confederacy?

When will the rapture of the Church occur? Is the devil actually preparing a lie to explain away the rapture, even as we speak? Could he actually be preparing more than one lie, for more than one group of people? Is he doing this under our noses?

While many of these were my own questions, sometimes family members and friends, also asked questions about prophecy, which caused me to do further study. Sometimes I would make a statement, and the answer would come back; *"Is that so?"* or "how do you know?" which would result in more study. Sometimes I would have to admit that I had spoken too hastily, but other times I found that there was substantial biblical evidence for my statements.

Over the years, as I came across answer after answer, I frequently said to myself, *"that's interesting"*, and filed it away in my mind. It made bible study very interesting, and I spoke about them with family and acquaintances, but it rarely went farther than that. Some of the answers I have found were startling, and even shocking to my western sensibilities, however as I continued studying I began to feel as if God wanted me to write about it. Ultimately, I came to the realization that the answers I have been given are not for me alone, but were meant to be shared with the whole world.

If I could sum up the thesis of this book, it is that the devil is real, and always has his counterfeits. His counterfeits are aimed primarily at Christians, since everyone else is already deceived. Because Christians usually know something about the Word of God, it is the purpose of the devil to make them think that biblical prophecy has already been fulfilled. He will try to convince people that the period Jesus referred to as "wars and rumours of wars" is actually the Tribulation period. In order to do this he will have to orchestrate events in a way that closely approximates the real

Tribulation events.

The bible does not specifically refer to this time period as the Great Tribulation, because it is not the Great Tribulation of God, but it does mention this time-frame many times. This book will examine the devil's *"Pseudo-Tribulation"*, and compare it to the real *"Time of Jacob's Trouble"*. While many claim that there is no prophecy that needs to be fulfilled before the rapture of the Church, the bible does indeed say that there will be signs before that event, though no man will be able to know the exact date. We will spend some time examining those signs.

A Word About the Bible Version Used in the Production of this Book

The King James Bible has been used almost exclusively throughout this work. I have found that the Text, translators, and translation methods, used in the Authorized Version are all superior to those used in the modern versions. Prophecy is actually clearer in the AV than it is in the NIV, RSV, NKJV, ESV, NASB, etc. Not only is prophecy clearer, but so is the gospel! This is simply amazing considering that the AV was four hundred years old in 2011!

I used the NIV almost exclusively for some twelve years, but have discarded it in favour of the AV. Every time I pick up a new version I am amazed at what looks, to me, like an attack on the Word of God. It is the same with all the new versions. I recently purchased a copy of the AV7, which claims to be an update of the AV, and after checking out some commonly corrupted passages I have not bothered to use it again.

Accordingly, I have included a lot of Scripture in this book. I know many in the western world have discarded the AV in favour of the new versions, and so this is for you. I encourage you to compare the quotes from the AV with your new version, if you are still using one. I think you will be amazed at the difference.

I do not think it is possible to get the true meaning of prophecy from the modern versions. You might understand some prophecies, but many are corrupted beyond recognition! The *"translators"* thought they knew what was being said, and gave us a paraphrase of their own thoughts. So much for them being *"clearer"*!

Let's do a quick comparison of Daniel 11:37. Here are three old versions, The AV, The Geneva Bible, and the Douay Rheims Catholic

Bible, and four new versions, the NIV, the ESV, the New Century Version, and the God's Word Version;

> *Neither shall he regard the God of his fathers, <u>nor the desire of women</u>, nor regard any god: for he shall magnify himself above all. (Authorized Version - King James Bible)*

> *Neither shall he regard the God of his fathers, nor the desires of women, nor care for any God: for he shall magnifie himselfe aboue all. [Geneva Bible 1599]*

> *And he shall make no account of the God of his fathers: <u>and he shall follow the lust of women</u>, and he shall not regard any gods: for he shall rise up against all things (Douay Rheims, 1582 & 1609)*

> *He will show no regard for the gods of his fathers or for the one desired by women, nor will he regard any god, but will exalt himself above them all. (New International Version)*

> *He shall pay no attention to the gods of his fathers, or to the one beloved by women. He shall not pay attention to any other god, for he shall magnify himself above all (English Standard Version)*

> *The king of the North will not care about the gods his ancestors worshiped or the god that women worship. He won't care about any god. Instead, he will make himself more important than any god. (New Century Version)*

> *He will have no interest in the gods of his ancestors or desire for women. He will have no interest in any god, because he will make himself greater than anyone else. (God's Word)*

Here we have utter confusion. The AV and Geneva bible tell us that the Antichrist, as a lawmaker, will not care for the desires of women. The Douay tells us that he will be a womanizer. The NIV, ESV, and NCV claim that he won't care for the god that women worship, and the "God's Word" translation tells us that he will not desire women, like a homosexual. There is no way that all these versions could be the Word of God. If they are, then God is very confused!

The AV and Geneva Bible are giving us the literal translation of the original language. That is, they simply translate word-for word from the original, and let the reader figure out what is being said. The truth is that, in this verse, the popular NKJV and NASB also give the literal translation of this passage, further evidence in favor of the AV, but the rest of the bibles quoted are giving a paraphrase.

In order for paraphrase to work as a translation method, the translator needs to understand exactly what the author is saying. While the translators of the NIV, ESV, Douay, God's Word, and NCV, imagined that they knew what was being said, the truth is that they did not. They inserted their own interpretations into scripture, ensuring that this generation would be the most confused, about the Antichrist and his policies, as well as the gospel of Jesus Christ.

Did the Antichrist's ancestors worship many gods or one God? According to the new versions, the Antichrist must come from a polythesitic family. Specifically It must be a family that had a belief in many gods, for many generations. This would rule out a Catholic, Protestant, Jewish, or Muslim family. All these faiths hold to one God.

Both the Geneva bible and the AV separate the God of gods in verse 36, from the God of his fathers in verse 37, with the word "neither", thus indicating that the God of his fathers could be a monotheistic God, and yet not the God of Gods. These two versions allow that the Antichrist could come from a Muslim family, but the new versions indicate that he would have to come from a polytheistic, family.

What god is worshiped exclusively by women? Most women in my life are Christians. They worship Jesus Christ. I do not know of too many women who worship a God different than their husband's or father's God. New Agers worship Gaia, or Sophia, but these goddesses are also worshiped by men. The new versions render this passage into gibberish. Why would it matter if the Antichrist did not concern himself with the god desired by women? Does such a god have any significance in the modern world? Just because words and phrases may have different possible interpretations, it does not mean that every possibility was meant by the author.

Notice that there seems to be a digression, where the subject goes from the God of his fathers, to the desire of women, and then back to point out that he will exalt himself above all gods. There seems to be a connection between the God of his fathers, and the desire of women. This is not referring to a *"God of women"*, but to his policy as a lawmaker, with respect to a policy regarding the desire of women, practiced by the followers of the God of his fathers. The answer is embedded in Scripture, and can be found, if we would only ask the Author.

We will discuss this issue in greater depth in chapter 8, but I wanted to point out one of the profound, and subtle, changes in the new versions.

The Bible has something very specific to say. Its language relates to the real world. It is not subject to interpretation, except the interpretation of the Holy Spirit Himself, and His interpretations are always backed up by Scripture. There are no real contradictions in the Word of God at all. Apparent contradictions always have a solution, which are revealed when the Author is consulted.

My point is simply that I want the most accurate, reliable, Bible which is available, and will not settle for less, and neither should you. The AV has stood the test of time, which is something no other bible can boast of. If I have to spend a little time learning some old English words, this is a small sacrifice to make for the sake of truth. The truth is more important than the pride, or lifestyle, of modern bible translators. My life, and yours, are at stake!

This is my commitment to you; I will tell you the truth, even if it is politically incorrect, even if it makes me look bad, even if it makes you angry with me. The truth is more important than any person on earth!

Don't take my word for it. I hope, and expect, that my readers will check out everything by the Word of God. Be like a Berean and compare what I am saying to the Bible. Read, and reread, every passage in context. Pray about everything!

These (Bereans) were more noble than those in Thessalonica, in that they received the word with all readiness of mind, and searched the scriptures daily, whether those things were so.(Acts 17:11)

One

The Foundation of Prophecy

All scripture is given by inspiration of God, and is profitable for doctrine, for reproof, for correction, for instruction in righteousness: (2 Timothy 3:16)

The ultimate issue, in scripture interpretation, is one of authority. Who has the authority to interpret Scripture? There are men who tell us that they alone have authority to interpret the Bible. They are telling us that we can't really trust the literal/natural sense of the words placed there by God and they must be filtered by themselves before we can understand what is being said.

There are other men who tell us that scripture is just a human book and modern scholars, "*science*", and academics have more authority. If we examine these men we find that what they are teaching today is different than what they taught five years ago. Someone writes an article full of smooth words and it is picked up and run with, for a time. Inevitably a new philosophy comes along and academia drops the old philosophies of last year. The one constant is that their focus is always on man, and God, if He exists at all, exists for man's benefit.

In spite of all the shifting sands of philosophy, the Word of God remains as the one authority that stands firm. Though under attack from the time it was written, it stands as the one standard toward which all other philosophies, and all its critics, ultimately will bow the knee.

Our generation has seen the greatest attack against the Bible in all of history, and much of it has been from within the ranks of professing Christians! In English we now have over two hundred different Bible *"translations"*! The translators of each new version tell us how hard the Bible is to understand, "*with all the thees and thous*", as if there was only one Bible to compare to. The truth is that there is only one Bible to compare to, and the plethora of new versions pale in comparison to the one Bible that has stood the test of time, the Authorized Version of 1611.

This document is not meant as a study of the textual or translational issues surrounding the Bible versions controversy. In my study of prophecy I have found that this version is clearer than any new version, not only in the prophetic passages but also in the gospel. The translators simply gave us a word-for-word translation of the original texts and left it up to the Holy Spirit to do the interpretation for us. Theirs was an attitude of faith that stands head and shoulders above the modern attempt at scholarship.

The translators of the Authorized Version (King James Bible) understood that they did not know all there is to know about the Word of God. They believed that the Spirit of God is capable of teaching you and me from His text, and therefore set out to give us a faithful copy of the original. They were successful, and this is the reason I will use this version for this book. Occasionally I will use new versions, but that is only for comparison purposes.

In any Bible study there are some rules and principles that apply if one is to allow God to speak through His Word. One should not formulate doctrine, and then pick out isolated verses that seem to support one's view. Any interpretation that is an apparent contradiction of other scriptures, shows that one or the other is in error. God, who sees the end from the beginning, cannot contradict Himself. We humans, with our limited understanding, frequently induce contradictions into scripture, because of our preconceived ideas and prejudices. It is necessary to approach scripture with the correct attitude and a teachable spirit.

In our post-modern age there is an unwillingness to disagree with anyone. We do not want to offend others, or make them feel bad about themselves. Our society wants to believe themselves "*good*", contrary to Jesus' teaching that there is none good but God. The basis of the Bible is that there is an objective truth, which is above and beyond mankind, and to which we have to answer. This makes us uncomfortable.

The truth is that everyone really believes in objective truth. Post-moderns still look both ways before crossing the street. When it comes to spirituality, however, they do not want to confront it, so they sidestep it. Jesus came preaching repentance and the society of that day hated Him for it, and ended up crucifying Him. Our society is not all that different from Israel two thousand years ago.

Christians teach our children to memorize Proverbs 3:5-6, but as we grow older we, more often than not, tend to lean on our own understanding: *"Trust in the LORD with all thine heart: and lean not unto thine own understanding. 6 In all thy ways acknowledge him, and he shall direct thy paths."* As we go on I will show you some things that will surprise and even shock you, but please bear with me and trust God, not yourself, nor me. Like a Berean believer God wants us to check everything by His word.

> *Beloved, **believe not every spirit**, but try the spirits whether they are of God: because many false prophets are gone out into the world. (1 John 4:1)*

> *These (Bereans) were more noble than those in Thessalonica, in that they received the word with all readiness of mind, and searched the scriptures daily, whether those things were so. (Acts 17:11)*

There are some things that must be covered first before one starts with prophecy. The one person who must be consulted in any Bible study is none other than the author Himself, the Holy Spirit. The Bible is written in such a way that it can't be received, accepted or understood, by persons unacquainted with the Author. It is not that it is unintelligible gibberish, but rather that prophecy reveals the character of God. Those who are His enemies, who have made a god in their own image, simply refuse to accept what it says about His character though it is in plain English, Greek, or the language of your choice. Everyone understands the principle of substitution, they just don't think it applies to them.

> *But the natural man receiveth not the things of the Spirit of God: for they are foolishness unto him: neither can he know them, because they are spiritually discerned. (1 Corinthians 2:14)*

If you are a natural man, a person unregenerated by the Spirit of God, you will not accept anything that truly comes from God. You must first accept Him, and the sacrifice He made on your behalf. Those who reject the sacrificial atonement of Jesus Christ will also reject the rapture of the Church, even when it actually occurs, and even though they may have personally known people who were caught up. This is the crux of the matter. You must be born-again.

Humans often try to create a God in their own image, rather than accept what He says about Himself. By doing so we actually claim to know the thoughts of God, ultimately deifying ourselves.

The word that God uses to describe himself is *"Holy"*. When the biblical authors wanted to emphasize something they would repeat it. Jesus often said *"verily, verily"* or *"Truly, truly"* to emphasize something he was saying. The only word that is emphasized three times is *"Holy"*, as in, *"Holy, holy, holy, is the Lord God almighty"*. This word means that God is completely separate from His creation. God is not a part of the creation, as is commonly taught in eastern religions. He is separate and distinct from creation and so different that you and I cannot truly grasp the difference. If you have had an experience that taught you that God is one with all of creation, I can assure you that that experience was deceptive, and did not come from God.

As Paul said on Mars hill, "(God) *is not far from each of us*". As we study scripture we find that God actually wants to reach us with important truth. In order for me to learn what God wants me to understand, I must to be willing to be a student and let God be the Master. Jesus said we must be like a little child if we would enter the kingdom of Heaven (Matthew 18:2-4, Mark 10:15, Luke 18:17). He did not mean to be childish, but to be trusting like a child, to trust God as a child trusts his or her father, even when that child doesn't understand everything his or her father says or does.

It is essential to listen to what He says, and accept it even if it goes against strongly held, preconceived ideas, even ideas we thought we knew about God Himself. We are fleshly persons and subject to all kinds of frailties and sins. Pride is an object that stands in the way of God's truth. So guard your heart against pride. Forget what your professors in college, university or seminary have said and look at the Word of God with fresh, unbiased eyes. This is not meant to be disrespectful of anyone, but only to show that truth is more important than our own, and other's, pride and pet doctrines.

If the Holy Spirit is not involved, the doctrines of the Word of God will be nonsense and foolishness! In order to have His participation we need to start with prayer.

But the Comforter, which is the Holy Ghost, whom the

Father will send in my name, he shall teach you all things, and bring all things to your remembrance, whatsoever I have said unto you. (John 14:26)

But when the Comforter is come, whom I will send unto you from the Father, even the Spirit of truth, which proceedeth from the Father, he shall testify of me: (John 15:26)

At that day ye shall ask in my name: **and I say not unto you, that I will pray the Father for you: For the Father himself loveth you, because ye have loved me,** *and have believed that I came out from God. (John 16:26-27)*

So we see in the above verses that the Holy Spirit wants to teach us, and will if we ask humbly in the name of Jesus. In John 15:26 it says that the Comforter teaches about Jesus Christ and this brings us to the title of this book for *"the testimony of Jesus is the Spirit of Prophecy"* Revelation 19:10b. Prophecy in the Bible is inextricably linked with the person and character of the Lord Jesus Christ, from the first prophecy in Genesis 3 until the very end of the book.

To ignore biblical prophecy is to ignore the Lord Jesus Christ, regardless of whether one says nice things about Him or not.

The Literal Interpretation Method

Jesus answered and said unto them, Ye do err, not knowing the scriptures, nor the power of God. (Matthew 22:29)

Search the scriptures; for in them ye think ye have eternal life: and they are they which testify of me. (John 5:39)

And Paul, as his manner was, went in unto them, and three sabbath days reasoned with them out of the scriptures, (Acts 17:2)

Over the years I have read many excellent articles on interpreting the Bible in its literal plain-sense meaning. The truth is that I can't remember all the authors and articles, I have read. Certainly David Cloud and Donald Waite were two of them. One of the triumphs of the reformation is the reestablishment of the literal/natural understanding of scripture, to a certain extent. Unfortunately even its champions, at times, seem to back-off when the plain sense conflicts with their world-view.

In their excellent article on the literal interpretation of scripture, *"Do I Interpret the Bible Literally?"*, Middletown Bible Church quotes Dr. David L. Cooper, the founder of The Biblical Research Society:

"When the plain sense of Scripture makes common sense, seek no other sense; Therefore, take every word at its primary, ordinary, usual, literal meaning unless the facts of the immediate context, studied in the light of related passages and axiomatic and fundamental truths indicate clearly otherwise."

[This rule was published regularly in Dr. Cooper's monthly magazine, Biblical Research Monthly.]

(*"Interpret the Bible Literally?"*, Middletown Bible Church)

The article goes on to say:

"A shortened form of the above rule goes like this:

" If the plain sense makes good sense seek no other sense lest it result in nonsense."

The opponents of dispensationalism sometimes depart from the above rule, and although they might not want to admit it, they seem to follow this rule:

" If the plain sense does not fit my theological system, then I will seek some other sense, lest I should end up agreeing with the dispensationalists!"

This is illustrated by an amillennialist, named Hamilton, who made this remarkable admission:

"Now we must frankly admit that a literal interpretation of the Old Testament prophecies gives us just such a picture of an earthly reign of the Messiah as the premillennialist pictures" [Cited by Charles Ryrie, The Basis of the Premillennial Faith, (Neptune, New Jersey: Loizeaux Brothers, 1981), 35].

When we get to the subject covered in chapter 8, we will see that even many who champion the literal approach to scripture will back-off when confronted with that particular subject. When we get there I will show you how the literal/natural approach makes the most sense, even when studying such controversial subjects.

God, who created man, created us with the capacity for language from the very first day. In Genesis 2:16 we see that God was able to give the man commands that he understood immediately after he was created. It follows that God is able to communicate through the spoken and written word. Today God has chosen to speak to us through the written word. Speaking through prophets only, would subject His word to the machinations of false prophets, and make salvation based on the proximity of the hearer to a true prophet. This happens anyway and people do follow false prophets, but God has made it so that anyone can get a copy of His word and understand what he wants to say to them.

The Bible is literally true. You do not need to interpret it in most cases, just believe what it says. Where it needs to be interpreted, is when it is obvious that the literal meaning isn't enough. If it says something is "like" something else, it is speaking in allegory. If it says something is a parable, this is another case where the meaning is hidden by a story, where spiritual truth is compared with something physical. Even where interpretation is necessary, however, the Bible itself provides the information necessary for interpretation. It just takes time, study, prayer, and faith.

The following is a theory that, while it can't be proved, makes the best sense of the facts as we know them:

It appears that Adam was the first man to develop some sort of writing system, which was probably some form of pictograph writing on clay tablets. It is likely that these tablets, or copies thereof, made it on to Noah's ark and ultimately into the hands of Shem and his descendants.

At the tower of Babel (Babylon) the one family that had not rebelled against God, or had rebelled the least, would have been the only family that did not have their language changed, and could still read the original script, or pictographs. This family would have been in possession of these tablets and would have passed them down from generation to generation.

Eventually these tablets found their way into the hands of the tribe of Levi and ultimately into a certain man of that tribe by the name of Moses. Moses then took the writings from these tablets and compiled them into the book of Genesis. This would explain why there are eleven different sections of that book and why the writing style of each section differs from the others. At times they are written in the present-tense and at other times in the past-tense. Moses was thus the editor, and not the author of the book of Genesis.

We have therefore, in the pages of the Bible itself, evidence that mankind could read from the very beginning of human history.

As we look at human languages both modern and ancient, we observe something else. Linguists observe that ancient languages were all more complicated than modern languages and, in fact, modern languages are less complicated than their immediate predecessors. There is a simplifying process going on around the world which can be observed in languages as diverse as English and Chinese.

All this is to say that there were intelligent people in the ancient world who were able to give an accurate eyewitness account of what they had seen, and had the ability to record it accurately in whatever medium was available to them, either on clay tablets, animal skins or papyrus.

The ancient Hebrews were scrupulous scribes and wrote what they saw, and described events in a literal/natural way. These men were not given to fanciful and fantastic writing as were the Greeks, Romans and other nations in the area.

If a biblical author wanted to compare spiritual truth with the physical world, he stated plainly that what he was writing was an allegory. As you go through scripture you will find phrases like these: *"I saw something like..."*, *"Jesus spoke a parable"*, *"like..."*, or *"like unto..."* In these instances the author is stating that something physical is used to describe something spiritual. In other words the spiritual thing that is being described has characteristics like something else, but the author either doesn't have the words or is intentionally using simplified language to make the meaning apparent to the reader.

Another parable put he forth unto them, saying, The kingdom of heaven is like to a grain of mustard seed, which a man took, and sowed in his field: Which indeed is the least of all seeds: but when it is grown, it is the greatest among herbs, and becometh a tree, so that the birds of the air come and lodge in the branches thereof. (Matthew13:31)

Jesus often used parables, which allows the Holy Spirit to provide the interpretation for us, and at the same time keeps the meaning veiled from His enemies.   Usually Jesus gave the interpretation to His disciples, but because of unbelief, the sceptics usually invent meanings in order to avoid the truth.

When the Bible describes something without using allegorical language it is because God wants us to understand the literal meaning.   Having said this, however, it is still important to understand the context.   When Jesus was standing before his disciples, in His body, he said to them *"This is my body which is broken for you".* (1 Cor. 11:24) He was not saying that the bread literally became His body, since he was still in that same body, standing in front of them. He meant it in an allegorical way, that they would be partaking of His body figuratively, not literally. If he meant it in a literal way He would have been commanding them to commit sin by eating human flesh.

Had Jesus been actually offering his body at the last supper, there would have been no reason for Him to go to the cross! He would have already been sacrificed!

The Church is called the *"body of Christ"*, yet He has a literal body. Again it is meant in a figurative way. We are here to do His work. We are His representatives, or ambassadors to our society.

Many of the prophetic passages in scripture speak in terms that are not allegorical but are very literal.   They are meant to be frightening. The language is meant to be a warning to the lost that the time is now to make things right between ourselves and our Maker. I think that when the time of the Great Tribulation comes, things will actually be far worse than our imaginations, or our most graphic movies could convey.

This was the greatest error of Augustine, the man who gave the Roman Catholic Church its basic philosophy. Augustine was schooled in the ideas of the ancient Greek and Roman philosophers. To them everything was allegorical, and therefore he assumed that the Hebrew prophets were writing in the same fashion.

Thus was born a system of biblical interpretation where every literal passage is taken as allegorical, but every allegorical passage was taken as literal. This is the system that also gave birth to the amillennial view of eschatology. Though the book of Revelation speaks of a thousand year period, at least six times, amillennialists deny that this could mean literally what it says and claim that it is a long indeterminate period of time. There are many time references in the book of Revelation and they all refer to literal periods of time. Some are to a certain number of days and others to months or years. There is nothing in the Word of God that would indicate that we should not take time references as literal.

It is true that a day with God can be a thousand years. This does not mean an indefinite period of time but a literal thousand years, a millennium. In other parts of the prophetic Scriptures a day can mean a year (Eze.4:5), or a literal day (Genesis 40:12). By far the main use of the word "*day*" in scripture is a literal 24 hour day. There must be scriptural evidence before we can take the term "*day*" to mean any other period of time. Careful study will show us which is which, whether it is a day from man's perspective or from God's.

John Calvin and Martin Luther were Augustinian scholars and allowed the philosophy of Augustine to colour their understanding of scripture. Consequently neither Luther nor Calvin wrote commentaries on the book of Revelation. They did not understand it, and I think, they knew in their heart that it wasn't meant for them, but for a future generation.

The philosophy of Calvinism is really a form of Augustinianism. These men, including Arminius, were attempting to put God into a box. They were trying to form a system that accurately describes God and predicts His behaviour, however, God is too big to put into a man-made box. There was some truth to what they said, but neither system really works in the light of scripture. Leave the "*isms*" alone and simply believe what the Lord says in His Word.

Please understand that if the "*box*" is the Bible, God does indeed fit into that box. He has purposely revealed something of himself in His Word and He will never go against it. Yes God does fit into a box, but it is a box of His own making, and because of this we can trust Him. He will not break one promise because of who He is.

> *For I am the LORD, I change not; therefore ye sons of Jacob are not consumed. (Malachi 3:6)*

> *"... thou hast magnified thy word above all thy name." (Psalms 138:2)*

Comparing Scripture with Scripture

> *Jesus answered and said unto them, Ye do err, not knowing the scriptures, nor the power of God. (Matthew 22:29)*

> *Search the scriptures; for in them ye think ye have eternal life: and they are they which testify of me. (John 5:39)*

> *And Paul, as his manner was, went in unto them, and three sabbath days reasoned with them out of the scriptures, (Acts 17:2)*

> *These were more noble than those in Thessalonica, in that they received the word with all readiness of mind, and searched the scriptures daily, whether those things were so. (Acts 17:11)*

> *Study to shew thyself approved unto God, a workman that needeth not to be ashamed, rightly dividing the word of truth. (2 Timothy 2:15)*

These verses are only a small example of the importance the Lord places on the Scriptures. As He says in John 5:39 "*Search the Scriptures*". It is important to search through the Scriptures and compare similar terminology in various books. Paul's authority is the Scriptures, not feelings, tradition, or some other book. He told Timothy to study to be able to rightly divide the Word of truth, the Scriptures. As we go on I will show some examples of this method.

Remember Jesus' words in Matthew 4:4: *"But he answered and said, It is written, Man shall not live by bread alone, but by every word that proceedeth out of the mouth of God."* Much more could be said about this principle, but let's just remember Jesus' emphasis on *"every word"*. Jesus is the *"Word of God"* not the *"thought of God"*. There are no accidents nor coincidences in the Bible. We are not to take the Word of God and boil it down into general thoughts or principles without considering every word. There are nuances of meaning that are lost in paraphrase translations. It is best to translate literally and educate the reader on the meaning of the words. Let the Holy Spirit do the interpretation.

> *All scripture is given by inspiration of God, and is profitable for doctrine, for reproof, for correction, for instruction in righteousness: (2 Timothy 3:16)*

The word *"inspiration"* means *"God Breathed"*. Remember, this includes the Old Testament including the Law. The Law is weak only in the sense that it cannot save. But it is correct! It was given to show us that we are sinners deserving God's Judgment. Galatians 3:24 states *"Wherefore the law was our schoolmaster to bring us unto Christ, that we might be justified by faith."* The Law condemns, but Christ saves! When we are in Christ we are not under the Law, but are set free!

> *For what man knoweth the things of a man, save the spirit of man which is in him? even so the things of God knoweth no man, but the Spirit of God. Now we have received, not the spirit of the world, but the spirit which is of God; that we might know the things that are freely given to us of God. Which things also we speak, not in the words which man's wisdom teacheth, but which the Holy Ghost teacheth; comparing spiritual things with spiritual. (1 Corinthians 2:11)*

In the above passage we see that since the Holy Spirit is responsible for the creation of the Scriptures, He is the one who is able to interpret them correctly. We are also told to compare spiritual things with spiritual. That is, to compare scripture with scripture.

As we read scripture we need to compare passages with similar language in order to understand what is being said. Usually the second passage will add to the context of the first and shed more light on what is meant. Comparing scripture to modern dictionaries is often a waste of time. Many words have lost meanings over long periods of time and modern dictionaries often only contain modern definitions.

Reading a word within its context often conveys the meaning without actually having it spelled out for you. One word that comes to mind is the word *"begotten"* or *"begat"*. As you read the many genealogies in scripture you will find these words frequently used, such as "David <u>begat</u> Solomon" (Mat. 1:6). By its use we understand that a son who is begotten is a son that comes from his father, and is made of the same substance. A begotten son is actually equal to his father.

In John 3:16 we read, *"For God so loved the world, that he gave his **only begotten Son**, that whosoever believeth in him should not perish, but have everlasting life."* This core verse of the Gospel of Jesus Christ makes a statement that many Bible translators have missed. Jesus Christ is the only <u>begotten</u> son of God. This verse is making the claim that Jesus is made of the same substance as God the Father, and thus is equal to God.

There are many passages in the Bible where other persons are called *"sons of God"*. In the Old Testament angelic beings are called *"sons of God"* (Gen. 6:2 & 4, Job 1:6, 2:1, 38:7, Daniel 3:25), but in the New Testament we are told that now human beings can become *"sons of God"* or *"children of God"*. This creates a contradiction in new versions that say that Jesus is the *"one and only son of God"*. He isn't. God has many sons.

When shopping for a new Bible I recommend that you open it to John 3:16 and if it says *"one and only"* put it back on the shelf and keep looking. The word in the original Greek has the same meaning as the English word *"begotten"*. If the translators can't give you an honest translation of this word, how do you know you can trust them anywhere else?

You see, the Bible claims that you and I can become children of God through adoption:

> *For ye have not received the spirit of bondage again to fear; but ye have received the Spirit of <u>adoption</u>, whereby we cry, Abba, Father. (Romans 8:15)*

*To redeem them that were under the law, that we might receive the **adoption** of sons. (Galatians 4:5)*

*Having predestinated us unto the **adoption** of children by Jesus Christ to himself, according to the good pleasure of his will, (Ephesians 1:5)*

This is why we were created in the first place. He desires fellowship and communion with beings who love Him for who he is and what he has done for us. God doesn't need us. He has a perfect fellowship within Himself, the three persons of the Godhead. He has such a good relationship within Himself, that He desired to share some of that goodness with other beings. That is why He created us. He allowed us to sin so that He could demonstrate His love for us, by saving us from the penalty we justly deserve: death and the Lake of Fire! God, in Jesus Christ, invites us to fellowship with Him! This is a privilege he has not extended to the angels!

At times I have sat under preachers who gave me the idea that God was lonely and wanted fellowship! This is a false idea and borders on blasphemy! God is complete in Himself, more than any one else, and more than all combined! What God has is so good that if we understood only a shadow of what He has, we would be on our faces begging Him to save us! In contrast, God's wrath is so fearsome that if we understood only a shadow of his anger, we would be on our faces begging Him to save us!

The Importance of Context

A lot of emphasis is placed on context as you listen to many preachers today and I agree, to a certain extent. We need to understand the cultural context in which the Scriptures were given. Some of the daily life of the original audience is important if it touches on the meaning of scripture.

Very often, however, Bible teachers mean that one has to get some text books on the ancient Middle-East in order to study the Word of God. On this point I disagree. If you understand the ancient Jewish way of thinking you will still be predisposed to reject the Gospel, since most of the ancient Jews rejected it. Even many who knew Jesus personally, like Judas, the Pharisees, and Sadducees, still rejected the gospel. The Gospel of Jesus Christ has always been a stumbling block to Jews, and foolishness to Gentiles. God exists outside of time and space and views all of human history at once. (Isaiah 57:15) Consequently He knew that times would change and the meanings of words would change. Accordingly He carefully placed definitions in the Bible so that His book would be independent of dictionaries. All the context you need is contained within the pages of scripture itself, though sometimes you may need to dig a little.

All man-made books are always below, and subject to, the Scriptures and not the other way around. In any clear contradiction between the Scriptures and a dictionary you can take the scriptural meaning over the dictionary's meaning every time.

Let me give you an example, found in the midst of a prophecy of the End Times:

And I heard a voice in the midst of the four beasts say, A measure of wheat for a penny, and three measures of barley for a penny; and see thou hurt not the oil and the wine. (Revelation 6:6)

Please note the word "penny". In the day the Authorized Version was translated, a general labourer in England would earn about a penny a day. The translators used a word that was equivalent in seventeenth century England to what a denarius meant in ancient Israel. Consequently this prophecy indicates that in the End Times a measure of wheat, about the amount needed to feed a man for a day, would cost a day's wages. A lot of inflation has occurred during the intervening four hundred years so that today a penny is almost worthless. A casual reader would be led to think that food would be cheap and plentiful in the last days, the exact opposite of what was intended!

The awesome God of the Bible was aware that this would be the situation and so he defined what he meant in the Scriptures. Let's discover the value of a biblical "penny" in the following:

And when he had agreed with the labourers for a penny a day, he sent them into his vineyard. (Matthew 20:2)

Modern translators simply transliterate the original Greek word denarius, which is not wrong so long as they consistently use it in every passage where it is used in the Greek, but this does not really qualify as translation. When was the last time you used "denarius" in a normal, average, every-day English conversation? Once again this says something about the honesty of the modern Bible translators.   Nevertheless the same principle applies.   Compare scripture with scripture.

> *Study to shew thyself approved unto God, a workman that needeth not to be ashamed, rightly dividing the word of truth. (2 Timothy 2:15)*

Everything important for context can be found within the pages of scripture itself, one need not go to other texts for any scriptural interpretation. Though at times it can be helpful, one must always place all other sources below the authority of scripture. The Bible is not a novel that can be picked up and understood in a few minutes of casual reading. There is a reason Paul told Timothy to study. Everything you really need is contained within scripture, but you won't find it with a brief or casual reading.

Another sort of context is found in other prophecies.

Abraham was told by God that he should sacrifice his only son to Him. Being of heavy heart, yet still believing that God could raise his son from the dead he took Isaac up to the place where God had told him to prepare an altar. As they were walking up to the appointed place Isaac questioned his father:

> *And Isaac spake unto Abraham his father, and said, My father: and he said, Here am I, my son. And he said, Behold the fire and the wood: but where is the lamb for a burnt offering? (Genesis 22:7)*

Please note Abraham's response, it is prophetic and has more than one context, or interpretation:

> *8 And Abraham said, My son, God will provide himself a lamb for a burnt offering: so they went both of them together.*

Abraham was answering his son's question in context; that is, that God would provide a lamb for himself. He was not lying but was referring to Isaac's miraculous birth, since Isaac was the intended sacrifice. God, however, actually provided a real ram for them to sacrifice in verse 13.

The way the prophecy is worded, however, provides a third context that is higher than either of the previous two, yet does not contradict them. *"God will provide himself a lamb"* can also mean that God will provide Himself AS a Lamb, to satisfy His own requirement for sacrifice. The third meaning is true in the context of the Messiah, and the Messiah's father, God, is the one who sacrificed Him for our sins. So Abraham's answer was true on three different levels, or three different contexts. The three different meanings are actually complimentary.

This principle is actually the exact opposite of Occult teachings which frequently contradict themselves, where initiates are told meanings that are later denied when they become adepts.

Jesus Himself, when quoting scripture showed that sometimes prophecies may be split in mid-sentence with different parts having their fulfilment many years apart. In other words the context can be split by as much as thousands of years, and the split is not readily apparent in the passage.

> *And there was delivered unto him the book of the prophet Esaias. And when he had opened the book, he found the place where it was written, The Spirit of the Lord is upon me, because he hath anointed me to preach the gospel to the poor; he hath sent me to heal the brokenhearted, to preach deliverance to the captives, and recovering of sight to the blind, to set at liberty them that are bruised,* **To preach the acceptable year of the Lord.** *And he closed the book, and he gave it again to the minister, and sat down. And the eyes of all them that were in the synagogue were fastened on him. And he began to say unto them, This day is this scripture fulfilled in your ears. (Luke 4:17-21)*

Jesus was quoting Isaiah 61:1-3. Please note verse 2 of that passage; Isaiah 61:2 **"To proclaim the acceptable year of the LORD, and the day of vengeance of our God;** *to comfort all that mourn;"* Jesus stopped in the middle of a sentence because only the first part was fulfilled. The *"day of vengeance of our God"* was still at least two thousand years future when He spoke. When God does this kind of thing with prophecy, it is impossible to understand all of the implications, without the intervention of the Holy Spirit of God. We must depend on Him.

Zechariah 11 is an example of a passage that has several different contexts one after another, that skip forward and backward in time by hundreds and even thousands of years:

1 Open thy doors, O Lebanon, that the fire may devour thy cedars. 2 Howl, fir tree; for the cedar is fallen; because the mighty are spoiled: howl, O ye oaks of Bashan; for the forest of the vintage is come down. 3 There is a voice of the howling of the shepherds; for their glory is spoiled: a voice of the roaring of young lions; for *the pride of Jordan* is spoiled.

The first three verses are a continuation of chapter 10 and are a description of the result of Asaph's war, an End Times prophecy from Psalm 83. Usually in Scripture, the word *"Jordan"* is a reference to the river, yet in this case it appears to be a reference to the nation, which did not exist at the time.

> *4 Thus saith the LORD my God; Feed the flock of the slaughter; 5 Whose possessors slay them, and hold themselves not guilty: and they that sell them say, Blessed be the LORD; for I am rich: and their own shepherds pity them not. 6 For I will no more pity the inhabitants of the land, saith the LORD: but, lo, I will deliver the men every one into his neighbour's hand, and into the hand of his king: and they shall smite the land, and out of their hand I will not deliver them. 7 And I will feed the flock of slaughter, even you, O poor of the flock. And I took unto me two staves; the one I called Beauty, and the other I called Bands; and I fed the flock. 8 **Three shepherds also I cut off in one month**; and my soul lothed them, and their soul also abhorred me. 9 **Then said I, I will not feed you: that that dieth, let it die**; and that that is to be cut off, let it be cut off; and let the rest eat every one the flesh of another. 10 And I took my staff, even Beauty, and cut it asunder, that **I might break my covenant which I had made with all the people**. 11 And it was broken in that day: and so the poor of the flock that waited upon me knew that it was the word of the LORD. (Zechariah 11:4-11)*

Verses 4 through 11 seem to be a prophecy of the End Times, even farther into the future than the first three verses. The three shepherds that were cut off in one month appear to be a reference to the three kings who will be uprooted by the Antichrist in Daniel 7:8, thus it would appear that the prophet, or the Lord, is acting out the role of the Antichrist in these verses. The fact that he does not feed the flock would be further evidence that this is the case. In verse 10 the fact that he breaks the covenant with the people seems to confirm this interpretation, for God is the covenant keeper, but then he skips back two thousand years:

> *12 And I said unto them, If ye think good, give me my price; and if not, forbear.* **So they weighed for my price thirty pieces of silver.** *13 And the LORD said unto me, Cast it unto the <u>potter</u>: a goodly price that I was prised at of them. And I took the thirty pieces of silver, and cast them to the potter in the house of the LORD.*

Here we have the crucifixion of Jesus Christ and the thirty pieces of silver refer to the money Judas was paid by the scribes and pharisees to betray him. This passage is further proof that Jesus is the God of the Old Testament, for the price is the price Jehovah/Yahweh/God was valued at. The reference to the potter is what they did with the money after Judas threw it back to them in the Temple, they bought a potter's field. With prophecy like this it is impossible to understand every part of it until it is fulfilled, or God reveals it to us.

> *14 Then I cut asunder mine other staff, even Bands, that I might break the brotherhood between Judah and Israel.*

Verse 14 is a reference to the split between Israel and Judah, during the reign of Rehoboam, Solomon's son, sometime around 900 BC. It could also be a reference to the two nations being captured separately by Assyria and Babylon and scattered in different parts of the world. In which case it was prophetic when it was written, but has since been fulfilled, long ago.

> *15 And the LORD said unto me, Take unto thee yet the instruments of a foolish shepherd. 16 For, lo,* **I will raise up a shepherd in the land,** *which shall not visit those that be cut off, neither shall seek the young one, nor heal that that is broken,* **nor feed that that standeth still:** *but he shall eat the flesh of the fat, and tear their claws in pieces. 17* **Woe to the idol shepherd that leaveth the flock!** *the sword shall be upon his arm, and upon his right eye:* **his arm shall be clean dried up, and his right eye shall be utterly darkened.**

Now we see he skips forward to the Tribulation again. The Idol Shepherd is a reference to the Antichrist. It might be possible to conclude that he will come from Israel because of the use of the term "*the land*", but I think that it could also mean that his ancestral land will become a part of Israel before this time. Thus he could be from "*the land*" of Israel, yet also from the "*sea of the nations*", the gentiles. Even today there are many Arabs living in Israel. Another possibility is that this reference to "*the land*" simply means that he will rule over the land of Israel.

Verse 16 states that it is God's will that he will arise and describes the way he governs. To "*eat the flesh of the fat*" is not a reference to cannibalism, but to the fact that he will take their substance without pity. Verse 17 describes a wound he will receive. This appears to be the wound spoken of in Revelation 13:3 and 12. As a result of the fatal head wound he receives, and is then healed from, it appears that he will become blind in his right eye and will lose the use of one arm. This will be another sign of the Antichrist to the people alive during the Great Tribulation.

In an interview with examiner.com Joel Richardson, the author of "*The Islamic Antichrist*", says about the Muslim apocalyptic view...

"The Islamic version of the Antichrist is called the Dajjal. He is supposed to be one eyed or blind in one eye (speculative) according to pop culture in Islam. Islam is filled with conspiracy theories. Some see the all seeing eye and freemasonry as an all encompassing Dajjal system. Similar to the way some conspiracy theorist view the "new world order." There's even a website called the Dajall News Network." (Interview, Larry Amon)

I find it interesting that some in Islam have come to the same conclusion that the Bible gives about this man, though from a different source. I see the hand of God here. Reasoning from the conspiracy theories, and the "*all seeing eye of Horus*" on the American dollar bill, some Muslims have come to the conclusion that the Dajjal, or Antichrist, will be blind in one eye. Zechariah chapter 11 says the same thing, and Revelation 13:3 speaks of the same event.

What they are missing is that this man will attain world power as an able bodied man, several years before he loses his eye. They will be following him, thinking he is the Imam Mahdi, and slaughtering believers, until he receives his fatal head wound. When he is resurrected, he will be blind in one eye and crippled in one arm. At that time the Muslim world will begin to reevaluate their support of him.

Indeed, the Muslim stories of the Imam Mahdi (the Twelfth Imam) and the returning Isa (Jesus) parallel the biblical story of the Beast and the false prophet. They will accept the Antichrist as the Mahdi and the false prophet as the Muslim Jesus until the Antichrist loses his eye. As he claims to have been raised from the dead for them, with only one eye, many will turn to the Scriptures for answers. I believe that at that time many Muslims will turn to the true Jesus Christ and will lay down their lives for Him. God is still in control.

It is unlikely that Zechariah knew all of the implications he was writing about when he penned these verses. God inspired him to write, but the full meaning was not apparent to him or even to the Church until the appropriate time approaches. The truth is that we can't understand these prophecies unless God shows us the meaning. Indeed, it is likely there are more hidden meanings that will become apparent only after the Rapture of the Church, and the Tribulation approaches.

This same principle also applies to many other prophecies, and there is yet another wrinkle, for God's adversary has an interest in seeing prophecy fulfilled. He is interested in deceiving people to believe that prophecy has been fulfilled before its intended time, in order to lull them into a false sense of security.

The devil is a real person who is active in our society today. Just pick up a newspaper, you will see his work on every page. As the originator of sin he was an angel, created holy and powerful, but pride got the better of him. Though he was created to be a ministering spirit for man, he was lifted up with pride and thought that man should worship and serve him instead. (Isaiah 14:12, Ezekiel 28:13 – 19, Hebrews 1:13 & 14)

Since Lucifer had seen God, and knew Him personally, he cannot be saved. Jesus died only for the descendants of Adam. Consequently Satan is trying to discredit God whenever he can. He is trying to destroy as many people as possible and is trying to make God out to be a liar. He wants to drag you down with him.

One of the many ways he is attacking God is to try to bring about prophecies before their time in order to cause confusion. Since Jesus told the Church to be vigilant and to watch for the signs of Christ's return, the devil is trying to make God's children believe several schemes that do not fit scripture. The historical view is closely related to the amillennial view in that they share a belief that

Nero, or perhaps Domitian, was the Antichrist, the Man of Sin, or the Beast. This belief ignores the fact that Nero was already dead long before John wrote the book of Revelation. Besides this there are many other reasons these views are wrong.

The Old Testament states that a prophet must be 100% correct to be a true prophet of God. Conversely it is also true that for a prophecy to be truly fulfilled it must be 100% fulfilled. We see that Antiochus Epiphanes did not fulfil exactly all the prophecies concerning the *"Little Horn"*, although he was very close. For one thing the persecutions of Antiochus did not last exactly three and a half years. His reign did not last until the Judgment of God spoken of in Daniel 7:9-11. Antiochus never did enact a law whereby the whole world would have to wear a mark on the right hand or the forehead in order to be able to buy or sell. Antiochus never did rule the whole world, neither did the ancient Roman empire...until now. (Antiochus Epiphanes, Burnside)

Antiochus Epiphanes IV

W hat Was Going On With Antiochus?

Antiochus Epiphanes was a fulfillment of parts of Daniel chapter 8. This chapter specifically states that this particular "Little Horn" will come from the kings of Greece:

> *Therefore the he goat waxed very great: and when he was strong, the great horn was broken; and for it came up four notable ones toward the four winds of heaven. And out of one of them came forth a little horn, which waxed exceeding great, toward the south, and toward the east, and toward the pleasant land (Daniel 8:8-9)*

> *21 And the rough goat is the king of Grecia: and the great horn that is between his eyes is the first king. (Alexander the Great) 22 Now that being broken, whereas four stood up for it, four kingdoms shall stand up out of the nation, but not in his power. (The Greek Antigonid, Ptolemaic, Seleucid, and Attalid dynasties) 23 And in the latter time of their kingdom, when the transgressors are come to the full, a king of fierce*

countenance, and understanding dark sentences, shall stand up. 24 And his power shall be mighty, but not by his own power: and he shall destroy wonderfully, and shall prosper, and practise, and shall destroy the mighty and the holy people. (Daniel 8:21-24)

We see here that verse 21 identifies this particular kingdom as being the kingdom of Greece. In verse 23 *"the latter time of their kingdom"* is still referring to the same Grecian kingdom. The kingdom of Rome, which is visible in Daniel's other prophecies, is not mentioned in this passage. The king specified here must have Greek origins, which is true of Antiochus Epiphanes. He was a part of the Greek Seleucid dynasty that ruled Syria, and is the fulfilment of this prophecy of "A Little Horn".

Of particular interest is the title that Antiochus Epiphanes IV gave himself. On several of the coins he had minted, the Greek inscription reads ΘΕΟΥ ΕΠΙΦΑΝΟΥΣ ΝΙΚΗΦΟΡΟΥ / ΒΑΣΙΛΕΩΣ ΑΝΤΙΟΧΟΥ (Antiochus, Image of God (or God Manifest), Bearer of Victory) (Antiochus, Smith) This is a perfect prototype of the Little Horn to come. This man will proclaim himself to be God, manifest in the flesh, and thus attempt to usurp the title and role of Jesus Christ.

The very next verse points to someone other than Antiochus:

*25 And through his policy also he shall cause craft to prosper in his hand; and he shall magnify himself in his heart, and by peace shall destroy many: **he shall also stand up against the Prince of princes; but he shall be broken without hand.***

Antiochus was not a man of peace, not even a false peace, and the Prince of princes is none other than the Lord Jesus Christ. Antiochus died in 164 BC, and couldn't fulfil this prophecy. The last part of this verse refers to Nebuchadnezzar's dream of the End Times, where the kingdoms of the world will be destroyed by a *"stone cut out **without hands"***. (Daniel 2:45)

There is a split in the prophecy between verses 24 and 25, where the giver of the prophecy jumps to *"another little horn"* who shall come in the distant future. Many have been confused because the second Little Horn comes earlier in the book of Daniel, while the first Little Horn comes second. Chapter 7 is an overview that encompasses much more time, while chapter 8 zeros in on a much smaller time frame.

If we compare chapters 7 and 8 we find *"another* Little Horn" spoken of. This time the Little Horn comes from the ten horns of the fourth beast, which is Rome, not the third, or Greece, which has four horns. The three horns that are plucked up are three of the ten, not the other three of Greece.

> *After this I saw in the night visions, and behold a fourth beast, dreadful and terrible, and strong exceedingly; and it had great iron teeth: it devoured and brake in pieces, and stamped the residue with the feet of it: and it was diverse from all the beasts that were before it; and it had ten horns. I considered the horns, and, behold, there came up among them* **another** *little horn, before whom there were three of the first horns plucked up by the roots: and, behold, in this horn were eyes like the eyes of man, and a mouth speaking great things. (Daniel 7:7-8)*

> *Thus he said, The fourth beast shall be the fourth kingdom upon earth, which shall be diverse from all kingdoms, and* **shall devour the whole earth,** *and shall tread it down, and break it in pieces. And the ten horns out of this kingdom are ten kings that shall arise: and another shall rise after them; and he shall be diverse from the first, and he shall subdue three kings. (Daniel 7:23-24)*

Comparing chapters 7 and 8 of Daniel we see that only two kingdoms are spoken of in the vision of chapter 8, Medo-Persia and Greece, whereas there are four kingdoms in chapter 7. These four kingdoms correspond to Nebuchadnezzars vision of a statue in chapter 2. The four are identified as Babylon, Medo-Persia, Greece, and another that combines all the worst features of the previous three...Rome.

This last kingdom is a world empire, beginning with Rome but spreading out, like a fungus or cancer, to encompass the entire earth. The Little Horn of chapter 7 is clearly identified as coming from the ten horns of the fourth kingdom. The four heads of the leopard like beast of verse 6 of chapter 7 correspond to the four horns of the he goat of chapter 8 (Greece).

In chapter 8 the first kingdom, Medo-Persia, is likened to a ram with two horns, and the second, Greece, is likened to a goat, with one notable horn, Alexander. The horn is broken at the peak of his power and is replaced by four horns (v. 8). Alexander died as a young man and was succeeded by four generals who divided the empire into four smaller kingdoms. This particular Little Horn comes up from one of the four horns of the *"he goat"* which is identified later as Greece (v. 21).

This contrasts to chapter 7 where the Little Horn comes up from one of the ten horns of the fourth beast. This fourth kingdom is prophesied to encompass the entire earth in verse 23. This did not occur in ancient Rome but awaits its final fulfilment in the near future. The ten kings are not European kings, but kings or presidents of ten regions that will encompass the globe. Europe itself will be only one of these ten nations.

Chapter eleven actually blurs the distinction between these two "Little Horns" even further. As we have seen there are two distinct Little Horns, but the similarities between them are so great that it appears that one chapter is sufficient to describe them both. It also may very well be, that Antiochus Epiphanes IV is a trap set for the Last Days Apostasy.

So, there are actually two Little Horns prophesied in Daniel 7 and 8, One from a Grecian background and the second from the fourth kingdom, the End Times world Empire. The terminology is similar, but the specifics are different, and the line between them is blurred because of the similarities, and because God views all of history at once. One is an Antichrist-type, and the other is the Antichrist himself, and they are separated by more than two thousand years.

As I began to write this book I thought the best explanation for Antiochus was that Satan had inspired this man to attempt to fulfil the prophecies of the book of Daniel. The reason was so that when the actual time came the Jews would not be looking for the signs, because they believe they are already fulfilled. What I have found is that while this is partly true, the actual truth is that God is ultimately in control. He is the one setting a trap for those who are self-deluded, and He is able to use His arch-enemy to do it.

The same is true for Christians who believe the false escatological systems. Even pretribulational premillennialists are told *"there is nothing to watch for, so don't bother looking"*! If Satan can slip the Antichrist in unnoticed he can do a lot more damage than he can if people are vigilant. God wants to save everyone, yet is quite willing to allow those who rebel from his grace to be deceived and destroyed.

Satan has been continually attempting to deceive the Christian Church since the resurrection of Christ nearly two thousand years ago. Nero, Domitian, Diocletian, Napoleon Bonaparte, Hitler, Stalin, and the popes, are only a few of the attempted Antichrists. When the true Antichrist comes along he will precicely fulfill all the prophecies regarding his tenure.

Many true Bible believing, blood-bought, born-again Christians have believed several of these false schemes. The truth has always been a minority viewpoint. Satan can't get you unsaved if you are truly born-again, but he can make you less effective for the Lord Jesus Christ. If he can get you to focus on other believers and to fight with them, to waste your energy in useless arguments, he will gain a partial victory. He can then go to the world and say *"Look at those Christians, they are always fighting among themselves. How can anything they say be of any value to you?"* The result is that people who believe his lies will suffer for all eternity!

The truth is that Christians have the most valuable gift that has ever been given to a human being: the Lord Jesus Christ, the Holy Spirit, and Eternal Life!

I hope that this chapter has shown you some of the principles of Bible interpretation that God intended we should use. As we go on we will use these principles frequently to dig deeper into the Word of God.

In Summary

• We cannot know God apart from the revelation He has given us, His Holy Word. (1 Corinthians 2:14, 2 Timothy 3:16)

• The true interpreter of scripture is the Holy Spirit, not any man or church. (John 14:26, 15:26)

• Scripture is a self-contained unit, with all the contextual information that you need.

• Scripture must interpret scripture. Any apparent contradiction always has a solution found in a closer inspection of the passages in question or somewhere else in scripture.

• Tradition is not a reliable interpreter of scripture, and is subject to

The Spirit of Prophecy

the plain teaching of the Word of God. (Matthew 15:6)

• Antiochus Epiphanes was a type of the final Antichrist, who is yet to come.

Resources:

"Interview with Joel Richardson: The Islamic Antichrist", Larry Amon, Baltimore Christian Conservative Examiner, Examiner.com, http://www.examiner.com/x-4291-Baltimore-Christian-Conservative-Examiner~y2009m9d21-Interview-with-Joel-Richardson-The-Islamic-Antichrist, accessed 05/08/2010

"Protection from al-Masih ad-Dajjal", The Dajjal System, accessed 05/08/2010, http://etori.tripod.com/dajjalsystem/protection.html

"Do I Interpret the Bible Literally? Seven Tests to See If I Truly Do", Middletown Bible Church, Middletown CT, accessed 05/08/2010, from www.middletownBiblechurch.org/dispen/literal.htm

"THE "NORMAL LITERAL" METHOD OF THE INTERPRETATION OF BIBLE PROPHECY", David Cloud, Way of Life Literature, accessed 05/08/2010, from www.wayoflife.org/files/64cd39027b2e673d1812ef383063e256-93.html

"What is a Christian Fundamentalist?, Modified and expanded by Craig Ledbetter from an article by David Cloud". Bible Baptist Church, Ballincollig, Cork, Ireland, www.Biblebc.com/Christian_Helps/what_is_a_christian_fundamentali.htm, accessed 05/08/2010

"Antiochus Epiphanes", George Burnside, Thursday 06, 2007, Accessed 20/11/2009, from www.whitehorsemedia.com/docs/ANTIOCHUS_EPIPHANES.pdf

Antiochus IV Epiphanes [ca. 215 -164 BCE], Smith, Mahlon H., Accessed 24/09/2010, from http://virtualreligion.net/iho/antiochus_4.html

36

Two

The Beginning of Sorrows

For nation shall rise against nation, and kingdom against kingdom: and there shall be earthquakes in divers places, and there shall be famines and troubles: these are the beginnings of sorrows. (Mark 13:8)

There are a myriad of interpretations of the biblical End Times prophecies. We have: Amillennialism, Preterism, Premillennialism, Dispensationalism, Pre-trib, Mid-trib, and Post-trib, and dozens of hybrid systems which fit in between these others. What we really need to know is which system of eschatology was God trying to convey to us?

Growing up in a conservative Baptist church I was in a good place to get some excellent bible teaching. One thing I noticed, however, is that different Sunday School teachers, and preachers, had different interpretations on certain passages. It turns out that in our church there were amillenialists, and premillenialists, and several variations from within each system.

Now, since amillenialists believe there will be no earthly reign of Christ, or that He is reigning today(?), and premillenialists, and millennarians, believe there will be a literal, visible, one thousand year reign of Christ on earth, it is clear somebody is wrong. These systems are mutually exclusive. Jesus can't reign and not reign at the same time.

Before I go on I want to state emphatically that any one who claims to be saved, by the shed blood of Christ alone, by faith alone, I accept as a brother or sister in Christ. Just because they disagree with me does not make them an unsaved person. They still may know Christ, though I might question how well they know Him. The standard for the Christian is the teaching of the Word of God and not some well-established doctrine, or tradition, handed down through Church history by well-meaning Christians. Interpretations of the Bible are suspect if they do not fit with the rest of scripture regardless of their origin.

The Doctrine of Imminence

What is meant by the term *"the Doctrine of Imminence"*? What did Jesus mean? Did it mean that He could have returned at any time from his ascension until now? Does it mean that there will be no signs before His return? Is there nothing to look for?

> But of that **day and hour** knoweth no man, no, not the angels of heaven, but my Father only. But as the days of Noe were, so shall also the coming of the Son of man be. 38 For as in the days that were before the flood they were eating and drinking, marrying and giving in marriage, until the day that Noe entered into the ark, And knew not until the flood came, and took them all away; so shall also the coming of the Son of man be. Then shall two be in the field; the one shall be taken, and the other left. Two women shall be grinding at the mill; the one shall be taken, and the other left. **Watch therefore:** for ye know not what hour your Lord doth come. (Matthew 24:36-42)

This passage includes some important clues as to what is meant by the doctrine of imminence. It is true that the term *"day"* in scripture can mean a long period of time, even a thousand years. Jesus' use of the qualifying term *"hour"* narrows down the meaning to a specific point within a literal 24 hour day. So He is not saying that we can't know a season or general signs, only that we won't know the actual day on the calendar, until it happens.

Notice that He commands us: *"Watch therefore"*. Now, what are we to watch for, if there is nothing to watch for? Luke 21 is a parallel passage. In it Jesus makes another, closely related statement:

> And when these things <u>begin</u> to come to pass, then look up, and lift up your heads; for your redemption draweth nigh. (Luke 21:28)

It is significant that He uses the word *"BEGIN"*. It is obvious that we won't see the END of these things, because our redemption shall arrive before this occurs. What *"things"* is he talking about? Well, look at what He had been discussing:

> *And they asked him, saying, Master, but when shall these things be? and what sign will there be when these things shall come to pass?* And he said, **Take heed that ye be not deceived:** *for many shall come in my name, saying, I am Christ; and the time draweth near: go ye not therefore after them. But* **when ye shall hear of wars and commotions, be not terrified:** *for these things must first come to pass; but the end is not by and by. Then said he unto them, Nation shall rise against nation, and kingdom against kingdom: And great earthquakes shall be in divers places, and famines, and pestilences; and* **fearful sights and great signs shall there be from heaven.** *But before all these, they shall lay their hands on you, and persecute you, delivering you up to the synagogues, and into prisons, being brought before kings and rulers for my name's sake. (Luke 21:7-12)*

So we can see that He was referring to false teachers, wars and commotions, but He says the end isn't just yet. In verse 12 he goes back to the beginning, to a general condition of the entire church age, so verses 10 and 11 must be very important. Many point out that there have been wars continually from that day until now, so is Jesus saying that things will be normal up until the day He comes for His Church?

Jesus, being the God of history, knew about all the wars this planet had experienced up to that point, and he knew about the wars the world would have to endure before He would return. He is not referring to war in general, but to a specific sequence of wars. He is likely referring to the series of prophetic wars beginning with the restoration of Israel and continuing up until the rapture itself. I also believe that this series of prophetic wars fits into a false Tribulation scenario. Why would Jesus' disciples be terrified because of just any war? The truth is that His disciples are not terrified of just any war, but of the wrath of God. He is saying that what may look like the Great Tribulation may actually be something else. He is implying that there will be a false Tribulation set up to deceive the world. Part of the devil's deception will be that *"the*

Tribulation is over, and now it is time for world peace".

Verse 11 appears to be a reference to the war of Gog and Magog, where God states that he will defeat the invading armies with an earthquake and with fire and brimstone from heaven. Notice the similarity of the language with Ezekiel 38:20-22 Famines and pestilence are an inevitable result of war, especially if nuclear or WMDs are used. It is possible, then, that He is saying that a sure sign of the imminent rapture of the Church is Ezekiel's war, but will there be other wars before Ezekiel's war? Hold on...

Paul echoes a similar thought in 1 Thessalonians:

> *But of the times and the seasons, brethren, ye have no need that I write unto you. For yourselves know perfectly that the day of the Lord so cometh as a thief in the night. For **when they shall say, Peace and safety; then sudden destruction cometh upon them**, as travail upon a woman with child; and they shall not escape. But ye, brethren, are not in darkness, that that day should overtake you as a thief. Ye are all the children of light, and the children of the day: we are not of the night, nor of darkness. Therefore let us not sleep, as do others; but **let us watch and be sober**. (1 Thessalonians 5:1-6)*

The question we need to ask ourselves is: *"Who is it, who is surprised by the day of the Lord, like a person who finds a thief in his house?"* By the context of this passage we see that it is not believers who are surprised, but unbelievers. Those in darkness will be taken by surprise. Everyone will see the signs, but those with a false explanation will be unprepared.

What of imminence? Were the early Christians wrong to be looking for the return of Christ in their lifetime? Clearly God was not planning the return of Christ for at least some two thousand years. The story of the rich fool in Luke 12 is instructive. The man was making plans for his future without concern for the will of God. After enlarging his barns and making provision for a long retirement he is suddenly called away in death:

> *But God said unto him, Thou fool, this night thy soul shall be required of thee: then whose shall those things be, which thou hast provided? (Luke 12:20)*

The day of your, or my, meeting with the Lord is, and has always been, imminent. No one has a guarantee that he or she will live until the rapture. We are not even guaranteed today! Christians of all ages should be looking toward their meeting with Christ, because it truly can happen any day. Unbelievers and believers alike, should prepare for their meeting with their Creator, because it is imminent!

This does not take away from the fact that the Rapture of the Church will come as a surprise to the world. No one knows the day nor the hour, the exact time, but this does not mean that we can't discern the signs of the times. We certainly will know the general season. We will know when it is fast approaching, by the signs the Lord has given us in His word. Those who are not looking, or do not want Him to return, will miss the signs and die in the Tribulation.

Behold, I come as a thief. Blessed is he that watcheth, and keepeth his garments, lest he walk naked, and they see his shame. (Revelation 16:15)

Here, in the midst of the chaos of Armageddon, Jesus is still saying *"I come as a thief"*. There is no way that the context of this passage would allow us to think that this coming is without warning. The armies of the world have no idea who they are up against. They know He is coming. They just don't accept what Christians have been saying about Him! They are not surprised that Jesus is returning, they are surprised by the power He commands! Their demons have told them that He is just an "alien" like them, but He is actually the Creator who spoke this world into existence! Not only this, but He is coming to take something they think is theirs, dominion over this planet, and their very lives!

Signs of the Times

Surely the Lord GOD will do nothing, but he revealeth his secret unto his servants the prophets. (Amos 3:7)

So, what prophetic war or series of wars was the Lord Jesus speaking of when he referred to these as a sign of the end? Did He reveal something of every major event of the last days to His prophets?

The most important fulfilment of prophecy to occur in the twentieth century was the re-establishment of the nation of Israel in 1948, followed by the taking of Jerusalem in 1967. Growing up in the 1970s I heard on occasion that Israel was the *"fig tree"* spoken of by Jesus in Matthew 24:

> *Now learn a parable of the fig tree; When his branch is yet tender, and putteth forth leaves, ye know that summer is nigh: So likewise ye, when ye shall see all these things, know that it is near, even at the doors. Verily I say unto you, This generation shall not pass, till all these things be fulfilled. (Matthew 24:32-34)*

Israel is indeed the fig tree in this passage, but how do we know this? I had often heard pastors, and prophecy speakers, state that Israel is referred to as a fig tree in the Old Testament, but they left it up to their audience to find it. I have found it and I want to show you a few places where it occurs:

> *I found Israel like grapes in the wilderness;* **I saw your fathers as the firstripe in the fig tree** *at her first time: but they went to Baal–peor, and separated themselves unto that shame; and their abominations were according as they loved. (Hosea 9:10)*

> *For a nation is come up upon my land, strong, and without number, whose teeth are the teeth of a lion, and he hath the cheek teeth of a great lion. He hath laid my vine waste, and* **barked my fig tree:** *he hath made it clean bare, and cast it away; the branches thereof are made white. (Joel 1:6-7)*

Jeremiah 24:5 is especially significant, since it is the same people who were scattered in this verse, who shall be gathered.

> *Thus saith the LORD, the God of Israel;* **Like these good figs, so will I acknowledge them that are carried away captive of Judah,** *whom I have sent out of this place into the land of the Chaldeans for their good. (Jeremiah 24:5)*

OK. We have established that Israel is the fig tree, so what does he mean by *"This generation shall not pass, till all these things be fulfilled."*?

When I was young I recall some preachers stating that a biblical generation is forty years. Likely they were referring to the Generation that left Egypt, and wandered in the wilderness for forty years, until they were all dead but Caleb and Joshua. The account is found in Numbers 14. Note that those who died in the wilderness were already adults when Israel left Egypt (verse 29). In fact the passage specifically states that they were twenty years of age and up before God decreed that they would die in the wilderness. They may also have been referring to the length of time some kings of Israel reigned; forty years, like David.

I do not believe Jesus was referring to Numbers 14, in Matthew 24, nor do I think He was referring to the length of David's reign. David was around thirty when he became king, after all. I think He was actually referring to the Psalm of Moses, Psalm 90, the oldest Psalm in the book, and one very significant to the study of Eschatology:

> For we are consumed by thine anger, and by thy wrath are we troubled. Thou hast set our iniquities before thee, our secret sins in the light of thy countenance. For all our days are passed away in thy wrath: we spend our years as a tale that is told. **The days of our years are threescore years and ten; and if by reason of strength they be fourscore years,** yet is their strength labour and sorrow; for it is soon cut off, and we fly away. (Psalm 90:7-10)

Today we use the expression "to pass away" to mean to die. So when Jesus was saying "This generation shall not **pass**" wasn't he saying that this generation shall not die, until all the pertinent prophecies are fulfilled? But the generation that fought for Israel's independence, in 1948, is already passing away. Most of them are already in their eighties (in 2010).

The generation he was referring to could be the generation that was born during the year Israel won her independence. Psalm 90 speaks of the whole lifespan of a person, or a generation. In 2008 that generation celebrated their sixtieth birthday, along with the nation of Israel. The nation of Israel began to bud in the year 1948, but it has yet to come into full bloom. If Jesus was referring to Moses' Psalm, there are only eight to eighteen years left for the events Jesus spoke of in Matthew 24 to be fulfilled (as of 2010).

Someone suggested that Jesus was referring to Genesis 6:3 with regard to the life of a generation, "And the LORD said, My spirit shall not always strive with man, for that he also is flesh: yet his days shall be an hundred and twenty years." The reason I do not think this is the case, is the context of the particular passage in question. In Genesis 6:3 the context is the destruction of the earth and sinful man in the flood of Noah. One hundred and twenty years is the time that Noah had to preach to that generation. It may be that one or two persons from most generations makes it to one hundred and twenty years old but the majority makes it to somewhere between seventy and eighty years old.

If Jesus was actually referring to Israel's taking the city of Jerusalem, then we could still have a long way to go. Is it possible He was referring to Luke 21:24 where he said; *"And they shall fall by the edge of the sword, and shall be led away captive into all nations: and **Jerusalem shall be trodden down of the Gentiles, until the times of the Gentiles be fulfilled.**"*? I personally do not think so, since I think the budding of the fig tree is a reference to Israel achieving nation status in 1948. Though the Temple mount is still in the hands of Muslims, I believe the times of the Gentiles ended in 1967, but the count-down actually began in 1948. The *"times of the Gentiles"* did not end suddenly in 1967, but have been fading away, and gradually giving way to apostasy.

If the earth makes it to 2033 without the Tribulation having begun, then we may have to revise our thinking along these lines, but at this point I douibt we'll have to wait that long. Things are moving too fast for either of these ideas to be true.

Does He mean that the final generation that returns to Israel, that completes the return of the twelve tribes from all around the world, shall not pass until the End Time prophecies are fulfilled? I believe He does, but I still think this will occur before the generation that was born in 1948 passes away. That generation will be young men when they perform their missionary ministry, for the Bible states that they will be virgins. Thus the time from their return until their calling must be very short, or they will have time to get married.

Peter, another New Testament prophet also referred to Psalm 90 in relation to the End Times. 2 Peter 3:8 is a direct reference to Psalm 90:4.

Knowing this first, that there shall come in the last days scoffers, walking after their own lusts, 4 And saying, Where is the promise of his coming? for since the fathers fell asleep, all things continue as they were from the beginning of the creation. 5 For this they willingly are ignorant of, that by the *word of God the heavens were of old, and the earth standing out of the water and in the water: 6 Whereby the world that then was, being overflowed with water, perished: 7 But the heavens and the earth, which are now, by the same word are kept in store, reserved unto fire against the day of judgment and perdition of ungodly men. 8 But, beloved, be not ignorant of this one thing, **that one day is with the Lord as a thousand years, and a thousand years as one day.** 9 The Lord is not slack concerning his promise, as some men count slackness; but is longsuffering to us-ward, not willing that any should perish, but that all should come to repentance. 10 But the day of the Lord will come as a thief in the night; in the which the heavens shall pass away with a great noise, and the elements shall melt with fervent heat, the earth also and the works that are therein shall be burned up. 11 Seeing then that all these things shall be dissolved, what manner of persons ought ye to be in all holy conversation and godliness, 12 Looking for and hasting unto the coming of the day of God, wherein the heavens being on fire shall be dissolved, and the elements shall melt with fervent heat? 13 Nevertheless we, according to his promise, look for new heavens and a new earth, wherein dwelleth righteousness.* (2 Peter 3:3-13)

Amillennialism rests mainly upon verses 10-13 of 2 Peter 3, but in order to do so they have to divorce the context of these verses from verse 8, just two verses prior. Peter is continuing with the same thought, that a day with the Lord is as a thousand years and a thousand years as a day. The phrase *"in the which"* means *"within which"* or *"during which"*. So the *"Day of the Lord"* is a thousand year day, that comes in like a thief in the night, and ends with the *"Day of God"* and the destruction of the entire earth, some one thousand years later. The trigger for the destruction of the earth will be when the nations rebel against the Lord's rule. This rebellion is mentioned in Revelation 20:7-9 and Psalm 2.

This would explain why the term *"the Day of the Lord"* in scripture has been somewhat puzzling at times. Sometimes it appears to refer to the Tribulation period and other times it appears to refer to the millennial reign of Christ. It appears now that *"the Day of the Lord"* includes both the tribulation and the millennial reign all rolled up into Moses' one-thousand-year-long day.

Elsewhere in Psalm 90 Moses wrote; (verse 13) *"Return, O*

LORD, how long? and let it repent thee concerning thy servants". No doubt Moses was referring to the return of Israel to the land of Canaan, while wandering for forty years in the desert. While this was Moses' intention, I believe the Lord Himself was referring to a much more important return, the return of the Lord Jesus Christ. He therefore gave us clues as to the return of the Messiah in this Psalm. It is referred to in the words of Jesus Himself, in the words of Peter, and also in the words of Hosea.

> *I will go and return to my place, till they acknowledge their offence, and seek my face: in their affliction they will seek me early. Come, and let us return unto the LORD: for he hath torn, and he will heal us; he hath smitten, and he will bind us up. After two days will he revive us: in the third day he will raise us up, and we shall live in his sight. Then shall we know, if we follow on to know the LORD: his going forth is prepared as the morning; and he shall come unto us as the rain, as the latter and former rain unto the earth. (Hosea 5:15- 6:3)*

Note that it is the Lord God who says He will return to his place. When did God leave his place and when did He return to it? Did He not leave his place in Heaven when He was conceived of a virgin? Did He not return to it when Jesus was taken up to Heaven after his resurrection? (Acts 1:9) He says that in their *"affliction"* they will seek Him. This is a reference to the Great Tribulation. Israel has not sought the Lord as a nation from that day until now. Rather, they have blasphemed His name wherever they have gone, and now He is gathering them back to the land and He will deal with them there.

The reference to Psalm 90 occurs in verse 2, when he says the Lord will return *"after two days"*. Two days from when? He will return two days from the day he left, from the ascension, forty days after His resurrection. The timing is from the day he returns to his place, not two days after they call on His name. **It is God who sets the time of His return, not they.** The time of Jesus' return is appointed by God the Father and does not depend on the Church, nor on Israel (Acts 1:7). If the Church fails to evangelize the world, the *"Gospel Angel"* of Revelation 14:6 & 7 will finish the job.

Some may accuse me of saying *"My Lord delayeth His coming"*. I am actually saying that Jesus will return exactly on schedule, at the time appointed by the Father, and not a moment too soon nor too late. For most people on this planet, however, including many professing Christians, Jesus will return too soon! It is those whose focus is on making the world a better place, who are saying "*my Lord delayeth His coming*" by their actions!

While the Church has been given the job of evangelizing the world, we have NOT been given the job of achieving dominion over the earth. The truth is that the gospel has gone out into all the world and is today in every nation, as was foretold by Jesus. It is not yet in every tribe, however, which would certainly indicate that the rapture of the Church is not yet imminent. Don't think that we can delay the Lord's second coming by prohibiting the spread of the gospel, for when one church abandons the gospel, the Holy Spirit will lead someone else to continue its spread! God will ensure it is spread around the world on schedule. Revelation 5:9, which takes place shortly after the rapture, shows us that the gospel will reach the whole world before the rapture takes place.

*And they sung a new song, saying, Thou art worthy to take the book, and to open the seals thereof: for thou wast slain, and hast redeemed us to God by thy blood **out of every kindred, and tongue, and people, and nation**; (Rev. 5:9)*

*And the gospel must first be published among **all nations**. (Mark 13:10)*

Note that Hosea says "*in the third day he will raise us up*". This is not a reference to the rapture since the "*us*" is Israel. This is a reference to Israel being given spiritual life after existing as a dead nation for some 2700 years. This could possibly indicate that he will come back any time during the third thousand years, but I do not believe this is the case. The prophet was a Jew and the "*us*" is a reference to Israel, not the Church. Since He is coming for Israel at the end of the seven year Tribulation period, in the third day, it is thus still possible that He may rapture the Church at some time before the end of the second "*day*".

Notice also that the coming of the Lord is "*as the rain*"? How does rain come? Doesn't it come down from the sky? This is the same way the Lord will return, which was also repeated in Acts 1:11. He will not be born of a woman the second time, but will return as the conquering king, from Heaven.

The rapture of the Church is an event that will happen before the Lord reverts to dealing through Israel as He did in the Old Testament.   Though He will revert to dealing through Israel, the greatest harvest of gentile souls will actually occur under their watch.

Daniel Chapter 2

An introduction to eschatology can not be complete without a look at Nebuchadnezzar's dream of Daniel chapter 2. While the book of Daniel is the foundation of End Times prophecy, Nebuchadnezzar's dream forms the basic framework upon which the rest of Daniel is based.

> *31 Thou, O king, sawest, and behold a great image. This great image, whose brightness was excellent, stood before thee; and the form thereof was terrible. 32 This image's head was of fine gold, his breast and his arms of silver, his belly and his thighs of brass, 33 His legs of iron, his feet part of iron and part of clay. 34 Thou sawest till that a stone was cut out without hands, which smote the image upon his feet that were of iron and clay, and brake them to pieces. 35 Then was the iron, the clay, the brass, the silver, and the gold, broken to pieces together, and became like the chaff of the summer threshingfloors; and the wind carried them away, that no place was found for them: and the stone that smote the image became a great mountain, and filled the whole earth. 36 This is the dream; and we will tell the interpretation thereof before the king. 37 Thou, O king, art a king of kings: for the God of heaven hath given thee a kingdom, power, and strength, and glory. 38 And wheresoever the children of men dwell, the beasts of the field and the fowls of the heaven hath he given into thine hand, and hath made thee ruler over them all. Thou art this head of gold. 39 And after thee shall arise another kingdom inferior to thee, and another third kingdom of brass, which shall bear rule over all the earth. 40 And the fourth kingdom shall be strong as iron: forasmuch as iron breaketh in pieces and subdueth all things: and as iron that breaketh all these, shall it break in pieces and bruise. 41 And whereas thou sawest the feet and toes, part of potters' clay, and part of iron, the kingdom shall be divided; but there shall be in it of*

the strength of the iron, forasmuch as thou sawest the iron mixed with miry clay. 42 And as the toes of the feet were part of iron, and part of clay, so the kingdom shall be partly strong, and partly broken. 43 And whereas thou sawest iron mixed with miry clay, they shall mingle themselves with the seed of men: but they shall not cleave one to another, even as iron is not mixed with clay. 44 And in the days of these kings shall the God of heaven set up a kingdom, which shall never be destroyed: and the kingdom shall not be left to other people, but it shall break in pieces and consume all these kingdoms, and it shall stand for ever. 45 Forasmuch as thou sawest that the stone was cut out of the mountain without hands, and that it brake in pieces the iron, the brass, the clay, the silver, and the gold; the great God hath made known to the king what shall come to pass hereafter: and the dream is certain, and the interpretation thereof sure. (Daniel 2:31-45)

I recommend reading the whole of Daniel chapter 2, but for brevity's sake I'll present a synopsis here: Nebuchadnezzar had a dream, which troubled him greatly, but when he awoke he couldn't remember it. He asked his astrologers, soothsayers, and wise men to recall the dream for him, and to give him the interpretation. When they replied that what he was asking was impossible, and no king had ever asked such a thing, the jig was up. They were exposed as frauds, and the king decided to put them, and their families, to death. Daniel had not heard about the incident, and when the soldiers came to take him away he went to the king and asked for some time. He and his friends prayed, and the Lord answered their prayer and gave Daniel the dream and its interpretation. The section of Daniel 2:31-45 is the dream and its interpretation.

An interesting, related, observation is that the law of Moses forbids the practise of divination, witchcraft, or necromancy, and provides the death penalty for those who practise it. (Exodus 22:18, Deuteronomy 18:9-14) Nebuchadnezzar had actually prescribed the biblical penalty for these people, so why did Daniel seek mercy for those who did not deserve it? I think there is more than one answer, but essentially God never did expect the complete keeping of the Law, for ultimately we all deserve the death penalty. The Law was given to show us that we deserve death. God was giving the witches, diviners, enchanters, astrologers, and Chaldeans, a second chance. He was going to show them that Daniel's God was more powerful than the spirits they had contact with. When they saw that Daniel's God could do what they could not, they should have repented and followed that God. While it is obvious the majority did not repent, I would not be surprised if a few of them did.

God knew that the philosophy of these magicians would one day infect the Jewish understanding of Scripture. By the time of Christ, the Sadducees, and many of the Pharisees, were following the oral tradition that was based on the teachings of these Babylonian witches and astrologers. Jesus Himself railed against that tradition (Matthew 15:3, Mark 7:8, 9, & 13), and was sentenced to death by its practitioners. Later that teaching was written down and is today known as the Babylonian Talmud, and is followed by many Jews.

God knew this would happen, so why did He allow it? I think one reason is His reluctance to interfere with your freedom of choice. You can choose destruction if you wish. He has given many warnings in His Word, and even the fact that pagan prophets are so frequently wrong should provide enough warning for us to avoid such persons and teachings. It is all about God's glory, and even those who choose death will ultimately glorify God. We see, in this incident, God directly intervening to allow his enemies to live, because it ultimately fits in with His purposes.

Let's get back to Nebuchadnezzar's dream: Note that this vision was to cover all the time left for the earth, from that time until the end. The head of the image represents Babylon. The chest and arms of silver represents the Medo-Persian kingdom. The belly and thighs of brass represent the kingdom of Greece. The legs of iron and feet of iron mixed with clay represent the kingdom of Rome, which is the last kingdom and is to remain until it is crushed by the stone cut out without hands. Note that that stone is to strike the image on the feet, not the legs, nor the hips. This means that the Roman empire still exists in some form, and will exist until the return of Christ.

The Ten Toes

The ten toes of the image are the final form of the Roman world government, and will encompass the entire world, not merely Europe. Note that the Roman empire was divided into two, the eastern and western halves. You do not normally grow ten toes on one foot, and neither did Nebuchadnezzar's image. This should indicate to us that the final form of this empire will not be one sided, from Europe alone, but will take in the whole earth, from east to west. This book is not intended to be an exposé of secret societies. Suffice it to say that there is a network of secret societies which encompasses such groups as the Freemasons, the Bilderburgers, The Trilateral Commission, the Club of Rome, and the Council on Foreign Relations, among others. While the actual minutes of the meetings of these organizations is secret, it is well known that their purpose is to create a world government. Today you will be hard pressed to find a person in a position of authority who is not a member of one of these, a sister organization, or at the very least is not surrounded by such people. Gary Kah's book *"En Route to Global Occupation"'* is an excellent resource for those interested in digging deeper into the world of secret societies. While there are some who think that we need to fight the manipulation of our nations by such groups, it is my contention that it is God's will that they will succeed, for a time, in forming a global government. The best way to fight them is to preach the gospel of Jesus Christ!

In 1974 the Club of Rome released a report called *"Mankind at the Turning Point: The Second Report to the Club of Rome"*, by Mihajlo Mesarovic and Eduard Pestel. This report speaks of dividing the world up into ten economic regions, which really amounts to ten super-states, or kingdoms. The basic premise of the report is that the human race is in a crisis and in order to save mankind, and the earth, we need to create a global government. If you read between the lines you will see that what they are saying is that "*in order to save mankind, and the planet, we need to create a global government, and we need to submit to it, even if it is totalitarian in nature.*"

This report is well written and compelling, but I think wrong in its basic premise. It is materialistic in its outlook, essentially saying that the human race is in control, that it is up to us to save the planet. On page 151 and 152 Aurelio Peccei, the founder of the Club of Rome is quoted speaking of *"the noosphere"* and *"communion with Nature and with the transcendent"*. By these statements we can see that both Peccei's, and the author's, mindset is New Age pantheism. *"Noosphere"* is a concept invented by Vladimir Vernadsky, and expanded upon by Peirre Teilhard de Chardin, one of the fathers of the New Age movement, and refers to the hypothetical *"Collective Consciousness"* of the human race. This concept is closely linked to both the New Age movement, and the evolutionary hypothesis.

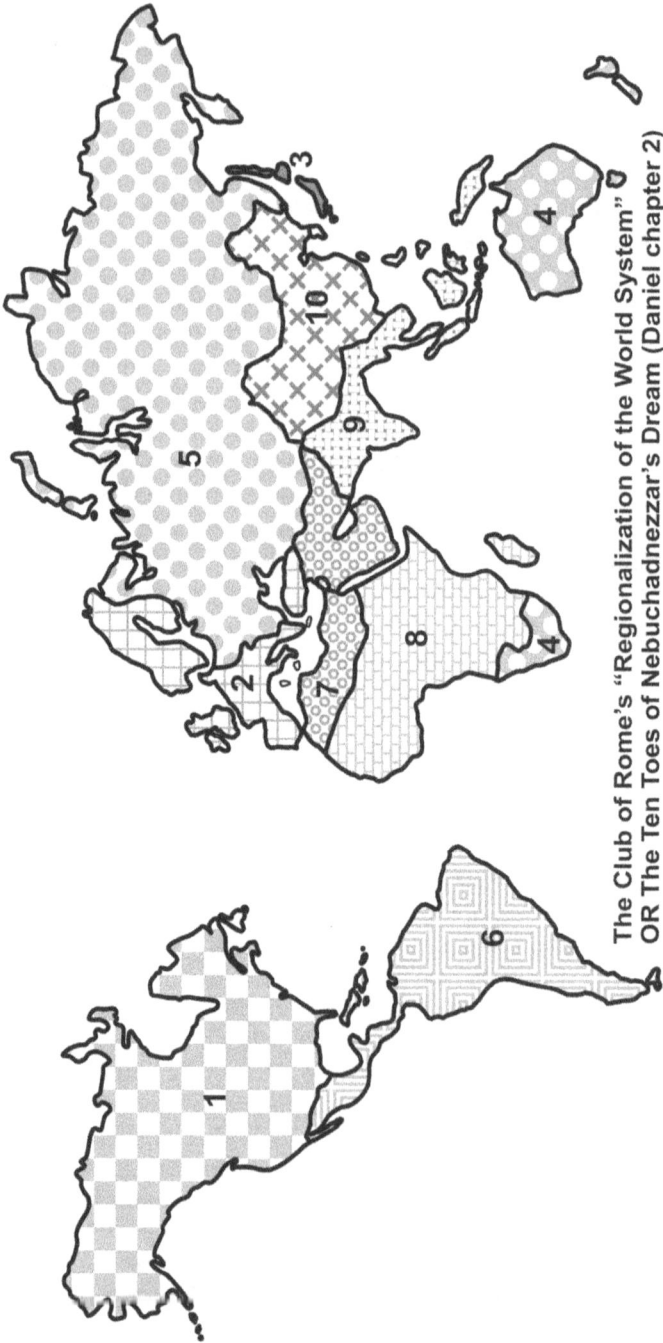

The Club of Rome's "Regionalization of the World System"
OR The Ten Toes of Nebuchadnezzar's Dream (Daniel chapter 2)

(Noosphere, Wikipedia)

In Appendix I the authors present two cases: Either there will be global warming, or global cooling, as a result of man's activity, and either is presented as evidence that the human race must accept their recommendations! They conveniently ignore the fact that past fluctuations in the earth's temperature were not the result of human activity. It is a known fact that the Ice Age, the global warming of two thousand years ago, and the mini-ice age of three hundred years ago, were not the result of human activity. There were not enough people on the planet to have that sort of effect. Neglecting relevant data in this fashion should certainly give us pause to consider whether the authors are truly scientific, as they claim, or whether they are following some other agenda. Nevertheless, it appears that many governments, and the UN, are following the advice presented in their book.

On page 38, figure 4-1 of *"Mankind at the Turning Point"* there is a map showing the world divided into ten regions. Appendix II identifies these regions as: 1. North America, 2. Western Europe, 3. Japan, 4. Rest of the Developed Market Economies (including Israel, Australia and South Africa), 5. Eastern Europe including the Soviet Union, 6. Latin America, 7. North Africa and the Middle East, 8. Main Africa, 9. South and Southeast Asia, 10. Centrally Planned Asia. This is the embryonic form of the ten toes of Nebuchadnezzar's vision. Already there have been changes, as we have seen Mexico being included in NAFTA, whereas it was originally included in the Latin American region. Originally Africa had been divided into three regions, but the African Union, formed on 9 July 2002, has taken in almost all of Africa, with the one exception currently being Morocco.

The Central Asian Union was proposed by the Kazakhstan President on April 26, 2007. This regional grouping has as its goal, the unification of the central Asian nations of Kazakhstan, Kyrgyzstan, Tajikistan, Turkmenistan, and Uzbekistan.

There are competing proposals on the table at the same time, such as the "South Asian Union", which would encompass the entire area from Lebanon in the west to Japan in the east, the southern border of Russia in the North, and The Pacific island nations in the south. (Proposal for Future South Asian Union (SAU)) Whether one or the other or some combination of these ideas takes root is immaterial. My point is only that there are groups worldwide working to form the Club of Rome's ten nation confederacy as a prelude to world government.

While the borders presented are not written in stone, this plan represents the basic framework for the final form of the Roman empire. It remains to be seen, just exactly where the borders will go, but it is obvious that some people take this idea very seriously, and in the end we will see exactly ten regional unions, or super-states formed, exactly as the bible predicts.

Daniel's Seventy Weeks Prophecy

Seventy weeks are determined upon thy people and upon thy holy city, to finish the transgression, and to make an end of sins, and to make reconciliation for iniquity, and to bring in everlasting righteousness, and to seal up the vision and prophecy, and to anoint the most Holy. Know therefore and understand, that **from the going forth of the commandment to restore and to build Jerusalem unto the Messiah the Prince shall be seven weeks, and threescore and two weeks:** the street shall be built again, and the wall, even in troublous times. And **after threescore and two weeks shall Messiah be cut off, but not for himself:** and the people of the prince that shall come shall destroy the city and the sanctuary; and the end thereof shall be with a flood, and unto the end of the war desolations are determined. And he shall confirm the covenant with many for one week: and in the midst of the week he shall cause the sacrifice and the oblation to cease, and for the overspreading of abominations he shall make it desolate, even until the consummation, and that determined shall be poured upon the desolate. (Daniel 9:24-27)

A lot of good men have explained these seventy sevens, or weeks, so I do not feel the need to do more than a brief review: From the time the king of Persia decreed that Jerusalem should be rebuilt until the Messiah would be *"cut off"* would be sixty nine weeks of years. There were apparently three decrees to rebuild Jerusalem, and for our purpose it doesn't matter which it refers to. God's timing is far more exact than our best calendars. Essentially, then, from the most significant decree to rebuild Jerusalem, until the Crucifixion, there were four hundred and eighty three years.

Daniel 9:24 decrees seventy weeks of years or four hundred and ninety years, which leaves a gap of seven years, for Israel to put away iniquity, and anoint the most Holy. There was an interruption of the time-line between the first four hundred and eighty three years and the last seven years. This interruption is the Church age, and was a mystery to the Old Testament saints. The last seven years is the Great Tribulation period or *"The Time of Jacob's Trouble"*.

There is some debate as to who or what Daniel 9:24 is referring to as the *"most Holy"*. Some think it refers to a place, but in context it must be the Messiah Himself. He is the one who is most Holy, and He is the one Israel has rejected. The Jews were loyal to the Temple, but they were not loyal to their God. Note that the A.V. Translators believed it to refer to Christ himself since they capitalized the first letter of the word Holy, which indicates deity. Kings are anointed in the Bible, and He is the King of kings and Lord of lords, so this is a reference to Jesus the Messiah himself. It's all about Him!

In verse 26 the subject changes to the *"prince that is to come"*, the Antichrist, and verse 27 starts the countdown of the last seven years. His confirmation of a covenant is the start of the seventieth week. From that point the day of Christ's return can be calculated. That's right, the day itself can be calculated! The exact number of days is written in Daniel chapter 12. It is the day of the Rapture of the Church that can't be calculated.

The Great Snatch

The system of Eschatology known as amillennialism has been around since its invention by Augustine, and is today the dominant view of the professing Christian Church. Many of its proponents are very hostile to the idea that Jesus will one day physically return and reign on earth, for a period of one thousand years. This view tends to spiritualize any passage that speaks of Christ's reign on earth. Some of them are hostile to the idea that there will be a Rapture of the Church at all. 1 Thessalonians 4:16-18 is a passage that speaks directly of the Lord snatching believers from off the earth and meeting us in the clouds. In view of this passage the debate must be about the timing of the Rapture, and not whether there is one or not. We find that if one disbelieves this passage, one likely has a low view of scripture itself:

16 For the Lord himself shall descend from heaven with a shout, with the voice of the archangel, and with the trump of God: and the dead in Christ shall rise first: 17 **Then we which are alive and remain shall be caught up together with them in the clouds, to meet the Lord in the air:** *and so shall we ever be with the Lord. 18 Wherefore comfort one another with these words. (1 Thessalonians 4:16-18)*

Here in 1 Thessalonians Paul gives us the clearest picture of the rapture in the Bible. This is not Jesus' second coming, but a part of it that precedes His actual arrival by some time. During this event the Lord will not actually touch down on the earth, but will meet his people in the clouds above. To say that the rapture happens at the end of the Tribulation period would hardly be a comfort to anyone, since that period will be characterized by unimaginable horrors. Verse 18 is given to show that the Church will not go through the Tribulation, which is a time of God's judgment against those who rebel against Him.

For **God hath not appointed us to wrath, but to obtain salvation** *by our Lord Jesus Christ, (1 Thessalonians 5:9)*

Much more then, being now justified by his blood, **we shall be saved from wrath through him.** *(Romans 5:9)*

No doubt these verses refer to Hell and the Lake of Fire, but they also refer to the wrath of God that is poured out on mankind during the Tribulation period, the Time of Jacob's Trouble. The wrath of God that begins during the tribulation will continue for all eternity for those who do not repent during this life. Jesus paid for the sins of believers and took away our wrath on the cross. Though we suffer tribulations in this life we will not suffer the wrath of God, which begins with the Great Tribulation.

The rapture and first resurrection, as a separate event from the Second coming of Christ, is not spoken of plainly in any part of the Bible. God has done this deliberately. He doesn't want to spoon feed his children, yet he does want to trap those who are wise in their own estimation. This doctrine is found *"between the lines"* and is arrived at by compiling and comparing the evidence found in scripture. This is not a new thing in Christianity. The doctrine of the Trinity was arrived at the same way.

Many attack this doctrine as wishful thinking on the part of rapture theorists, and claim it to be heresy. Their objection is mainly based on tradition, that *"Since it was not taught before the early 1800s it can't be true"*. The truth is that it is a legitimate doctrine <u>if</u> the Bible teaches it, even if no one ever saw it before 1800, or 2010. In the book of Daniel the angel told the prophet: *"And he said, Go thy way, Daniel: for the words are closed up and sealed till the time of the end."* (Daniel 12:9) Thus the Bible itself predicts that more of the End Times prophecies will be unveiled as the world comes closer to the end. The question is not, *"What did Christians traditionally believe?"* but *"what does the Bible teach?"*.

The truth is that the rapture of the Church was taught from time to time in ancient times, but that teaching was suppressed and its believers persecuted. Before the founding of the Roman Catholic Church by Constantine, the majority of Christians were futurists, and some taught the rapture. A man from the sixth century AD, one Pseudo-Ephraem wrote very clearly of the rapture of the Church. His sermon was translated into at least two other languages, which would indicate that it was widely received. It is a common tactic of the devil to attempt to kill off all those who believe something true, and then say *"See, no-one believes it"*! It seems to me to be a miracle that since the devil tried so hard to suppress this teaching, that it keeps on being revived!

For interest's sake here are a couple of quotes from Pseudo-Ephraem's sermon:

> "Why therefore do we not reject every care of earthly actions and prepare ourselves for the meeting of the Lord Christ, so that he may draw us from the confusion, which overwhelms all the world? For all the saints and elect of God are gathered, prior to the tribulation that is to come, and are taken to the Lord lest they see the confusion that is to overwhelm the world because of our sins." (Pseudo-Ephraem)

During the last seven years of Daniel's seventy weeks, the Lord will revert to dealing with the nation of Israel as He did in the Old Testament. To do this He must first remove the Church from this planet. This event is known as the Rapture of the Church. This word comes from the Greek *"harpazo"*, translated into Latin as *"rapere"* or *"raptus"* which means to snatch or take by force. This word is translated in English as *"caught up"* in 1 Thessalonians 4:17.

(Stewart, Study of Harpazo)(PRETRIBULATION RAPTURE, Rapture Ready)

There is another reason that the Lord will remove the Church from the earth. That reason is found in the writings of Moses, of all people!

> They have moved me to jealousy with that which is not God; they have provoked me to anger with their vanities: and I will move them to jealousy with those which are not a people; I will provoke them to anger with a foolish nation. (Deuteronomy 32:21)

This verse poses a riddle which is answered by the Church. The apostle Paul quotes this verse in Romans 10:19 and identifies the "people who are not a people", and "a foolish nation" as the Church of Jesus Christ. Christians come from all the tribes of the earth, not from any one people group, so we are a "People that are not a people". We are considered foolish by the unsaved and especially the Jews because of the large number of denominations who identify themselves as Christian.

Paul does not specifically state how the Lord will make Israel jealous, but He does give clues. A few years ago I was lying in bed one Saturday morning and I was meditating on this verse. I thought to myself "It is nearly two thousand years since the founding of the Church, and Israel is still not jealous." Now it is true that some Jews see the love of Christians for each other, and also for them, and come to Christ as a result, but the majority of Israel are still far away from God. They are not jealous. As I thought this thought the answer suddenly came to me; "The Rapture"! No I did not hear an audible voice, it was just a thought, but as I investigated, I became convinced that it was a thought given to me by God Himself.

As I meditated I realized we do not get jealous unless we see someone receive a favour that we perceive as unmerited, which we do not receive ourselves. When a parent shows favour to one child and not to another, the second child becomes jealous. To date, Israel has not seen the Christian world receive any great favour from God. When Christians die they immediately go to be with Jesus in Heaven, but this is something Jews do not actually see. To them, Christians live much the same way as Jews. We have to work for a living and we get sick and die in the same way as anyone else.

Israel will become jealous when God Himself shows a great

favour to the Church, that He does not show to Israel. When He snatches His bride from off this earth, at a time that He is about to bring unimaginable horrors to those who are left, Israel will be as jealous as a wife who is left at home, to mind the children, while her husband goes out and marries a second woman! What's more is that the Church does not deserve this favour, and they know it, as does Israel.

Every truly born again, regenerated believer in Christ will be caught up in the rapture including all gentile and Jewish believers. For one moment of one day the world will be full of unsaved people! There will be believers among them, but you can believe in the true God without being saved. Many of those unsaved persons think they have a special place with God. When they realize that they have been left behind they will become jealous. This will not only be the reaction of Israel but, I believe, of nominal Christians around the world. This event will cause these people to search the Scriptures like never before!

Note that in order for this interpretation to be true, the rapture must occur before the Great Tribulation period. Otherwise this jealousy of Israel would occur on Judgment day. God is not interested in making Jews jealous as he tosses them into the Lake of Fire. Everyone in that predicament will be jealous of the saints, not merely the Jews. The jealousy spoken of in Deuteronomy is for a purpose: to bring natural Israel to Christ!

It is true that the Gospel was initially given to Israel, and the apostles were obedient and preached it to Israel and the Gentiles, however, shortly thereafter the Jews dropped the ball, as it were, and it was picked up by the Gentile Church. Since that time the missionary work of the Church has largely been done by Gentile Christians. This is "the times of the Gentiles" that Jesus spoke about in Luke 21:24. Did it end in 1967 when Israel retook Jerusalem? I'm not sure. It may have began ending at that date, but Israel does not yet control the Temple mount. Regardless of the timing, there is definitely a "times of the gentiles" which Paul also spoke about in Romans 9-11. God is going to graft Israel into the tree again during the seven year, Great Tribulation period, shortly after the rapture of the Church.

Meanwhile, the devil is preparing a lie to explain away the rapture. He has been working on this lie for a long time now. After the rapture, the Antichrist, and false prophet, will pick up the lie and run with it! Any one who believes their lie will be lost for all eternity! We'll examine the lie in the last chapter.

Deuteronomy is not the only place in the Old Testament where the rapture is mentioned. A pre-trib rapture can be seen in Zephaniah chapter 2. Here we see Israel, the *"undesired nation"*, gathered together and then the Church, *"the meek of the earth"*, are hidden in Heaven during the day of the Lords anger. Why does he say *"may be hid"*? Because not all professing Christians will be taken, only those that know the Lord personally, and are faithful to Him. Only those He knows are in view here. Does He know you?

> Gather yourselves together, yea, gather together, O nation not desired; Before the decree bring forth, before the day pass as the chaff, before the fierce anger of the LORD come upon you, before the day of the LORD'S anger come upon you. Seek ye the LORD, all ye meek of the earth, which have wrought his judgment; seek righteousness, seek meekness: it may be ye shall be hid in the day of the LORD'S anger. (Zephaniah 2:1-3)

They will be hid in a totally secure place, God's Heaven, not somewhere on earth. The bible says in no uncertain terms, that the Antichrist will have power over the saints and will kill them in great numbers. Here we have a promise that these people will be hid in the day of the Lord's anger. They can't be the same group of people as the saints who will be beheaded for Jesus. There is a third group who survive the Tribulation and repopulate the earth. We will discuss them later.

By laying down their lives this way the saints will actually have victory over the Beast! These people will have seen God's power in rapturing the Church and they will know that He has power to resurrect them as well. Millions of Christians have been called upon to lay down their lives as the supreme act of faith. The saints of the Tribulation will lay down their lives as the greatest act of defiance, and faith, this world will ever know. Jesus will certainly see it and will reward those people in the sight of their enemies!

It will be an act of faith, but these people will also have the *"sight"* of having been witness to the rapture of the Church. They will have the *"sight"* of having seen many prophecies come to pass in a way that has not been seen from the resurrection of Christ until now. They will also have the *"sight"* of seeing the 144,000 Jewish evangelists successfully evade death at the hands of the Antichrist, and they will also have seen the two witnesses in Jerusalem and the miracles they perform. These people will see so many things, that confirm the Bible, that it is amazing that anyone would not come to Jesus Christ in faith.

And he (the Antichrist) shall speak great words against the most High, and shall wear out the saints of the most High, and think to change times and laws: and they shall be given into his hand until a time and times and the dividing of time. (Daniel 7:25)

And they overcame him by the blood of the Lamb, and by the word of their testimony; and they loved not their lives unto the death. (Revelation 12:11)

And it was given unto him to make war with the saints, and to overcome them: and power was given him over all kindreds, and tongues, and nations. (Revelation 13:7)

In Psalm 50 the Lord comes and gathers his saints, the ones who have made a covenant with him by His sacrifice on the cross:

Our God shall come, and shall not keep silence: **a fire shall devour before him,** *and it shall be very tempestuous round about him.* **He shall call to the heavens from above, and to the earth, that he may judge his people. Gather my saints together unto me; those that have made a covenant with me by sacrifice.** *And the heavens shall declare his righteousness: for God is judge himself. (Psalm 50:3-6)*

The *"fire"* that shall devour before Him refers to the Great Tribulation period, generally, and the return of Christ specifically. Notice that there are two simultaneous judgments in view here. There is one in Heaven for the saved, and one on earth, the Tribulation, for the lost. Both of these judgments are different from the Great White Throne judgment, and the lost who die during the Tribulation will ultimately stand for Judgment before the Great White Throne. In the Heavenly judgment it is only His people who are being judged, not the unsaved. He calls them to the heavens first in the rapture. This Judgment is referred to as the "Bema Seat", and is like the judgment at a sports meet, for which it is named. There will be no condemnation here, only rewards and the loss of rewards. The unsaved dead are in Hell, and the living are on the earth. If He has any words of rebuke for His people it is not the business of the lost!

Later on, after the Millennium, the unsaved dead will be raised and will face the Great White Throne Judgment. At that time the saved will be there as witnesses and will approve of the Judgment handed down from God. What a horrid place to be, to have God condemn you and then all the saints and angels agreeing with the verdict! Then to have an angel pick you up and toss you into the Lake of Fire, like a piece of garbage! This will be the fate of the majority of mankind, who have not received Jesus Christ as their Lord and Saviour. I am sure there will be many tears coming from the eyes of the saints, but they will acknowledge that the sentence is just. You have had the same chance as they have. There is no other Saviour! He is your only hope to escape this fate!

Psalm 144:5-8 also speaks of the Lord reaching down from Heaven to rescue His people during a time of earthly upheaval:

> Bow thy heavens, O LORD, and **come down**: *touch the mountains, and they shall smoke. Cast forth lightning, and scatter them: shoot out thine arrows, and destroy them.* **Send thine hand from above;** *rid me,* **and deliver me out of great waters, from the hand of strange children;** *Whose mouth speaketh vanity, and their right hand is a right hand of falsehood.*

Isaiah also speaks of the Rapture of the Church, in the clearest picture of the Rapture in the Old Testament. This has been in the Word of God for some 2700 years, why is it that few have seen it until now?

> *Like as a woman with child, that draweth near the time of her delivery, is in pain, and crieth out in her pangs; so have we been in thy sight, O LORD. We have been with child, we have been in pain, we have as it were brought forth wind;* **we have not wrought any deliverance in the earth; neither have the inhabitants of the world fallen. Thy dead men shall live, together with my dead body shall they arise. Awake and sing, ye that dwell in dust:** *for thy dew is as the dew of herbs, and the earth shall cast out the dead.* **Come,**

my people, enter thou into thy chambers, and shut thy doors about thee: hide thyself as it were for a little moment, until the indignation be overpast. For, behold, the LORD cometh out of his place to punish the inhabitants of the earth for their iniquity: the earth also shall disclose her blood, and shall no more cover her slain. (Isaiah 26:17 - 21)

Verses 17 and 18 refer to a pregnant woman beginning her labour pains. This is a reference to the wars and commotions that Jesus spoke about as signs of the end. The time leading up to the Great Tribulation is compared to a woman in labour. The pangs are first mild and far apart, but soon come closer and closer and more intense, until the child is born. Jesus referred to this time in Matthew 24:8 *"All these are the beginning of sorrows"*. Many new translations render this passage *"All these are but the beginning of the birth pains."*

Many times in the Bible the period leading up to the Great Tribulation period is compared to labour pains. *"And they shall be afraid: pangs and sorrows shall take hold of them; they shall be in pain as a woman that travaileth: they shall be amazed one at another; their faces shall be as flames."* (Isaiah 13:8) The same terminology and context is in view in Jeremiah 13:21, 49:24, Hosea 13:13, Mark 13:8, and John 16:21. As men we often do not think that labour could be that severe, but remember, many women have died in child-birth.

The prophet laments that Israel has not wrought deliverance upon the earth, as indeed they have not. They were commissioned to lead the nations to God but instead they have abandoned Him. They have been wasting their time for the last 2700 years! The implication of verse 18 is that Israel is being recalled, like a defective product, back to the land where their manufacturer will correct their deficiencies.

In verse 19 we see the first resurrection of the saints in the term *"Thy dead men shall live"*. The unsaved are not resurrected at this time, they are not *"His"* dead men, but children of the Devil. We see the saints singing, and the prophet himself anticipates being resurrected at this time! This is not a general resurrection which includes the lost, for at their resurrection they will not be singing, but in mourning and fear! We need to base our lives on the knowledge of the resurrection, and not the here-and-now.

In verse 20 we see the Rapture of the Church, occurring

immediately after the resurrection of the saints. The chambers spoken of in verse 20 are the *"rooms"* or *"mansions"* in Heaven that Jesus spoke about. The comparison here is to the Jewish wedding where the bride is sequestered, with her husband, in her chambers for seven days, and is later presented as his wife. The *"Indignation"* is the Great Tribulation period, and verse 21 is a brief description of that event. The term *"cometh out of His place"* is a reference to Hosea 5:15 and 6:1-2 which takes place two *"days"* after he returned there. Very clearly the contents of this passage are an actual, physical, literal event, coming very soon to a planet near you.

In the next chapter of Isaiah, chapter 27 verses 12 and 13 speak of another event that is closely related to the preceding:

> And it shall come to pass in that day, that the LORD shall beat off from the channel of the river unto the stream of Egypt, and ye shall be gathered one by one, O ye children of Israel. And it shall come to pass in that day, **that the great trumpet shall be blown,** and they shall come which were ready to perish in the land of Assyria, and the outcasts in the land of Egypt, and shall worship the LORD in the holy mount at Jerusalem. (Isaiah 27:12-13)

This passage is a reference to the war of Psalm 83. The phrase *"beat off"* is a reference to Israel beating her enemies from the Euphrates river to the Nile in Egypt. This is the land that God promised Abraham in Genesis 15:18. The *"great trumpet"* here is likely the trumpet Paul spoke of in I Corinthians:

> "Behold, I shew you a mystery; We shall not all sleep, but we shall all be changed, In a moment, in the twinkling of an eye, at the last trump: for the trumpet shall sound, and the dead shall be raised incorruptible, and we shall be changed." (1 Corinthians 15:51 & 52)

> "For the Lord himself shall descend from heaven with a shout, with the voice of the archangel, and with the trump of God: and the dead in Christ shall rise first": (1 Thessalonians 4:16)

Ignorance over this trumpet has caused many to conclude that the trumpet in 1 Corinthians, and 1 Thessalonians, refers to the last of the seven trumpet judgments found in Revelation 8-10.

Actually the book of Revelation had not even been written at the time that Paul wrote these passages. Paul could not have been referring to anything written in that book, but to the trumpets spoken of in the Old Testament. Paul was ignorant of the book of Revelation, and while God knew what was going to be written in it, I don't think He has that book in mind here at all. It was something that could be found in the Scriptures of Paul's day.

There are several trumpets referred to by the Old Testament prophets, relating to the judgments of Israel, the last of which is the trumpet in Isaiah 27:13 and Joel 2:1.

> *Blow ye the trumpet in Zion, and sound an alarm in my holy mountain: let all the inhabitants of the land tremble:* ***for the day of the LORD cometh, for it is nigh at hand;*** *(Joel 2:1)*

It appears that this is the *"Last Trumpet"* that Paul was referring to in 1 Corinthians, and 1 Thessalonians. The Rapture of the Church will coincide with the final return of the lost tribes of Israel, near the beginning of the day of the LORD. Large numbers of the southern kingdom of Judah, the Jews, have already returned, but there are still many elsewhere, plus there is as yet very little representation from the tribes of the northern kingdom of Israel. We shall look at this subject a little later.

> *And they shall be mine, saith the LORD of hosts, in that day when I make up my jewels; and* ***I will spare them, as a man spareth his own son that serveth him.*** *Then shall ye return, and discern between the righteous and the wicked, between him that serveth God and him that serveth him not. (Malachi 3:17)*

Malachi is also referring to a pre-tribulation rapture in this passage. His sparing of them is a reference to the rapture of the Church, when He spares his people from the Wrath of God during the Tribulation. The "return" spoken of in verse 18 appears to be when the Church and Old Testament saints return to rule the world with Jesus during the millennium, or perhaps the spiritual awakening of Israel during the Tribulation. During the Tribulation Israel will finally discern between the Antichrist and Jesus Christ. 1

Thessalonians 3:13 also speaks of this same event.

The Rapture of the Church will be the most amazing event in the History of the World. For this reason many have doubted its existence. Why isn't there more about it in Scripture? Well, how much do you need? As I have shown it is very clearly there in the Old Testament, and I predict that it will be found in more places there as more study the amazing Word of God, especially after the event. They will have sight added to their faith, but God in His mercy will still be able to save millions. While we're on the subject let's take a look at it in the New Testament:

> *Immediately after the tribulation of those days shall the sun be darkened, and the moon shall not give her light, and the stars shall fall from heaven, and the powers of the heavens shall be shaken: And then shall appear the sign of the Son of man in heaven: and then shall all the tribes of the earth mourn, and they shall see the Son of man coming in the clouds of heaven with power and great glory. (Matthew 24:29-30)*

As we have seen before in prophecy, Jesus now skips from the end, back to the beginning of the Tribulation period:

> *But as the days of Noe were, so shall also the coming of the Son of man be. For as in the days that were before the flood they were eating and drinking, marrying and giving in marriage, until the day that Noe entered into the ark, And knew not until the flood came, and took them all away; so shall also the coming of the Son of man be. Then shall two be in the field; the one shall be taken, and the other left. Two women shall be grinding at the mill; the one shall be taken, and the other left. Watch therefore: for ye know not what hour your Lord doth come. (Matthew 24:37-42)*

Note that Jesus is saying that when the ark was complete, Noah and his family were first taken to a place of safety and then the flood came and destroyed the whole world. Those left behind were destroyed.

> *And as it was in the days of Noe, so shall it be also in the days of the Son of man. 27 They did eat, they drank, they married wives, they were given in marriage, until the day that*

Noe entered into the ark, and the flood came, and destroyed them all. 28 Likewise also as it was in the days of Lot; they did eat, they drank, they bought, they sold, they planted, they builded; 29 But the same day that Lot went out of Sodom it rained fire and brimstone from heaven, and destroyed them all. 30 Even thus shall it be in the day when the Son of man is revealed. 31 In that day, he which shall be upon the housetop, and his stuff in the house, let him not come down to take it away: and he that is in the field, let him likewise not return back. 32 Remember Lot's wife. 33 Whosoever shall seek to save his life shall lose it; and whosoever shall lose his life shall preserve it. 34 I tell you, in that night there shall be two men in one bed; the one shall be taken, and the other shall be left. 35 Two women shall be grinding together; the one shall be taken, and the other left. 36 Two men shall be in the field; the one shall be taken, and the other left. (Mark 17:26-36)

When God was about to bring destruction on Sodom and Gomorrah, He first brought Lot and His family out of the city. The Lord reminds us of Lot's wife who looked back and was destroyed. If we think we can combat the Antichrist ourselves, if we think we can somehow survive through the Tribulation period through our own strength we will certainly lose everything including our lives. The only security is in Christ Jesus.

This passage shows the Lord's knowledge of the earth's time zones, for he shows that the event will happen simultaneously all over the world. Some will be sleeping and others will be awake and working.

The first resurrection has actually already begun. This is a multi-staged event. Jesus Himself is called the firstfruits from the dead in 1 Corinthians 15:20. He is not the only one already risen, for Matthew 27 records that many of the Old Testament saints were resurrected around the same time as Jesus. He states that they appeared to many in Jerusalem, however there is nothing written about them after this. It appears that when Jesus ascended to Heaven these saints went with Him. We could also add Enoch and Elijah to this list, since they were the first to be raptured, and are still alive in Heaven. God wants His saints with Him, not left here on the earth.

And the graves were opened; and many bodies of the saints

which slept arose, And came out of the graves after his resurrection, and went into the holy city, and appeared unto many. (Matthew 27:52)

As already stated, there is a debate over the timing of the rapture among millennialists. Some teach that it will occur before the Tribulation, while others claim that it will occur at the mid point, around the time the Antichrist sets up the abomination of desolation in the Temple. The other choice is that it could occur after the Tribulation at the time when Jesus Christ returns.

Could it be that all three rapture scenarios are correct? Like the famous multiple choice question D, is it possible that A, B, and C are all correct? Actually I do not think so. The Resurrection is definitely a multi-stage event, since it has already begun and will continue in the future. We have already seen this, so what is happening in Matthew 24:31 and Mark 13:27? Go back and look at the verses regarding the rapture of the Church. Are there any angels in those passages? No, there are not, and the reason is that at the rapture of the Church the believers will receive bodies like Jesus Christ Himself. When He calls He will empower us to come to Him! As He says: "My sheep know my voice". (John 10:3, 4, 16, 27) In Isaiah 26:20 and in Revelation 4:1 Jesus calls his people to Him. It is an invitation that we can not resist! His children want to be with Him more than anything else!

*And then shall he **send his angels, and shall gather together his elect from the four winds, from the uttermost part of the earth to the uttermost part of heaven.** (Mark 13:27)*

*And <u>**he shall send his angels with a great sound of a trumpet, and they shall gather together his elect from the four winds, from one end of heaven to the other.**</u> (Matthew 24:31)*

This event is a gathering of God's people from the earth, in preparation for His second coming. This passage is often used as support for a post-trib Rapture. We have already seen strong evidence that the rapture will be before the Tribulation. Is it possible that He will actually snatch His people off the earth more than once? He certainly did it twice in the Old Testament. Before the flood He raptured Enoch, and later He took Elijah directly to Heaven without having seen death! Though this event is certainly near the end of the Tribulation period, it doesn't appear to be the rapture.

Notice the differences between these two passages. Though they are recordings of the same discourse Jesus had with His disciples the differences are significant. The reference to *"heaven"* in these passages is not a reference to God's home, but to the atmosphere. This is why there is the reference to *"the four winds"*. This event will take place within the confines of the atmosphere of the earth.

Please do not get this event confused with Jesus' story of the rich man and Lazarus, where the angel takes Lazarus to Abraham's Bosom. That story was given in the past tense. It was the story of an Old Testament Jew, not indwelt with the Holy Spirit, being taken to the waiting place of the Old Testament saints, to await the cross. That story and that type of event is not in view here.

So who are the elect who are gathered by the angels in these two verses? This is not the Church of Jesus Christ, since the Church will be Raptured before the Great Tribulation period. These are the believers who were saved during, and have survived through, the Great Tribulation period. These people are snatched off the earth in their natural bodies and taken to a safe place while Jesus brings destruction and judgment to the unbelieving humanity on the earth. The bible says in many places that the mountains will fall at the return of Christ, so this earth will be a very dangerous place to be when He returns. (see Deuteronomy 32:22, Psalms 97:5, 144:5, Isaiah 34:3, Isaiah 40:4, Isaiah 64:1, 3, Amos 9:13, Nahum 1:5)

*The mountains quake at him, and **the hills melt, and the earth is burned at his presence**, yea, the world, and all that dwell therein. (Nahum 1:5)*

Could this possibly be a reference to the end of the millennial reign of Christ? No. If the mountains were to exist for a thousand years during the reign of Christ, it could not be said that they fell at His presence. For this to happen it must occur when He physically returns to set up the Kingdom on earth, at the end of the Tribulation. Besides this the other verses listed speak of the hills falling, or melting in the context of the Lord's second coming. This gives new meaning to Jesus' words *"Then shall they begin to say to the mountains, Fall on us; and to the hills, Cover us."* (Luke 23:30) The Lord elaborated on this event in Revelation 6:12-17. It appears that when the people of earth crawl into holes in the rocks to hide from the Returning Christ they shall indeed be crushed as the mountains fall and the earth returns to its pre-flood state. Be vigilant to make sure you are not one of those people!

> *And there shall be signs in the sun, and in the moon, and in the stars; and upon the earth distress of nations, with perplexity; the **sea and the waves roaring;** (Luke 21:25)*

We have seen tremendous destruction, in recent years, as tsunamis have devastated coastlines of various parts of the world. How much more powerful will the tsunamis be at the time when the mountains fall? Cities like New York, Vancouver, London, and many others will be destroyed as huge waves overcome them. Other cities will be destroyed by earthquakes and the resultant fires. This world will not be a safe place to live at that time. In order for the Lord to keep His people safe, they will have to be lifted off of the surface of the planet.

The word *"heaven"* in scripture has three meanings: It is used for the atmosphere, the space between the stars, and the place where God dwells. Geneses 1:20 tells us that God created the birds *"that may fly above the earth in the open firmament of heaven."* In Revelation 14:6 we have an angel flying throughout "heaven" proclaiming the gospel to those who dwell on the earth. Again we see that the term *"heaven"* can actually refer to the atmosphere of the earth.

The reference to *"heaven"* in these two verses is thus likely a reference to the atmosphere, perhaps to just a few thousand feet above the surface of the earth. This group, gathered by the angels, will likely contain the believing remnants of both Israel and the Gentiles. Once God's enemies have been destroyed these people will be brought back down to repopulate the planet. In the mean time they will be eye witnesses to what He is able to do. They will tell their children of that which they have seen, and will be able to show them the ruins, but a thousand years later many of their descendants will have forgotten all about it.

Much confusion is caused because events separated by thousands of years are often spoken of in the same passage, and often in the same sentence. At other times different passages which use similar terminology, are speaking of separate events. Also, pay attention to who is speaking. The disciples often asked questions not fully realizing what they were asking. In Matthew 13 Jesus spoke with similar terminology to Matthew 24 and Mark 13, yet was speaking of separate events:

> *The enemy that sowed them is the devil; the harvest is the end of the world; and the reapers are the angels. As therefore the tares are gathered and burned in the fire;* **so shall it be in the end of this world.** *The Son of man shall send forth his angels, and they shall gather out of his kingdom all things that offend, and them which do iniquity;* (Matt. 13:39-41)

In verse 39 and 40 most new translations change "*end of the world*" to "*end of the age*". **This seemingly small change actually changes the timing of the passage by at least one thousand years!** The "*end of the age*" is the return of Christ and the setting up of the millennial kingdom. The "*End of the world*" will occur at the end of the millennial kingdom, a thousand years later! That will be the time when this earth is destroyed and a new earth is created. It is Jesus who says this event will occur at the end of the world. Thus we know that this is a reference to the end of the millennial kingdom.

Confusing these two events could be fatal to your soul. If, at the rapture of the Church, you think God has removed the "*evil people*", so the "Church" can create the kingdom of God on earth, you will be set-up to accept the Antichrist as the Messiah, or Christ. This is part of the strong delusion.

In the Matthew 24 passage similar terminology is used, but it is important to note who is saying what:

> *And as he sat upon the mount of Olives, the* **disciples** *came unto him privately, saying, Tell us, when shall these things be?* *and* **what shall be the sign of thy coming, and of the end of the world?** *(Matthew 24:3)*

Note that at this time it had not yet been revealed that the Kingdom of Christ on earth will last one thousand years. The disciples did not know how much separation there would be between these two events. In Jesus' answer he mainly spoke on His second coming, only speaking of the end of the world briefly in verse 35. Just because he says "*Heaven and earth shall pass away*" in the middle of speaking of his return, it does not mean that Heaven and earth will be destroyed at the time he returns. He is actually emphasizing the eternal nature of his Word, that his Word will outlast heaven and earth.

In the Matthew 24 and Mark 13 passages it is the elect who are gathered at the return of Christ, while in the Matthew 13 passage it is the unbelievers who are gathered for destruction at the end of the millennium. Matthew 13:47-49 indicates that both unbelievers and the believers will be gathered at the same time. The believers themselves will be gathered and moved to a place of safety as earth and Heaven are destroyed and recreated, so that the eternal kingdom can begin. At that time the unbelievers too shall be gathered, but for them it is for their final Judgment and the assignment of a place in the Lake of Fire.

Rapture Timing

I f the rapture timing is based on the ascension of our Lord we need to ask *"When was the crucifixion, resurrection, and ascension of the Lord Jesus Christ?"*

Many have mocked Anglican Bishop James Ussher for his monumental work *"The Annals of the World"*. I do not believe such mocking is warranted, Bishop Ussher was a greater scholar than his critics, and I have found that often mocking is a sign of ignorance on the part of the mockers. This is not to say that he made no errors...we all do.

Bishop Ussher dates the birth of Jesus Christ to the year of 5 BC. His reasons are sound; that Herod is believed to have died in 4 BC and therefore Jesus had to be born some time before that. There had to be enough time, also, for the wise men from the east to visit, as well as Herod's killing of the babies of the Bethlehem area.

Ussher and many other scholars have come to the conclusion that Jesus was crucified in 33 AD, which would make him thirty seven or thirty eight years old at the time. The bible itself does not say how old He was at his death, although it does say he was about thirty years old when he was baptized by John (Luke 3:23). The editors of the recent reprint of Ussher's Annals believe that there may have been a gap of three years from the time of Jesus' baptism until the beginning of his earthly ministry. (Annals, p. 822)

Luke records, in Acts 1:22, that when replacing Judas Iscariot, the Apostles chose two men who had been with Jesus from the time of His baptism. This would effectively eliminate any idea of a gap between His baptism and the beginning of His ministry. His baptism was the beginning of His ministry! There is not enough material in the gospels for an eight year ministry of Jesus Christ, so it appears that the date of 33 AD for the crucifixion is incorrect.

There is at least one book that argues for a birth of Jesus Christ as early as 15 BC (Important Dates, Conte). The author makes a compelling case, based on historical celestial observations and modern computer calculations of eclipses and comets, that many of the commonly accepted dates are inaccurate, not only for the birth of Christ, but for the dates of the reigns of many ancient kings. If he is correct then another question that needs to be asked is: *Which of the three decrees to rebuild Jerusalem does Daniel 9:25 refer to?* It seems that the commonly accepted crucifixion year of 33 AD may be out by as much as fifteen years! If the crucifixion and ascension of our Lord were actually between 18-28 AD the dates would line up perfectly.

The modern Jewish method of calculating Passover was only established around AD 359 by Sanhedrin president Hillel (The Jewish Calendar). The truth is that we just do not have an accurate Jewish calendar dating from the first century. If we assume that Jesus was born during the year 5 BC, and began his ministry when he was thirty, that would have been in 25 AD. If His ministry lasted three years the crucifixion would have been in 28 AD. (This assumption may be too late, by as much as ten years.) The gospel of John chronologically records three Passovers which occurred while Jesus was performing His ministry, in chapters 2, 6, and 11-19. It does not say that there were no other Passovers during his time of ministry, however, so theoretically there could have been more than three. There may have been one, but it's unlikely that there would have been five passovers passing by without notice from the disciples, especially since Jesus came to fulfill the Passover.

I find it astounding that our calendars could be out by as much as fifteen years, yet as I read through Ronald Conte's website, I am forced to admit that he makes a compelling case. Jesus may have actually been born in 15 BC, and this would mean that the two thousand year anniversary of the resurrection could be as near as 2018! (www.BiblicalChronology.com)

I cannot give you an exact date for the return of Christ for either the Church or Israel, but it appears to be approaching very quickly. Even if we could calculate the exact date referred to by Jesus in

Matthew 24:34, we would still not know the date of the Rapture of the Church. That date is hidden and not knowable to anyone until it occurs.

Eight to eighteen years does not seem like a very long time. I find it hard to believe that all the things of Matthew 24 could be accomplished in such a short time, but that is how I read the Scriptures. The Temple in Jerusalem must be rebuilt before the middle of the Tribulation, and sacrifices must be restarted before that time.

Herod's temple was started by Herod the Great before the birth of Christ and not completed until shortly before it was destroyed. It may be that the third temple will not be as elaborate as Herod's temple, and modern transportation and building methods may be faster, but it must still take some time to build. For this reason it is likely that the Rapture of the Church will occur some time before the beginning of the Tribulation period itself or, failing this, the rebuilding of the Temple must begin before this event.

As it stands, the Temple mount is currently under Muslim control, and any attempt on the part of Israel to begin the reconstruction of the Temple will immediately result in a major war.

The lack of a temple is not the only obstacle to a soon fulfilment of the End Times prophecies. While Israel was reestablished in 1948, the majority of the tribes of Israel have yet to return. The fig tree has been in bud for a long time, but it has yet to bloom.

I say these things are obstacles to the soon fulfilment of prophecy, but God is quite capable of rapidly changing the situation in ways that will take our breath away! Obstacles to us are merely opportunities to God! I look forward to see what He is about to do!

All Israel?

The people known today as Jews are mainly the descendants of the southern kingdom of Judah, from the time when Israel split into two nations. The word "Jew" is derived from the word Judah. The Jewish prisoners in German Nationalist Socialist (Nazi) concentration camps wore yellow stars of David with the word "Jude" in the middle of it. This is one of the unfortunate problems with the modern English language, we often do not see the connection to history in the words we use every day.

The kingdom of Judah was mainly made up of the tribes of Judah, Benjamin and some of the Levites. The Northern kingdom was made up of the tribes of Reuben, Gad, Simeon, Naphtali, Ephraim, Manasseh, Asher, Zabulun, Issachar, Dan and the balance of Levi. The two nations had a rocky relationship for three hundred years until Israel was carried off by the Assyrians. When Nebuchadnezzar conquered the Assyrians those people were transported even farther away from their homeland. The ten tribes of Israel seemed to disappear from history and few are seen again in the Bible.

While there is little representation of the northern kingdom in modern day Israel, there are numerous passages that describe the return of these people:

> *And he shall set up an ensign for the nations, and shall assemble the outcasts of Israel, and gather together the dispersed of Judah from the four corners of the earth. The envy also of Ephraim shall depart, and the adversaries of Judah shall be cut off: Ephraim shall not envy Judah, and Judah shall not vex Ephraim.* (Isaiah 11:12-13)

> *Thus saith the LORD; I am returned unto Zion, and will dwell in the midst of Jerusalem: and Jerusalem shall be called a city of truth; and the mountain of the LORD of hosts the holy mountain. Thus saith the LORD of hosts; There shall yet old men and old women dwell in the streets of Jerusalem, and every man with his staff in his hand for very age. And the streets of the city shall be full of boys and girls playing in the streets thereof. Thus saith the LORD of hosts; If it be marvellous in the eyes of the remnant of this people in these days, should it also be marvellous in mine eyes? saith the LORD of hosts. Thus saith the LORD of hosts; Behold, I will save my people from the east country, and from the west country; And I will bring them, and they shall dwell in the midst of Jerusalem: and they shall be my people, and I will be their God, in truth and in righteousness.* (Zechariah 8:3-8)

Note that the house of Joseph consists of the tribe of Ephraim and the tribe of Manasseh. Both Ephraim and Joseph are used as catch-all phrases to refer to the entire northern kingdom:

> *And I will strengthen the house of Judah, and I will save*

*the house of Joseph, and I will bring them again to place them; for I have mercy upon them: and they shall be as though I had not cast them off: for I am the LORD their God, and will hear them. And they of Ephraim shall be like a mighty man, and their heart shall rejoice as through wine: yea, their children shall see it, and be glad; their heart shall rejoice in the LORD. I will hiss for them, and gather them; for I have redeemed them: and they shall increase as they have increased. And I will sow them among the people: and they shall remember me in far countries; and they shall live with their children, and turn again. I will bring them again also out of the land of Egypt, and gather them out of Assyria; and **I will bring them into the land of Gilead and Lebanon;** and place shall not be found for them. (Zechariah 11:6-10)*

The land of Gilead is on the East side of the Jordan river and the sea of Galilee, and the Golan is only a part of that territory. The Golan was partially returned to Israel during the 1967 war, though Syria still controls 30% of it. Lebanon is self explanatory. God says that these territories will belong to Israel when the rest of Israel returns. There is more than one place in Scripture where God has promised the land of Lebanon to Israel. (Deuteronomy 11:24, Joshua 13:5, Isaiah 12:12 & 13)

Historically the Land of Gilead belonged to the tribes of Reuben, Gad and half of Manasseh, however Obadiah predicts that when it is restored it will initially belong to Benjamin.

*And they of the south shall possess the mount of Esau; and they of the plain the Philistines: and they shall possess the fields of Ephraim, and the fields of Samaria: and **Benjamin shall possess Gilead.** (Obadiah 1:19)*

I find it interesting that the first part of Israel to return is Judah, of whom Benjamin is a partner. I take it then, that the other tribes will not return until Benjamin has already captured Gilead. Those tribes will indeed return, for God says all of Israel shall return, but I suspect that they shall live together with the other tribes, at least initially, and not necessarily in tribally allocated land. Eventually they will possess all the land God has promised to them, including what was theirs historically, and it shall be divided up tribally as it was in the Old Testament.

*For, lo, the days come, saith the LORD, that I will bring again the captivity of my people **Israel and Judah**, saith the LORD: and I will cause them to return to the land that I gave to their fathers, and they shall possess it. (Jeremiah 30:3)*

Therefore fear thou not, O my servant Jacob, saith the LORD; neither be dismayed, O Israel: for, lo, I will save thee from afar, and thy seed from the land of their captivity; and Jacob shall return, and shall be in rest, and be quiet, and none shall make him afraid. (Jeremiah 30:10)

*Again I will build thee, and thou shalt be built, O virgin of Israel: thou shalt again be adorned with thy tabrets, and shalt go forth in the dances of them that make merry. 5 Thou shalt yet plant vines upon the mountains of Samaria: the planters shall plant, and shall eat them as common things. (Samaria was a part of Israel not Judah) 6 For there shall be a day, that the watchmen upon the mount **Ephraim** shall cry, Arise ye, and let us go up to Zion unto the LORD our God. 7 For thus saith the LORD; Sing with gladness for Jacob, and shout among the chief of the nations: publish ye, praise ye, and say, O LORD, save thy people, the remnant of Israel. 8 Behold, I will bring them from the north country, and gather them from the coasts of the earth, and with them the blind and the lame, the woman with child and her that travaileth with child together: a great company shall return thither. 9 They shall come with weeping, and with supplications will I lead them: I will cause them to walk by the rivers of waters in a straight way, wherein they shall not stumble: for I am a father to Israel, and **Ephraim** is my firstborn. (Jeremiah 31:4-9)*

*And **I will cause the captivity of Judah and the captivity of Israel to return,** and will build them, as at the first. And I will cleanse them from all their iniquity, whereby they have sinned against me; and I will pardon all their iniquities, whereby they have sinned, and whereby they have transgressed against me. And it shall be to me a name of joy, a praise and an honour before all the nations of the earth,* *which shall hear all the good that I do unto them: and they shall fear and tremble for all the goodness and for all the prosperity that I procure unto it.* (Jeremiah 33:7-9)

For the children of Israel shall abide many days without a king, and without a prince, and without a sacrifice, and without an image, and without an ephod, and without teraphim: **Afterward** *shall the children of Israel return, and seek the LORD their God, and David their king; and shall fear the LORD and his goodness in the latter days.* (Hosea 3:4-5)

Israel has indeed waited many days without a king, a prince, and a sacrifice as they have been scattered among the nations for some 2700 years. We are now in the "Afterward" part of this prophecy. Watch the news, they are coming!

The famous *"dry bones"* passage is found in Ezekiel chapter 37. In this passage the prophet sees dry bones come together and then flesh comes upon them, yet there is still no life in them. The Lord gives this explanation:

Then he said unto me, Son of man, these bones are the **whole house of Israel:** *behold, they say, Our bones are dried, and our hope is lost: we are cut off for our parts. Therefore prophesy and say unto them, Thus saith the Lord GOD; Behold, O my people, I will open your graves, and cause you to come up out of your graves, and bring you into the land of Israel.* (Ezekiel 37:11 & 12)

Moreover, thou son of man, take thee one stick, and write upon it, For Judah, and for the children of Israel his companions: then take another stick, and write upon it, For **Joseph, the stick of Ephraim,** *and for all the house of Israel his companions: And join them one to another into one stick; and they shall become one in thine hand. And when the children of thy people shall speak unto thee, saying, Wilt thou not shew us what thou meanest by these? Say unto them, Thus saith the Lord GOD; Behold,* **I will take the stick of Joseph, which is in the hand of Ephraim,** *and the tribes of Israel his fellows, and* **will put them with him, even with** *the stick of Judah, and make them one stick, and they shall be one in mine hand. And the sticks whereon thou writest shall be in thine hand before their eyes. And say unto them, Thus saith the Lord GOD; Behold, I will take the children of Israel from among the heathen, whither they be gone, and will gather them on every side, and bring them into their own land: And I will make them one nation in the land upon the mountains of Israel; and one king shall be king to them all: and they shall be no more two nations, neither shall they be divided into two kingdoms any more at all: (Ezekiel 37:16-22)*

All of Israel shall return and not just Judah, this is the Word of the Lord!

A few years ago a Jewish movie maker by the name of Simcha Jacobovici made a documentary on the lost tribes of Israel, called; *"Quest for the Lost Tribes"*. In this movie Mr. Jacobovici found remnants of all but one of the ten tribes of the northern kingdom of Israel. Of some of the tribes he only found a small remnant, just a few thousand, in places like Calcutta, India. In the border region between Burma and India there is a tribe called Manmasseh, or Manasseh. This tribe firmly believes that they are the tribe of Manasseh, so firmly that some have converted to Judaism and have already returned and are serving in the Israeli army. The flag that this tribe has chosen for themselves has a star of David in the centre of it.

The most astounding group that Mr. Jacobovici had contact with is a very large group of tribes in Afghanistan and Pakistan totalling some fifteen million people, plus! The Pathan tribes contain a remnant of the Northern kingdom of Israel. These tribes still live in traditional tribal units, and even dress in the manner of ancient Israel. Their tribal names are corruptions of the names of the tribes of Israel: Ephraim is Afridi, Naphtali is Daftani, Levi is Levani, Jaji is Gad, Asher is Ashuri, etc. One large group of Pathan call themselves Josefzai, or sons of Joseph! (*"Quest for the Lost Tribes"*, By Simcha Jacobovici)(also see *"Lost Tribes from Assyria"*, by A. Avihail and A. Brin)

There is one big problem with the Pathan tribes; though they are indeed tribes of Israel they have converted to Islam. They can't return to Israel as long as they are Muslims. Israel was founded as a

Jewish state and will not allow such a large group of Muslims to return, though they are indeed brothers of the Jews. Even in their conversion, however, they have incorporated a part of the Law of Moses into their version of Islam. Rather than this fact adding to the problem, these people are a living fulfilment of prophecy themselves:

> And the LORD shall scatter you among the nations, and ye shall be left few in number among the heathen, whither the LORD shall lead you. And **there ye shall serve gods, the work of men's hands, wood and stone, which neither see, nor hear, nor eat, nor smell.** (Deuteronomy 4:27 & 28)

> The LORD shall bring thee, and thy king which thou shalt set over thee, unto a nation which neither thou nor thy fathers have known; **and there shalt thou serve other gods,** wood and stone. (Deuteronomy 28:36)

> And the LORD shall scatter thee among all people, from the one end of the earth even unto the other; and **there thou shalt serve other gods, which neither thou nor thy fathers have known,** even wood and stone. (Deuteronomy 28:64)

> Therefore will I cast you out of this land into a land that ye know not, neither ye nor your fathers; and **there shall ye serve other gods day and night; where I will not shew you favour.** (Jeremiah 16:13)

This is a pattern that Israel set almost immediately after Solomon died. Actually it began during his life, since he gave in to his pagan wives and built shrines and altars to their false gods. After the nation split in two the northern kingdom quickly followed the pagan gods of their neighbours and incurred the wrath of God. Consequently the northern tribes were taken captive first by Assyria, and in time made their way to India and ultimately to Afghanistan, Pakistan, India and China. At some point around AD900 large numbers of them converted to Islam.

When the 911 hijackers attacked the USA in September 2001, Osama bin Laden was hiding out among the Pathan tribes in the hills of Afghanistan. While many Pathan acknowledge their common history with Israel, many others are uncomfortable with the connection. It is very clear that for there to be a reconciliation between the ten northern tribes and the southern tribes of Judah, they will have to abandon their faith in Allah. Something major must occur for them to return to the God of their fathers, the God of the Bible. I believe that this will be the same event that will allow Israel to rebuild the Temple, and it is mentioned in prophecies which we will examine in chapter 4.

Resources

"*The Annals of the World*", Ussher, James, Revised and Updated by Larry and Marion Pierce, copyright 2003 by Larry and Marion Pierce, sixth printing November 2006, Master Books, Inc. P.O. Box 726, Green Forest, AR 72638

"*Isralestine, the Ancient Blueprints of the Future Middle East*", Sallus, Bill, HighWay, A division of Anomalous Publishing House, Crane 65633, 2008

"*The Prophecy That Is Shaping History: New Research on Ezekiel's Vision of the End.*" Ruthven, Jon, PhD, and Griess, Ihab, PhD, Fairfax, VA: Xulon Press, 2003

"*The Israeli Source of the Pathan Tribes*", From the book, Lost Tribes from Assyria, by A. Avihail and A. Brin, 1978, in Hebrew, by Issachar Katzir, http://www.dangoor.com/74069.html, Website of the Scribe Magazine, Autumn 2001 Accessed 05/08/2010

"*Quest for the Lost Tribes*" Movie Documentary, Simcha Jacobovici, A&E Home Video, July 29, 2008

"*Mankind at the Turning Point: The Second Report to the Club of Rome*", Mesarovic, Mihajlo, and Pestel, Eduard, Clarke, Irwin and Company, Toronto and Vancouver, 1974

"*Noosphere*", Wikipedia, the Free Encyclopedia, Accessed 17/08/2010, from http://en.wikipedia.org/wiki/Noosphere,

"*Proposal for Future South Asian Union (SAU)*", accessed

17/08/2010, from http://www.southasianunion.net/,

"*The Jewish Calendar. In Calendars through the Ages.*" Douma, M., curator.   (2008).   Retrieved   08/24/2010,   from http://www.webexhibits.org/calendars/calendar-jewish.html, Calendars Through the Ages

"*Harpazo: The Scriptural Concept of Rapture*", Steward, Tom 27 March   2007,   Accessed   28/09/2010,   from http://www.raptureready.com/resource/steward/7.htm

"*A PRETRIBULATION RAPTURE OF THE CHURCH – DOES THE BIBLE TEACH   IT?*", Rapture Ready, Accessed 28/09/2010, from http://www.raptureready.com/soap/pretrib.htm

"*Important Dates In The Lives Of Jesus And Mary*", Conte, Ronald L. Jr., Catholic Planet, Copyright Ronald Conte Jr. 2002-2007, (June 13, 2007), See the book's website at www.BiblicalChronology.com, accessed 19/10/2010

Three

The Abandonment

Now we beseech you, brethren, by the coming of our Lord Jesus Christ, and by our gathering together unto him... Let no man deceive you by any means: for that day (Day of the Lord) shall not come, except there come a falling away first, and that man of sin be revealed, the son of perdition; (2 Thessalonians 2:1 & 3)

*Now the Spirit speaketh expressly, that **in the latter times some shall depart from the faith, giving heed to seducing spirits, and doctrines of devils;** (1 Timothy 4:1)*

***For the time will come when they will not endure sound doctrine; but after their own lusts shall they heap to themselves teachers, having itching ears;** (2 Timothy 4:3)*

*Beloved, believe not every spirit, **but try the spirits whether they are of God: because many false prophets are gone out into the world.** (1 John 4:1)*

Apostasy [a-pos'ta-si] *n* abandonment, or desertion of one's religion, principles, or political party - *n* apost'ate, one guilty of apostasy;-Also *adj*- vi apost'atize. [Gr *apostasis*, a revolt or "standing away" - *apo*, from, *histanai*, to stand.] (Websters Integrated Dictionary)

I s evidence of a worldwide Christian apostasy relevant to the study of Eschatology? I believe it is, and I think this movement will ultimately result in the creation of the Harlot of Revelation 17 and 18, culminating in the crowning of the Antichrist. So many talk about *"Jesus"* today, but which Jesus are they referring to? There are many Jesuses out there. It is apparent in this section from Matthew's gospel that one can say Jesus is the Christ and still be a deceiver:

> And as he sat upon the mount of Olives, the disciples came unto him privately, saying, Tell us, when shall these things be? and what shall be the sign of thy coming, and of the end of the world? And Jesus answered and said unto them, Take heed that no man deceive you. For many shall come in my name, saying, I am Christ; and shall deceive many. (Matthew 24:3-5)

This statement has many applications and I believe all of them are relevant. In fact the plain reading is that many will claim to be Christ, and this appears to be what is happening today. The New Age movement has infiltrated all areas of our society, including the Christian Church. One goal of this movement is to reduce Jesus Christ to being one of many Christs, and only a partaker of the *"Christ Consciousness"*. The New Age teaches that you too can partake of the *"Christ Consciousness"* yourself, making you another Christ! There are not just a few who claim to be Christ, there are many.

Like the church of Laodicea, modern evangelical Christians have deluded themselves into thinking that we are rich and in need of nothing. The truth is that our modern churches are wretched, miserable, poor, blind, and naked. We are heaping up teachers who say the things our itching ears want to hear! In verse 5 Jesus states that many shall be deceived and in turn shall deceive others.

A couple of things that all false belief systems have in common is that they demote Jesus Christ, and they remove or replace the people of Israel. The Angel in Daniel 9:24-27 specifically speaks of Israel to Daniel as *"thy people"*. This is not the Church, nor is it the Jehovah's Witnesses, nor the Palestinians or Arabs. Daniel was a member of the royal family of Judah, and likely a descendant of David. His people are the people of Israel. His people were given 490 years to *"put away iniquity"*, yet the iniquity of the Church was put away on the Cross. Of that 490 years Israel still has seven to go. It is about Israel and their relationship with their God. It is about His plan to reap the greatest harvest of souls in the history of the world, of both Jews and Gentiles. It is about His plan to bring in the Messianic age of the earth.

Reconstructionism, Dominionism, Amillennialism, Preterism, Replacement Theology and related philosophies deny that God has any use for national Israel in His plan. This is an incredibly dangerous idea, and will lead many professing Christians to support the Antichrist, and ultimately end up in the Lake of Fire. I have been shocked, at times, when speaking with members of the Church I attend, as I have found that many deny the literal/natural interpretation of scripture. Many who claim to believe in the literal plain sense of scripture, still allegorize the content when the plain understanding goes against their beliefs. To be fair I was once like that myself, even as I began writing this book I found I had to battle my old beliefs, and yield to the plain sense of the Word of God.

> *I say then, Hath God cast away his people? God forbid. For I also am an Israelite, of the seed of Abraham, of the tribe of Benjamin. (Romans 11:1)*

> *31 Behold, the days come, saith the LORD, that_I will make a new covenant with the house of Israel, and with the house of Judah: 34 And they shall teach no more every man his neighbour, and every man his brother, saying, Know the LORD: for they shall all know me, from the least of them unto the greatest of them, saith the LORD: for I will forgive their iniquity, and I will remember their sin no more. 35 Thus saith the LORD, which giveth the sun for a light by day, and the ordinances of the moon and of the stars for a light by night, which divideth the sea when the waves thereof roar; The LORD of hosts is his name: 36 If those ordinances depart from before me, saith the LORD, then the seed of Israel also shall cease from being a nation before me for ever. 37 Thus saith the LORD; If heaven above can be measured, and the foundations of the earth searched out beneath, I will also cast off all the seed of Israel for all that they have done, saith the LORD. (Jeremiah 31:31, 34-37)*

Very clearly these passages speak of the nation of Israel, the physical descendants of Jacob. His promises to national Israel are unconditional. That is, it doesn't depend on their faithfulness, but on His. God's plan for the End Times has the nation of Israel at the centre. In the past they abandoned Him, but in the near future he will call a remnant of Israel to be His witnesses to the nations and they will be faithful. At the end of the Tribulation period, all that remain of Israel will be saved (Romans 11:26). This shows the wonderful love and mercy of God that though the people He called were unfaithful and rebellious for thousands of years, yet He is faithful to them and will restore them, and keep all His promises to them! As He says, it is not ultimately about them, but about Him! (Ezekiel 36:22 & 32) He is the one with a name to keep (Isaiah 48:9)!

The number of eschatologies that replace or deny Israel's place in the plan of God is staggering. Those who believe that God has a plan for Israel are actually a small minority. Essentially it is only Jews and Dispensational Premillennialists (Bible believing Christians) who believe God has a plan for national Israel. Others may claim to love the Jews, but when you examine what they really believe they actually replace Israel with someone else...usually themselves!

In stating that God would break His promises to Israel, because of something they did, these groups are making a statement about the character of God. Essentially these theologies are stating that God can break His word. If He can break His word to Israel, then He could break His word to you! What is to stop God from getting bored and throwing His glorified saints into the Lake of Fire a million years into Eternity? It is His character and only His character that we can count on!

> For **I am the LORD, I change not;** *therefore ye sons of Jacob are not consumed.* (Malachi 3:6)

> *Therefore say unto the house of Israel, Thus saith the Lord GOD;* **I do not this for your sakes, O house of Israel, but for mine holy name's sake,** *which ye have profaned among the heathen, whither ye went.* (Ezekiel 36:22)

Islam claims to honor Jesus, but on close examination you find that their Jesus is not the Jesus of the Bible. The Isa (Jesus) of Islam was born of a virgin, and is called the *"breath of God"*, yet he was too cowardly to die on the cross, and someone else took his place. He is not the son of God, for the God of Islam has no son.(Qur'an, Suras 5:73, 116, 9:30, 17:111) Muslims claim to honour Jesus yet they belittle Him and claim that anyone who says Jesus is God is worthy of death. Islam denies the need for a Saviour and claims that you have to work your own way to Heaven. This is contrary to the Bible which claims that *"all have sinned and come short of the glory of God"*, and in fact is identical to the teachings of every false religion in the world. **The bible denies the ability of any person to make his, or her, own way to Heaven.** (Isaiah 53:6, 64:6, John 14:6, Romans 3:4, 9-20, 5:12, 6:23)

It is my belief that Islam is a key player in the events leading up to the last days. I think, however, that there is a far greater enemy who is far more subtle than Islam. I think Islam, or at least radical Islam, may end up being a scapegoat for the Antichrist. I have no doubt that Islam is going to unleash some horrors on this planet. When the world is focused on a major conflict with Islam, it will give the Antichrist the opportunity to slip in unnoticed. When the Antichrist arises from the ashes he will be seen as a *"Christian"* and a breath of fresh air!

It is pretty easy to document the differences between Islam and biblical Christianity. All one has to do is compare the Bible and the Qur'an. An even greater threat is arising from within the ranks of professing Christianity itself. It is impossible to document all the heresies floating around in "*Christian*" circles these days, but I want to make note of some of the most notable ones, and some that are more subtle.

In the second and third chapters of the book of Revelation there are several references to the apostasy and the End Times. It is common among pre-trib eschatology teachers to speak of the seven churches in Asia Minor as being seven ages, or stages, the Church would go through. This may actually be true in a general sense, however, there are statements directed at each church which indicate that each type of church will still be in existence up until and even during the Great Tribulation itself.

The only church that is promised to be kept out of the Great Tribulation is Philadelphia in 3:10. Now, if the chronological view, that these churches represent ages, is true, and since this is the second last church, these believers would be kept out of the Tribulation period by virtue of the fact that they would all be dead before it starts! We are now in the *"Laodicean Age"*, and the

"Philadelphian Age" is over. The truth is that, while this view may be generally true, each of these types of churches has always existed and still has representation today.

The final statement to the church in Ephesus is repeated for each church:

> *He that hath an ear, let him hear what the Spirit saith unto the churches; To him that overcometh will I give to eat of the tree of life, which is in the midst of the paradise of God. (Revelation 2:7)*

Later we see what Jesus is referring to with the word *"overcometh"*: *"And they overcame him by the blood of the Lamb, and by the word of their testimony; and they loved not their lives unto the death."* (Revelation 12:11) Thus it follows that some members of each church will be alive during the Tribulation and will overcome the Antichrist by giving up their lives for Jesus. They will refuse to accept the mark of the beast and will be beheaded.

To Smyrna:

> *11 He that hath an ear, let him hear what the Spirit saith unto the churches; He that **overcometh** shall not be hurt of the second death. 12 And to the angel of the church in Pergamos write; These things saith he which hath the sharp sword with two edges; 13 I know thy works, and where thou dwellest, even where Satan's seat is: and thou holdest fast my name, and hast not denied my faith, even in those days wherein Antipas was my faithful martyr, who was slain among you, where Satan dwelleth. 14 But I have a few things against thee, because thou hast there them that hold the doctrine of Balaam, who taught Balac to cast a stumblingblock before the children of Israel, to eat things sacrificed unto idols, and to commit fornication. 15 So hast thou also them that hold the doctrine of the **Nicolaitans**, which thing I hate. 16 Repent; **or else I will come unto thee quickly, and will fight against them with the sword of my mouth.** (Revelation 2:11-16)*

Notice that Jesus is the one with the sharp two-edged sword. He is coming to fight against churches who hold false doctrines! Specifically, the doctrine of the Nicolaitans is what makes Him angry. This passage links the Nicolaitans with the teaching of

Balaam. The bible does not say specifically what Balaam taught, but it shows what the Midianites did after he taught them. Essentially it appears that he said that they could be true to God in their heart, while at the same time fornicating with their bodies. This teaching led to a war where Balaam himself was killed along with the Midianite men, boys and all the women who listened to him.

The reference to the two edged sword is referring to His second coming, when he defeats his enemies with the *"Sword of His mouth"* (Psalms 55:21, Isaiah 49:2, Rev. 19:15). There will thus be many members, and even whole churches who align themselves with the Antichrist! There will be churches that Jesus will actually fight against at his return! Nevertheless His promise to this church is the same as to the other churches:

*17 He that hath an ear, let him hear what the Spirit saith unto the churches; To him that overcometh will I give to eat of the hidden manna, and will give him a white stone, and in the stone a new name written, which no man knoweth saving he that receiveth it. 18 And unto the angel of the church in Thyatira write; These things saith the Son of God, who hath his eyes like unto a flame of fire, and his feet are like fine brass; 20 Notwithstanding I have a few things against thee, because thou sufferest that woman Jezebel, which calleth herself a prophetess, to teach and to seduce my servants to commit fornication, and to eat things sacrificed unto idols. 21 And I gave her space to repent of her fornication; and she repented not. 22 Behold, I will cast her into a bed, and them that commit adultery with her into **great tribulation**, except they repent of their deeds. 23 And I will kill her children with death; and all the churches shall know that I am he which searcheth the reins and hearts: and I will give unto every one of you according to your works. 24 But unto you I say, and unto the rest in Thyatira, as many as have not this doctrine, and which have not known the depths of Satan, as they speak; I will put upon you none other burden. 25 But that which ye have already hold fast till I come. 26 And he that overcometh, and keepeth my works unto the end, to him will I give power over the nations: 27 And he shall rule them with a rod of iron; as the vessels of a potter shall they be broken to shivers: even as I received of my Father. (Revelation 2:17-27)*

The term *"great tribulation"* used in verse 22 can be none other than the Great Tribulation of the End Times. Very clearly some (many) church members will be going through the Great Tribulation. As stated before, there are many unsaved persons in Christian churches. They will be left behind at the rapture, but I think some of them will get saved at that time. This will be an opportunity for them to show their love for the Lord by laying down their lives for Him. If a person prays a *"prayer of salvation"* but doesn't repent, it is a sign they are not regenerated spiritually. He says similar things to the church in Sardis:

> 3 Remember therefore how thou hast received and heard, and hold fast, and repent. If therefore thou shalt not watch, I will come on thee as a thief, and thou shalt not know what hour I will come upon thee. 4 Thou hast a few names even in Sardis which have not defiled their garments; and **they shall walk with me in white: for they are worthy.** 5 He that overcometh, the same shall be clothed in white raiment; and I will not blot out his name out of the book of life, but I will confess his name before my Father, and before his angels. (Revelation 3:1)

In verse 3 we see the terminology is the same as He uses toward the unsaved. If they do not watch, He will come upon this church as a thief! I do not believe this verse is referring to the rapture, it is referring to those who are left behind after the rapture! This is a threat of judgment to those who will not watch for His coming. The next verse is referring to those who are taken in the rapture, the Great Snatch! They will walk with Jesus in white, while judgment comes upon the rest of the church. Notice the similar terminology to Luke 21:36, where we are told to watch and pray that we are counted worthy to escape the Judgments of God.

> Watch ye therefore, and pray always, that ye may be accounted worthy to escape all these things that shall come to pass, and to stand before the Son of man. (Luke 21:36)

Very clearly those who escape the Great Tribulation will be standing before Jesus, at the same time that event unfolds on earth.

There is a pre-flood passage that also echoes the teaching of this verse:

And Enoch walked with God: and he was not; for God took him. (Genesis 5:24)

By faith Enoch was translated that he should not see death; and was not found, because God had translated him: for before his translation he had this testimony, that he pleased God. (Hebrews 11:5)

The word *"translate"* means to move from one place to another. Enoch was moved from earth to Heaven because he pleased God. God is not pleased with *"Christians"* who walk in sin. If a person prays a prayer but never walks with God he needs to ask himself *"Am I really saved?"* The bible promises us that the Holy Spirit will never leave us nor forsake us. The only answer to this dilemma must be that many professing Christians were not really saved to begin with. Will the Holy Spirit enter a place where He is not welcome? Will He cohabit with sin? Will He enter a place where you think you have to do the clean-up yourself (works salvation)? We ourselves are not able to clean up our own lives, but if we are not willing to allow Him to do the clean-up, the question remains: Will He actually enter in and dwell with us? The bible tells us that man looks at the outside but God looks at the heart.

In Luke 21:36 Jesus tells us to pray that we may be accounted worthy to escape the things that shall come upon the earth. It sounds like saying a prayer is no guarantee that the person saying it will escape the Great Tribulation. It sounds like those who actually receive Jesus as Lord and Saviour will be obedient to His commands, and ultimately He will determine them to be worthy.

Verse 5 speaks to those who are left behind after the rapture. Those who overcome will not have their name blotted out of the book of Life. Again a reference to Revelation 12:11, that those who overcome will do so by giving up their lives for Jesus.

As for the church in Philadelphia Jesus has no words of judgment but only words of comfort, yet at the same time he warns them to hold on to what they have:

*10 Because thou hast kept the word of my patience, **I also will keep thee from the hour of temptation**, which shall come upon all the world, to try them that dwell upon the earth. 11 Behold, I come quickly: hold that fast which thou hast, that no man take thy crown. 12 Him that overcometh* *will I make a pillar in the temple of my God, and he shall go no more out: and I will write upon him the name of my God, and the name of the city of my God, which is new Jerusalem, which cometh down out of heaven from my God: and I will write upon him my new name.* (Revelation 3:10-12)

Verse 10 is a promise that this church will escape the hour of temptation that shall come upon the whole world, which seems to be a promise of rapture. Yet even in this promise there seems to be a condition attached: *"Because thou hast kept the word of my patience"*. In verse 12 we have yet another reference to some being left behind.

The church of Laodicea is the saddest church in this book. There are no commendations, only warnings. Yet even to this church there are promises given:

*14 And unto the angel of the church of the Laodiceans write; These things saith the Amen, the faithful and true witness, the beginning of the creation of God; 15 I know thy works, that thou art neither cold nor hot: I would thou wert cold or hot. 16 So then **because thou art lukewarm, and neither cold nor hot, I will spue thee out of my mouth.** 17 Because thou sayest, I am rich, and increased with goods, and have need of nothing; and knowest not that thou art wretched, and miserable, and poor, and blind, and naked: 18 I counsel thee to buy of me gold tried in the fire, that thou mayest be rich; and white raiment, that thou mayest be clothed, and that the shame of thy nakedness do not appear; and anoint thine eyes with eyesalve, that thou mayest see. 19 As many as I love, I rebuke and chasten: be zealous therefore, and repent. 20 Behold, I stand at the door, and knock: **if any man hear my voice, and open the door, I will come in to him, and will sup with him, and he with me.** 21 To him that overcometh will I grant to sit with me in my throne, even as I also overcame, and am set down with my Father in his throne.* (Revelation 3:14-21)

Verse 16 would certainly indicate that not everyone in this church will be raptured. It is inconceivable that He would rapture to Heaven, the same person He wants to vomit out of His mouth! However, He says He loves these people and invites them to receive Him. Evidently this church is made up of unbelievers. To those who receive Him he invites them to sup (eat) with Him. These will be raptured, but the rest of this church will go through the Tribulation. Those who miss out on the rapture, however, still have a second chance. They have the opportunity to receive Jesus Christ, and overcome the Antichrist by giving up their lives for Jesus. Many have stated, and I agree, that those who have heard the gospel and rejected it, before the rapture, are not likely to receive it after the rapture. This is why it says "*Now is the day of salvation*" (2 Corinthians 6:2).

> *When the boughs thereof are withered, they shall be broken off: the women come, and set them on fire: for it is a people of no understanding: therefore he that made them will not have mercy on them, and he that formed them will shew them no favour. (Isaiah 27:11)*

Jesus alluded to this passage in John 15:2, as did Paul in Romans 11. While the subject at hand is Israel, I think it extends to all who call themselves "*His people*". The clear implication is that some of the professing Church will indeed go through the Tribulation period. Some churches that identify themselves as "*Christian*" do not have a single born-again member!

If we go back to the feasts of Israel we can see the Church in the feast of Pentecost (Shavuot, the Feast of Weeks, the Feast of Harvest, or the Latter Firstfruits). The Church officially began on this day, fifty days after the Passover when Jesus was crucified, when the Holy Spirit came on the disciples with power. (Acts chapter 2) The Church is symbolized in the two wave loaves that were offered. The two loaves symbolized the two branches of the Church, Israel and the Gentiles. Today the Jews weave, or braid, the two loaves into one, creating a perfect picture of the church. Of particular interest is the fact that the loaves were to be mixed with yeast, or leaven.

> *Ye shall bring out of your habitations two wave loaves of two tenth deals: they shall be of fine flour; **they shall be baken with leaven;** they are the firstfruits unto the LORD. (Leviticus 23:17)*

As in the Passover feast, yeast retains its symbolism of sin. From the beginning, God was saying that the Church would be a mixture of saved and lost people. Jesus Himself stated that the Church would be a place where sinners would come for shelter. Note in Matthew 13:31-32, that the kingdom is the tree, and the birds resting on the branches symbolize something that doesn't belong there, as Jesus said elsewhere *"I am the vine and ye are the branches"*. (John 15:5)

The wave loaves of Leviticus show that the Church will be mixed with unbelievers and Paul states that *"A little leaven leaveneth the whole lump."* (Galatians 5:9) What can this mean but that eventually the Church will fall into apostasy? Of course it doesn't mean that the entire Church will become apostate, because God always leaves Himself a remnant of believers. This must be a general condition of the Church in the last days.

The parable of the mustard seed restates the same concept. The Church, the believers, are the tree, and the birds, the unbelievers, rest in its branches, but do not belong there. In these last days there are more and more birds, and the tree is bending over with the weight. There is a parallel here with Israel in the Old Testament. When the Messiah finally came most of Israel was apostate. We should not be surprised that history repeats itself.

> *Another parable put he forth unto them, saying, The kingdom of heaven is like to a grain of mustard seed, which a man took, and sowed in his field: Which indeed is the least of all seeds: but when it is grown, it is the greatest among herbs, and becometh a tree, so that the birds of the air come and lodge in the branches thereof. (Matthew 13:31-32)*

The prophet Zephaniah, when speaking about the Great Tribulation, states that God will rid Jerusalem of those who worship (and swear by) the Lord. When I first read this I was taken aback, but the more I thought about it the more I realized that it is true.

> *I will also stretch out mine hand upon Judah, and upon all the inhabitants of Jerusalem; and **I will cut off** the remnant of Baal from this place, and the name of the Chemarims with the priests; And them that worship the host of heaven upon the housetops; and **them that worship and that swear by the LORD**, and that swear by Malcham; And them that are turned back from the LORD; and those that have not sought the LORD, nor enquired for him. Hold thy peace at the presence of the Lord GOD: for the day of the LORD is at hand: for the LORD hath prepared a sacrifice, he hath bid his guests. (Zephaniah 1:4-7)*

The Lord wants more than worship from you. He wants your

life, your heart, your obedience, everything! Jesus Himself is the one who said *"Don't swear an oath"*. So many pray a prayer to receive Jesus, and then go away and act as if nothing has happened. Many go to church on Sunday and sincerely worship Him, then go to work the next day and act like the world. Jesus wants to be your all-in-all and will accept nothing less! Those who receive Jesus in spirit and in truth will do more than merely worship God, they have the Holy Spirit within them and develop a relationship with Him!

> *If any man come to me, and hate not his father, and mother, and wife, and children, and brethren, and sisters, yea, and his own life also, he cannot be my disciple. And whosoever doth not bear his cross, and come after me, cannot be my disciple. So likewise, whosoever he be of you that forsaketh not all that he hath, he cannot be my disciple. (Luke 14:26-33)*

Jesus is not saying that we must literally hate our family, for that would be a contradiction. He is saying that our love for Him must be so much greater than our love for family that the difference would seem like hate. He is very serious that we are not to love the things of this world. We are to hold on to possessions very loosely, knowing that they truly belong to Him and are loaned to us for a time, and for His purposes.

Modern prosperity teachers say that God wants to make you rich and comfortable. They say God wants to make you happy and healthy: *"You can have your best life now!"* This is a false teaching, but these men prosper because this is what people want to hear. They do not want to hear about sacrifice and struggle, which is what Jesus taught. I am not saying that a man shouldn't own property. I am only saying that everything you have is on loan to you from God, and belongs to Him. He expects you to use it for His glory.

I tried to ignore this apostasy, and hope it isn't happening, but the evidence keeps on piling up, and can't be ignored any more. We need to take a brief look at what is happening around us. This will help us understand just where we are in the last days.

There has always been a stream of apostasy in the Church. As the apostle John says: *"Little children, it is the last time: and as ye have heard that antichrist shall come, even now are there many antichrists; whereby we know that it is the last time."* (1 John 2:18) The teaching of the Bible is that a type of abandonment will be a general characteristic of many churches shortly before Christ's return. Please note that just because there are many antichrists it does not preclude the fact that there is one final, personal Antichrist. All of the popes have been antichrists. Years ago I read a book by David Yallop, "In God's Name", about the one month reign of pope John Paul I. In the book Mr. Yallop documents how John-Paul I was actually trying to clean-up the Vatican of its secret societies, and really believed he was there as a servant of Jesus Christ.

Mr. Yallop's thesis was that pope John Paul I was murdered, and he makes a strong case for his point. Nevertheless, in spite of his good intentions, John Paul I was actually an antichrist. The term "Vicar of Christ" means "In the place of Christ". The Greek word "anti", not only has the connotation of being against, but also means "in the place of", the same meaning as the Latin word "vicar", from which we get the English word "vicarious". Therefore anyone who takes the title "Vicar of Christ" is actually an antichrist, regardless of their intentions or actions.

In the days of the apostles there was a conflict with a group of heretics known as Gnostics. Among their heresies, these people taught that there is hidden knowledge that only a select group of adepts are worthy of receiving. This heresy is totally contrary to the teachings of Jesus Christ. For Jesus said "Come unto me all ye who are weary and heavy laden and I will give you rest". (Matthew 11:28) Christianity is for anyone, but those who are puffed up in their own pride will be kept out.

In the third century the Emperor Constantine formed the state church of Rome and began the process of paganizing Christianity. We see the results of this compromise in the mixed grace-plus-works, false gospel of Rome, still being propagated today. A careful study of the Book of Romans, or John, will show that salvation is a free gift, and is by the grace of God, without works of any kind.

There has always been a remnant of Christians who believed in salvation by grace alone, through faith alone, in the shed blood of Christ alone, but today that remnant is shrinking as modern Christians seek a visible unity at the expense of truth.

The whole world does not contain enough paper to itemize the teachings of each of the false teachers in circulation today. Of necessity, then, this chapter will be more of an overview of some of the leaders of the modern apostate movement among professing Christians. The word "apostasy" simply means "an abandonment" or a *"falling away"* from something, in this case it is a falling away from the true faith.

I really did not want to name names. I am aware that by naming names and organizations I will incur the wrath of many. I do not see how I can be faithful to my calling, however, without speaking of individuals. I do not know whether any person named here is saved or not. They may actually be born-again Christians. It is possible for truly saved individuals to embrace false teachings. Why else would the Bible spend so much time warning about error? The bible, however, tells us to mark and avoid those who teach things contrary to scripture.

> *Now I beseech you, brethren, mark them which cause divisions and offences contrary to the doctrine which ye have learned; and avoid them.* (Romans 16:17)

> *But though we, or an angel from heaven, preach any other gospel unto you than that which we have preached unto you, let him be accursed. As we said before, so say I now again, If any man preach any other gospel unto you than that ye have received, let him be accursed.* (Galatians 1:8-9)

This is not a comprehensive list of all persons and organizations that teach error. Neither am I making a statement on the eternal destination of any person named herein. For all I know, we all have some error in our understanding. As the Holy Spirit brings our errors to our attention, through the Scriptures, we need to repent and change our way of thinking. It is those who refuse to repent who should be avoided:

> *Now I beseech you, brethren, **mark them which cause divisions and offences contrary to the doctrine which ye have learned; and avoid them.*** (Romans 16:17)

Alpha

The Alpha course is one program that professing Christians seem to be able to agree on regardless of denomination. In my home town there are very few churches that do not use the Alpha course, and most of the ones that don't use it just can't afford it. What is the history of this movement? Who are these people that we allow into our churches via the TV screen?

In the early nineties I remember seeing videos of the *"Toronto Blessing"* phenomenon in our adult Sunday school class. I remember thinking *"this is very strange"*. The consensus in our church, at the time, was that *"this is not of God"*. There is no place in scripture where Christians bark like dogs or growl like lions. Christians are taught to test the spirits (1 John 4:1).

The role of the Holy Spirit on the Day of Pentecost, and ever since, is to point to the Lord Jesus Christ. The purpose of tongues on the day of Pentecost was so that people of diverse backgrounds could hear and understand the gospel. There may actually be an angelic tongue but its use is for prayer, and Paul said it should not be done in the Church assembly without an interpreter. (2 Cor. 14:18-19) The truth is, however, that these modern phenomena go far beyond tongues. We have phenomena like *"being drunk in the spirit"*, *"roaring like lions"*, *"barking like dogs"*, and *"holy laughter"*. There is a place in scripture where these phenomena are actually spoken of, but the context is one of judgment. In Jeremiah 51 God brings judgment against Babylon because of their sins and unbelief;

> 38 **They shall roar together like lions: they shall yell as lions' whelps.** 39 In their heat I will make their feasts, and I will make them drunken, that they may rejoice, and sleep a perpetual sleep, and not wake, saith the LORD. 40 I will bring them down like lambs to the slaughter, like rams with he goats. 57 And **I will make drunk her princes, and her wise men, her captains, and her rulers,** and her mighty men: and they shall sleep a perpetual sleep, and not wake, saith the King, whose name is the LORD of hosts. (Jeremiah 51:38 - 40, 57)

As you read through Jeremiah 51 you will notice that the context of the passage is Judgment against Babylon. Some of it was meant for Babylon in the time of Nebuchadnezzar's grandson, but if you compare this chapter with chapters 17 and 18 of the book of Revelation you will see that the Babylon spoken of is not only ancient Babylon, but more specifically a future End Times Babylon. These judgments are actually a prophecy of the day in which we live!

Some of the verses in Revelation are direct quotations from this chapter of Jeremiah. Jeremiah 51:7 is quoted in Revelation 17:2 and speaks of the nations of the world growing drunken with the wine of her fornication, her spiritual compromise with pagan religions. Jeremiah 51:13 and Revelation 17:1 identify Babylon as the whore who sits on many waters, meaning that she is a religious prostitute who covers the whole earth. She is a city, but also a religious/political system that ultimately takes over the earth. As each world empire took over its predecessor it absorbed the system of Babylon into itself, thus Persia became Babylon, and then Greece and then Rome. Rome has morphed and twisted and grown until, like the roots of a tree, or a giant fungus, she has spread throughout the whole world. This is not to deny that there may actually be one or more literal End Time cities that have all of the characteristics of Babylon.

An interesting aside is the origin of the term *"diocese"*- an administrative territory presided over by a Bishop. The original administrative unit of the ancient Roman empire was also called a diocese, which gives us pause to consider where, exactly, this church came from.

Jeremiah 51:45 is quoted in Revelation 18:4 where it says *"come out of her my people, that ye be not partakers of her sins, and that ye receive not of her plagues"*. These verses indicate that some of God's people will be a part of this End Times political/religious system, and city, and are warned to get out before God's judgment comes against it.

So we see then, that the signs of Jeremiah 51:38-40 and 57 are signs of the times within which we live, and not just a judgment against ancient Babylon. This spiritual drunkenness is a judgment from God and a precursor to destruction!

Isaiah echoes the thought, that a spiritual drunkenness is a judgment from God and not a blessing! Both Isaiah 29 and 63 are End Times passages:

> *Stay yourselves, and wonder; cry ye out, and cry:* **they are drunken, but not with wine; they stagger, but not with strong drink.** *For* **the LORD hath poured out upon you the spirit of deep sleep,** *and hath closed your eyes: the prophets and your rulers, the seers hath he covered. (Isaiah 29:9-10)*

> *And I will tread down the people in mine anger, and make*

them drunk in my fury, and I will bring down their strength to the earth. (Isaiah 63:6)

Benjamin Creme is known as a *"prophet"* of the New Age Maitreya, a false Christ. He was able to induce Toronto Blessing type phenomena at his meetings without any pretense of Christianinty.

> "Just to emphasise the close connection between the TB and these other non-Christian religious experiences, Benjamin Creme was recently asked what he thought of the TB. His response was that **he thought the TB was a good thing; it is, according to him, the method being used by his spiritual Masters to soften up Christian Fundamentalists to accept the New Age Christ when He appears.** "(Needham, The Toronto Blessing)

If there is anything from God in the Toronto *"Blessing"* it is Judgment. As Jesus himself said *"An evil and adulterous generation seeketh after a sign;"* (Matthew 12:39a) Seeking a sign from God when your heart is not right will only bring judgment.

Eleanor Mumford, a member of of the South-West London Vineyard church (associated with John Wimber) came to Toronto and brought back the *"laughing revival"* back with her to England. In a meeting in her home she imparted the *"Toronto Blessing"* to Nicky Gumbel, the man behind the Alpha course. Here is Gumbel's testimony of that meeting:

> "We went to their house...where a group of leaders of their church was meeting...Ellie Mumford told us a little bit of what she had seen in Toronto...it was obvious that Ellie was just dying to pray for all of us...then she said, "Now we'll invite the Holy Spirit to come," and the moment she said that, one of the people was thrown, literally, across the room and was lying on the floor, just howling and laughing...making the most incredible noise...I experienced the power of the Spirit in a way I hadn't experienced for years, like massive electricity going through my body...One of the guys was prophesying. He was just lying there prophesying...[Gumbel returns to HTB, closes the meeting there in prayer]...I prayed "Lord, thank you so much for all you are doing and we pray you'll send your Spirit" and I was

just about to say "in Jesus' name, Amen" and go out the door when the Spirit came on the people who were in the room. One of them starting laughing like a hyena." [video 3, talk 9, Alpha course, Christian Witness Ministries]

Since that time Holy Trinity Brompton became the centre of the *"Laughing Revival"* in Europe and, as we have noted, is also the producer of the Alpha course. The connection, therefore, between the demonic Laughing *"Revival"* and thousands of churches around the world is the Alpha course. We have already covered some, but there are many theological problems with the Alpha course. The biggest problem of Alpha is that it is mostly true. The devil knows that Christians won't be deceived by a very big lie so he has to give a little poison with a cup of truth. Alpha may actually be 90% true. The truth is not the problem, the lie is. Would you drink a glass of 90% pure water with only 10% cyanide? What about 99% water and 1% cyanide? Remember, Paul said *"a little leaven leaveneth the whole lump"*(1 Cor. 5:6 & 7, Gal. 5:9), meaning that any error, if left alone, will corrupt the entire Church. No error is acceptable to God!

People come away from Alpha feeling affirmed, and having their self-esteem enhanced. This cannot be evidence of the true gospel, for God says things like this:

> *Let nothing be done through strife or vainglory; but **in lowliness of mind let each esteem other better than themselves**. (Philippians 2:3)*

> *And the times of this ignorance God winked at; but **now commandeth all men every where to repent**: (Acts 17:30)*

> *For **I know that in me (that is, in my flesh,) dwelleth no good thing**: for to will is present with me; but how to perform that which is good I find not. (Romans 7:18)*

True faith in Jesus Christ always comes with brokenness over sin. We cannot appreciate what Christ has done for us without having some idea of just how horrible our own sin is, and how much we deserve His wrath!

Talk 5 of Alpha says *"There are moral problems with the Bible(?), there are [also] historical problems"**, but the Bible itself says: "All scripture is given by inspiration of God, and is profitable for doctrine, *for reproof, for correction, for instruction in righteousness:"* (2 Timothy 3:16) We will cover the alleged moral problems with the Bible in the chapter on marriage. Any moral problems are with Christians, and not with the Word of God. For Nicky Gumbel to say this, is evidence that he is leaning on his own understanding, and setting it above the Word of God, which is a very dangerous predicament to be in.

Talk 5 also says: *"God has given us his guide book"**, yet the Bible itself says: *"If any man think himself to be a prophet, or spiritual, let him acknowledge that the things that I write unto you are the* **commandments** *of the Lord."* (1 Corinthians 14:37) Do we understand the difference between a *"guide book"* and "*commandments*"? In life, if you ignore your guide books, you might still make it to your destination on your own, but if you reject the Word of God you will not make it to Heaven, guaranteed! (*Nicky Gumbel, quoted in *The New Age of Alpha*, Dusty Peterson)

> The <u>law</u> of the LORD is perfect, converting the soul: the testimony of the LORD is sure, making wise the simple. The **statutes** of the LORD are right, rejoicing the heart: the **commandment** of the LORD is pure, enlightening the eyes. The **fear** of the LORD is clean, enduring for ever: the <u>judgments</u> of the LORD are true and righteous altogether. More to be desired are they than gold, yea, than much fine gold: sweeter also than honey and the honeycomb. (Psalm 19:7-10)

The doctrine of Hell is not a popular subject these days and Alpha is no exception in this regard. Hell, and the Lake of Fire, get very little mention in the Alpha course. It seems the God of Alpha is a one dimensional God of Love only. The God of the Bible is a multi faceted personality. God, as revealed in the pages of scripture, is Love, but He is also Just. He is a balanced personality not some Santa Claus type of caricature, not some doting grandfather figure. Justice is who He is. He is Holy and Jealous, and He knows what you have done!

If there is anything God owes to anyone it is Justice. God doesn't owe anyone entrance into Heaven, but He does owe Justice to sinners. *"For the wages of sin is death"* (Rom. 6:23a) This is why Jesus came and died for us. He came and took the just reward of our sins upon Himself. He was protecting us from Himself, and His pure

Holiness, but being the absolute gentleman He is, He will not force Himself on anyone. He will respect the choice of those who choose to live without Him. Though they will change their mind when they see Him, it will be too late.

People talk about the Love of Jesus, but they neglect to mention that Jesus Christ spoke more about Hell, and the Lake of Fire, than any of the prophets. He spoke more about Hell than he did about Heaven. People truly do not like to talk of Judgment and the Lake of Fire, but the God who created that Lake died so you do not have to go there. God has offered the free gift of salvation, but like any gift it must be received to be yours. (Rom. 6:23, John 3:16) What is Love without there being an alternative?

For God to accept Adolph Hitler, or a petty thief, or a liar, into Heaven without demanding justice would be evil! What if a judge had a pedophile and child killer before him, and he were to dismiss the charges saying, *"though you are guilty, I am a loving judge, therefore I am dismissing your charges in the name of love"*. Wouldn't that judge be more evil than the criminal before him?

In order for God to be good justice must be satisfied. Jesus Christ satisfied justice, on the Cross. Only God could have done this for He is eternal in nature and unlimited. Had He been only a man, even a perfect man, He could have died for only one person. Thus His penalty could cover all sin of all time, for all who believe. If you insist on doing it your way, however, you will pay the full penalty for your sin, for by rejecting His sacrifice you have insulted God and trampled His love into the ground. The truth is that no man can ever pay the full penalty for their sin. If they could they would be let out of the Lake of Fire sometime during eternity.

He that justifieth the wicked, and he that condemneth the just, even they both are abomination to the LORD. (Proverbs 17:15)

Jesus Christ was accursed of God, because He justifies the wicked! God's wrath was poured out on Him for your sake. His terror at Calvary was not fear of the beating, the nails, or the crown of thorns, but fear of the righteous anger of His Father that was to be poured out on Him for your and my sake! God, both Father and Son, became an abomination to Himself on your behalf! Don't ever underestimate the value of the blood of Christ. It is worth more than all of humanity, the sun, the moon and the entire universe put together!

Ecumenism is probably the most significant error of the Alpha course. Nicky Gumbel downplays the differences between Protestants and Catholics. Catholic churches are running the Alpha course without change, although they have added sessions on the sacraments and Mary. Rather than repudiating these additions the Alpha website speaks of them as if they are essential for true faith. Here is a quote from the Alpha USA website:

"ALPHA IN A CATHOLIC CONTEXT

Alpha is an effective initial presentation of the core of the Gospel, 'the Kerygma'. It is wholly compatible with Catholic teaching, its name is most appropriate as it is the beginning of faith. Once the foundation who is Jesus is laid, a range of follow on material is available to address specific Catholic teachings and ecclesiology. Alpha in a Catholic Context is a wonderful tool at the stage of inquiry for those seeking the RCIA process.

Not a substitute for catechetical programs, Alpha works best as part of an ongoing process of evangelization and catechesis within a parish.

(Alpha in a Catholic Context, Alpha USA website)

What do they mean "*It is wholly compatible with Catholic teaching*"? The Catholic Church still teaches a faith-plus-works gospel. They teach the infallibility of the pope, and the equality of their traditions to scripture! The Catholic Church teaches that the Pope is God's representative on earth, thus usurping the role of the Holy Spirit! If Alpha is wholly compatible with Catholic teaching, then it is incompatible with the Word of God!

Another heresy of the Catholic Church is the teaching that punishment is purgative, hence the teaching on purgatory. This word, and this concept, is not found anywhere in scripture. Hell and the Lake of Fire are the true biblical doctrines on the fate of the lost, there is no second chance after death. Once a person enters the Lake of Fire there is no way out. Evil is unrestrained in that place, and those who find themselves there will find their evil will grow throughout eternity. Those who go there will start off being angry at

God and His saints, and that anger will grow into a pure, unadulterated, hatred! After all, many in Hell will have lived better lives on earth than many of the saints. There are murderers in Heaven, like David, Moses, Paul, and others, and many in the Lake will not have committed such heinous crimes. They refuse to accept that it is not about them, but about the Grace of God, and what Christ did on the cross.

And fear not them which kill the body, but are not able to kill the soul: but rather fear him which is able to destroy both soul and body in hell. (Matthew 10:28)

Then shall he say also unto them on the left hand, Depart from me, ye cursed, into everlasting fire, prepared for the devil and his angels: (Matthew 25:41)

And if thy hand offend thee, cut it off: it is better for thee to enter into life maimed, than having two hands to go into hell, into the fire that never shall be quenched: (Mark 9:43)

We often speak of Hell and the Lake of Fire as being synonymous, and indeed a person who enters Hell has no chance of ever going to Heaven. Hell is indeed spoken of as a place of torment and regret. It appears that Hell is more like a holding cell for condemned spirits, rather than a place of eternal destruction. At the end of history the inhabitants of Hell will be reunited with their bodies and stand before God on Judgment Day. This Judgment is not to determine whether one goes to Heaven or the Lake of Fire, but to determine the place of the condemned, in the Lake of Fire. In this sense the White Throne Judgment is more like a sentencing hearing. As Jesus said:

He that believeth on him is not condemned: **but he that believeth not is condemned already,** *because he hath not believed in the name of the only begotten Son of God.* (John 3:18)

If you are not a believer in Jesus Christ as your Lord and Saviour, you stand condemned today! You are already under a death sentence! Judgment day for you is to determine your place in the Lake of Fire! This is why Jesus came saying *"Repent"*!

God does not owe anyone an explanation for what He is going to do with them. He could justifiably toss the entire human race into the Lake of Fire today without an explanation. *"For all have sinned, and come short of the glory of God;"* (Romans 3:23) and *"**For the wages of sin is death**; but the gift of God is eternal life through Jesus Christ our Lord.* (Romans 6:23) We have His word that He won't do that, however. God had a plan to save many, from even before the creation of the world. Every person who ends up in Heaven owes his/her presence there to the grace of God and Christ's sacrificial death on the cross, and to nothing else!

The Catholic Church lifts up her *"ecclesiastical"* traditions above the Word of God, and actually nullifies the Bible by her traditions. This was the error of the Pharisees in Jesus' day, and He railed against their traditions: *"Making the word of God of none effect through your tradition, which ye have delivered: and many such like things do ye."* (Mark 7:13) Read the whole passage as well as Matthew 15.

Many Christians do the same thing on different subjects: Baptists are famous for their tradition prohibiting the consumption of alcohol, because the Bible says *"be not drunk with wine"*. Jesus, however, stated *"Not that which goeth into the mouth defileth a man; but that which cometh out of the mouth, this defileth a man."* (Matthew 15:11) As Christians we are commanded to believe Jesus, and not lift up our traditions above His Word.

What does the Bible say about itself, and how does this compare to your churches view?

> **All scripture is given by inspiration of God**, *and is profitable for doctrine, for reproof, for correction, for instruction in righteousness: That the man of God may be perfect, throughly furnished unto all good works.* (2 Timothy 3:16 & 17)

If you are thoroughly furnished you are lacking nothing, you do not need any man-made traditions to make you complete in Christ.

> *(The Bereans) were more noble than those in Thessalonica, in that they received the word with all readiness of mind, and searched the scriptures daily, whether those things were so. (Acts 17:11)*

Search the scriptures; for in them ye think ye have eternal life: and they are they which testify of me. (John 5:39)

Any person who says you need their traditions to be a complete Christian is a false teacher. The same goes for any who say you need their training to interpret the Scriptures. The bible was inspired by the inventor of language. It is to be read literally for what it says. God's message is for everyone, not for an educated elite. Look at 2 Timothy 3:16 again. The Holy Spirit is our only interpreter of scripture. Human teachers have a role, to point out the Scriptures, but any that steps beyond that role should be avoided. Any who add to, or take away from, the message of the Bible should be avoided.

Why this digression into the authority of scripture? It is because Alpha tends to give credibility to the Roman Church. There is an Ecumenical movement today that is attempting to unite all churches, and indeed all religions, under one umbrella. This Super-Church will be the one to support the Antichrist and he will use them to gain power, before he destroys it like a piece of garbage. As we enter the End Times there may actually be a couple of iterations of this ecumentical movement.

In the New Age movement, the term for the altered state of consciousness, where one is open to spiritual entities, is called the *"alpha"* state. I know the producers of Alpha would tell us that the name of their course is related to Jesus' words in Revelation 1:8 where he says *"I am the Alpha and Omega"*, but I am not so sure. I think it is a reference to the New Age term, and the blurring of terms is deliberate doublespeak. Had it been truly biblical it would have been called the *"Alpha and Omega Course"*. That would have eliminated confusion.

Purpose Driven?

One of the most popular books written in the last couple of decades would have to be Rick Warren's "The Purpose Driven Life" (hereafter PDL). Rick Warren is the pastor of Saddleback Church of Saddleback valley, California. Warren's book has soared to international best-seller status, with sales of over one million copies per month at times.

My greatest joy is simply reading and meditating on the Word of God, so reading PDL was quite a chore. My heart was grieved as I read error on almost every single page of this book. One of the problems is that there is a lot of truth contained in it, but there is also a lot of error and it takes great discernment to tell the difference. It is not my purpose to do a lengthy discourse on the dangers of Warren's Purpose Driven heresies. Others have done excellent work to that end. I am only giving a thumbnail sketch of some of the more glaring errors I have found in his book. There are so many errors in PDL that one could write a full volume merely refuting the things Warren says.

One of the first things I noticed was the multitude of bible versions, and perversions, that Warren quotes. His favourite version seems to be Eugene Petersen's *"The Message"*, which is not really a translation of the text, but more of a bible commentary. The Message claims to be a paraphrase, but is really a New Age reinterpretation of the Bible. Even with The Message, however, Warren leaves out parts of verses to make them say things they do not say when read in context.

Warren's method of quoting bible verses is to bury references at the back of the book, which makes it difficult to check-up on what he is saying. I believe this was planned this way to minimize scrutiny. It's much easier to just go with the flow rather than exercise discernment with this book.

On page 9, on the first page of his introduction, he says *"Whenever God wanted to prepare someone for his purposes, he took 40 days"*. He then goes on to give eight examples, all taken out of context. But, what does the word *"whenever"* mean? Doesn't it mean *"always, without exception"*? If we could find one exception to this rule we could prove him to be a liar.

On the next page he gives eight examples to support his *"forty day claim"*. Every single one of these eight examples is taken out of context. The first one reads, *"Noah's life was transformed by 40 days of rain."*(Genesis 7:12) Now, Noah preached righteousness for 120 years before the flood. Noah was already a believer and transformed well before the 40 days began. Actually Noah was in the ark for a whole year, and the people left outside were the ones transformed by the forty days of rain!

He then states, *"Moses was transformed by 40 days on Mount Sinai."*(Exodus 34) Again, Moses was a believer and prophet of God, before he went up on the mountain. He was not conformed to the world before he went up the mountain. His face shone with the Glory of God when he came down, but in time that faded away.

"The spies were transformed by 40 days in the Promised Land."(Numbers 13) Of the twelve spies only two had confidence in God after the 40 days, but they were believers before they went. The others dissuaded Israel from possessing the Holy Land. As a result the nation wandered in the wilderness until all the men who were over 20 years old at that time had died. None of the twelve were transformed by their forty day experience.

I'm not going to discuss all of the eight points, but I want to note the second last, since it is especially grievous: *"Jesus was empowered by 40 days in the wilderness."* Jesus was the Son of God from eternity past. He always had the ability to take up all the power of God whenever he chose to use it. The 40 days in the wilderness was actually a time of trial and temptation. He was not empowered by 40 days in the wilderness. Warren is implying that Jesus was a mere man before this event.(Mat. 4:2, Mark 1:13, Luke 4:2)

We have not even left the introduction of PDL and we have already proved its author to be ethically challenged! This deceptive use of scripture sets the tone for the rest of the book!

At the end of the introduction the author wants us to sign his written covenant. This is before we have read his book to see if it is biblical or not! There are enough warnings in the introduction that any Christian, with any amount of discernment, should put it down immediately, but some will go on, ignoring the promptings of the Holy Spirit.

The book starts with an excellent line on page 17, *"It's not about you"*, but probably the best quote in the book is found on page 20, *"To Discover your purpose in life you must turn to God's Word, not the world's wisdom"*. Unfortunately the rest of the book is all about the world's wisdom and manipulating scripture to fit the Purpose Driven agenda.

Look at the titles of the sections of the Purpose Driven Life, they are all about "you".

PURPOSE #1:   <u>You</u> Were Planned for God's Pleasure

PURPOSE #2:   <u>You</u> Were Formed for God's Family

PURPOSE #3:   <u>You</u> Were Created to Become like Christ

PURPOSE #4:   You Were Shaped for Serving God

PURPOSE #5:   You Were Made for a Mission

The subject of each of these titles is *"You"*. God is reduced to someone who exists to help *"You"*! It's all about you! As Tamara Hartzell says *"You, not God, are the subject of this "spiritual journey." God is merely the means to purpose, meaning, and significance in life."* (p.48, In the Name of Purpose)

In chapter 2 Warren's selective quote from the New Century Version changes the subject of scripture from the nation of Israel to *"You"*, the reader. This is dishonest:

"(God) wasn't lonely. But he wanted to make you in order to express his love. God says, 'I have carried you since you were born; I have taken care of you from your birth. Even when you are old, I will be the same. Even when your hair has turned gray, I will take care of you. I made you and will take care of you.'" (PDL p. 25)

The bible actually says:

*Hearken unto me, **O house of Jacob, and all the remnant of the house of Israel**, which are borne by me from the belly, which are carried from the womb: And even to your old age I am he; and even to hoar hairs will I carry you: I have made, and I will bear; even I will carry, and will deliver you. (Isaiah 46:3-4)*

On the previous page Warren begins to misrepresent God's character: *"The bible tells us, 'God is Love.' It doesn't say God has love. He is love! Love is the essence of God's character."*

The bible does indeed say *"God is Love"* (1 John 4:8) but it also reveals that the character of God has much more depth than the one dimensional, Santa Claus type of caricature which Warren presents. You will look long and hard to find any mention of God's justice, wrath or holiness in PDL God's love is nothing without His wrath! Jesus died to save us from His own wrath, which we justly deserve! Jesus Christ hates sin with as much passion as the Father, and the Holy Spirit! What a horrendous burden it was to take your, and my, sin on Himself! God's character demands that there is a penalty for sin! God's eternal nature demands an eternal punishment for sin.

This is why only God Himself could be our sacrifice, for all eternity!

Day 3, on page 34, says *"God won't ask about your religious background or doctrinal views."* Here the author is prophesying in the name of God, but is he correct? Jesus spoke a lot about doctrine:

> *"Jesus answered them, and said, My doctrine is not mine, but his that sent me."* *(John 7:16)*

> *"But in vain they do worship me, teaching for doctrines the commandments of men."* *(Matthew 15:9)*

Paul taught Doctrine:

> *That we henceforth be no more children, tossed to and fro, and carried about with every wind of doctrine, by the sleight of men, and cunning craftiness, whereby they lie in wait to deceive; (Ephesians 4:14)*

> *All scripture [is] given by inspiration of God, and [is] profitable for doctrine, for reproof, for correction, for instruction in righteousness: (2 Timothy 3:16)*

> *For the time will come when they will not endure sound doctrine; but after their own lusts shall they heap to themselves teachers, having itching ears; (2 Timothy 4:3)*

> *Holding fast the faithful word as he hath been taught, that he may be able by sound doctrine both to exhort and to convince the gainsayers. (Titus 1:9)*

What did the Apostle John think of doctrine?

> *If there come any unto you, and bring not this doctrine, receive him not into [your] house, neither bid him God speed (2 John 1:10)*

(See also: Matthew 7:28, 15:9, 16:22, 22:33, Mark 1:22, 4:2, 7:7, 11:18, 12:38, Luke 4:32, John 7:16 & 17, 18:19, Acts 2:42, 5:28, 13:12, 17:19, Romans 6:17, 16:17, 1 Corinthians 14:6 & 26,

Ephesians 4:14, Colossians 2:22, 1 Timothy 1:3, 1:10, 4:1, 4:6, 4:13, 4:13, 4:16, 5:17, 6:1 & 3, 2 Timothy 3:10 & 16, Titus 1:9, 2:1, 2:7, 2:10, Hebrews 6:2, 13:9, 2 John 1:9 & 10, Revelation 2:14, 15 & 24)

The bible repeatedly emphasizes the importance of sound doctrine, and the danger of false doctrine. Warren shows that he is not only a false teacher but a false prophet, speaking what God does not say!

I could not have said it better than Tamara Hartzell:

> "God's Word is clear that the nature of God is the basis for what He wants from us. Therefore, increasing our knowledge of God Himself also increases our knowledge of His purposes. Yet not much is said in The Purpose Driven Life about the nature of God. In a man centered "spiritual journey," helping people deepen their knowledge of God isn't the primary issue. " (p.48, In the Name of Purpose, By Tamara Hartzell, 2006)

In chapter 4 Rick does mention Hell in passing, but never defines it, rather he says *"if you reject his love, forgiveness, and salvation, you will spend eternity apart from God forever."* This is a half truth. Those who do not like Jesus Christ and His Holiness will not find this too threatening. The book of Revelation, however, says this about the lost:

> *The same shall drink of the wine of the wrath of God, which is poured out without mixture into the cup of his indignation; and* **he shall be tormented with fire and brimstone in the presence of the holy angels, and in the presence of the Lamb:** *And the smoke of their torment ascendeth up for ever and ever: and they have no rest day nor night, who worship the beast and his image, and whosoever receiveth the mark of his name. (Revelation 14:10-11)*

To *"drink of the wine of the wrath of God"* implies that God's wrath is taken in, and becomes a part of you! Jesus is not in the Lake of Fire, but in a position where He can observe the Lake of Fire, and the torment of those who rejected His offer of forgiveness. If you read the passage carefully you will see that those in the Lake of Fire are also in the presence of the holy angels. We know the holy angels are not suffering in the Lake of Fire since they have never sinned, nor did they die for mankind, therefore the only explanation for this passage is that Jesus and the angels are in a place where they can observe what happens in that Lake, without being in it themselves. Jesus is not in the Lake, for He suffered Hell on the Cross. He is not in a position where those suffering God's wrath could mock him.

Those inhabiting the Lake of Fire will be apart from the kindness of Jesus, who walked the earth in Israel and died for them, they will be without His loving presence, but they will know He is observing their torment. Their hatred will be bound by the shores of that lake and they will become so evil that they will not be recognizable as members of the family of man. So, evil will exist for all eternity in the Lake of Fire, and they will glorify God by their presence there.

Jesus took our Hell on the cross, and since He is an eternal being He suffered an eternity separated from the Father in those few hours. God declares that what Christ did at that time is sufficient for all sin of all time. He is not in the Lake of Fire today, but at the right hand of God the Father (Acts 7:55 & 56, Heb. 1:3, 10:12, Rev. 4:2). The bible says *"Jesus died once for all"*. (Hebrews 10:10)

In chapter 6 Warren says *"your identity is in eternity, and your homeland is heaven"* (PDL p. 48) Here he is making the assumption that his audience is all saved. This is dangerous since there is no doubt that many who read this book are lost. He is giving them false hope. His presentation of *"the gospel"* is not made until chapter 7, so this statement is certainly very premature. The apostle Paul made similar statements, but always qualified it to identify the audience as *"the saints"* or those who have received Christ. Such a statement is not applicable to the lost and hints of universalism.

PDL makes its presentation of *"the gospel"* on page 58. This presentation says nothing about the holiness of God, nor the just wrath that we deserve. This is a *"feel good"* presentation that is probably the most shallow I have seen. Acknowledgement of one's sinful condition and depravity is not mentioned. It is almost as if he is trying to sneak his readers into the family of God against their will. As Dave Hunt has been heard to say: *"A man convinced against his will is of the same opinion still"*.

Just before this *"gospel"* presentation the author quotes the Message version of John 3:36 *"Whoever accepts and trusts the Son gets in on everything, life complete and forever!"* The actual bible reads differently: *"He that believeth on the Son hath everlasting life:*

and he that believeth not the Son shall not see life; but the wrath of God abideth on him".

Warren invites his readers to *"whisper the prayer that will change your eternity: 'Jesus, I believe in you and I receive you.' Go ahead."* Many will place their trust in this prayer and be lost forever! It is only Jesus who can save, not prayer... especially a prayer this shallow! Recognize you are a sinner deserving Hell and judgment, repent and fall at the feet of Jesus and beg for mercy. Today!

In the next paragraph he says: *"If you sincerely meant that prayer, congratulations! Welcome to the family of God!"* How does he know the reader is saved? Does he think that saying a certain prayer is a magic formula that saves the speaker? It is not up to any man to tell another that they are saved! Salvation is not based on how sincere you think you were when you prayed a prayer. You can't trust your own heart: *"The heart is deceitful above all things, and desperately wicked: who can know it?"* (Jeremiah 17:9) Confirmation of salvation is something that is reserved for the Holy Spirit. This treatment of the gospel is demeaning to the Lord Jesus Christ and is secondary to the purpose of Warren's book. The truth is that the Gospel is glorious, invincible, and at the centre of Christ's command to teach all nations. (Matthew 28:19 & 20, Mark 16:15, Luke 24:47, John 20:21 & 31)

The indictment of these modern false teachers is found in Ezekiel 13:22:

> *Because with lies ye have made the heart of the righteous sad, whom I have not made sad; and strengthened the hands of the wicked, that he should not return from his wicked way, by promising him life:*

Chapter 8 is entitled *"Planned for God's Pleasure"*. This chapter begins by stating that you bring pleasure to God just by being *"you"*. This chapter is pure *"Self-Esteem gospel"*, that lifts up man and makes God dependant on him. He never stops to point out that you are depraved!

The God of The Purpose Driven Life is a mushy, fuzzy, Santa Claus type, who is desperate for you to love Him. Warren's Jesus says *"I'd rather die than live without you."*(P. 79) I do not find such a God attractive, do you? The God of scripture is Holy and is His own standard. You can't get into Heaven without the Holiness of God! *"Because it is written, Be ye holy; for I am holy"*. (1 Peter 1:16)

On Page 31 Warren says *"Your purpose becomes the standard you use to evaluate which activities are essential and which aren't."* The standard that a Christian uses is the Word of God, not some purpose that you make up yourself. In the next paragraph he says *"Without a clear purpose you have no foundation on which you base decisions, allocate your time, and use your resources."* In neither paragraph does he quote any scripture, so let's see what God has to say:

"For other foundation can no man lay than that is laid, which is Jesus Christ".(1 Corinthians 3:11) If you are saved you have a sure foundation, the Lord Jesus Christ.

On page 81 Warren says *"Retirement is not the goal of a surrendered life, because it competes with God for the primary attention of our lives."* The truth is the Bible speaks often about wise stewardship. Growing old and feeble is inevitable, unless we die or the Rapture occurs first. Planning for retirement is not serving money like a god, it is wise stewardship. It is not the same as hoarding wealth. Rick is afraid that his audience will not give what he considers enough to their churches, and so attempts to manipulate his audience into giving! Born-again Christians, who have the Holy Spirit within, will give out of love, but unbelievers need to be coaxed into giving. I wonder if Warren knows something he is not letting on?

Rick Warren's Saddleback Church demands a written commitment of their members, to tithe a minimum of ten percent of their income to the Church. This is not a command to New Testament believers, but pastors like it because it brings money into the coffers. Just because it works does not mean it is of God!

Tithing was instituted in the Old Testament for Israel, and essentially was the income tax to run the country, since Israel was a theocracy at the time. A careful study of tithing reveals that only land owners and farmers were required to tithe, not tradesmen. Furthermore a shepherd was to bring in the *"tenth under the rod"* (Leviticus 27:32) not the first. In other words a young shepherd who only had eight lambs that year was not required to tithe at all. Yes they were to bring in the firstfruits, but that offering was not considered part of the tithe.

There was an element of mercy built into the Law that many modern preachers miss. There were actually two tithes of ten percent each plus an additional ten percent, for the poor, every third year. The total annual tithe was actually 23 1/3 percent, however, Israel was a theocracy and the tithe was a tax to run its government.

Israel was the first "welfare state" with 3 1/3 percent of income being allocated for the poor. Most pastors forget that in modern countries like Canada, our total tax burden is often in excess of fifty percent of our annual income! (Figure it out: we have income tax, property tax, license fees, vehicle license fees, building permits, sales tax, and even sales tax on goods for which sales taxes have already been paid, like used automobiles. And don't forget hidden taxes!) Though the amount taxed is less in the United States, it is still far in excess of the 23 1/3 percent that God required of Israel! The truth is that our modern welfare states are so irresponsible that they are almost all on the brink of financial collapse!

The New Testament rule for giving is that we are to give sacrificially and willingly. Paul spoke of giving in 1 Corinthians 16:2 *"Upon the first day of the week let every one of you lay **by him in store**, as God hath prospered him, that there be no gatherings when I come."* We are to set aside as God has prospered us, and please note that it is to be kept *"by him"*, that is; close at hand where the man of the house has access to it, to use it for God's business. The Church is not the storehouse as was the temple, and these funds are to be kept separate and secure, by the believer, but ready for needs that arise among the brethren.

Am I saying not to give to your church? Absolutely not! Give joyfully, and until it hurts, but remember there is no general rule about how much you should give. For some single mothers, working in the service industry, even two percent will hurt. If they can't put food on the table for their children, it would be irresponsible to give of their children's substance! On the other hand it might be better to give than to buy them violent video games. Give as the Holy Spirit leads you. Be wise. Pray about it, and do not be manipulated into giving on the basis of emotions.

Warren is careless with regard to whom he quotes:

> "The Bible is crystal clear about how you benefit when you fully surrender your life to God. First you experience peace", "Stop quarreling with God! If you agree with him, you will have peace at last, and things will go well for you" (p. 82, Endnote: Job 22:21)

Considering the fact that millions of Christians, throughout the ages, have suffered martyrdom, I wonder what he is talking about? Warren is actually quoting Eliphaz the Temanite, one of the three *"friends"* who came to *"comfort"* Job when tragedy befell him.

Eliphaz was actually in the middle of a speech expounding the virtues of Works righteousness! The Lord eventually appeared to Eliphaz and this is what He said to him:

> *And it was so, that after the LORD had spoken these words unto Job, the LORD said to Eliphaz the Temanite, **My wrath is kindled against thee, and against thy two friends: for ye have not spoken of me the thing that is right, as my servant Job hath**. (Job 42:7)*

Isn't it rather unwise to be quoting Eliphaz, since what he says is a false teaching about God, and is identified so by God Himself? Does Warren actually agree with Eliphaz?

Warren has a habit of quoting, unwisely, from Catholic Mystics. On page 88 he recommends the book *"Practicing the Presence of God"* by a Catholic mystic by the name of Brother Lawrence. Brother Lawrence's book doesn't quote scripture, but is full of mystical methods, and techniques, for communicating with the spiritual realm, none of which appear in scripture. This man was a Carmelite monk, an order that was in the lead in Mary worship, and in mysticism. Both John of the Cross, and Teresa of Avila were also Carmelites and are also quoted in PDL *"Practicing the Presence of God"* is a New Age, pagan, practise whereby the practitioner attains an altered state of consciousness, and opens his or her mind to influence by demonic spirits!

> "The Bible says, 'He rules everything and is everywhere *and is in everything*.' (Ephesians 4:6b, NCV, PDL, p. 88)

This quote from the New Century version is stating the New Age idea of panentheism, which is closely related to pantheism. Pantheism states that God *is* everything, while panentheism states that God is *in* everything. This comes from the pagan practise of mantra prayers where the participant experiences *"God is in everything and in everyone"*. This practise undermines the gospel message. While God is present everywhere, He only indwells believers in the Lord Jesus Christ. Had Warren quoted from the true bible his quote would have read, *"One God and Father of all, who is above all, and through all, and in you all."* Keep in mind that this letter is addressed to the believers in Ephesus, not to all people everywhere. Only born-again Christians have God in them.

Warren is subtly slipping in New Age pagan practises under the guise of Christian teaching. For a more in-depth study of this foundational belief of New Age Paganism in Warren's book, please see Tamara Hartzell's book *"In The Name Of Purpose"*.

On Page 89 Warren recommends *"Breath Prayers"*, an occult, mystical practise. He explains...

> "You choose a brief sentence or a simple phrase that can be repeated to Jesus in one breath: "You are with me." "I receive your grace." "I'm Depending on you." "I want to know you." & etc. "Pray it as often as possible so it is rooted deep in your heart. Just be sure that your motive is to honor God, not control him."

Now, if God wants a personal relationship with his creation, how is He going to react to us saying the same thing over and over, hundreds or thousands of times a day? How would you react to a good friend saying the same thing repeatedly, ad nauseum, to you? You'd be sick wouldn't you? What did Jesus say about this kind of prayer? *"But when ye pray, use not vain repetitions, as the heathen do: for they think that they shall be heard for their much speaking."* (Matthew 6:7) This recommendation of Warren's is enough, in itself, to reject the entire book. How could there be anything worth salvaging when it contains such blatant anti-Christ statements?

Going back to the last sentence of his quote I have to ask: *"Does Warren actually think that one could control God by saying this type of prayer?"* Does he actually think that God listens to this type of prayer? Jesus indicates in Matthew 6:7 that you won't be heard when you pray this way! Warren is actually promoting disobedience to Jesus Christ! The truth is that this type of prayer can induce altered states of consciousness, and can lead to mystical experiences, where the practitioner encounters demonic spirits masquerading as angels, or as Jesus himself!

Later in page 103 Warren contradicts himself: *"Jesus called thoughtless worship 'vain repetitions'"*. Well, what does he think he had just said on page 89? Actually Jesus said *"They think they will be heard for their much speaking"*, so it really isn't thoughtless prayer but repeated prayer exactly like Rick is recommending. What a glaring contradiction! It's almost as if more than one person wrote this book and they forgot to compare notes before going to print!

In chapter 13 he quotes a book by Gary Thomas, *"Sacred Pathways"*. Warren identifies nine ways people draw near to God.

As I read through this list I found that most of them are not biblical, and in fact smack of the New Age movement. My comments are in parentheses:

"Naturalists are most inspired to love God out-of-doors, in natural settings" (Like Wicca, maybe? Wicca is a religion that worships nature, and the creation, rather than the creator.) (See Romans 1:18-25)

"Sensates love God with their senses and appreciate beautiful worship services that involve their sight, taste, smell, and touch not just their ears" (This sounds again like some kind of nature worship, mixed with Catholicism.)

"Traditionalists draw closer to God through rituals, liturgies, symbols and unchanging structures" (This sounds like the Catholic, orthodox and Anglican churches. Jesus said *"Full well ye reject the commandment of God, that ye may keep your own tradition."* Mark 7:9)

"Ascetics prefer to love God in solitude and simplicity". (But we are commanded to preach the gospel to every creature, not lock ourselves away in a monastery or convent.)

"Activists love God through confronting evil, battling injustice, and working to make the world a better place". (You will have a hard time finding a command to join activists in scripture, nor will you find an example there. Activists often make up their own standard of right and wrong, and then attempt to force it on others. This sounds like the shameful liberal social gospel.)

"Caregivers love God by loving others and meeting their needs". (We are all commanded to care for others, there is no special group set out for this in scripture.)

"Enthusiasts love God through celebration", (But doesn't everyone love a good party? So you can party and consider that to be worship?)

"Contemplatives love God through adoration". (This is a reference to Eastern Mystical methods, breath prayers, mantra prayers and yoga. Not only are these practises not condoned in scripture, they are actually condemned by it.)

"Intellectuals love God by studying with their minds", (But Jesus told us ALL to love God with ALL our mind. (Matthew 22:37, Mark 12:30, Luke 10:27) Many *"scientists"* ignore the Word of God and raise their own intellect to the same level as God. You love God with the intellect by studying God's word, and then applying it to your life.)

While Caregivers are obeying God, and Jesus did command us to Love God with all our mind, you will not find any reference to the other seven of these *"pathways"* in scripture. Each of these groups make up their own methods for reaching God, and Rick lends them credibility in this passage! Most of these ways of *"loving God"* are not only unbiblical, but anti-biblical and dangerous. Only what Scripture says is of any value in loving God.

On page 124 Warren continues his attack on the Word of God: *"Jesus said our love for each other-- not our doctrinal beliefs-- is our greatest witness to the world."* The implication in Warren's statement is that doctrinal belief is not important, but the truth is that it is our doctrinal beliefs that make us love each other. Furthermore it is what Jesus said that constitutes our doctrinal beliefs. If Rick is correct Jesus would have been saying that what He said wasn't important! This constitutes another of Rick Warren's contradictions.

Rick Warren promotes Alpha and actually has a YouTube video of his endorsement on the Alpha website. (*Alpha USA: What Church Leaders Say*)

"If an organ is somehow severed from its body, it will shrivel and die. It cannot exist on its own, and neither can you. Disconnected and cut off from the lifeblood of a local body, your spiritual life will wither and eventually cease to exist. [PDL p.131, endnote: Ephesians 4:16 (no version listed)]"

But speaking the truth in love, may grow up into him in all things, which is the head, even Christ: From whom the whole body fitly joined together and compacted by that which every joint supplieth, according to the effectual working in the measure of every part, maketh increase of the body unto the edifying of itself in love. (Ephesians 4:15-16)

Comparing what the author says to the Bible we see a substantial amount of manipulation has to be done to go from pure scripture to Warren's pronouncements. When we are without the camp, we are not without Christ. He is the one who supplies our spiritual life, not the Church. Yes we should fellowship with other believers, but not with churches that sell-out the gospel for some man-made church-growth formula. Warren is implying that our salvation depends on church attendance, that the Church is an agent of salvation! This is heresy!

Be it known unto you all, and to all the people of Israel, that by the name of Jesus Christ of Nazareth, whom ye crucified, whom God raised from the dead, even by him doth this man stand here before you whole. This is the stone which was set at nought of you builders, which is become the head of the corner. Neither is there salvation in any other: for there is none other name under heaven given among men, whereby we must be saved. (Acts 4:10-12)

"Contrary to popular book titles, there are no Easy Steps to Maturity or Secrets of Instant Sainthood." (PDL; p. 222)

While maturity, and sanctification, truly is a process, here he is implying that there is some validity to the Catholic method of creating saints. The truth is that all who are in Christ Jesus are saints. We become saints instantly when we repent of our sin and trust Jesus Christ and His sacrifice alone to save us. This process is instantaneous and is an act of the Holy Spirit. All true believers have the Holy Spirit dwelling in them and those who do not are not saved.

But ye are not in the flesh, but in the Spirit, if so be that the Spirit of God dwell in you. Now if any man have not the Spirit of Christ, he is none of his. (Romans 8:9)

All true believers are saints. The apostles wrote to the entire Church and called them saints. The bible speaks of ministering to living saints, yet according to the Catholic Church you have to be dead at least five years before you can be considered for sainthood:

To all that be in Rome, beloved of God, called to be saints: Grace to you and peace from God our Father, and the Lord Jesus Christ. (Romans 1:7)

Unto the church of God which is at Corinth, to them that are sanctified in Christ Jesus, called to be saints, with all that in every place call upon the name of Jesus Christ our Lord, both theirs and ours: (1 Corinthians 1:2)

Paul, an apostle of Jesus Christ by the will of God, to the saints which are at Ephesus, and to the faithful in Christ

Jesus: (Ephesians 1:1)

> *Paul and Timotheus, the servants of Jesus Christ,* **to all the saints in Christ Jesus which are at Philippi,** *with the bishops and deacons: (Philippians 1:1)*

It is apparent that Warren is confusing terms like salvation and sanctification, terms that every pastor should be aware of. Sanctification is a process, but salvation is instantaneous.

> "God wants you to have a Christlike ministry on earth. That means other people are going to find healing in your wounds. Your greatest life messages and your most effective ministry will come out of your deepest hurts. The things you're most embarrassed about, most ashamed of, and most reluctant to share are the very tools God can use most powerfully to heal others." (PDL; p. 275)

I was so amazed when I read this passage. The things I am most embarrassed about are my sins. Is he saying that our sins can heal others? Is he saying we should confess our sins to the unsaved so they do not feel too bad about theirs?   This is upside-down, black-is-white, nonsense. It was prophesied by Isaiah:

> *Woe unto them that call evil good, and good evil; that put darkness for light, and light for darkness; that put bitter for sweet, and sweet for bitter! (Isaiah 5:20)*

The truth is that the victories we have in Christ can be an encouragement to others. It is the wounds of Jesus that heal, it is His power that saves, and it is His life that is given to sinners who repent and believe. It is the gospel of Jesus Christ that changes lives, the Word of God is the Sword of the Spirit.

Both Warren and the Emergent Church are condescending towards the study of eschatology, or prophecies of the End Times. On page 285 he says,

> "When the disciples wanted to talk about prophecy, Jesus quickly switched the conversation to evangelism.   He wanted them to concentrate on their mission in the world. He said in essence, "the details of my return are none of your business. What is your business is the mission I've

given you. Focus on that." (See Acts 1:7)

Warren is conveniently forgetting that by this time Jesus had already given His disciples lengthy discourses on the End Times in Matthew 13 & 24, Mark 13, Luke 21 and many other passages. Furthermore, he later gave lengthy End Times prophecies to some of the men who were standing there that day. Peter's second book, and the Book of Revelation, written by John, have added much to the study of eschatology. Though not there that day, Paul also wrote extensively on End Times prophecy, under inspiration of the Holy Spirit. Every book of the New Testament touches on prophecy, in one way or another.

The reason that many men today ignore eschatology is that such a study would reveal them as false teachers. Another reason is that truth always divides. In these days of deep ecumenism, anything that divides is rejected. Jesus said:

> *Think not that I am come to send peace on earth: I came not to send peace, but a sword. For I am come to set a man at variance against his father, and the daughter against her mother, and the daughter in law against her mother in law. And a man's foes shall be they of his own household. He that loveth father or mother more than me is not worthy of me: and he that loveth son or daughter more than me is not worthy of me. And he that taketh not his cross, and followeth after me, is not worthy of me. He that findeth his life shall lose it: and he that loseth his life for my sake shall find it. (Matthew 10:34-39)*

"The last thing many believers need today is to go to another Bible study. They already know far more than they are putting into practice. What they need are serving experiences in which they can exercise their spiritual muscles." (PDL; p. 231)

It is true that we need to apply the Scriptures we already know to our lives, but the truth is that modern Christians are probably the most biblically illiterate generation that has ever walked the earth. Christians do not apply the Word because they do not know the Word. We need the Word of God more than ever. I find this quote to be deceitful and arrogant. This is insulting to the Spirit of God

and to the Lord Jesus Christ. Warren's emphasis is how you fit into
this world.

There is so much wrong with The Purpose Driven Life, and Rick
Warren's philosophy, that many books could, and have been, written
about it. I have included the names of several at the end of this
chapter. Please avail yourself of these resources, and pass them
around.

Regarding Rick Warren's books: Don't waste you money or your
time. If you feel that you must read it, borrow it from a library, get
a good commentary on it, and read it with your King James bible
open beside you. Check out each quotation.

The Emerging or Emergent Church

C losely related to Rick Warren is a movement that is
gathering steam known as the Emergent, or Emerging
Church. He has had members of this group, like Leonard
Sweet, speak at his church. While there technically is a difference
between these terms, they are so closely related that I will use them
synonymously.

The Emergent Church is a reaction to post modernism. Actually
it is a surrender to it. This movement seeks to redefine Christianity
based on changes within the culture. While it accurately defines
real problems in protestant and evangelical Christianity, their
solution is to reject the Bible entirely as authoritative, and to accept
other religious writings as equally valid. Mysticism is at the core of
this movement and though they use similar terminology to biblical
Christianity, they have redefined most words to reflect their own
views and practises. Remember, when dealing with false teachers,
always make them define their words.

Why should we pay attention to these fringe groups? Aren't
they just another fad? They may be a fad, but I think the evidence
is that there is something else going on. If they are a fad, I am
certain that they will be replaced by something even more
dangerous. These groups are growing and some older churches
have gone or are leaning the *"Emergent"* way. Actually it is
beginning to look like there will be a merging of the Emergent
groups with the New Apostolic Reformation in the near future.

Some of the names of leaders of this movement are, and this is
not a comprehensive list. Brian McLaren, Rob Bell, Alan Jones,
Tony Jones, Doug Pagit, Peter Scazzero, Leonard Sweet, Phyllis

Tickle, Richard Rohr, Jason Clark, Dan Kimball, Dallas Willard, Calvin Miller, and Brennan Manning. By the time this book goes to press I'm sure this list will have expanded.

On the surface the Emergents claim to be bringing something new to Christianity, but in reality it is just the same old stuff. Essentially it is nineteenth century liberalism mixed with Contemplative Spirituality/Mysticism. The mix with pagan spirituality actually makes the movement more acceptable, and thus more dangerous. These people teach Breath prayers, mantra prayers and even yoga, practises expressly forbidden by Jesus. (Matthew 6:7) Spiritual experiences replace faith and lead to a rejection of biblical doctrines.

Ikons are another feature of the Emergent movement. Ikons are pictures of "saints" and even of Jesus, "to help you focus your worship" and are blatant disobedience to the second commandment:

> Thou shalt not make unto thee any graven image, or any likeness of any thing that is in heaven above, or that is in the earth beneath, or that is in the water under the earth: (Exodus 20:4)

Some make the excuse that what they are doing is using the image to worship the prototype. This is a lie. As we go throughout scripture we see that God has no problem with art, or with creating images of angels, for the ark of the covenant for instance, or any other thing so long as it is not worshipped. The clear intent of scripture is that we ought not to make images of the divine. We are not to think that God is like anything on earth.

> Forasmuch then as we are the offspring of God, we ought not to think that the Godhead is like unto gold, or silver, or stone, graven by art and man's device. (Acts 17:29)

Rick Warren has had Emergent leader, Leonard Sweet, speak at Saddleback Church. (From the Lighthouse, Nov. 27, 2007) Like Warren, the Emergents often quote the same Catholic mystics, such as Brother Lawrence, Teresa of Avilla, and John of the Cross.

What is the point of all of this? There is a movement back to the Roman Catholic Church, and Alpha, Purpose Driven and the Emergent Church are all part of this stream. There is a rejection of biblical doctrine in favour of experience, especially mystical experiences. There is an assumption that any kind of spiritual experience is a good experience. Unfortunately the type of experience that those who practise contemplative spirituality encounter is an identical experience to that which Buddhist, Hindu, and Sufi Muslim mystics experience. When some spirit tells you that you have achieved a *"state of oneness"* with God, and then you find that people in these other religions have the same experience, it results in a denial of the gospel of Jesus Christ. If Buddhists, Hindus and Sufis can all experience oneness with God without Jesus Christ, then Jesus Christ is not necessary!

The primary meaning of the word *"Holy"* is separation. This is the word that God uses to describe himself and is the only attribute of God that is repeated three times: *"Holy, holy, holy is the Lord God Almighty"*. God is separate from His creation. This is a message that is diametrically opposed to the message of mystics, both modern and ancient.

While man is made in the image of God, man is not God. The lie of mysticism goes back to the garden of Eden, and has been taught by His enemies since that time: *"You are one with God, You are God!"* When you read the experiences of mystics this is the common experience they speak of, and it matter's not which tradition they come from. They can be Buddhist, Hindu, Sufi, New Age or *"Christian"*, yet they all speak of an experience of oneness with God, and with all creation! Thus creation itself becomes God! If a person who denies the cross can be one with God equally with a Christian, then the cross is of no importance! Remember, however, that experiences can be deceitful.

> *But we preach Christ crucified, unto the Jews a stumblingblock, and unto the Greeks foolishness; (1 Corinthians 1:23)*

Jesus Christ said *"...I am the way, the truth, and the life: no man cometh unto the Father, but by me.."* (John 14:6) which leads us to the conclusion that either Jesus Christ is mistaken, or the Contemplatives are mistaken. Both can't be correct. As the Bible itself says: *"Beloved, believe not every spirit, but try (test) the spirits whether they are of God: because many false prophets are gone out into the world."* (1 John 4:1)

The only way we can test the spirits of contemplative spirituality is to compare what they say to the Word of God. This we have done above, and throughout this chapter. Very clearly the Christianity practised by modern evangelicals, emergents and Catholics is not that which is taught and practised in the pages of scripture.

What is happening is the the rebellion spoken of in 2 Timothy 4:3, and 2 Thessalonians 2:3. It is no accident that many of these groups are also involved in communist or Marxist philosophy. Richard Bennet, a former Dominican priest, states in his testimony that he was involved with Liberation Theology as a Catholic priest, and supported communist rebels in Nicaragua, along with other priests.

The Purpose Driven P.E.A.C.E. plan is simply old line Liberation Theology repackaged for a new generation, with the added twist of mystical, spiritual experiences. The emphasis is on making this life better, rather than preaching the gospel of Jesus Christ. The truth is that most people who have a good life here on earth do not think they need a Saviour. This is why the majority of Christians come from poor backgrounds, and why there is so much apostasy in the western world.

The Shack

While attending a witnessing seminar at my church, in the spring of 2009, the leader of the seminar recommended a book called *"The Shack"* by Wm. Paul Young. His recommendation was accompanied by applause from several attendees of the seminar.

At the time I had not even heard of this book, and assumed that a person from Evangelism Explosion would not recommend anything unhealthy, however since I was very busy and did not have time to read it I just filed the name in the back of my mind and went on with other things.

In the course of researching for this book, however, the name *"The Shack"* kept coming up again and again. Finally I decided to read one of the articles about this book. I was shocked by what people were saying. They were saying things like *"This book teaches a form of universalism"* and *"The God of the Shack is not the God of the Bible"*!

Well, I had to get it out of the library and check it out. Indeed it is true that the God presented in *"The Shack"* is not the God of the Bible. The God of this book is a pantheistic (God is all things) or panentheistic (God is in all things) God, that has more in common with Santa Claus than the God of the Bible.

The Shack is a cleverly crafted fable that sucks the reader in with the use of emotion, but in the end it teaches a false view of God.

God the Father is portrayed as an African-American woman, named Eloise, but called *"Papa"*, who has scars on her hands. This is turning God into a goddess. The scars on her hands are extreme heresy since it was the Father who sacrificed His Son for mankind. The Father did not suffer on the cross, it was Jesus alone who died for our sins! The Father abandoned His Son on the cross, and he did it for you! He did not suffer as did His Son. If He did suffer at all it was emotional, but the atonement was done by Christ alone!

While it is true that Jesus did come as a man, to portray God the Father and the Holy Spirit in this way is definitely idolatry. (Exodus 20:4) Our culture is so used to this that we do not see it when it happens right in front of us.

What does the God of the Shack have to say about sin? *"I don't need to punish people for sin. Sin is its own punishment, devouring from the inside. It's not my purpose to punish it; it's my joy to cure it"* (The Shack, page 120).

What does the God of the bible say about the punishment of sin?

> *And the devil that deceived them was **cast into the lake of fire and brimstone**, where the beast and the false prophet are, and **shall be tormented day and night for ever and ever.** And I saw a great white throne, and him that sat on it, from whose face the earth and the heaven fled away; and there was found no place for them. And I saw the dead, small and great, stand before God; and the books were opened: and another book was opened, which is the book of life: and the dead were judged out of those things which were written in the books, according to their works. And the sea gave up the dead which were in it; and death and hell delivered up the dead which were in them: and they were judged every man according to their works. And death and hell were cast into the lake of fire. This is the second death. And **whosoever was not found written in the book of life was cast into the lake of fire.** (Revelation 20:10-15)*

The Father was satisfied by His Son's sacrifice! It was actually the Father who demanded the sacrifice, though Jesus is just as Holy as His Father.

The Jesus of the Shack is not the Jesus of the Bible, but "*another Jesus*". This guy is a Jewish carpenter who goes around fixing things, and is some sort of "*good old boy*".

Paul Young elevates experience to a level equal to or even above Scripture, and is demeaning to the reformation doctrine of "Sola Scriptura". He also subtly promotes a form of Universalism, called Universal Reconcilliation, or Christian Universalism. Though he publically denies this, nevertheless this is what is presented in the pages of this book.

Dr. Michael Youssef has counted thirteen heresies promoted in "The Shack". (13 Heresies, Youssef) As an engaging read, the author sneaks these ideas into your head while you are preoccupied with the emotion of the story. The ideas presented serve to undermine biblical Christianity. The "Jesus" of the Shack says "*I am the best way any human can relate to Papa (God the Father), or Sarayu (God the Holy Spirit)*.(p. 110) The clear implication is that there are are other ways to relate to God. The Jesus of the bible says something very different:

> *Jesus saith unto him, I am the way, the truth, and the life: no man cometh unto the Father, but by me. (John 14:6)*

Some will point out that I too question some traditional "*Christian*" ideas, so why should I challenge Mr. Young? This is not really true. I question ideas that do not come from the infallible source, the bible. I question ideas that twist the plain teaching of the Word of God, but I do not question any Christian teaching that is based on the clear teaching of the bible. Salvation is based on faith, and not works, and this is taught from the first book all the way to the last, and was emphasized by the reformation. Unfortunately, the reformers, like Laban's daughters, clung to some ideas that did not come from the Word of God, and these I reject.

I have listed several resources related to "*The Shack*" at the end of this chapter. Some are free online, and others are available from book stores and Christian ministries. If you have read "*The Shack*" or know someone who has, please take the time to read them.

The New Apostolic Reformation and Related Groups

I have already touched on Dominionism, and Reconstructionism briefly. These groups along with the Prosperity Gospel and Kingdom Now theology are all closely related. There are several key teachings of these groups including:

· "They believe that God is restoring the office of prophet and apostles to the church
· Claim that they alone have the power and authority to execute the plans and purposes of God
· Believe they are building a new foundation for a global church.
· Believe they will literally establish the Kingdom of Heaven on earth
· Believe in a coming "civil war" in the church where they will overcome all (true Christian) opposition.
· Place an inordinate emphasis on angels and the supernatural
· Claim extra biblical revelations that can not be scripturally proven (progressive revelation)
· Claim that God is doing a "new thing"
· Frequently say that those not accepting their heretical teaching are "Putting God in a box"
· Teach that we should never question their authority.
· They use the term "Touch not God's anointed" frequently when questions are raised.
· They peg those that question their authority as bound by religion, legalistic, divisive, narrow minded, rebellious, and demonic
· Place a greater emphasis on dreams, visions and extra-biblical revelation than they do on the Word of God
· They believe they will be the corporate incarnation of Christ
· They believe they will execute judgment upon those who oppose them (up to and including death).
· They believe in a one world religion operating in sync with a one world government.
· They believe in complete unity and believe that there is nothing they can not accomplish through this unity.
· They believe they can bring Heaven down to earth (Yoism- see link   below   for   more   information) (http://herescope.blogspot.com/2006/05/yoism-creating-heaven-

on-earth.html)
· They believe that we will be perfected here on earth
· They believe in aggressively organizing small group networks
· They believe in the organization of apostles under pre-eminent apostles
· They believe that ALL local churches must be under the authority of a regional or trans-local apostle
· They believe each city must have an apostle- men given extraordinary authority in spiritual matters over the other Christian leaders in the same city
· They consider themselves divine, little gods and equal to Christ (although they loosely veil this)
· They believe they will attain perfection on earth
· They consider themselves the "Defenders of the Faith"
· Place a great deal of emphasis on mysticism and hidden knowledge (Gnosis)
· Do not believe in the rapture (or believe the wicked are the ones that will be raptured)
· Stress unity over doctrine and reject the literal/natural interpretation of the Bible"
(A Strong Delusion, McCumber)

The undisputed leader and "Chief Apostle" of this movement is Dr. C. Peter Wagner, a former Fuller Seminary professor, and associate of John Wimber, the founder of the Vineyard denomination. Dr. Wagner was an advisor to Rick Warren while he was working on his Doctoral Thesis.

The May Day 2010 rally at the Lincoln Memorial in Washington DC featured New Apostolic teachers Dutch Sheets, Cindy Jacobs and Stacy Campbell. The brochure for the event, on page seven, features an article about *"Prayers of Repentance for the Seven Mountains of Culture"*. These seven mountains include Family, Religion, Education, Arts & Entertainment, Business, Government, and Media. The stated goals of these people is to take over every area of these *"mountains"*. Jesus Christ stated, however, that *"My kingdom is not of this world"*. (John 18:36) His instructions to His disciples is to win the lost one soul at a time, using love and persuasion, by the preaching of the gospel, not through coercion!

I know thy works, and thy labour, and thy patience, and how thou canst not bear them which are evil: and __thou hast__ _tried them which say they are apostles, and are not, and hast found them liars_: (Revelation 2:2)

I cannot help but notice the similarity of the terminology between this group and the Harlot of chapters 17 and 18 of the book of Revelation. Given the "_Seven Mountain_" terminology and the doctrines of this group as stated above, I would not be surprised if this is indeed a significant part of the last-days movement of apostasy spoken of by Jesus, Peter and Paul, though it may not yet be in its final form.

In a video on YouTube, _"Apostle"_ Dr. Lance Wallnau states that a huge problem for the Church is _"The mischief of eschatology"_. He goes on to state that Christians are _"Afraid to take dominion"_ over the earth. He then goes on to take scripture out of context. According to Mr. Wallnau it is the job of the Church to take dominion for God, and to occupy until Jesus comes. Unfortunately they have redefined the word "occupy". It originally meant to keep busy, to get a job, and to be occupied with preaching the gospel to the lost. Now the _"New Apostles"_ use the word _"occupy"_ in the military sense: To take over a kingdom, or nation, and force your way on it! This is not God's way! Even when the lost are ultimately thrown into the Lake of Fire, they can be as evil as they want! (Lance Wallnau - Taking mountain (1))

Walnau quotes Psalms 110:1 "_The LORD said unto my Lord, Sit thou at my right hand, until I make thine enemies thy footstool._" Here is another example of taking one verse and pitting it against the rest of scripture. Walnau says that it is the job of the Church to take over the world, but every other End Times passage states that Jesus Christ Himself will defeat the Antichrist and his armies at His second coming. Don't forget that the "_I_" in this passage is God, not the Church.

I hope you have noticed the connections between all of these groups as we have gone through this list. The same names and doctrines keep on popping up over and over again. While they may seem to be disconnected they all have the same goals and are heading in the same direction... Apostasy.

I could go on, but this book was not written to be an expose of false teachers. We have only touched on a few notable ones, but there are more all the time. It is easy to find the truth. Just pick up a bible (King James or AV) and read it. Study it. Believe it. Pray to the God of that bible, the God of all creation. Ask His Son to save you and He will do it because He loves you and died for you. Cling to Him with all your strength, but know this; if you are truly His, He will never let go of you!

For whosoever shall call upon the name of the Lord shall be saved.

Romans 10:13

Resources:

"The Berean Beacon", The website of former Roman Catholic priest Richard Bennet, Accessed 10/02/2010, www.bereanbeacon.org

"Rick Warren Connections,especially to the ecumenical Third Wave New Apostolic Reformation (NAR) and "Positive Thinking" Movement" compiled by Sandy Simpson, 1/04 Appologetics Coordination Team, Accessed 07/08/2010, www.deceptioninthechurch.com/warrenquotes.html

"The Serious Problems with Rick Warren's Purpose Driven Movement", Lighthouse Trails Research Project, Accessed 07/08/2010, www.lighthousetrailsresearch.com/warren.htm,

"The Emerging Church, Revival Or Return To Darkness?" Commentary by Roger Oakland, Roger Oakland, Understand the Times International, Accessed 07/08/2010, from http://www.understandthetimes.org/commentary/c29.shtml

"Cross + Word", an archive of articles from Banner Ministries by Trish Tillin, Accessed 07/08/2010, www.intotruth.org/misc/alpha.html, Cross + Word, an archive of articles from Banner Ministries by Trish Tillin, Accessed 07/08/2010

"Index page of articles about the Alpha Course", Bible Theology Ministries, Accessed 07/08/2010, www.christiandoctrine.net/doctrine/topics/topic_1_web.htm#Alpha %20Course

Jan Markell's Olive Tree Ministries website, featuring articles and radio .mp3 downloads on prophecy related topics, Accessed 07/08/2010, www.olivetreeviews.org,

Eric Bargers "Take a Stand Ministries", a discernment ministry featuring articles exposing the New Age infiltration into the Christian Church, accessed 07/08/2010, www.ericbarger.com

"Concerned Nazarenes exposing the infiltration of the Emergent Church movement into the Nazarene denomination", accessed 07/08/2010, www.concernednazarenes.org

The website of Southwest Radio Church Ministries, a discernment resource since 1933, accessed 07/08/2010, http://www.swrc.com

"The "New Apostolic" Church Movement", Let Us Reason Ministries, 2009,   accessed   06/10/2010, http://www.letusreason.org/Latrain21.htm

"The Devil in the Shack", a resource page featuring several articles exposing the errors of "The Shack", accessed 07/08/2010, from http://www.infointersect.com/the_devil_in_the_shack.html,

"THE SHACK: Exposing The Deception", Spiritual Research Network, a discernment ministry, accessed 07/08/2010, http://www.spiritual-research-network.com/theshack.html

A Reader's Review of The Shack, Challies, Tim, Tue 20 May 2008, Accessed   07/10/2010,   from   http://www.challies.com/book-reviews/a-review-of-the-shack-download-it-here

Thirteen Heresies in The Shack", Youssef, Dr. Michael, Accessed 09/10/2010,   from http://www.leadingtheway.org/site/PageServer?pagename=sto_TheShack_13heresies

"Norm Geisler Takes "The Shack" to the Wood Shed", Geisler, Norman, Novermer 12, 2008, posted on Christian Wworldview Blog, Accessed   09/10/2010,   from http://thechristianworldview.com/tcwblog/archives/934

Online Book: "HIDDEN SECRETS OF THE ALPHA COURSE ~The dark agenda behind Alpha~" John D. Christian, Published by Underground Press, New Zealand, First published in New Zealand,

April 2005, http://www.scribd.com/doc/15118047/Hidden-Secrets-of-the-Alpha-Course

"A Tale Of Two Cities -TORONTO", Richardson, Neil, Christian Witness Ministries, Accessed 08/08/2010, http://www.christian-witness.org/archives/van1998/alpha2_98.html

"Alpha USA: What Church Leaders Say", Alpha North America website, accessed 08/08/2010, from http://www.alphana.org/Groups/1000047512/What_Church_Leaders.aspx

"A Wonderful Deception: The Further New Age Implications of the Emerging Purpose Driven Movement" by Warren Smith, Published by Lighthouse Trails Publishing, Silverton, Oregon (July 2009)

"A Time of Departing" by Ray Yungen, STL Distribution North America, 2 edition (April 15 2006)

"The New Age of Alpha", by Dusty Peterson, 2009, Accessed 18/03/2010, from http://www.users.globalnet.co.uk/~emcd/TheNewAgeOfAlpha.pdf

"Alpha: The Unofficial Guide – Overview", McDonald, Elizabeth and Peterson, Dusty, published by St. Matthew Publishing Ltd., Cambridge, UK (2004)

"In God's Name" by Yallop, David, Carroll and Graff Publishers 245 W 17th, St., 11th floor, New York, New York 10011-5300, Published in the UK by Jonathan Cape Ltd. (1984)

"The Purpose Driven Life", Warren, Rick, Copyright 2002 by Rick Warren, Zondervan Books, Grand Rapids, Michigan 49530

"Faith Undone: The Emerging Church: A New Reformation Or An End-Time Deception?" by Roger Oakland, Lighthouse Trails Publishing, Silverton, Oregon, (August 2007)

"Who's Driving the Purpose Driven Church?: A Documentary on the Teachings of Rick Warren" by James Sundquist, Bible Belt Publishing, (January 2004)

"Tithing: Low-Realm, Obsolete & Defunct"   by Matthew E.

Narramore, Tekoa Publishing (May 2004)

"In The Name of Purpose: Sacrificing Truth on the Altar of Unity", by Tamara Hartzell, 2006, Accessed 25/01/2010, from www.inthenameofpurpose.org/,

"The Toronto Blessing", by Needham, Dr Nick, Orthodox Christian Information Center, Accessed 14/09/2010, from http://www.orthodoxinfo.com/inquirers/toronto.aspx

"A STRONG DELUSION - The New Apostolic Reformation", by McCumber, Mishel, Deception Bytes, Accessed 29/09/2010, from http://www.deceptionbytes.com/content/strong-delusion-new-apostolic-reformation

Four

Wars and Rumours

And ye shall hear of wars and rumours of wars: see that ye be not troubled: for all these things must come to pass, but the end is not yet. For nation shall rise against nation, and kingdom against kingdom: and there shall be famines, and pestilences, and earthquakes, in divers places. All these are the beginning of sorrows. (Matthew 24:6-8)

There have been several significant wars in the Middle-East since the founding of Israel in 1948. To date, however, the only two that had obvious prophetic significance were the war of independence, and the 1967 war. Every conflict that Israel has been involved with has been important, and a result of the End Times *"Controversy of Zion"* (Isaiah 34:8) but the most significant wars have been prophesied in scripture.

For years I had puzzled over the fact that the references to the war of Gog and Magog in Ezekiel 38 and 39 listed a group of nations that do not share borders with Israel. Since Israel's founding in 1948 her greatest enemies have all shared borders with her. Sometime in 2008 I received an email update from Cutting Edge ministries, which had a description of a new book by Bill Salus called *"Israelestine: The Ancient Blueprints of the Future Middle East"*. As I read the blurb I became excited, immediately read Psalm 83, and ordered the book. Bill has discovered a previously overlooked passage, Psalm 83, is a prophecy of an End Times war.

I am convinced that this war answers the question as to why Israel's immediate neighbours are not involved in the Gog and Magog war. In the process of time I came to some slightly different conclusions about some minor details, but I still believe that Salus is essentially correct, and his book has made a great contribution to the study of eschatology.

137

In Jesus' statements about *"wars and rumours of wars"*, I believe He was referring to a series of wars that are actually prophesied in the Old Testament scriptures.   The bible doesn't specifically say precisely every detail, nor the exact sequence in which they occur, but it does give us clues.   Read Psalm 83, and compare it to a map of the Middle East, and you will notice that this Psalm lists a group of nations that will attack Israel.   These nations form a "ring" around the nation of Israel.

Asaph's War

1 Keep not thou silence, O God: hold not thy peace, and be not still, O God. 2 For, lo, thine enemies make a tumult: and they that hate thee have lifted up the head. 3 They have taken crafty counsel against thy people, and consulted against thy hidden ones. 4 They have said, Come, and let us cut them off from being a nation; that the name of Israel may be no more in remembrance. 5 For they have consulted together with one consent: they are confederate against thee: 6 The tabernacles of Edom, and the Ishmaelites; of Moab, and the Hagarenes (Hagarites); 7 Gebal, and Ammon, and Amalek; the Philistines with the inhabitants of Tyre; 8 Assur also is joined with them: they have holpen the children of Lot. Selah. 9 Do unto them as unto the Midianites; as to Sisera, as to Jabin, at the brook of Kison: 10 Which perished at Endor: they became as dung for the earth. 11 Make their nobles like Oreb, and like Zeeb: yea, all their princes as Zebah, and as Zalmunna: 12 Who said, Let us take to ourselves the houses of God in possession. 13 O my God, make them like a wheel; as the stubble before the wind. 14 As the fire burneth a wood, and as the flame setteth the mountains on fire; 15 So persecute them with thy tempest, and make them afraid with thy storm. 16 Fill their faces with shame; that they may seek thy name, O LORD. 17 Let them be confounded and troubled for ever; yea, let them be put to shame, and perish: 18 That men may know that thou, whose name alone is JEHOVAH, art the most high over all the earth. (Psalm 83:1-18)

Today the goal of the Arab nations is stated precisely in verse 4. They have openly stated that their goal is to push Israel into the sea. Any western leader who thinks he can broker a negotiated settlement between these two warring peoples is deluded. Any concession that Israel makes to the Arabs is seen as weakness and encourages their enemies to continue in their present course of action. (In each of these nations is a small minority who love the Lord, and who love Israel. I am not speaking of them, but of the official policy of these governments)

Verses six through eight list a group of nations and tribes. Most of the names refer to old tribal names, and have little relation to the modern nations that occupy the same land today. Several of the names represent small parts of the respective modern nation, but I believe that what is being said is that the descendants of the tribes in question will have enough influence in the modern governments, to drag the entire nation into this war.

Edom, Moab, and Ammon lived on the land included within the boundaries of the modern nation of Jordan. These tribes were scattered, like Israel, for a time, but have always had a presence on that land, and have returned, and still occupy the land of their ancestors. These tribes, especially Edom, have great significance during the times in which we live.

Some of the Palestinians are descendants of the ancient Philistines of Gaza, although some have intermarried with Edomites, who moved in after Israel was exiled by Rome in the early second century A.D. This intermarriage between the Philistines and Edomites is significant for the subject of the identification of the Antichrist, but has little significance to this section, simply because both of these peoples are a part of the confederacy that will attack Israel.

Assur was the patriarch of Assyria, which is in northern Iraq. While there are people of Assyrian background living in many areas of the world, including Syria, Europe and the USA, I do not believe any of these populations are large enough to be in view here. This reference is to the location where Assyria matured as a nation, and where a sizable population still exists: northern Iraq. Today, with the American occupation of Iraq, we have an impediment to their inclusion in this confederacy; but with President Obama's determination to pull out, it is becoming clear that this war is looming on the horizon.

The city of Tyre is a major city of Lebanon. According to the on-

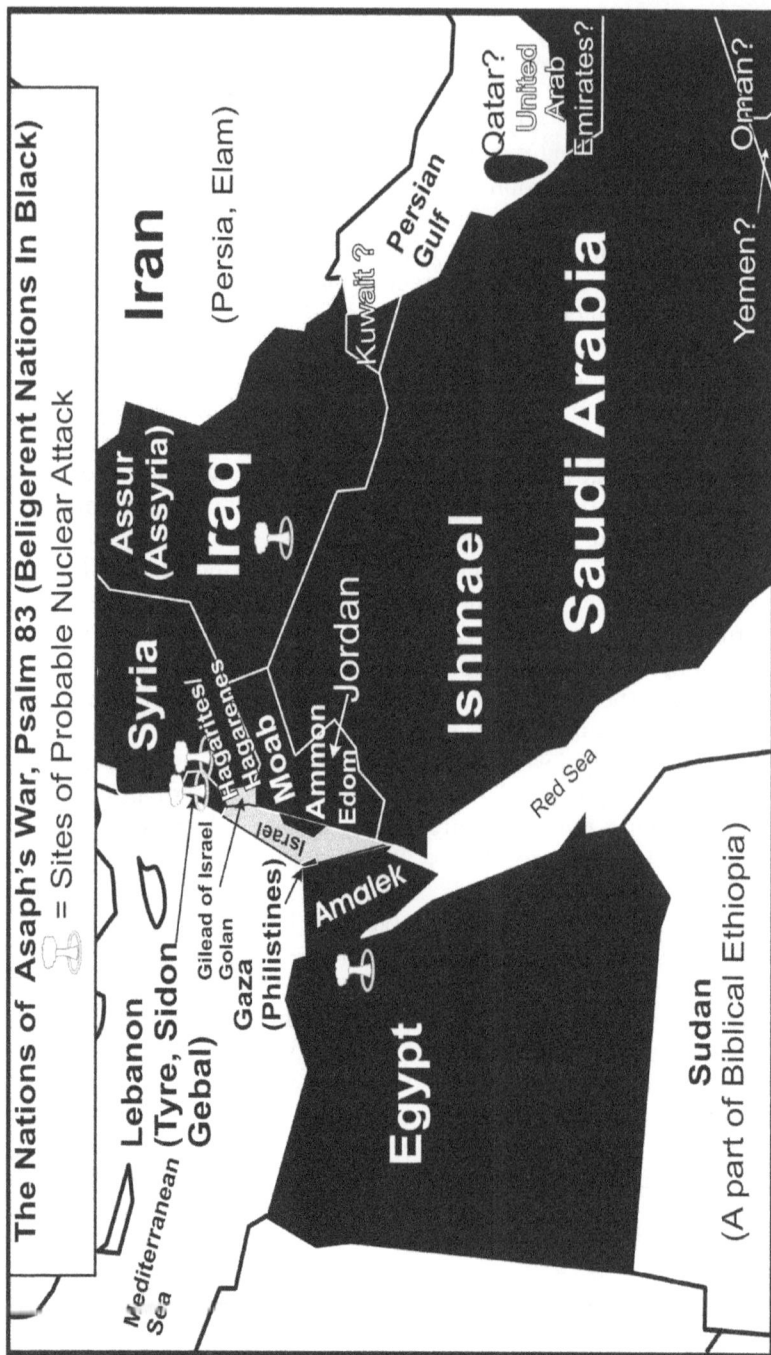

The Nations of **Asaph's War, Psalm 83** (Beligerent Nations In Black)
= Sites of Probable Nuclear Attack

Iran
(Persia, Elam)

Persian Gulf

Kuwait ?

Qatar?

United Arab Emirates?

Oman ?

Yemen?

Saudi Arabia

Assur (Assyria)

Iraq

Syria

Jordan

Hagarites/ Hagarenes

Moab

Ammon

Edom

Ishmael

Israel

Gilead of Israel
Golan
Gaza (Philistines)

Amalek

Lebanon (Tyre, Sidon Gebal)

Mediterranean Sea

Red Sea

Egypt

Sudan
(A part of Biblical Ethiopia)

line bible dictionary, Gebal is either another name for the port of Byblus in Phoenicia, or a mountainous region south of the dead sea in Edom (Net Bible Dictionary, *GEBAL*). In context it is most likely a reference to the Phoenician port which is today a part of Lebanon. The bible identifies Gebal as a group of people who worked in Tyre as either mariners or shipwrights (Ezekiel 27:9), thus giving evidence for the Lebanese town by implying that they had a marine heritage.

The Ishmaelites are a group of Arabs who descended from Abraham and Hagar's son, Ishmael, who today reside in Saudi Arabia. Considering that there is some mystery regarding the Hagarenes, who are sometimes referred to synonymously with Ishmaelites or with Egypt, this begs the question *"Who are the Hagarenes in this passage?"* Is Asaph's mention of the Hagarenes redundant? Is the prophet simply repeating himself? Salus believes that the term Hagarenes is a reference to Egypt, since Hagar came from Egypt, however, since Egypt had a sizeable population before Hagar was born, I find it unlikely that the term *"Hagarenes"* could be a reference to that nation. (p. 20, Isralestine)

Could it be that Ishmael's descendants split into two groups and went their separate ways? As I studied I found that the Bible actually gives us the location and identities of who the Hagarenes, or Hagarites, were.

> *And in the days of Saul they made war with the* **Hagarites,** *who fell by their hand: and they dwelt in their tents throughout all the* **east land of Gilead.** *And the* **children of God dwelt over against them, in the land of Bashan** *unto Salchah: Joel the chief, and Shapham the next, and Jaanai, and Shaphat in Bashan. (1 Chronicles 5:10-12)*

> *And they made war with the* **Hagarites, with Jetur, and Nephish,** *and Nodab. (1 Chronicles 5:19)*

We see then, that the Hagarites were located in the area of the east side of Gilead, and into Bashan. Asaph actually lists the Hagarites with the people who were their close geographical neighbours, Moab. They are likely still there, though they would call themselves Syrians today. This land is on the east side of the Jordan river and the sea of Galilee, known today as the Golan.

The Bible also tells us the origin of these tribes. They came from two of Ishmael's sons, Jetur and Nephish (Genesis 25:15). Since Ishmael had twelve sons it appears that there was a split, with two tribes calling themselves Hagarenes or Hagarites after Ishmael's mother, while the rest kept the association with Ishmael. I am not sure who Nodab was, but it is likely a reference to a sub-group of one of the other Ishmaelite tribes. It is unlikely then, that Hagarenes, or Hagarites, is a reference to Egypt.

The Hagarites are the people who will drag Damascus, and Syria, into the war with Israel. They are the people who live close to and even on the Israelite territory of Gilead and Bashan. They claim that this territory is a part of Syria known as the Golan, and it is this disagreement that will ultimately lead to their demise.

Zechariah 10:11 links the destruction of Lebanon, and Egypt with the destruction of *"the Pride of Assyria"*, which would seem to indicate that Egypt is somehow included in this Psalm 83 war. Damascus is not the pride of Assyria, it is not even in Assyria, though it is possible that Babylon, or perhaps Baghdad, might fit that description. I believe the *"Pride of Assyria"* is a reference to the pride of the people who live in the cradle of civilization.

> *And he shall pass through the sea with affliction, and shall smite the waves in the sea, and all the deeps of the river shall dry up: and the* **pride of Assyria shall be brought down,** *and the* **sceptre of Egypt** *shall depart away.* (Zechariah 10:11)

As I searched for a connection to Egypt in this passage I stumbled upon the answer. The Amalekites, mentioned in Psalm 83:7 are the connection. The Amalekites are descendants of Esau's son Amalek, who moved away from the other Edomites. In the flight from Egypt the Israelites were wandering in the wilderness of Sin, or Sinai, and were attacked there by the Amalekites. The account takes place in Exodus 17. The Israelites and Amalekites were still at war hundreds of years later when Saul was king. Notice also that this passage gives us the geographic location of these people:

> *And Saul smote the Amalekites from Havilah until thou comest to Shur,* **that is over against Egypt.** (1 Samuel 15:7)

The term *"Against Egypt"* means *"Opposite Egypt"*, as in *"The opposite side of the Red sea from Egypt".* The land described here is the Negev desert of the Sinai peninsula, and is today in Egyptian hands. Today these people are involved in building tunnels into Gaza, and smuggling weapons and contraband into the hands of the terrorist group, Hamas. This land is the same land spoken of in the Exodus 17, and 1 Samuel 15, and it is likely that the people are, at least in part, descendants of the same tribes who used to live there. We can conclude then, that the Amalekite citizens of Egypt will drag their nation into this war, and they will lose the Sinai permanently. The permanent loss of the Sinai peninsula will be compensation for their breaking the Anwar Sadat-brokered peace treaty.

Some have stated that the Psalm 83 war has already been fulfilled, but a careful study reveals that it has not. The war of 2 Chronicles 20 has been suggested as a fulfilment, but there are not enough nations mentioned. They were defeated by turning their swords against each other rather than being destroyed by fire. Remember that in order for prophecy to be fulfilled it must be 100%, not just a portion. The war of independence in 1948 and also the 1967 wars have also been suggested as fulfilment, but again, there were more nations involved in the 1948 war and less in the 1967 war. So, no, the Psalm 83 war is a yet future prophecy. Even if there were historically a war with the same combatants, it cannot be the same war if the result is not that which the Bible prophesies.

In verses nine through eighteen we see the prophet (inspired by God) praying for divine retribution against these enemies of God. In verse thirteen we see the enemies likened to stubble, the residue left after the harvest which is of no value, and is burned or blown away by the wind. The next verse calls for fire to devour them and their mountains. This is very similar language to some other passages regarding the same nations.

> *Open thy doors, O Lebanon, **that the fire may devour thy cedars.** Howl, fir tree; for the cedar is fallen; because the mighty are spoiled: howl, O ye oaks of Bashan; for the forest of the vintage is come down. (Zechariah 11: 1-2)*

No doubt the cedars mentioned are a euphemism which includes not only the trees of Lebanon, but the enemies of God themselves. Bashan was a part of Gilead, known as the Golan today. This passage appears to be a reference to the same event as Psalm 83. It is likely that the fire spoken of is a reference to some sort of nuclear attack.

Another fact that is terribly relevant is that there is no huge clamour of the Lost Tribes of Israel to settle back in the land. The majority of these people are happy worshipping their pagan gods in the land they have settled, the largest group being the Pathan tribes of Afghanistan and Pakistan. A major defeat of Islam by the tiny nation of Israel is needed for them to come back to the land, and God, of their fathers. Just such a defeat as described in Psalm 83, Zechariah chapters 10 & 11, and Isaiah 17.

Isaiah 49 also echoes the fact that the land of Israel is too small for all the returning exiles to inhabit. They will need all of the land God has promised them:

> For thy waste and thy desolate places, and the land of thy destruction, shall even now be too narrow by reason of the inhabitants, and they that swallowed thee up shall be far away. The children which thou shalt have, after thou hast lost the other, shall say again in thine ears, **The place is too strait for me: give place to me that I may dwell.** (Isaiah 49:19-20)

Another implication of this passage, and Zechariah 10:10, is that while Israel may inherit the land from the Nile to the Euphrates during Asaph's war, it appears that they may not get the land all the way to the Persian Gulf at that time. These passages are saying that when all of Israel returns they will be crowded in their land, but I can't see that being the case if they have all of their promised land, all the way to the Persian Gulf. It may be however, that the area around Damascus will be contaminated with nuclear debris and since the area east of there is largely desert, the inhabitable land area will be much smaller than their total land possessions. The timing is the question, not the fact that Israel's influence will grow immensely.

> But I will send a fire on the wall of Gaza, which shall devour the palaces thereof: And I will cut off the inhabitant from Ashdod, and him that holdeth the sceptre from Ashkelon, and I will turn mine hand against Ekron: and the remnant of the Philistines shall perish, saith the Lord GOD. (Amos 1:7-8)

Today Ashdod, Ashkelon and Ekron are in Israeli hands, but Gaza is still a thorn in their side. The Philistines are still there sending suicide bombers, and rockets, into Israel on a regular basis. Again we see that this prophecy is intended for a yet future fulfilment, and the judgment against Gaza shall coincide with that of Lebanon and Damascus, and shall be a fulfillment of the prayer of the prophet in Psalm 83:14.

Ezekiel 30:1-19 is another prophecy that appears to have a split fulfilment. *"And they shall know that I am the LORD, when I have set a fire in Egypt, and when all her helpers shall be destroyed."* (Ezekiel 30:8) Verse 3 speaks of the *"Day of the Lord"* being near. Verse 5 speaks of Ethiopia, Libya and Lydia, which are nations that attack during the war of Gog and Magog. Verse 9 separates the destruction of Egypt, and Ethiopia by saying *"as in the day of Egypt"* indicating that Egypt's destruction has been completed some time prior to this event. It is likely, therefore, that the destruction of Egypt and Ethiopia could be separated by a few years. The passage implies that fear comes upon them because they have witnessed the destruction of Egypt themselves. In other words these events are separated by less than a life time.

Verse 10 mentions Nebuchadnezzar, which would seem to indicate an ancient fulfilment, however, since verse 3 also points out *"the day of the Lord is near"*, this in itself would indicate a split time frame. We would expect that the final fulfilment of this prophecy will occur shortly before the Great Tribulation begins. In other words the fulfillment may actually occur before the Rapture of the Church, not only the fulfillment of the first part, the destruction of Egypt, but also the destruction of Ethiopia.

Egypt will lose some territory to Israel during the Psalm 83 war, and will make peace with her at that time.

*17 And **the land of Judah shall be a terror unto Egypt,** every one that maketh mention thereof shall be afraid in himself, because of the counsel of the LORD of hosts, which he hath determined against it. 18 **In that day shall five cities in the land of Egypt speak the language of Canaan, and swear to the LORD of hosts; one shall be called, The city of destruction.** 19 In that day shall there be an altar to the LORD in the midst of the land of Egypt, and a pillar at the border thereof to the LORD. 20 And it shall be for a sign and for a witness unto the LORD of hosts in the land of Egypt: **for they shall cry unto the LORD because of the oppressors, and he shall send them a saviour, and a great one, and he*** *shall deliver them. 21 And the LORD shall be known to Egypt, and the Egyptians shall know the LORD in that day, and shall do sacrifice and oblation; yea, they shall vow a vow unto the LORD, and perform it. 22 And the LORD shall smite Egypt: he shall smite and heal it: and they shall return even to the LORD, and he shall be intreated of them, and shall heal them. (Isaiah 19:17-22)*

This passage is a description of Israel possessing a part of Egypt, and the Millennial reign of Christ, but because they do not accept the New Testament, Israel will think this passage has been fulfilled after the war of Psalm 83, or more likely, later after the war of Gog and Magog. This will leave them vulnerable to deception by the Antichrist. His conquering of Egypt will be a sign to them that he is the messiah. It will be another example of partial or incomplete fulfilment.

I am not exactly sure how it fits in, but verse 20 appears to be ripe for a misapplication by the Antichrist and the false prophet. It very well may be that the Antichrist will initially appear as a saviour to Egypt, though the verse is really referring to the Lord Jesus Christ returning and saving the remnant of Egypt from the Antichrist.

What about Edom? Is the same language used regarding the Judgment of Edom, Esau's descendants? How about Obadiah 1:15?

*For the **day of the LORD is near** upon all the heathen: as thou hast done, it shall be done unto thee: thy reward shall return upon thine own head. For as ye have drunk upon my holy mountain, so shall all the heathen drink continually, yea, they shall drink, and they shall swallow down, and they shall be as though they had not been. But upon mount Zion shall be deliverance, and **there shall be holiness;** and the house of Jacob shall possess their possessions. And **the house of Jacob shall be a fire, and the house of Joseph a flame, and the house of Esau for stubble,** and they shall kindle in them, and devour them; and **there shall not be any remaining of the house of Esau;** for the LORD hath spoken it. (Obadiah 1:15-18)*

The same phrase is used here: *"the day of the Lord is near"*, so we see that it is in the same general time frame as Ezekiel 30, though it still could precede the tribulation by a few years. In verse 17, however, we are given a clue when we are told *"there shall be deliverance and there shall be* **holiness**". This event shall not happen until the return of the Lord. In verse 18 we are given another clue when it says *"and there shall not be any remaining of the house of Esau"*. Edom still exists today. They are one of the tribes that make up the nation of Jordan. Edom's Judgment is reserved for the time when Israel's iniquities come to an end, during the latter half of the Great Tribulation. Note that *"Mount Seir"* is a euphemism for the people of Edom.

> *Son of man, set thy face against* **mount Seir**, *and prophesy against it, And say unto it, Thus saith the Lord GOD; Behold, O mount Seir, I am against thee, and I will stretch out mine hand against thee, and I will make thee most desolate. I will lay thy cities waste, and thou shalt be desolate, and thou shalt know that I am the LORD.* **Because thou hast had a perpetual hatred, and hast shed the blood of the children of Israel by the force of the sword in the time of their calamity, in the time that their iniquity had an end:** *Therefore, as I live, saith the Lord GOD, I will prepare thee unto blood, and blood shall pursue thee: sith (since) thou hast not hated blood, even blood shall pursue thee. Thus will I make mount Seir most desolate, and cut off from it him that passeth out and him that returneth. (Ezekiel 35:2-7)*

Again the bible repeats that Edom's judgment will begin at the time when Israel's judgment ends, at the end of the Great Tribulation period. Therefore, the fire spoken of in relation to this nation is a reference to a later time and not to the battle of Psalm 83. It appears that the judgment by fire during Asaph's war is reserved for Lebanon, Iraq, Syria, and Egypt, though the other combatants will also lose the battle to Israel. Jordan may sue for peace, and since Israel is the brother to Esau, Israel will be predisposed to kindness. I suspect that Edom will get off lightly after this war, and its judgment will not really occur until the Lord brings it Himself, at His second coming.

Is the stage set for Asaph's war? All the nations mentioned are enemies of Israel and are talking of war, but today if they were to attack they would be joined by Iran. This nation can't be in the group that attacks Israel, or it would not be the same war. Something will happen to stop them from attacking at this time. In the next war we see that Iran will be involved, but their plans to

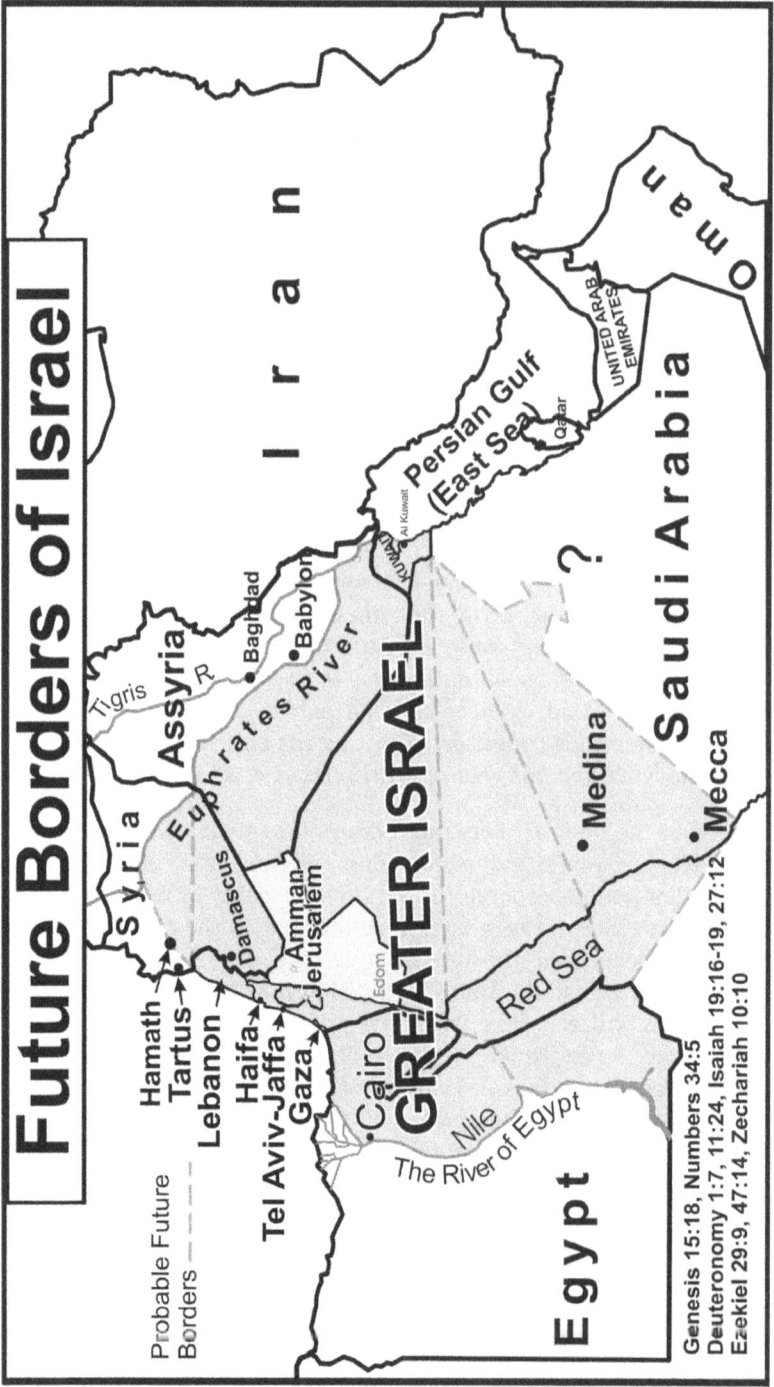

Future Borders of Israel

GREATER ISRAEL

Iran

Syria

Assyria

Saudi Arabia

Oman

UNITED ARAB EMIRATES

Qatar

Persian Gulf (East Sea)

Al Kuwait

Kuwait

?

Tigris R.

Baghdad

Babylon

Euphrates River

Medina

Mecca

Damascus

Amman

Jerusalem

Edom

Red Sea

Hamath

Tartus

Lebanon

Haifa

Tel Aviv-Jaffa

Gaza

Cairo

Nile

The River of Egypt

Egypt

Probable Future
Borders — — — —

Genesis 15:18, Numbers 34:5
Deuteronomy 1:7, 11:24, Isaiah 19:16-19, 27:12
Ezekiel 29:9, 47:14, Zechariah 10:10

attack must be set back, so that they sit it out when the Arabs go after Israel.

It is interesting to note that today Iran is busy in the process of enriching uranium, a part of the process of producing nuclear bombs. The Iranian administration has been very clever in their placement of nuclear facilities. While Iraq's Osirak reactor was out in the open and far from any population centre, the Iranians have placed most of their nuclear facilities deep underground below residential areas, thus ensuring many civilian casualties and world-wide condemnation of any Israeli strike.

The current American administration is committed to negotiations as a solution to the Middle-East crisis. As long as the USA is governed by the Obama administration it is not likely that they will attack Iran's nuclear facilities. They do not appear to appreciate the danger these facilities pose to the peaceful existence of the tiny nation of Israel and to the entire region. It thus appears that Israel will be forced to go alone against Iran, or wait for Iran to strike first.

An Israeli attack against Iran's Nuclear facilities poses serious implications for Israel. Will the USA back-off in their support of Israel, if they go ahead with this strike? If they do then we have the Psalm 83 scenario being built before our eyes. It is the perceived American support for Israel that has intimidated the Arab nations from attacking. Should this support disappear they will see the green light to proceed. Iran, recovering from some sort of Israeli strike, will not be in a position to join them at that time. It appears that, in the fall of 2010 we are within one to two years of Asaph's war from becoming reality.

It is also possible that the USA could be involved in a strike on Iran, and then use this fact to blackmail Israel into giving up *"land for peace"*. Should Israel balk at this suggestion, we could still see the USA stop supporting Israel. Should this occur, I would expect the Lord will allow some terrorist group to succeed in an attack against a major American target. The USA would then be so involved in their own disaster clean-up that they would be too preoccupied to come to Israel's aid.

The USA has already begun backing away from Israel, perhaps thinking that this will appease the Islamic terrorists. The truth is that such a move is seen as weakness and will be exploited by the Islamists. Don't discount the fact that there is a God in Heaven who has made unconditional promises to Israel. He is quite able to judge the USA for her unfaithfulness!

> (God's promise to Abraham) *And I will bless them that bless thee, and curse him that curseth thee: and in thee shall all families of the earth be blessed. (Genesis 12:3)*

> *For thus saith the LORD of hosts; After the glory hath he sent me unto the nations which spoiled you [Israel]: for he that toucheth you toucheth the apple of his eye. (Zechariah 2:8)*

I do not get any sort of pleasure in predicting the destruction of Damascus, or any other city. I am stating these things because they are a part of the End Times prophecies of the Word of God. In the mean time the Christians of Damascus should go about their business and preach the gospel to their neighbours. When the time comes that you see an army made up of Israel's neighbours, massing on the border of Israel, that would be the time to leave your city. This goes for the inhabitants of all these nations. When you see your army heading for Israel, you head for the hills!

The Name of the Son of God

The Hebrew name of the Messiah may seem irrelevant to the study of eschatology, but it is actually most important. Zechariah actually prophesied the human name of the Messiah in chapter 6 of his book. The amazing thing is that it was done in such a way that the meaning did not become clear for hundreds of years.

> *Then take silver and gold, and make crowns, and set them upon the head of Joshua the son of Josedech, the high priest; And speak unto him, saying, Thus speaketh the LORD of hosts, saying, Behold the man whose name is The BRANCH; and he shall grow up out of his place, and he shall build the temple of the LORD: (Zechariah 6:11-12)*

Joshua the high priest was not the BRANCH. He did not do the things that the BRANCH was prophesied to do. The BRANCH was an Old Testament name of the Messiah. What the Lord is actually saying in this passage is *"Behold, the man who has a name which is the same as the name of the Messiah"*. In the intervening years Israel adopted Greek as their main language. When Mary was pregnant by the Holy Spirit she was told to name her son Jesus. Jesus, or Iasous, is the Greek form of the Hebrew Joshua, or Yehoshua. Many commentaries note that verses 12 and 13 refer to the Messiah, but few note that His human name was predicted in these pages.

In the future when the Antichrist arises, he will be involved with the rebuilding of the temple in Jerusalem, and this prophecy will be important proof that he is NOT the Messiah of Israel, for the Messiah's name is Joshua, or Jesus, and none other!

And he came and dwelt in a city called Nazareth: that it might be fulfilled which was spoken by the prophets, He shall be called a Nazarene. (Matthew 2:23)

I have heard pastors refer to this passage, implying that Jesus of Nazareth must be a Nazirite. They are referring to Manoah's promise in Judges 13, that Samson would be a Nazirite from his mother's womb, thinking that this is a prophecy of the Messiah. They may also be referring to Hannah's promise that Samuel would also be a Nazirite from the womb. If these passages are prophetic at all they must refer to John the Baptizer and not to Jesus Christ. John was a Nazirite from birth. This cannot be a reference to the Messiah, for it is a sin for a Nazirite to drink wine, or grape juice. Regardless of whether the beverage served at the Last Supper was either, it would have been a sin for Jesus to consume it if he was a Nazirite. Had he been a sinner he could not be our Saviour.

The root of the name Nazareth is Netzer which means *"branch"* in Hebrew. In Hebrew both words use the equivalent of NZR as their main letters. Thus it appears that Matthew was identifying Jesus as *"the Branch"* because of his living in Nazareth. (Bratcher, the Branch)

A Covenant

Covenant: [kuv'enant] *n.* A mutual agreement, esp. for the performance of some action; the writing containing the agreement; the common-law action to recover damages for breach of a covenant.-*vt* to promise by a covenant. -*vi* to enter into an agreement. (Websters Integrated Dictionary)

Every war ends with some sort of *"covenant"*: a peace treaty, surrender, or armistice. If the losing nation does not agree to a formal surrender, a state of war continues to exist, and they could end up being completely annihilated! The nations of World Wars I and II signed agreements at the end of each war. If the Germans had not signed a surrender the state of war would have continued until every German soldier was killed or captured, and their soldiers could have been shot on sight. The same was true for the other combatants. In 70AD Jerusalem refused to surrender, and when the Roman armies entered the city, over one million persons were killed, and the survivors sent into exile and slavery.

A covenant can be one sided, which depends on only one individual. We see one of these in Genesis 15 where God made a covenant with Abraham, by Himself. It does not matter what the behaviour of Abraham's descendants is, God will keep that covenant because He made it by Himself, and His name is at stake. Other covenants may be two sided, which involve two equal sides, or they may involve unequal sides. A covenant is simply an agreement.

As we look throughout Scripture we see that most of the nations involved in the Psalm 83 war, with the exception of Edom, will actually continue on throughout the millennial reign of Jesus Christ (Isaiah 19:23). This shows us that this war will end in some sort of formal surrender, peace treaty, or covenant. This agreement will also likely be the one that allows Israel to rebuild its Temple. I do not have a direct revelation from God on this, it is only a logical deduction. With Israel's major enemies subdued there will be nothing to stop the reconstruction of the Temple. The surrender, or armistice agreement, will specifically allow Israel to rebuild the Temple without fear of reprisal from the Arab Muslims.

I would expect that a third party may be involved in the negotiations with regard to the end of this war. I do not believe that this third party will actually be the man ultimately known as the Antichrist, but more likely one of the ten "kings" who put the Antichrist on the throne. He may actually become a decoy, or surrogate Antichrist, and a patsy the Antichrist destroys as "*the Antichrist*".

Israel is looking for a Messiah who will build a new Temple in Jerusalem. I believe the covenant that the Antichrist "confirms" (Daniel 9:27) will allow Israel to finish the rebuilding of the Temple, which they will have already begun under that same agreement The language is rather interesting in this regard. The word *"confirm"* indicates that the Little Horn will not actually originate this agreement, but he will merely confirm, or acknowledge, an agreement that is already in existence.

> *And Jesus went out, and departed from the temple: and his disciples came to him for to shew him the **buildings of the temple**. And Jesus said unto them, **See ye not all these things?** verily I say unto you, There shall not be left here **one** stone upon another, that shall not be thrown down. (Matthew 24:1 & 2)*

Most scholars believe that Jesus' words in Matthew 24, Mark 13:2 and Luke 21:6 were fulfilled in the Roman destruction of Jerusalem in or around 70 AD. Indeed the city was in ruins, the Temple was destroyed, and over a million Jews had been killed. If Jesus was speaking in generalities then what He said did indeed come true.

There are a couple of small problems with this interpretation, however, for one wall of the old Temple complext still stands. Jesus was referring to the entire Temple complex, when He said that there would not be one stone upon another. Jesus was not given to speaking in generalities. He could simply have said *"the Temple will be destroyed"* and leave it at that, but God always has a reason for the specific wording of the Bible. Today there are many stones still standing upon each other, as there have been from that day until now. This is a detail that God has not overlooked. He will not give Satan the oportunity to say *"Lord, you lied! You said that there would not be one stone upon another, of the Temple complex, and here that wall stands, since that day, proving you a liar!"*

Sometimes Jesus did speak in the idioms of his age, but I do not believe He was doing so here. God's own standard is 100% fulfilment of prophecy. He Himself insists that if a prophet is not completely accurate he is not a prophet of God (Deut. 18:22). God is capable of bringing every prophecy to complete fulfilment. It ultimately, comes down to our view of God, His character, and His power. If you read carefully the passages in Matthew, Mark and Luke you will find that the context of each passage is the End Times. Immediately after making this statement Jesus began to give His disciples signs of the End Times. He was already giving them these signs, even before they asked. When He said *"There shall not be left here one stone upon another"* He was actually speaking of our day,

NOT OF 70 AD!

When Jesus said that the Temple complex would not have one stone upon another, the disciples question was *"When?"*(Matt. 24:3). His answer was to give them signs of the End Times. In other words there shall not be one stone upon another, of the complete Temple complex, shortly before the fulfilment of all the End Times prophecies. At the time of Titus' destruction of Jerusalem, many interpreted the prophecies of the destruction of the Temple to be fulfilled, but that one wall is still standing in defiance of the prophecies of Christ.

Jesus' statement that "Heaven and earth shall pass away, but my words shall not pass away", (Matthew 24:35) was directly related to the destruction of the Temple. When Jesus spoke of this event as being a sign of the end of the age, was He confused because it actually occurred at the beginning of the age?

The Wailing Wall has been standing for two thousand years waiting for Jesus' words to be finally fulfilled.

The Dome of the Rock sits atop the Holy of Holies on the Temple mount in Jerusalem, and any attempt on the part of Israel to destroy that shrine will result in a major war with the Muslim nations. Israel itself is fiercely protective of the Wailing Wall (ha Kotel) since it is the last remaining link they have to Solomon's Temple. Sometime in the near future Jesus' words will come true, and at the same time the Dome of the Rock will come down.

A stray SCUD missile is likely to begin the destruction, but is not likely to bring down the entire Western wall, as I first thought. I doubt that even a direct hit by a nuclear device would take down every stone, and I don't think God would allow that possibility anyway. What is most likely to happen is that a missile or bomb from one of the Arab nations will hit the wall and knock out a few stones. When the dust clears the world will see an amazing treasure exposed from behind the missing blocks. I am not sure if the exposed treasure will be the Ark of the Covenant, or some of the ancient Temple implements, but that exposure will give Israel the incentive they need to remove the rest of the blocks, to see what is behind that wall. In the process, and in the sight of the world's televison cameras, I believe Israel will find the Ark of the Covenant. Having such a great witness, the Arabs will have no grounds to say that the Ark is of recent manufacture, and thus a fake! This find will be the spark that ignites the rebuilding of the Temple.

I expect this event to occur around the time of the Psalm 83 war, and the right of Israel to rebuild the Temple will be written into the resulting peace treaty with the Arabs. The deal may actually allow the Arabs to keep the Al Aqsa mosque on the sight, this may be why the angel told John not to measure the outer court, in Rev. 11:2, but the Dome of the Rock will have to be torn down or moved because it is situated on the Holy of Holies, and this is not subject to negotiation.

I expect that this peace deal will be brokered by the leader of the European Union. It will look to many to be the agreement Daniel spoke of regarding the Antichrist in Daniel 9:27, and indeed it will likely be the very same covenant that he will ultimately confirm, though at some time later. This European leader will appear to be the Antichrist, and will ultimately be destroyed as "the Antichrist". He will be one of the three world leaders destroyed as being pretenders to the throne of Antichrist. As a result of his demise the world will say *"at last, peace and safety, we've gotten rid of the Antichrist"*, and sudden destruction shall come upon them and they shall not escape (1 Thes. 5:3).

Asaph's war will set the stage for the next war, but in between these conflicts there will be a time of peace. I am not sure how long it will be, but it will be long enough to be called a *"peace"*, and for the construction of the Temple to begin.

A Pseudo-Armageddon

At a prophecy conference I attended in the mid-1990s, with both Grant Jeffrey and Hal Lindsay speaking, one of them stated *"the Devil always has his counterfeits"* in context of the war of Gog and Magog. Whatever disagreements I may have with these gentlemen, this statement is absolutely true, and has been one of the foundations of this book.

In whatever is true or good, you can be sure that the devil will have a counterfeit, and likely more than one. This statement is also true in whatever is evil. We have seen a number of counterfeit Antichrists over the last two thousand years or so, including Antiochus Epiphanes IV, Nero, the popes, Stalin, and Hitler. The truth is that they were real antichrists, but they were not the one final Antichrist. At the time some even thought that World War Two was Armageddon. Pilots flying over Europe could see pillars of smoke rising from the burning cities, and later the same thing happened in Japan, culminating with the two nuclear bombs. That war was actually a prototype for wars to come.

What of the war described in Ezekiel 38 and 39? Is it possible that this war is the same war as that described in Psalm 83? Given the fact that verses 6 and 9 of chapter 38 say *"and many people with thee"*, is it not possible that the nations listed in Psalm 83 could be included?

Since not one of the nations of Psalm 83 is mentioned as an antagonist in the Ezekiel passage it would seem unlikely that it is the same conflict. The nations of Egypt, Lebanon, Syria, Edom, Moab and Ammon, feature frequently in the accounts of the Old Testament. It is unlikely that prophecies of a major conflict that included them would not name them. There is internal evidence, however, that Asaph's war will take place at an earlier time. If you study the defeat of the invading armies you will see some conditions that indicate a chronological order. Actually it does appear that they are named in the Ezekiel passage, but not as antagonists.

Ezekiel Chapter 38

> *1 And the word of the LORD came unto me, saying, 2 Son of man, set thy face against Gog, the land of Magog, the chief prince of Meshech and Tubal, and prophesy against him, 3 And say, Thus saith the Lord GOD; Behold, I am against thee, O Gog, the chief prince of Meshech and Tubal: 4 And I will turn thee back, and put hooks into thy jaws, and I will bring thee forth, and all thine army, horses and horsemen, all of them clothed with all sorts of armour, even a great company with bucklers and shields, all of them handling swords: 5 Persia, Ethiopia, and Libya with them; all of them with shield and helmet: 6 Gomer, and all his bands; the house of Togarmah of the north quarters, and all his bands: and many people with thee. 7 Be thou prepared, and prepare for thyself, thou, and all thy company that are assembled unto thee, and be thou a guard unto them. 8 After many days thou shalt be visited: in the latter years thou shalt come into the land that is brought back from the sword, and is gathered out of many people, against the mountains of Israel, which have been always waste: but it is brought forth out of the nations, and they shall dwell safely all of them. 9 Thou shalt ascend and come like a storm, thou shalt be like a cloud to cover the land, thou, and all thy bands, and many people with thee. 10 Thus*

*saith the Lord GOD; It shall also come to pass, that at the same time shall things come into thy mind, and thou shalt think an evil thought: 11 And thou shalt say, I will go up to the land of unwalled villages; I will go to them that are at rest, that dwell safely, all of them dwelling without walls, and having neither bars nor gates, 12 To take a spoil, and to take a prey; to turn thine hand upon the desolate places that are now inhabited, and upon the people that are gathered out of the nations, which have gotten cattle and goods, that dwell in the midst of the land. 13 **Sheba, and Dedan, and the merchants of Tarshish**, with all the young lions thereof, shall say unto thee, Art thou come to take a spoil? hast thou gathered thy company to take a prey? to carry away silver and gold, to take away cattle and goods, to take a great spoil? 14 Therefore, son of man, prophesy and say unto Gog, Thus saith the Lord GOD; In that day when my people of Israel dwelleth safely, shalt thou not know it? 15 And thou shalt come from thy place out of the north parts, thou, and many people with thee, all of them riding upon horses, a great company, and a mighty army: 16 And thou shalt come up against my people of Israel, as a cloud to cover the land; it shall be in the latter days, and I will bring thee against my land, that the heathen may know me, when I shall be sanctified in thee, O Gog, before their eyes. 17 Thus saith the Lord GOD; Art thou he of whom I have spoken in old time by my servants the prophets of Israel, which prophesied in those days many years that I would bring thee against them? 18 And it shall come to pass at the same time when Gog shall come against the land of Israel, saith the Lord GOD, that my fury shall come up in my face. 19 For in my jealousy and in the fire of my wrath have I spoken, Surely in that day there shall be a great shaking in the land of Israel; 20 So that the fishes of the sea, and the fowls of the heaven, and the beasts of the field, and all creeping things that creep upon the earth, and all the men that are upon the face of the earth, shall shake at my presence, and the mountains shall be thrown down, and the steep places shall fall, and every wall shall fall to the ground. 21 And I will call for a sword against him throughout all my mountains, saith the Lord GOD: every man's sword shall be against his brother. 22 And I will plead against him with pestilence and with blood; and I will rain upon him, and upon* *his bands, and upon the many people that are with him, an overflowing rain, and great hailstones, fire, and brimstone. 23 Thus will I magnify myself, and sanctify myself; and I will be known in the eyes of many nations, and they shall know that I am the LORD.*

This war comprises an *"outer ring"* of nations which excludes the nations of the Psalm 83 conflict. Asaph's war will have occurred some time before this, and those nations will have been defeated, and made their peace with Israel. Israel will have expanded to a size much closer to the borders God gave them in the Old Testament.

> *In the same day the LORD made a covenant with Abram, saying, Unto thy seed have I given this land, from the river of Egypt unto the great river, the river* **Euphrates:** *(Genesis 15:18)*

There is still a lot of debate over the boundaries specified here. I am not certain as to exactly where the borders will actually go, but I am certain they will be much larger than they are today, or ever were. We do know for a fact where the Euphrates river is situated, and have a definite northern boundary. If Israel gets control of Middle Eastern oil they will become a world power-broker, as the Arabs are today.

> *In that day shall five cities in the land of Egypt speak the language of Canaan, and swear to the LORD of hosts; one shall be called, The city of destruction. (Isaiah 19:18)*

This passage is indeed a reference to the millennial reign of Christ, but the time that Israel first receives this land could still be pre-millennial. I think they will receive it during Asaph's war. These cities are on the eastern side of the Nile, and quite possibly Cairo may be the city of destruction. It may be the victim of a nuclear attack when Egypt joins the Arabs in an all-out attack on Israel.

Ancient Jewish scholars believed that the river of Egypt was the Nile, or at least the eastern branch of the Nile, known as the Pelusian. When the Pelusian branch dried up the scholars began to think that Israel's borders would only go as far as the Wadi-el-Arish, only some fifty miles from the current southern border of Israel. I think God dried up the Pelusian branch of the Nile because He wanted the border to go further west, to the next branch, the Tanitic.

According to Wikepedia; *"Genesis gives the border with Egypt as Nahar Miztrayim -- nahar denotes a large river in Hebrew never a wadi."* (Wikipedia, Land of Israel)

> *Every place whereon the soles of your feet shall tread shall be yours: from the wilderness and Lebanon, from the river, **the river Euphrates, even unto the uttermost sea** shall your coast be. (Deuteronomy 11:24)*

Think about what God is saying here. I know that he said this after they were almost done their wandering, yet it appears from the descriptions of the land they will inherit, that He ultimately is applying this retroactively to every place they went after leaving Egypt. Where did the journey of the Israelites begin? Did it not begin in Goshen in Egypt? The area of Goshen is near the eastern branch of the Nile. I think that the implications of this verse are that Israel will get back the land they lived on when they were slaves building the cities of Egypt, and I think they will get some of those cities. What does God say to Egypt about their river?

> *And the land of Egypt shall be desolate and waste; and they shall know that I am the LORD: because he hath said, **The river is mine, and I have made it.** (Ezekiel 29:9)*

Egypt does not care much about the Wadi-el-Arish, but they do care a whole lot about the Nile. Isn't God saying that He is the Sovereign Creator and can give the Nile to whom He will? It appears that Israel will inherit one bank of the Nile, perhaps all the way to the Sudanese border, which was known as Ethiopia at the time. They took the entire Sinai peninsula in 1956 and again in 1973. They gave it back, but some day soon Egypt will provoke them, and this time they will go all the way to the Nile!

Where else did Israel travel in their journey from Egypt? Did they not cover a large part of the Arabian peninsula? How will Islam react if Israel takes control of Mecca and Medina? Keep an open mind, and watch the news.

Some prophecy scholars have stated that Israel will only get all of their promised land during the Millennial reign of Christ. I doubt it. You see, God is powerful enough to give Israel their land even when the world is controlled by His enemies! When the UN, or a

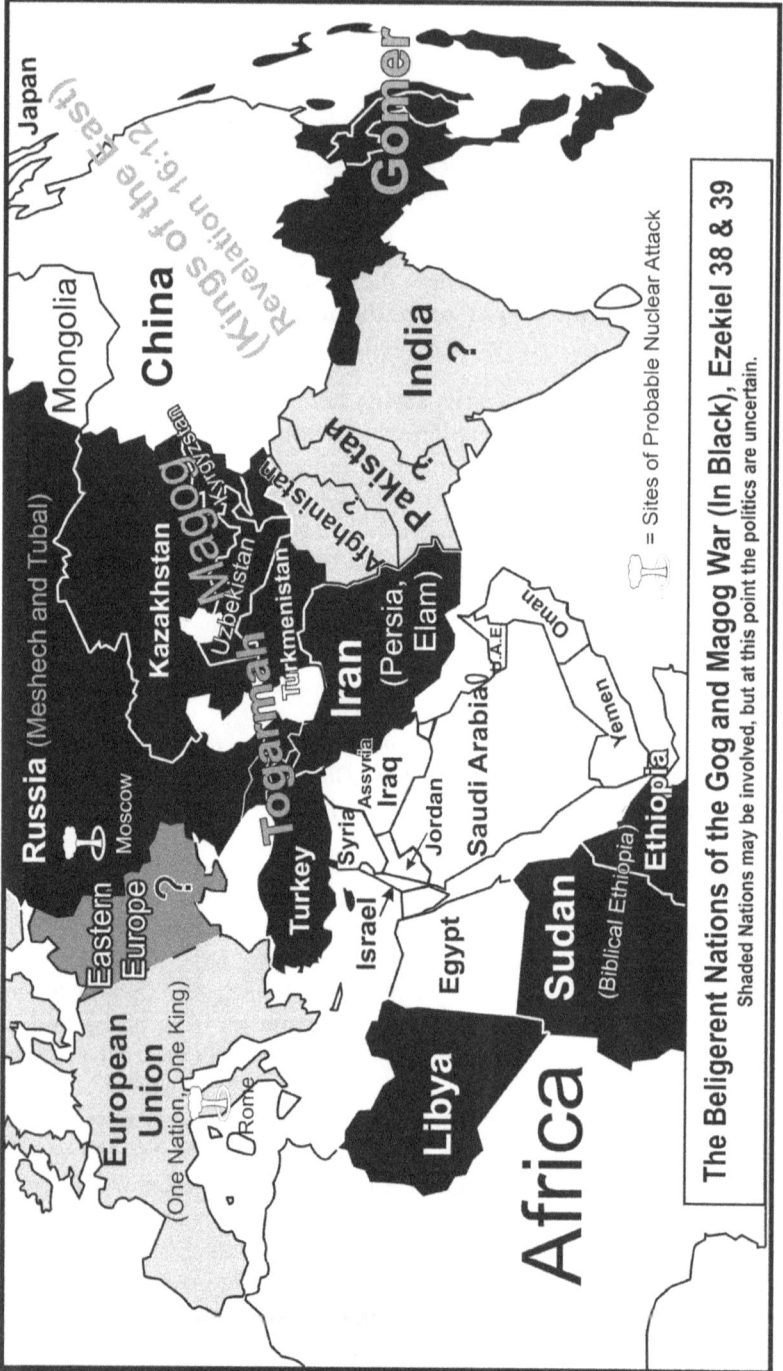

The Belligerent Nations of the Gog and Magog War (In Black), Ezekiel 38 & 39

Shaded Nations may be involved, but at this point the politics are uncertain.

⚓ = Sites of Probable Nuclear Attack

world dictator tries to tell Israel where their borders should go, God is capable of overruling them! I think He wants to show His power to both Israel and their enemies, while man is still "in control".

God Himself is capable of engineering Israel's return to, and possession of, the promised land, in spite of world-wide opposition. Of this I am certain. At the same time I believe that God will actually use Satan to accomplish His goals! Satan himself has a motivation for wanting Israel to have their promised land! You see Satan's ultimate goal is to destroy the people of Israel. Israel's army is one of the best trained and best equipped armies in the world, and hundreds of millions of Arabs are no match for five million Jews.

In order for Satan to get Israel to drop their guard, he has to make them believe the worst is over. He will have to make them think that they have already been through the Time of Jacob's trouble. He will also have to get Christians to confirm to Israel that the Tribulation, and Armageddon is over, and that it was the same conflict as Gog and Magog's war. Remember, Jesus said that deception is the first and biggest issue facing the world in the last days. (Matthew 24:4)

And so, after some horrific wars, Israel will possess their land. A false Antichrist will have been defeated, and a false Babylon destroyed, and then the world will say *"peace and safety..."*

*And the east side ye shall measure from Hauran, and from Damascus, and from Gilead, and from the land of Israel by Jordan, from the **border unto the east sea**. And this is the east side. (Ezekiel 47:18)*

Hauran, or Howran is the district of Syria within which Damascus is located.

In the Old Testament the Dead Sea was known as the *"Salt sea"*, and Lake Genessaret was known as the Sea of Chinnereth. The Sea of Galilee was actually fully surrounded by Israel, so this passage could not be a reference to that body of water. It could be a reference to the Dead Sea, but I do not see it called the *"East Sea"* anywhere in Scripture. Several passages speak of Israel extending to the Euphrates river, and this passage in Ezekiel speaks of it extending to the *"East Sea"*. If you follow the Euphrates river, you will find that it flows **eastward** into the Persian Gulf, which is the East Sea. The only other reference I have found in scripture to the *"East Sea"* is found in Joel, which appears to be a reference to the

war of Gog and Magog, and also appears to be a reference to the
Persian Gulf:

> *But I will remove far off from you the northern army, and
> will **drive him into a land barren and desolate, with his
> face toward the east sea,** and his hinder part toward the
> utmost sea, and his stink shall come up, and his ill savour
> shall come up, because he hath done great things.* (Joel 2:20)

It would appear that these forces have their backs to the sea of
Galilee, or perhaps the Mediterranean, and are retreating eastward,
through the Arabian Desert toward the Persian Gulf. The Arabian
Desert is "*a land baren and desolate*", to the east of Israel. We know,
from Ezekiel 38 & 39, that they shall fall in the hills of Israel **east** of
the sea, so putting two and two together we come up with the
Persian Gulf.

At some point Israel's influence will likely reach as far as Kuwait
and Iraq south of the Euphrates. When God is done with Israel,
their territory will include parts of present day Syria, Iraq, Egypt,
and Kuwait, and all of Lebanon and Jordan, and perhaps all of the
Arabian peninsula! Now that is a cup of trembling!

Many Arabs have accused Israel of wanting their land. I suspect
that some of them have read these things in the bible. I do not
believe Israel has designs on any of this territory. They just want
what they once had, a place where they can live in safety, but God
Himself will ensure that they receive all the land He promised them
in His Word. I expect that Israel will find themselves in a situation
where they must take the territory or face extinction! They won't
have any choice in the matter. God is about to show the world that
His Word is trustworthy!

Don't forget the last part of Deuteronomy 11:24: *"from the river,
the river Euphrates, even unto the uttermost sea shall your coast be."*
The word *"uttermost"* means "*the farthest"*, and if you follow the
Euphrates to its farthest end, you end up in the Persian Gulf, which
is the first sea you get to when you go to the east of Israel.

I cannot see the Arabs suing for peace with Israel, unless they
lose a large amount of land in a major battle, and neither can I see
the Jews who have turned to Islam, returning to the God of Israel
unless their false god is proven powerless. The exact future borders
of Israel are in God's hands. I am only following the logical
conclusions of the Word of God, as to where they will ultimately be

situated.

Balaam, a prophet hired by the king of Moab, was one of the first to prophesy that Edom would one day become a possession of Israel. Numbers 24:14-19, among other passages, indicates that Moab and Edom would be subjugated by Israel in the last days, and so it is safe to conclude that Israel's borders will eventually include all of Jordan. Since Edom, a part of Jordan, was on the opposite side of the Dead Sea, and if Israel possesses Edom, then that body of water would be ruled out as being the *"East Sea"*. It will be fully surrounded by Israel, and actually west of parts of Israel.

In Ezekiel 38:8 and 11 we see that Gog's army is coming against a people who are at peace and rest, who have returned from all nations where they were scattered. This situation does not describe Israel today. From the establishment of Israel in 1948 until now (2010) Israel has been in a state of constant warfare. Hezbollah and Hamas regularly launch rockets over the border, and suicide bombers are a regular part of the scene. We have already seen that there are many members of the nation of Israel still living in the far off nations where they were sent some 2700 years ago. This war cannot occur today since these conditions have not yet been met.

Who are the armies named in the Ezekiel account? Many have speculated on the identities of these nations, though the consensus seems to centre on Russia as being the driving force. Gog is actually a person, probably a charismatic, unifying leader and probably from Russia, or the republics that were once part of the Soviet Union. Meshech is likely a reference to the founder of the tribe for whom Moscow is named, and Tubal is likely his brother, the grandson of Noah for whom the city of Tobolsk, Russia, and the Tubal river is named.

The Creation-wiki website says...

"The descendants of Meshech were well-known to the people of the Middle East centuries after the great and terrible flood of Noah."

"The Assyrians knew them as the Mushku, the Greeks as the Moskhi and by others as Musku, Muskaaia, Moshi and Moska. Herodotus, a well-known ancient historian, calls them Moschi and Tibarenoi. And the ancient capital of Cappadocia was Mazaca. While in Asia Minor they were inseparable from the Toboli. They were the "natural" or hereditary enemies of the Assyrians and were largely the cause of the Assyrians losing power over other peoples from time to time."

"They migrated with Tubal up to the Black Sea and into the Russian plains. Dr. Gesenius wrote, in the nineteenth century, that Meshech became the Moschi, a very barbaric people. They dwelt, he said, in the Moschian Mountains. The Moschian Mountains were the connecting chain between the Caucasus and Anti Taurus Mountains. The Scofield Reference Bible says that the "reference to Meshech and Tubal (Moscow and Tobolosk) is a clear mark of identification". Strabo claimed that here was a district named "Moschice", a very barbaric people, while Lempriere stated in his dictionary that the Moschi were a people to the west of the Caspian Sea." (Creation-wiki, Meshech)

It is important to remember that people alive at the time of Ezekiel, did not necessarily live in the same location that their descendants would live some 2700 years later. When the tribes of the earth dispersed at Babel they did not have to go too far to separate from each other. As populations increased they found themselves having to move farther away than their ancestors had gone. The city of Turin, Italy, was named for Celtic peoples who used to live there. Bohemia, in the Czech Republic, is named after Celtic tribes who lived there at one time. Those tribes migrated throughout Europe and ultimately made it to France and England where many of them still reside, though of course, many moved further west to North America. The same is true of many other people groups around the world.

The people of Meshech and Tubal are mentioned in Ezekiel 27:13 as being people who traded with Tyre. No doubt these Scythians/Russians came down from the Black sea through the Bosphorus and Dardanelles to the Mediterranean sea.

The city of Moscow did not exist at the time of Ezekiel, nor at the time of Christ. The first mention of Moscow in Russian is from 1147 AD in a letter by Yuri Dolgoruki, the Russian prince, to whom is attributed the founding of that city. (The Moscow Guide, Russian Sun Site) Ezekiel could not have been referring to that city, but to the founder of the tribe for whom the city is named. That tribe has lived over a large territory throughout the centuries and has lent its name to many localities within that area, not just Moscow. The key to the identity of these peoples is found in verse 15 with the phrase *"north parts"*. If you check on a map of Europe and the Middle East you will find that Moscow is situated directly north of Israel. This is distinguished from Turkey (Togarmah) which is in the *"north quarters"*, which would seem to indicate a location somewhat closer to Israel, though still to the north.

Some claim that Russia will not be involved in the armies that attack Israel, that these armies will be exclusively Muslim in origin. I agree that there will be a majority of Muslims in the Ezekiel 38 and 39 war, but can't see how Russia is not involved. Russia has constantly sided with the Arabs since the founding of Israel, and is heavily involved with them in arms sales, military advisors, and other joint ventures. Verse 4 speaks of God putting hooks into the jaw of Gog and bringing him down against Israel. This term speaks of an unnatural alliance of the people of Meshech and Tubal with the other involved nations. There may be something personal that causes this man to pledge his people to fight along side the Muslim nations.

Iran was known as Persia until 1935, and Libya is still Libya. The name Ethiopia may be the modern Ethiopia, but probably also includes Sudan. Magog most likely represents the former Soviet republics of Uzbekistan, Kyrgyzstan, Kazakhstan, Tajikistan, Dagestan, and Azerbaijan.

Gomer is a name of much discussion. Some have identified this name with eastern Europe, Spain, and Asia. Gomer was a brother of Ashkenaz, who is believed to be the ancestor of the Germanic peoples. It appears, however, that Gomer, or some of his descendants migrated eastwards. The CreationWiki website states that Khmer, of Cambodia and Vietnam, is a corruption of the name Gomer.

"Gomer gave rise to the Siamese, Burmese, Indonesians, Filipinos, Vietnamese, Laotians, and Cambodians who all have the same sub-racial anthropological classifications."

"The Cambodians' real name is the Khmer which is very likely derived from Gomer. Similarly, the Burmese state of Keng Tung was classically known as Khemarata. Also, Khemara was the original name of Sumatra and a region in Sumatra is known as Kampar. We also find the area of

Khemarat in Thailand and the Guimaras island in the Philippines. Given the aforementioned, it is highly likely, that these place and ethnic names are ultimately traceable back to Gomer." (http://creationwiki.org/Gomer)

Given the above evidence I think it is likely this claim is true. If the author of the CreationWiki article is correct, these nations could be mistaken for the *"Kings of the East"*, and *"proof"* that this war was Armageddon. The Ezekiel war will be unmistakable since the results are spelled out for us in Ezekiel 38 and 39, but the evidence is that some will confuse it with the battle of Armageddon, and this error could be fatal. The bible tells us that Armageddon will include the armies of the whole world. Every nation will be represented at that conflict.

<u>Sheba, Dedan, and Tarshish</u>

I n verse 13 we see Sheba, Dedan and Tarshish are mentioned as not being involved, but lodging a diplomatic protest. In each case there have been more than one of each entity mentioned in scripture or in other literature, so the question arises: which of each is being spoken of here? Notice the language of their protests. Each of them says *"Art thou come to take a spoil?"* The word *"come"* is an indication that each of these nations is geographically located between the invading nations and Israel. The invading armies are too large for these people to fight, so they just make a feeble protest and allow them through. Sheba is an Arab city, thus representing Saudi Arabia or Ishmael. Dedan is often referred to as an Arab city, but there are at least two places in scripture where it is referred to in relation to the nation of Edom. Ezekiel 25:13 and Jeremiah 49:8 both seem to indicate that this reference to Dedan is actually a reference to the descendants of Esau, or southern Jordan today.

> *Therefore thus saith the Lord GOD; I will also stretch out mine hand upon **Edom**, and will cut off man and beast from it; and I will make it **desolate from Teman; and they of Dedan shall fall by the sword**. (Ezekiel 25:13)*

> ***Concerning Edom**, thus saith the LORD of hosts; Is wisdom no more in Teman? is counsel perished from the prudent? is their wisdom vanished? **Flee ye, turn back,***

dwell deep, O inhabitants of Dedan; for I will bring the
calamity of Esau upon him, the time that I will visit him.
(Jeremiah 49:7 & 8)

Even Isaiah 21:13 which seems to identify Dedan as Arabia
actually also associates Dedan with Esau's descendants. Verse 11
speaks of Seir, a prominent area of Edom. The reference to Arabia is
a reference to the Arabian peninsula of which Jordan is a part. On a
map of Jordan you will notice that parts of that nation jut out into
the Arabian desert, consequently I do not believe that the
association of Edom with Dedan is beyond the realm of possibility.

*The burden of Dumah. He calleth to me out of **Seir**,*
Watchman, what of the night? Watchman, what of the night?
The watchman said, The morning cometh, and also the night:
if ye will enquire, enquire ye: return, come. The burden upon
Arabia. In the forest in Arabia shall ye lodge, O ye travelling
*companies of **Dedanim**. (Isaiah 21:11-13)*

Whether Dedan is Arabia, or related to Edom is immaterial to
my point. Either way it is one of the nations that is defeated in
Asaph's war, and is not involved in the Gog and Magog conflict.

Various sources indicate that Tarshish is either: the city of Tarsus
in Turkey; a Phoenician port in Spain, Tartessos; another name for
Carthage, Tunisia; or perhaps a port in India or Sri Lanka, since
some ships may have sailed there from Ezion-Geber on the Red Sea
(1 Kings 9:26). I think these possibilities are unlikely because of
the distance to Israel from these places, i.e. they do not fit the
context.

As I studied this problem I found that there is a port in Syria,
just north of the Lebanese border called Tartus. If the Isaiah 17:1
prophecy of the destruction of Damascus occurs during the Psalm 83
war, it will be uninhabitable, and Syria will have to relocate its
capital. Could this be a reference to Tartus as the new capital of
Syria? Tartus is Syria's second most important port on the
Mediterranean sea. It might be the natural choice for a replacement
capital city. It is most likely then that Tarshish is a reference to a
new Syrian capital, probably Tartus. Given the fact that Israel has
been promised the land of Lebanon, and from there to the
Euphrates river, it is likely that the remnant of Syria will not possess
Damascus, or any area of southern Syria by that time.

The Turkish city of Tarsus is a strange and unlikely possibility, since Togarmah appears to be a reference to the Turkic peoples, the most notable nation of which is Turkey. This would give us the unlikely scenario of Turkey joining Iran and Russia in attacking Israel, yet having one of its own cities protesting the war. The only faint possibility would be if Tarsus is earlier given to Syria as a new capital after Damascus is destroyed. I doubt this scenario, since most countries are very jealous of their land, and for Turkey to give a city of two million people to Syria would be pretty much out of the question. Still, Tarsus is fairly close to the Syrian border and, if it were given in exchange for some Syrian land Turkey desires, it is not beyond the realm of possibility. I tend to believe the Syrian city of Tartus is in view here, but the exact understanding of the fulfilment of this prophecy awaits the aftermath of Asaph's war.

Whatever the exact location, these three cities appear to represent nations that will establish some kind of peace with Israel after the Psalm 83 war, but before the Ezekiel 38/39 conflict. This peace will not be an alliance in which they will come to her aid, but some sort of non-aggression treaty. Today these people are Muslims and avowed enemies of Israel. If this war were to occur today they would be at the front of the line to volunteer.

Verse 22 speaks of fire and brimstone coming down from Heaven to destroy the invading armies. Some believe that this must occur during the battle of Armageddon as a result of this celestial bombardment. There is, however, evidence that this celestial attack will occur before the Tribulation period. In verse 2 of chapter 39 God says that he will leave a sixth part of the invading armies alive. In Revelation 19:21 it is stated that one hundred percent of the armies that come against the Lord will be slain. There will be no survivors at all. This must therefore be another battle which will occur some time before the battle of Armageddon.

> *Therefore, thou son of man, prophesy against Gog, and say, Thus saith the Lord GOD; Behold, I am against thee, O Gog, the chief prince of Meshech and Tubal: And I will turn thee back, and leave but the sixth part of thee, and will cause thee to come up from the north parts, and will bring thee upon the mountains of Israel: And I will smite thy bow out of thy left hand, and will cause thine arrows to fall out of thy right hand. Thou shalt fall upon the mountains of Israel, thou, and all thy bands, and the people that is with thee: I will give thee unto the ravenous birds of every sort, and to the beasts of the field*

to be devoured. (Ezekiel 39:1-4)

Notice that these armies will fall upon the mountains of Israel. Which mountains of Israel are being referred to here? Note verse 11:

> *And it shall come to pass in that day, that I will give unto Gog a place there of graves in Israel, the valley of the passengers on the **east of the sea:** and it shall stop the noses of the passengers: and there shall they bury Gog and all his multitude: and they shall call it The valley of Hamon–gog.*

The ruler of the invading armies, referred to as Gog, is not the same person as the Antichrist for the simple reason that Gog will be buried in the mountains of Israel; whereas the Antichrist himself, along with the false prophet, will be raptured alive and taken straight to the Lake of Fire (Rev. 19:20). This seemingly small detail makes all the difference in the world! Those who think Gog was the Antichrist will now be looking for a saviour to bring peace to the world. That *"saviour"* will actually be the Antichrist.

The sea referred to here is not the Mediterranean, since all of Israel is east of this sea, but rather it is likely a reference to the Dead Sea. The *"valley of the passengers"* is likely the same as *"the Valley of the Travellers"*, a valley that runs from mount Moab toward the Dead Sea. In the past this valley was a part of Moab, and is today a part of Jordan, yet the prophet identifies this land as *"the Mountains of Israel"*. Something must happen in the mean time for this land to become possessed by Israel. That question is answered by the war of Psalm 83.

As stated earlier, this war will be regarded by many as having been Armageddon. If the people of the world believe Armageddon, the final battle, has already been fought they will be looking for a saviour to bring peace to the world. In fact they will be looking for "the Christ". Unfortunately they will not be looking for Jesus Christ, but for someone who embodies the New Age *"Christ Consciousness"*. They will accept a man who has been born on this planet, and who has some sort of *"Christianish"* value system.

In both Daniel 7:8 & 24, and in Revelation 17 we see three of the world rulers will be subdued by the Antichrist. When he uses the word "subdue" I am not sure if he means they surrender to him, or he has them killed and replaced by a puppet, or rules their kingdom personally. I suspect that each of these three rulers will have some characteristics of the Antichrist himself, and will be defeated for their ambition. When Adolf Hitler had Ernst Roehm killed, during the Night of the Long Knives, he claimed it was because of Roehm's homosexuality. In actual fact Roehm had become very popular and was a threat to his power. (The Pink Swastika, p. 206) In the same way these three kings will be vying for the throne of Antichrist.

Most bible commentators concentrate on the Antichrist himself and say very little about these other rulers. These ten men represent ten regions encompassing the entire earth, not merely Europe. I suspect that the man of sin will point at three of these people and say that they are each the Antichrist. He may be able to point to the teachings of Christians to back himself up, and when the last is subdued he will claim that "*now is the time to set up the kingdom of God on earth, a kingdom of peace and harmony*".

Very likely one of these three leaders will closely match the popular idea that western Christendom has of the Antichrist. He will likely be from Rome, Italy, or perhaps Romania. He will likely be handsome, gay, charismatic, Catholic, and the leader of the European Union. At some time prior to his downfall he will have brokered an agreement with Israel, probably to allow them to rebuild the Temple in Jerusalem. I suspect the timing of that agreement will coincide with the end of Asaph's war, and the establishment of Greater Israel. When he is defeated the world will believe that *"the Antichrist has been defeated and now we will enter a time of world peace"*! He will actually be a counterfeit, or decoy, Antichrist. Unfortunately, it will be the real Antichrist who defeats him!

> *For when they shall say, Peace and safety; then sudden destruction cometh upon them, as travail upon a woman with child; and they shall not escape. (1 Thessalonians 5:3)*

It is often stated that it is odd that there is no mention of the United States of America in prophecy. Considering that the USA has been the dominant nation in the world for nearly a century this omission is conspicuous by its absence. I personally believe that the USA is included in this prophecy, though not by name.

> *And I will send a fire on Magog, **and among them that dwell carelessly in the isles**: and they shall know that I am the LORD. (Ezekiel 39:6)*

The three continents in scripture are Europe, Asia and Africa. All three of these continents are connected in the Middle East. You can drive a car from Beijing to Moscow, to Paris, to Cape Town. To a person who inhabits this great land mass, the continents of North and South America, and Australia appear as islands. I think the reference to *"them that dwell carelessly in the isles"* is a reference to these continents. The term *"careless"* certainly would describe the lifestyle practised in the developed areas of these continents. I am not certain that this passage describes these nations as joining this war, but it appears that this judgment occurs because they fail to come to the aid of Israel in her time of deepest distress.

The other reference to these three continents would be some of the ten toes of Nebuchadnezzar's dream in Daniel chapter 2 and Revelation 13 and 18. At one time the British Empire was the greatest empire on earth, but Britain has faded to back-water status today, and is now a small part of the European Union. I am sure the same will shortly be said of the USA. Once they have stopped supporting Israel, the Lord will stop protecting them. Ultimately the USA will become a part of the North American representation in the World Government, but it will only be one of ten and not the dominant one.

If the leader of the North American Union aspires to the position of World President he would likely be a second *"king"* exposed as an Antichrist by the Antichrist. Given the dominant role the USA has played on the world stage for so long, I expect that the person presiding over this union would likely have ambitions for a greater role.

*And they that dwell in the cities of Israel shall go forth, and shall set on fire and **burn the weapons**, both the shields and the bucklers, the bows and the arrows, and the handstaves, and the spears, and they shall burn them with fire seven years: So that they shall take no wood out of the field, neither cut down any out of the forests; for they shall burn the weapons with fire: and **they shall spoil those that spoiled them, and rob those that robbed them**, saith the Lord GOD. (Ezekiel 39:9-10)*

Considering that weapons have changed since the Bible was written, there has been a lot of speculation as to what these verses might mean. It seems fair then that I might add my two cents worth: Modern armies are equipped with tanks, trucks, guns, helicopters and airplanes. These machines require fuel for propulsion, so it is likely that the fuel will be used for household, and cooking heat. These weapons are mainly made of steel, plus a few other metals. These verses talk of Israel spoiling those who came to spoil them.

Metals have intrinsic value in themselves, and Israel will turn their enemies' weapons into wealth. A Russian T90 tank weighs 46.5 metric tonnes or 102,765 lbs., the bulk of which is steel. If the Israeli army has access to a few thousand tank hulks they would have a lot of steel with which to produce wealth! Russia is also the world's largest producer of titanium, a very light weight, and expensive metal. No doubt some of this material has made it into their weapon systems. What could Israel do with large amounts of titanium?

How is metal turned from one form into another? You put it into an oven and melt it down...with fire! So when it says that Israel will burn the weapons I think it means that they will melt them down and produce consumer products with them. You could produce many passenger cars from one tank! One tank could provide the sheet metal for the chassis for thousands of computers!

Aluminum is one of the most expensive metals to produce, because the process requires large amounts of electricity. What are most airplanes made of? Aluminum, of course. With hundreds, or perhaps thousands, of airplanes destroyed in Israeli airspace, there will be a lot of aluminum to recycle.

In bringing their weapons to Israel the Russian/Iranian coalition will be handing a supply of wealth to their enemies! The Jews, who often escaped from those countries with only the clothes on their backs, will be given a source of wealth by those very same nations!

> *11 And it shall come to pass in that day,* **that I will give unto Gog a place there of graves in Israel,** *the valley of the passengers on the* **east of the sea:** *and it shall stop the noses of the passengers: and there shall they bury Gog and all his multitude: and they shall call it The valley of Hamon–gog. 12 And seven months shall the house of Israel be burying of them, that they may cleanse the land. (Ezekiel 39:11-12)*

Verse 11 is key in differentiating between the Gog and Magog war, and Armageddon. Gog, the leader of the Russian forces, will die in Israel and be buried there. At Armageddon the Antichrist will not physically die but will be picked up bodily and cast into the Lake of Fire (Rev. 19:20).

The danger of allegorizing scripture can be seen here; **If you think that the passage means that Gog is the Antichrist, and is killed, buried, and only his spirit is thrown into the Lake of Fire, you will then be looking for the return of Christ at that moment.** Gog will spend the millennial reign of Christ in Hell, and only after will he be resurrected, judged, and thrown into the Lake of Fire. Those who allegorize parts of scripture will also spiritualize the return of Christ. They will believe that *"the Christ"* (consciousness) could be born as a man, or will reside in one living human individual. This would be the perfect opportunity for the Antichrist to arise. Only those who believe the literal, plain sense of scripture will understand what is going on, and will be prepared.

Ezekiel 39:17 and Revelation 19:17 are very similar in their language. The only way one can tell the difference is to look at details and the context. The end of Gog and the end of the Beast are very different. Confusing these two events, will allow the man of sin to rise at that time and deceive the nations, who are looking for peace. The Antichrist will arise at the end of a false Armageddon, from the nations of earth. Jesus Christ will literally return at the end of Armageddon the same way he left, from the sky (Acts 1:11).

The war of Ezekiel 38 and 39 is a more limited war in which some nations do not participate, Revelation 19 and Zechariah 14 state that all the armies of the earth will be involved in Armageddon. This does not mean some troops from every continent, but every army of every nation. All means all! All the armies of the earth will be destroyed at Armageddon, (Rev. 19:18 & 20) while one sixth of the armies of the Gog and Magog conflict shall return to their homes (Eze. 39:2).

This will be a perfect opportunity for a misinterpretation of Isaiah 2:4, for swords will indeed be turned into plowshares, but it is not yet the beginning of the millennial reign of Christ! The Time of Jacob's Trouble is just around the corner!

It is impossible to overstate the differences in the details of these two conflicts. Mistaking one for the other can mean the difference between life and death! God is doing these things to bring glory to His name. Those who see these things come to pass, and fail to search the Scriptures, will misinterpret them, support the

Antichrist, and condemn themselves!

Resources

"Isralestine, the Ancient Blueprints of the Future Middle East", Salus, Bill, HighWay a division of Anomalous Publishing House, Crane 65633, USA (July 7, 2008)

"The Prophecy That Is Shaping History: New Research on Ezekiel's Vision of the End." Ruthven, Jon, PhD, and Griess, Ihab, PhD, Fairfax, VA: Xulon Press, 2003

"The Pink Swastika, Homosexuality in the Nazi Party", by Lively,Scott and Abrams,Kevin E., Published by Veritas Aeterna Press, January, 2002

"The Encyclopedia of Creation Science, Meshech", accessed 2/22/2010, from http://creationwiki.org/Meshech

"The Encyclopedia of Creation Science, Gomer", accessed 2/22/2010, http://creationwiki.org/Gomer

"NET Bible ™ Learning Environment", Gebal", accessed 09/08/2010, from http://net.bible.org/dictionary.php?word=GEBAL,

"Nazareth and The Branch, Matthew 2:23 and Interpretation of the Old Testament", CRI/Voice, Institute, by Dennis Bratcher, accessed 02/06/2010, from www.crivoice.org/branch.html

"Websters Integrated Dictionary and Thesaurus", Geddes & Grosset, 2006, David Dale House, New Lanark ML11 9DJ, Scotland

"The Moscow Guide: History", Russian SunSITE, accessed 10/05/2010, from http://redsun.cs.msu.su/moscow/history.html

"Land of Israel", Wikipedia, the free encyclopedia, 13 September 2010, accessed 16/09/2010, from http://en.wikipedia.org/wiki/Land_of_Israel

"The Shack, Where Tragedy Confronts Eternity", Young, Wm. Paul, 2007, Windblown Media, 4680 Calle Norte, Newbury Park, CA 91320

Chapter 5

The Unveiling

*1 Now we beseech you, brethren, **by the coming of our Lord Jesus Christ, and by our gathering together unto him**, 2 That ye be not soon shaken in mind, or be troubled, neither by spirit, nor by word, nor by letter as from us, as that the day of Christ is at hand. 3 Let no man deceive you by any means: **for that day shall not come, except there come a falling away first, and that man of sin be revealed**, the son of perdition; 4 Who opposeth and exalteth himself above all that is called God, or that is worshipped; so that he as God sitteth in the temple of God, shewing himself that he is God. 5 Remember ye not, that, when I was yet with you, I told you these things? 6 And now ye know what withholdeth that he might be revealed in his time. 7 For the mystery of iniquity doth already work: only **he who now letteth (hinders) will let, until he be taken out of the way. 8 And then shall that Wicked be revealed**, whom the Lord shall consume with the spirit of his mouth, and shall destroy with the brightness of his coming: 9 Even him, whose coming is after the working of Satan with all power and signs and lying wonders, 10 And with all deceivableness of unrighteousness in them that perish; because they received not the love of the truth, that they might be saved. 11 And for this cause God shall send them strong delusion, that they should believe a lie: 12 That they all might be damned who believed not the truth, but had pleasure in unrighteousness. (1 Thessalonians 2:1-12)*

As I read this chapter, over and over again, I was left with the impression, from the first three verses, that *"the coming of our Lord Jesus, and our gathering together unto Him"*, which is the rapture, shall not occur until there is a general falling away (apostasy) of the Church, and the revealing of the Man of Sin. In other words the Antichrist shall be revealed before the rapture of the Church. Then in verse 6 we are told that whatever hinders the spirit of Antichrist, that is the Church, shall be removed and then the *"Man of Sin"* will be revealed. In other words it looks like the rapture of the Church will occur before the Antichrist is revealed!

This could look like a contradiction, except it appears that what is being said is that there will be a dual revealing of the man of sin. First, the Antichrist will be revealed to the Church, and the Church will endeavour to warn the unsaved, to no avail. Then the Church will be taken out of the way in the rapture. After the Church is raptured and the Antichrist tries to explain it away, then he will be revealed to the world in general. Only then will some of the unsaved begin to understand.

The confusion over the *"he"* in this passage stems from the different roles the Church has in relation to different persons or groups. Being made up of persons of both genders, the Church actually is sexless, but in relation to the Lord Jesus Christ, the Church takes on a submissive, feminine role. She is His bride. In relation to this world, and the devil, however, the Church takes on the masculine role of a soldier.

If you look for the different roles of the Church throughout Scripture you will see them: The Church is a "bride" in Matthew 9:15, John 3:29 and Revelation 22:17. In 1 Timothy 6:12, however, we are told to *"fight the good fight of faith"*. In 2 Timothy 4:7 Paul says he has *"fought the good fight"*. In Philippians 2:25 Paul calls Epaphroditus a *"fellow soldier"*. In 2 Timothy 2:3, Timothy is told to *"endure hardship as a good soldier of Christ"*. In Philemon 1:2 Archippus is called a *"fellow soldier"*. In 2 Corinthians 10:3-5 Paul speaks of the *"weapons of our warfare"* which are not carnal but spiritual. In Revelation 19:14 all the saints are called *"armies"* as we descend to the earth with the Lord Jesus Christ.

Please do not misunderstand me, I am not saying the Church is meant to subjugate the earth, as the New Apostolic Reformers and other Dominionists say. The Christian is a soldier who is called to be gentle and even lay down his life for the cause of Christ. Our weapons are not fleshly, physical arms, but powerful spiritual weapons.

> *Behold, I send you forth as sheep in the midst of wolves: be*
> *ye therefore wise as serpents, and* **harmless as doves***.*

(Matthew 10:16)

> *For we wrestle not against flesh and blood, but against principalities, against powers, against the rulers of the darkness of this world, against spiritual wickedness in high places. Wherefore take unto you the whole armour of God, that ye may be able to withstand in the evil day, and having done all, to stand. Stand therefore, having your loins girt about with* **truth**, *and having on the breastplate of* **righteousness**; *And your feet shod with the preparation of the* **gospel of peace**; *Above all, taking the* **shield of faith**, *wherewith ye shall be able to quench all the fiery darts of the wicked. And take the* **helmet of salvation**, *and the* **sword of the Spirit, which is the word of God**: *(Ephesians 6:12-17)*

Because Christians think of the Church as a bride they fail to understand that it is the Church that is referred to in verse 7. Who is *"he"* hindering? Is it not the spirit of Antichrist? This spirit is revealed as the devil himself in Revelation 12:9. The Church of Jesus Christ is the soldier who is standing in the way of Antichrist. The Church is a soldier because of the special, unprecedented, relationship he has with the Holy Spirit. Once we are out of the way, the Antichrist will be able to fully deceive the world. The Holy Spirit indwells each believer in a special way, yet remaining omnipresent. He will not leave the earth nor will he stop saving souls, but His relationship with the saved on earth will revert to that which He had with the Old-Testament saints. They will not be permanently indwelt with the Holy Spirit as Church Age saints are.

During the age of Israel, the Spirit's relationship with mankind is different than it is during the Church age. I am not certain of all the details of how it is different, I only know that salvation has always been by grace through faith, but the heavenly status of pre and post-Christian believers is somewhat less than for Church-age saints. No one was ever saved by works, from Adam until the end of history.

> *Verily I say unto you, Among them that are born of women there hath not risen a greater than John the Baptist:* **notwithstanding he that is least in the kingdom of heaven is greater than he.** *(Matthew 11:11)*

Very clearly this passage indicates that there is a difference between Church age saints and Old Testament saints. All saints of every age are saved, but there is a difference in status. The Old Testament saints were not indwelt by the Holy Spirit like Church age saints, and the same will be the rule during the Tribulation. Tribulation saints are Old Testament saints. They are saved by grace alone, through faith alone, in the shed blood of Christ alone, but they are not promised to be indwelt by the Holy Spirit like Church age saints. God is good, and we can trust Him to do what is best in every age.

Another item of confusion is the fact that so many professing *"Christians"* do not live any differently than the world. As Jesus said, the Church is like a tree where many birds take shelter in its branches, but the birds are not the branches (Luke 13:19). The Church is full of unbelievers who do not have the Holy Spirit, and really do not belong there. They are not really a part of His Church though they are members of churches, and receive some benefit from being there.

The clock of the seven year tribulation period will start with the confirmation of a pre-existing covenant for a seven year period. This confirmation will also coincide with the rapture of the Church within a very short period, perhaps even days.

The Land and the Sea

There is a lot of debate in Christian circles as to the identity of the Beast of Revelation 13:1. Many Catholics and Protestants have identified him as being Jewish because Jesus said, *"I am come in my Father's name, and ye receive me not: if another shall come in his own name, him ye will receive."* (John 5:43) The reasoning goes like this, "Israel will not accept anyone as Messiah unless he is Jewish". This is an example of taking one verse out of context and using it against all the other evidence in Scripture. Jesus may have not even been referring to the Antichrist at all but may have been referring to the false Prophet. Lets have a look at the verses relating to the Antichrist in this chapter.

> *1 And I stood upon the sand of the sea, and saw a beast rise up out of the sea, having seven heads and ten horns, and upon his horns ten crowns, and upon his heads the name of blasphemy. 2 And the beast which I saw was like unto a leopard, and his feet were as the feet of a bear, and his mouth*

as the mouth of a lion: and the dragon gave him his power, and his seat, and great authority. 3 And I saw one of his heads as it were wounded to death; and his deadly wound was healed: and all the world wondered after the beast. 4 And they worshipped the dragon which gave power unto the beast: and they worshipped the beast, saying, Who is like unto the beast? who is able to make war with him? 5 And there was given unto him a mouth speaking great things and blasphemies; and power was given unto him to continue forty and two months. 6 And he opened his mouth in blasphemy against God, to blaspheme his name, and his tabernacle, and them that dwell in heaven. (Revelation 13:1-6)

Daniel 7 is a parallel passage. The two passages need to be consulted if we are to understand either:

*2 Daniel spake and said, I saw in my vision by night, and, behold, the four winds of the heaven strove upon the great sea. 3 And **four great beasts came up from the sea,** diverse one from another. 4 The first was like a lion, and had eagle's wings: I beheld till the wings thereof were plucked, and it was lifted up from the earth, and made stand upon the feet as a man, and a man's heart was given to it. 5 And behold another beast, a second, like to a bear, and it raised up itself on one side, and it had three ribs in the mouth of it between the teeth of it: and they said thus unto it, Arise, devour much flesh. 6 After this I beheld, and lo another, like a leopard, which had upon the back of it four wings of a fowl; the beast had also four heads; and dominion was given to it. 7 After this I saw in the night visions, and behold a fourth beast, dreadful and terrible, and strong exceedingly; and it had great iron teeth: it devoured and brake in pieces, and stamped the residue with the feet of it: and it was diverse from all the beasts that were before it; and it had ten horns. 8 I considered the horns, and, behold, there came up among them another little horn, before whom there were three of the first horns plucked up by the roots: and, behold, in this horn were eyes like the eyes of man, and a mouth speaking great things. 9 I beheld till the thrones were cast down, and the Ancient of days did sit, whose garment was white as snow, and the hair of his head like the pure wool: his throne was like the fiery flame, and his wheels* *as burning fire. 10 A fiery stream issued and came forth from before him: thousand thousands ministered unto him, and ten thousand times ten thousand stood before him: the judgment was set, and the books were opened. 11 I beheld then because of the voice of the great words which the horn spake: I beheld even till the* **beast was slain, and his body destroyed, and given to the burning flame.** (Thrown bodily into the Lake of Fire) *12 As concerning the rest of the beasts, they had their dominion taken away: yet their lives were prolonged for a season and time. 13 I saw in the night visions, and, behold, one like the* **Son of man** *came with the clouds of heaven, and came to the Ancient of days, and they brought him near before him. 14 And there was given him dominion, and glory, and a kingdom, that all people, nations, and languages, should serve him: his dominion is an everlasting dominion, which shall not pass away, and his kingdom that which shall not be destroyed. 15 I Daniel was grieved in my spirit in the midst of my body, and the visions of my head troubled me. 16 I came near unto one of them that stood by, and asked him the truth of all this. So he told me, and made me know the interpretation of the things. 17 These great beasts, which are four, are four kings, which shall arise out of the earth. 18 But the saints of the most High shall take the kingdom, and possess the kingdom for ever, even for ever and ever. 19 Then I would know the truth of the fourth beast, which was diverse from all the others, exceeding dreadful, whose teeth were of iron, and his nails of brass; which devoured, brake in pieces, and stamped the residue with his feet; 20 And of the ten horns that were in his head, and of the other which came up, and before whom three fell; even of that horn that had eyes, and a mouth that spake very great things, whose look was more stout than his fellows. 21 I beheld,* **and the same horn made war with the saints, and prevailed against them; 22 Until the Ancient of days came,** *and judgment was given to the saints of the most High; and the time came that the saints possessed the kingdom. 23 Thus he said, The fourth beast shall be the fourth kingdom upon earth, which shall be diverse from all kingdoms, and shall devour the whole earth, and shall tread it down, and break it in pieces. 24 And the* **ten horns out of this kingdom are ten kings that shall arise: and another shall rise after them; and he shall be diverse from the first, and he shall** *subdue three kings. 25 And he shall speak great words against the most High, and shall wear out the saints of the most High, and think to change times and laws: and they shall be given into his hand until a time and times and the dividing of time. 26 But the judgment shall sit, and they shall take away his dominion, to consume and to destroy it unto the end. 27 And the kingdom and dominion, and the greatness of the kingdom under the whole heaven, shall be given to the people of the saints of the most High, whose kingdom is an everlasting kingdom, and all dominions shall serve and obey him.*

The first thing we need to notice is the use of the word *"sea"*. In the Daniel passage we see that the four kings all come from the sea. We know from other parts of Daniel, and elsewhere, that these four kings represent the empires of Babylon, Medo-Persia, Greece and Rome. The fact that they all came from the sea as does the *"Beast from the sea"* should indicate to us that they all have a common origin, which is the gentile nations or *"kings of the earth"*. This is very apparent in this passage, but we can check it out in other Scriptures to confirm our thesis:

The Sea represents the nations of the world, the gentiles:

> *Woe to the **multitude of many people, which make a noise like the noise of the seas;** and to the **rushing of nations, that make a rushing like the rushing of mighty waters!** The nations shall rush like the rushing of many waters: but God shall rebuke them, and they shall flee far off, and shall be chased as the chaff of the mountains before the wind, and like a rolling thing before the whirlwind. (Isaiah 17:12 & 13)*

> *Therefore thus saith the Lord GOD; Behold, I am against thee, O Tyrus, and will cause **many nations** to come up against thee, as the **sea causeth his waves to come up.** (Ezekiel 26:3)*

> *And there came one of the seven angels which had the seven vials, and talked with me, saying unto me, Come hither; I will shew unto thee the judgment of the great whore that*

*sitteth upon **many waters**: (Revelation 17:1)*

I know that these four kings are spoken of as coming out of the earth, in Daniel 7:17. This is not a contradiction, it's a different context. The kings are kings of the earth, men, but they come from the sea of the nations, the gentiles, not Israel. We know this because we have seen that the nations referred to are Babylon, Medo-Persia, Greece, and Rome. The "land" is often spoken of synonymously with the people of Israel:

*LORD, thou hast been favourable unto thy **land**: thou hast brought back the captivity of **Jacob**. (Psalms 85:1)*

When thou criest, let thy companies deliver thee; but the wind shall carry them all away; vanity shall take them: but he that putteth his trust in me shall possess the land, and shall inherit my holy mountain; (Isaiah 57:13)

Violence shall no more be heard in thy land, wasting nor destruction within thy borders; but thou shalt call thy walls Salvation, and thy gates Praise. (Isaiah 60:18)

Thy people also shall be all righteous: they shall inherit the land for ever, the branch of my planting, the work of my hands, that I may be glorified. (Isaiah 60:21)

For your shame ye shall have double; and for confusion they shall rejoice in their portion: therefore in their land they shall possess the double: everlasting joy shall be unto them. (Isaiah 61:7)

But neither he, nor his servants, nor the people of the land, did hearken unto the words of the LORD, which he spake by the prophet Jeremiah. (Jeremiah 37:2)

*Then said he unto me, The **iniquity of the house of Israel and Judah is exceeding great, and the land is full of blood**, and the city full of perverseness: for they say, The LORD* *hath forsaken the earth, and the LORD seeth not. (Ezekiel 9:9)*

*Therefore say, Thus saith the Lord GOD; I will even gather you from the people, and assemble you out of the countries where ye have been scattered, and I will give you the **land of Israel**. (Ezekiel 11:17)*

Son of man, when the land sinneth against me by trespassing grievously, then will I stretch out mine hand upon it, and will break the staff of the bread thereof, and will send famine upon it, and will cut off man and beast from it: (Ezekiel 14:13) (Land can't sin by itself, can it?)

And it shall come to pass, that in all the land, saith the LORD, two parts therein shall be cut off and die; but the third shall be left therein. (Zechariah 13:8)

There are a lot of verses here, but I think it is necessary to include them. While there are other verses that speak of land and sea in other contexts, I think that there is abundant evidence that the passage in question is indicating that the Antichrist shall be from a gentile background, and the false prophet shall be from a Hebrew, or Israelite, background.

Some say that the Beast of Revelation is a kingdom because the term *"Beasts"* in this passage is a reference to kingdoms, or empires. This is indeed the terminology that is used here, however God makes an exception in Revelation 13:18, *"Here is wisdom. Let him that hath understanding **count the number of the beast: for it is the number of a man**; and his number is Six hundred threescore and six."* Note that the number of the beast is the number of a man. This is not the number of mankind in general, nor is it the number of a system or a kingdom, it is the personal number of a certain man. I suspect that he will want his number incorporated in your mark as a way of guaranteeing your personal security...in effect, by taking his mark you are placing your trust in him.

The Book of Revelation

The prophecies about events of the Tribulation, and the establishment of a Messianic kingdom on earth, are scattered throughout the Old Testament prophets in great detail. It is impossible to establish the order of events from these references, however, and this is one of the great contributions of the Book of Revelation. This book gives a chronological order of the End Times with several parentheses, which go back and explain events that overlap events already underway.

As we have already seen, the millennial reign of Christ is found in books like Ezekiel, Isaiah, Haggai and others, but the length of that reign is not stated in any of these passages. The only place in the bible where the length of Christ's earthly kingdom is stated is found in Revelation chapter 20.

Of necessity this chapter will only be an overview. Since we have already started on chapters 2 and 3 we will skip those and concentrate on the rest of the book:

This book is popularly called *"The Revelation of John"* but it is properly *"The Revelation of Jesus Christ, as given to John"*. While some of the things in Revelation are symbolic, the interpretation is given in the Word of God itself. Prayer, and careful study, comparing Scripture with Scripture, will give us what God has for us. Commentaries can be helpful but remember they are subservient to the Word of God.

In the first chapter we have an introduction and a description of the one giving the revelation; the Lord Jesus Christ. Note that the description of Him is frightening. He is dressed as a warrior and there is fire in His eyes, and a sword comes from His mouth. John fell at His feet as if dead. This description should put away any idea of *"the big guy upstairs"* or *"God as my buddy"*! Don't ever think of Him as existing for your benefit. You depend on Him for literally everything. Every breath you have ever taken has been a gift from Him to you. He doesn't owe you anything.

Have you ever noticed in the popular media; TV, Movies and video games, that evil creatures and demons often have their eyes glowing red? Satan is preparing his followers to interpret this as a sign of evil. When Jesus returns, and is seen by the world He will likely appear as He does in this passage, with fire in His eyes. Those who have read this book and believed it will be terrified, though prepared, and will receive Him. The unbelievers will just be terrified, as well they should be. They will attempt to hide from Him, or to fight Him, to no avail.

Notice that in verse 18 Jesus is the one who has the keys of Hell and of Death. He is the key to eternal life. He is the door, and rejecting Him is the key to eternal death. In chapter 3 verse 7 Jesus has the key of David. He is the son of David who will reign on earth. David's throne is in Jerusalem.

As we have discussed before the second and third chapters of Revelation concern a group of seven Churches, or types of Churches. These Church types will exist up until the Great Tribulation period and some members will actually support the Antichrist, and be destroyed with the unbelievers! The *"Big picture"* view of these Churches is that they represent ages the Church will go through before the second coming of Christ. This understanding leads to the view that verse one of chapter four is a picture of the rapture. The voice sounds like a trumpet and invites John to *"come up here"*. It appears that this may be the case:

> *After this I looked, and, behold, a door was opened in heaven: and the first voice which I heard was as it were of a trumpet talking with me; which said, Come up hither, and I will shew thee things which must be hereafter. (Revelation 4:1)*

Immediately John finds himself in Heaven observing a gathering around the throne of God. Four angelic beasts surround the throne and give glory to the one seated upon it. I was amazed by the fact that these beastly angels give *"glory and honour and thanks to him that sat on the throne"*. Angels are in Heaven by virtue of the fact that they do not sin, but even these have reason to give thanks to God! They owe their existence to Him. Sinners like us ought to give thanks to Him every day!

Those occupying the twenty four thrones surrounding the throne of God are also of particular interest. Who are these people? Chapter 5 gives us the answer:

> *9 And they sung a new song, saying, Thou art worthy to take the book, and to open the seals thereof: for thou wast slain, **and hast redeemed us to God by thy blood out of every kindred, and tongue, and people, and nation;** 10 And hast made us unto our God kings and priests: and we shall reign on the earth.*

These twenty four elders represent the raptured Church of Jesus Christ. The fact that they come from *"every family, language, tribe and nation"* is proof of their identity. There are more than 24 families, languages, and tribes, on the earth, therefore this group represents a much larger group that is actually from every kindred, tongue, people and nation. In verse 10 they state, in future tense, that they shall reign on the earth. This statement very strongly implies that they will return to the earth after having already been to Heaven! This scene in Heaven therefore takes place after the rapture of the Church and before they return with Christ when He sets up His kingdom here on the earth.

Note that Jesus is the only one worthy to open the seals of the scroll. This scroll contains the judgments of God against mankind. Jesus is in control of the disasters that shall come upon earth. He is the only one worthy to bring this era of earth's history to an end. He is not an aloof God who doesn't know what it is like to live as a fleshly man. He lived as a man, was subject to temptation as we are, yet He never sinned. He was not worthy of death, but since He died on a cross He earned salvation for all who believe. He, as God, paid the penalty for your sin and mine. Jesus Christ is the righteous judge, He is incorruptible and cannot be bribed. He has earned the last word.

Note carefully the subject of verse 11.

> *And I beheld, and I heard the voice of many angels round about the throne and the beasts and the elders: and the number of them was ten thousand times ten thousand, and thousands of thousands:*

In the preceding verses we are told the number of the beasts, four, and the number of the elders, twenty four, so the number here is the number of angels around the throne. Ten thousand times ten thousand is one hundred million. Thousands of thousands is a limited, yet indefinite number. Any more than 9,999 would be ten thousand, so it appears that the greatest number this statement could represent is 9,999 X 9,999 or 99,980,001. The maximum number of angels in view here is therefore 199,980,001 although it could be less, but for the sake of argument let's round it to the nearest million, or two hundred million. It seems strange that God would give us a particular number of angels. He could create trillions of angels if He wanted, so why is the number given here, and why does it seem so small?

Earlier we have looked at the sending of the angels to gather the elect in Matthew 24:31, and Mark 13:27, and as we have discussed, the term *"heaven"* in these passages is not God's home but the first heaven, which is the atmosphere. We see in Psalm 50:3 that a fire will precede immediately in front of the Lord as He returns, so it logically follows that the angels will gather the elect and hold them aloft in the atmosphere, out of harm's way, as the earth is destroyed by fire.

This is not the same fire as is spoken of by Peter in 2 Peter 3:10 for that fire will completely destroy the earth. This fire will be to cleanse the world of the pollution of the last few thousand years, especially the Great Tribulation period itself. God will not want the elect to have access to computer hard drives full of pornography, nor to Church buildings, and temples full of idols. He will not want them to be able to watch videos full of Occult teachings, nor will He want them to be couch potatoes!

If these angels are built like men, and most biblical angels are, they have two arms with which to carry people aloft. This leaves us with the formula of two hundred million times two, for a total of four hundred million elect. It may be possible that the fire will not burn the entire earth at once, but will precede at a pace from the point where Jesus touches down. If that is the case then the angels could pick up people and then put them back down again after the fire passes by. They could then go elsewhere to save other individuals. This is a best-case scenario, and I am not sure there is enough Scripture to support it.

Maybe God in his grace will save more than four hundred million to go into the millennium, but let's assume that this is the best case scenario. Four hundred million elect, divided by the current world population of about seven billion, gives us a formula like this: 400,000,000/7,000,000,000 which can be simplified to 4/70 or 1/17.5. In other words any person left alive after the rapture of the Church will have a 1 in 17.5 chance of surviving the Great Tribulation. This is a 5.7 percent chance of survival! Any person who takes the mark of the Beast will have a zero percent chance of survival! If you are an unbeliever on the day of the rapture, the odds are greatly against you. My calculations, though speculative, are actually on the optimistic side, it could actually be much worse! Don't make a sucker's bet!

This is why the Bible tells us,

*For he saith, I have heard thee in a time accepted, and in the day of salvation have I succoured thee: **behold, now is the accepted time; behold, now is the day of salvation.** (2 Corinthians 6:2)*

In chapter six we see the seals of the scroll broken in sequence. The first seal is a man on a white horse who has a crown and a bow. Notice that he does not have an arrow with his bow. This is the Antichrist and he goes about conquering the earth by the use of peace, and the threat of war. His crown is given to him, likely by some sort of democratic process. This man is the chosen representative of the human race.

The second seal reveals a red horse, which takes peace from the earth. By this seal we know that the first seal represents peace, or at least a false peace. The rider of this horse has a great sword. The bow represents the threat of war, but the great sword represents the ability to make war and is logically followed by the third seal.

The third seal is a black horse, representing famine. Famine usually follows war as a logical result. Crops are burned during war, and food is taken by enemies as spoils of war. Today we have the additional threat of nuclear war. With large amounts of dust kicked up into the upper atmosphere the sunlight will be reduced and crops will fail. Add to this the nuclear fallout, and some crops will become radioactively contaminated, and poisonous!

Later on in Revelation chapter 6 the same language is used. This is a reference to the same event as those described in Joel 2:1-11, 3:15, and Matthew 24:29. The pillars of smoke in the earlier reference appear to describe either the Gog and Magog war or a nuclear exchange between nations during the Psalm 83 war. Perhaps both. The second is caused by a great shaking from God, during Armageddon, that not only affects the earth but also the sun, moon and even the stars. The cause of these events appears to be different, and the second is worse than the first.

In Joel 2:30 - 31 we see a very similar situation. Note that these signs occur BEFORE the Day of the Lord, and could even occur before the Rapture of the Church! If these signs occur before the Day of the Lord, the Tribulation, how much worse will the latter judgments be?

As we have seen, the book of Joel speaks of similar situations in three places. The question is *"Do these three references refer to one event, or are they references to separate events?"* The evidence is that this phenomenon will occur at least twice in the last days. Mistaking the first for the second can have fatal results!

*The earth shall quake before them; the heavens shall tremble: the sun and the moon shall be dark, and the stars shall withdraw their shining: And the LORD shall utter his voice before his army: for his camp is very great: for he is strong that executeth his word: **for the day of the LORD is great and very terrible**; and who can abide it? (Joel 2:10-11)*

*And I will shew wonders in the heavens and in the **earth, blood, and fire, and pillars of smoke. 31 The sun shall be turned into darkness, and the moon into blood, before the great and the terrible day of the LORD come.** And it shall come to pass, that whosoever shall call on the name of the LORD shall be delivered: for in mount Zion and in Jerusalem shall be deliverance, as the LORD hath said, and in the remnant whom the LORD shall call. (Joel 2:30-31)*

*Multitudes, multitudes in the valley of decision: **for the day of the LORD is near** in the valley of decision. **The sun and the moon shall be darkened, and the stars shall withdraw their shining.** The LORD also shall roar out of Zion, and utter his voice from Jerusalem; and the heavens and the earth shall shake: but the LORD will be the hope of his people, and the strength of the children of Israel. (Joel 3:14-16)*

*Immediately **after the tribulation of those days** shall the sun be darkened, and the moon shall not give her light, and the stars shall fall from heaven, and the powers of the heavens shall be shaken: (Matthew 24: 29)*

In Joel 2:10 we have a passage referring to *"Joel's army"*. The context is the return of Christ with His army. This army will be so invincible that weapons of war will not hurt them. This passage occurs late in the Great Tribulation period, not the beginning. This army is locusts, not men, and it could actually be a reference to the demonic locust army seen in Revelation 9, or it may be a literal plague of locusts that eat the crops, and cause famine. In verse 30 Joel skips back to a time before the Day of the Lord begins, when there will be a similar phenomenon with the sun darkened and the moon turned red like blood. In chapter 3 he advances forward in time to the battle of Armageddon in the valley of Jehoshaphat. This reference is a repeat of the events of 2:10, likely for emphasis. This event is the Day of the Lord, in contrast to verse 30, which is *before* the Day of the Lord. This is strong evidence that there will be a pseudo-tribulation before the real thing begins.

The voice from the midst of the four beasts, in Revelation 6:6, is Jesus Christ Himself. Here He tells us that the wages for a days work will buy a measure of wheat, roughly a quart (or a litre in metric). This is enough for an average day's food for one person. Three measures of barley would feed a family, though barley is a lower grade food usually reserved for animals.

The fourth seal is a pale horse, symbolizing death and Hell. As a result of the wars and famines occurring at this time, death will be everywhere. Simultaneously occurring with these events will be the mass murder of Christians worldwide. The Antichrist will be telling the people of the earth that the only thing standing between them, and an earthly Utopia, is the Christians and Jews.

This brings us to the fifth seal; The souls of those who have died for Jesus during the Tribulation are seen beneath the Altar. They cry to the Lord asking when He will avenge their blood on those who have killed them. This is not the Church age, nor are these Church age saints, for Christians are told to love, and pray for our enemies. Those who take the mark of the Beast will have no chance of forgiveness. Thus the call for vengeance. It will be a very different time than that which we have experienced to date, but it will be soon.

These souls, beneath the altar, are proof that the idea of "*soul sleep*" is in error. These souls, though separated from their bodies, are conscious, in Heaven, and able to communicate with God and other believers.

The sixth seal in verse 12 reveals a great earthquake that will shake the entire earth and even the heavens! Here again the sun is darkened and the moon appears as blood. This is the same phenomenon as that referred to by the prophet Joel in chapter three. The other passages in Joel will occur before the Great Tribulation period, while this event will occur near the end of that seven year period. People looking for general agreement in the Bible will not understand that the events of Joel 2:30-31 are not the same as the events of Revelation 6:12. Read the two passages carefully.

Joel's event occurs with pillars of smoke, BEFORE the Day of the Lord. If the Day of the Lord includes the entire Tribulation period then this must occur before Daniel's seven years begin, and possibly before the Rapture of the Church. Revelation 6:12 occurs fairly early during the Tribulation, and is followed by the stars falling to earth and the sky opening like a scroll.

At this point the mighty men of earth, the rich men and rulers, free men and slaves will hide in bomb shelters, and caves, from the Wrath of Jesus Christ. They will know who it is and why He has returned. To me this a strange placement of this event. It almost appears that the people will hide in caves and rocks, and then, when the worst doesn't happen, they begin to crawl out and to think that they might be able to fight God after all! They get stung by the locust plague but they do not die! They will think something like, *"If this is all God can do to us, then maybe we can actually fight Him and win!"* The truth is He's holding back!

Revelation chapter 7 is a parenthesis which introduces us to the one hundred and forty four thousand Jewish servants of God. Not only are these men of Hebrew descent, but we find out in chapter 14 that they are virgins. If you are not male, Jewish (Hebrew), or a virgin, you cannot be in this number. This is the only group of people who are supernaturally protected by God throughout the Great Tribulation period. The vast majority of believers during this period will die for their faith. The second group of Tribulation saints appears in verses 9 – 17, although we have already seen them in chapter 6:9–11. It would appear then that chapter 7 is a parenthesis which goes back in time to the beginning of the seven year tribulation period. This group of one hundred and forty four thousand witnesses is likely responsible for preaching the gospel to the second group which receives it in record numbers.

A side benefit of the diaspora to these Jewish witnesses is the fact that they have physical features and languages from the places where they spent their exile. There are Jews who look like Arabs. There are Jews who look Chinese. There are black Jews, not only from Ethiopia, but also South Africa, and likely from other locations in between. There are blond, blue eyed Jews from Europe, and I once met a South American Jew who looks like an Inca Indian! These Jewish witnesses will be able to blend in with the populations where they spent their exile, and where God will send them, to the point that they will be virtually invisible!

It follows, therefore, that the final return of the Israelites will not happen until very close to the Tribulation period. If the returning exiles were in Israel for more than a generation, the children born there would speak Hebrew as their first language and would speak any language with a Hebrew accent, negating any advantage they would have. These Jewish witnesses are all virgins, which would indicate that they are relatively young, yet at the rapture of the Church they will all be unbelievers. Again this indicates a very short time frame for these events to occur.

In Revelation 8:13 and 14:6 we have further evidence that the word "*heaven*" does not necessarily mean God's home. In both examples an angel flies in "*heaven*" but is speaking to the people of earth. The meaning of "*heaven*" in these verses is the atmosphere of earth, as it is in Genesis 1:20, Matthew 24:31, and Mark 13:27.

By the time of the mid point in the Tribulation, between the sixth and seventh trumpet judgments, one half of the human race has been killed. In Revelation 6:8 we see one quarter of the earth's inhabitants die during the wars at the beginning of the tribulation. Later in chapter 9:15 and 18, we see a third of the remnant killed at that time. These two figures do not include the number of saints killed by the Antichrist.

> *And the rest of the men which were not killed by these plagues yet repented not of the works of their hands, that they should not worship devils, and idols of gold, and silver, and brass, and stone, and of wood: which neither can see, nor hear, nor walk: (Revelation 9:20)*

The people who do not repent by this time will have been so totally deluded that even these events will not cause them to repent. This seems bizarre, until we remember that **it is their interpretation of these events that keeps them deluded.** The events described in the book of Revelation are so similar to fictitious events portrayed in science fiction movies that the earth's inhabitants will think they are undergoing an alien attack! They will know that it is Jesus Christ who is bringing the plagues on the earth, but they will be deluded into thinking that He is an alien, instead of recognizing that He is the Creator God who owns the earth.

> *And sware by him that liveth for ever and ever, who created heaven, and the things that therein are, and the earth, and the*

things that therein are, and the sea, and the things which are therein, ***that there should be time no longer:*** *But in the days of the voice of the seventh angel, when he shall begin to sound,* ***the mystery of God should be finished,*** *as he hath declared to his servants the prophets.* (Revelation 10:6 & 7)

Many scholars have stated that the angel here is saying that time itself will exist no longer. This is a result of not following through with the thought of these two verses. Verse 7 is actually continuing with the thought of verse 6. It is the time of the *"mystery of God"* which will be finished, not time itself! God will reveal Himself at this time! Woe to the inhabitants of the earth! If you have not been saved by the time you see Him you are lost!

We know that the eternal state is not *"existence without time"*, for later, describing the eternal state John tells us: *"In the midst of the street of it, and on either side of the river, was there the tree of life, which bare twelve manner of fruits, and yielded her fruit every* ***month:*** *and the leaves of the tree were for the healing of the nations."* (Rev. 22:2) The word *"month"* is a unit of time, and thus we are informed that eternity, for us, is *"time without end"*, and not *"existence without time"*.

The centre of the Tribulation period is a very busy time. One of the events that occurs during this time is the killing of the two witnesses in Revelation 11:1 – 13. In this parenthesis we see these two witnesses, having supernatural power, standing against the Antichrist in Jerusalem for 1230 days. (this is days, not years) During this time these two men are invincible and are able to kill those who come against them by merely speaking, and fire comes out of their mouths! At the end of their ministry the Antichrist overcomes and kills them. Here we have evidence that advanced technology is required for the End Times events, for verse 9 states *"And* ***they of the people and kindreds and tongues and nations shall see their dead bodies three days and an half,*** *and shall not suffer their dead bodies to be put in graves."* The people of earth will rejoice for three and a half days until they see these two men resurrected. The world will know the prophecies regarding these two men, and will set up web-cams, and TV cameras, to view their bodies, daring God to do something!

Until the age of satellites, TV networks, and the Internet it was impossible for people around the earth to witness a single event, but not any longer! After their resurrection these men will be raptured to Heaven and their ascent will be witnessed by the world.

Other events which occur around this time will include: the Antichrist's breaking of his covenant with Israel; his receiving of a fatal wound; the translation of the Ark of the Covenant to Heaven; and his setting himself up as God in the Jewish Temple. I expect that the Antichrist's resurrection will occur some time shortly before his victory over these two prophets. The world will think that his resurrection has been an example of the power of God. His victory over these two men will be viewed as proof of God's approval, so when his enemies are resurrected and raptured before their eyes it will cause a great confusion and fear throughout the world! How could God raise people so totally different as the Antichrist and the two prophets he has killed? Obviously the pagan idea that God is everything, or is in everything, will be taking a beating by this time. Very clearly there is more than one power at work here, and the power behind these two prophets is the greater!

The Antichrist's *"resurrection"* will be accomplished with one eye sightless, and one arm paralysed, as a result of his fatal wound (Zechariah 11:17). These two prophets of God, however, will be raised whole and will be seen to ascend out of sight! He will be the one claiming to have an inside track with God, and aliens, yet here his enemies have power over life and death! He will be totally upstaged by these two prophets and it will infuriate him! This would be the logical time for the Ark of the Covenant to be moved to Heaven. In his anger he will go to the Temple to destroy it, and when he gets there it will be gone!

Many have wondered where the ark of the covenant went, and I am not sure where it is today. It will likely resurface at some time prior to the rebuilding of the temple, and at some time it will be transferred to Heaven! It looks like verse 19 is giving the timing of this transfer to be some time around the ascension of the two prophets, probably to prevent its destruction at the hands of the Antichrist. As we go through the outline of the time of Jacob's trouble it is apparent that the Little Horn is not the one in control at all.

Throughout the Tribulation period God will be progressively showing more and more power. In His Word, He has stated that all power belongs to Him, but because of the idea of evolution, few believe Him. Instead of Jesus Christ, the world will choose the Beast as their leader, and in the process the world will be nearly destroyed by this man!

And the nations were angry, and thy wrath is come, and the time of the dead, that they should be judged, and that thou shouldest give reward unto thy servants the prophets, and to the saints, and them that fear thy name, small and great; and shouldest destroy them which destroy the earth. And the temple of God was opened in heaven, and there was seen in his temple the ark of his testament: and there were lightnings, and voices, and thunderings, and an earthquake, and great hail. (Revelation 11:18 & 19)

I find it interesting that in verse 18 it is the nations who are angry at the wrath of God! People tend to believe that their body belongs to them, and that they can do with it what they want. I remember saying that to my parents when I was a teenager, but I was wrong. In the same way, those who occupy certain bodies of land tend to think it belongs to them, or their nation, but it does not!

The world is angry when Christians state that God has a right to judge them, and they will be angry when God Himself comes in judgment over them. Another reason, which is not stated, is that many will actually believe they are following God when they kill the saints and set up a world government! When He turns and brings judgment upon them they will be flabbergasted! They thought they were serving Him! Well, actually, they weren't! They were serving Satan, who makes a close impersonation of God! Had they read their bibles they would have seen the difference.

Your body belongs to its Creator. It is only on loan to you, and can be removed from you whenever He decides to do so. If it really belonged to you, you would not have to answer to another and you would live forever. I know this, for no one wants to die, but you cannot will your body to live beyond your time. Your time is decided by another.

At the time that God is dealing in judgment with the Antichrist and his followers on earth, He will be rewarding his people in Heaven. This passage is parallel with Psalm 50:4 – 5 and is not a general judgment but only a time of rewards for the saints in heaven.

Chapters 12 and 13 appear to be another parenthesis, this time dealing with Israel, the devil, the Beast, and his mark. Chapter 13:3 & 12 indicate that the world will worship the Beast because his wound was healed.

The 144,000 witnesses appear again in chapter 14, in which they are first seen on mount Zion in Jerusalem, with Jesus, and then they are seen in Heaven. Some have speculated that this group will die and then make their entrance into Heaven. I do not see that in this passage. Jesus is physically with them on mount Zion, on earth. I know that this goes against the conventional wisdom that He will not return until he does so to rescue national Israel, but this is the time after the seventh angel sounds. Since the mystery of God will be over by this time, He can come and go as He pleases! There appears to be no gap between their presence on Zion and then the Heavenly scene. If they did die I think they would appear with the larger group of believers in verses 9-17. It would thus appear that these Jewish servants of God are raptured at the end of their ministry.

Immediately after the scene of Heaven we are introduced to the *"Gospel Angel"* who preaches the gospel throughout the earth's atmosphere. This appears to be the last chance for mankind, the last time the gospel is preached before God's ultimate judgment falls on the earth. The few who have not heard by this time will hear it now. Some claim that there is a difference between the "*Gospel of the Kingdom*" and the "*Gospel of Grace*". I do not think there is any difference, for only those who receive the Gospel of Grace will be allowed to enter into the Kingdom.

Chapter 15 introduces the final seven *"bowl"* judgments. These are the worst of the judgments for verse one states that *"in them is filled up the wrath of God"*. In chapter 16 they are poured out on the earth. These plagues are natural disasters that devastate the earth. Those who worship the earth will be confused, and likely blame the believers for these disasters. The truth is that it is they who have brought this upon the earth! Those who have taken the mark of the Beast or worshipped him are given painful sores. The oceans of the world cease to support life, and then the fresh water becomes like blood (poisonous and stinking). The fourth angel causes the sun to produce great heat and to scorch the population of the earth. This scorching will make *"global warming"* look like a cool winter's day. The fifth angel then pours out darkness on the earth, which combined with the heat will give men a taste of Hell.

The sixth angel dries up the Euphrates river to make way for the kings of the East. The original language speaks of the *"kings of the rising sun"* or the *"sun rising"* (Even at the Doors Blog, *"Is the way being prepared"*). Considering that Japan is known as the *"Land of the Rising Sun"* there can be no doubt that Japan will be included, but they will not be the only eastern army involved in Armageddon. At this point the Euphrates is Israel's northern border, and its drying up leaves Israel vulnerable to these armies. Of course Israel has already fled to the wilderness, so it appears that these armies are initially coming to fight the Antichrist, but I expect that he will convince them to turn and fight their common enemy, the Lord Jesus Christ.

In our scenario of a *"Pseudo-Armageddon"* we should expect that this event will occur more than once...

Since 1913, a series of dams have been built on the Euphrates river system in Turkey, Syria and Iraq. These dams do indeed have the ability to stop, or severely restrict the flow, of the Euphrates river, so that it could be crossed on foot or in vehicles, and I expect that it will be used for this purpose during the war of Gog and Magog. This will then result in the false interpretation that Revelation 16:12 has been fulfilled during that conflict.

The event described here in the book of Revelation is a supernatural event. This will occur as a direct result of the action of this angel and not because some dam worker, or a group of dam workers, pushes a button to stop the flow of the river. It appears that the combination of a prolonged three-and-one-half-year drought in 11:6, plus the Lord's judgment of excessive solar heat in 16:9 may have a direct effect on the flow of this river.

From the mouth of the false Prophet, the Antichrist, and the Devil now come three unclean spirits to gather the kings of the earth for the final battle. John describes them as looking like frogs. As I have stated elsewhere, John was not familiar with twentieth, and twenty first, century popular media ideas of aliens appearing as *"little green men"*, so to him they look like frogs. I suspect that these *"little green men"* will appear physically to the people of the earth, since it says they perform miracles. No doubt they will have other fallen angels about them to carry out the deception and perform the miracles. These miracles will convince the world rulers, and their followers, that they have supernatural alien beings on their side, who can guarantee a victory.

The seventh and last bowl judgment brings the return of Christ. Now, it doesn't actually say that this is His return, but it says that there will be the greatest earthquake the world has ever seen, Jerusalem will be divided into three sections, and the mountains and islands will disappear at this point. Elsewhere in Scripture we are told that the mountains will flee at the presence of the Lord. (Isaiah 64:1 & 3, Ezekiel 38:20, Nahum 1:5) It thus follows that this is His return, and it is accompanied by a hail storm of one hundred pound hail.

Verse 19 states that now God will remember *"Great Babylon"* and will give her the fierceness of the wine of His wrath. The fact that God *"remembers"* Babylon, should indicate to us that there was a time when He *"forgot"* about her, or set her aside. She has been set aside for a long time, but ultimately Babylon will pick-up where she left-off.

The Harlots of Revelation 17 & 18

These two chapters are probably two of the most contentious chapters in the book of Revelation, if not the whole bible. They are full of symbolism, yet make some very definite statements. This section presented some of the greatest challenges to me. If you take Babylon literally you can't take the seven mountains literally and vice-versa. I eventually had to come to the point that I took the passage literally, that Babylon is Babylon, and then the pieces started to come together. We need to read them in their entirety before we move on:

Revelation 17

1 And there came one of the seven angels which had the seven vials, and talked with me, saying unto me, Come hither; I will shew unto thee the judgment of the great whore that sitteth upon many waters: 2 With whom the kings of the earth have committed fornication, and the inhabitants of the earth have been made drunk with the wine of her fornication. 3 So he carried me away in the spirit into the wilderness: and I saw a woman sit upon a scarlet coloured beast, full of names of blasphemy, having seven heads and ten horns. 4 And the woman was arrayed in purple and scarlet colour, and decked with gold and precious stones and pearls, having a golden cup in her hand full of abominations and filthiness of her fornication: 5 And upon her forehead was a name written, MYSTERY, BABYLON THE GREAT, THE MOTHER OF HARLOTS AND ABOMINATIONS OF THE EARTH. 6 And I saw the woman drunken with the blood of the saints, and with the blood of the martyrs of Jesus: and when I saw her, I wondered with great admiration. *7 And the angel said unto me, Wherefore didst thou marvel? I will tell thee the mystery of the woman, and of the beast that carrieth her, which hath the seven heads and ten horns. 8 The beast that thou sawest was, and is not; and shall ascend out of the bottomless pit, and go into perdition: and they that dwell on the earth shall wonder, whose names were not written in the book of life from the foundation of the world, when they behold the beast that was, and is not, and yet is. 9 And here is the mind which hath wisdom. The seven heads are seven mountains, on which the woman sitteth. 10 And there are seven kings: five are fallen, and one is, and the other is not yet come; and when he cometh, he must continue a short space. 11 And the beast that was, and is not, even he is the eighth, and is of the seven, and goeth into perdition. 12 And the ten horns which thou sawest are ten kings, which have received no kingdom as yet; but receive power as kings one hour with the beast. 13 These have one mind, and shall give their power and strength unto the beast. 14 These shall make war with the Lamb, and the Lamb shall overcome them: for he is Lord of lords, and King of kings: and they that are with him are called, and chosen, and faithful. 15 And he saith unto me, The waters which thou sawest, where the whore sitteth, are peoples, and multitudes, and nations, and tongues. 16 And the ten horns which thou sawest upon the beast, these shall hate the whore, and shall make her desolate and naked, and shall eat her flesh, and burn her with fire. 17 For God hath put in their hearts to fulfil his will, and to agree, and give their kingdom unto the beast, until the words of God shall be fulfilled. 18 And the woman which thou sawest is that great city, which reigneth over the kings of the earth.*

Revelation 18

*1 And **after these things** I saw another angel come down from heaven, having great power; and the earth was lightened with his glory. 2 And he cried mightily with a strong voice,* *saying, Babylon the great is fallen, is fallen, and is become the habitation of devils, and the hold of every foul spirit, and a cage of every unclean and hateful bird. 3 For all nations have drunk of the wine of the wrath of her fornication, and the kings of the earth have committed fornication with her, and the merchants of the earth are waxed rich through the abundance of her delicacies. 4 And I heard another voice from heaven, saying, Come out of her, my people, that ye be not partakers of her sins, and that ye receive not of her plagues. 5 For her sins have reached unto heaven, and God hath remembered her iniquities. 6 Reward her even as she rewarded you, and double unto her double according to her works: in the cup which she hath filled fill to her double. 7 How much she hath glorified herself, and lived deliciously, so much torment and sorrow give her: for she saith in her heart, I sit a queen, and am no widow, and shall see no sorrow. 8 Therefore shall her plagues come in one day, death, and mourning, and famine; and she shall be utterly burned with fire: for strong is the Lord God who judgeth her. 9 And the kings of the earth, who have committed fornication and lived deliciously with her, shall bewail her, and lament for her, when they shall see the smoke of her burning, 10 Standing afar off for the fear of her torment, saying, Alas, alas, that great city Babylon, that mighty city! for in one hour is thy judgment come. 11 And the merchants of the earth shall weep and mourn over her; for no man buyeth their merchandise any more: 12 The merchandise of gold, and silver, and precious stones, and of pearls, and fine linen, and purple, and silk, and scarlet, and all thyine wood, and all manner vessels of ivory, and all manner vessels of most precious wood, and of brass, and iron, and marble, 13 And cinnamon, and odours, and ointments, and frankincense, and wine, and oil, and fine flour, and wheat, and beasts, and sheep, and horses, and chariots, and slaves, and souls of men. 14 And the fruits that thy soul lusted after are departed from thee, and all things which were dainty and goodly are departed from thee, and thou shalt find them no more at all. 15 The merchants of these things, which were made rich by her, shall stand afar off for the fear of her torment, weeping and wailing, 16 And saying, Alas, alas, that great city, that was clothed in fine linen, and purple, and scarlet, and decked with gold, and precious stones, and pearls! 17 For in one hour so great riches is come to nought. And every shipmaster, and all the company in ships, and sailors, and as many as trade by sea, stood afar off, 18 And cried when they saw the smoke of her burning, saying, What city is like unto this great city! 19 And they cast dust on their heads, and cried, weeping and wailing, saying, Alas, alas, that great city, wherein were made rich all that had ships in the sea by reason of her costliness! for in one hour is she made desolate. 20 Rejoice over her, thou heaven, and ye holy apostles and prophets; for God hath avenged you on her. 21 And a mighty angel took up a stone like a great millstone, and cast it into the sea, saying, Thus with violence shall that great city Babylon be thrown down, and shall be found no more at all. 22 And the voice of harpers, and musicians, and of pipers, and trumpeters, shall be heard no more at all in thee; and no craftsman, of whatsoever craft he be, shall be found any more in thee; and the sound of a millstone shall be heard no more at all in thee; 23 And the light of a candle shall shine no more at all in thee; and the voice of the bridegroom and of the bride shall be heard no more at all in thee: for thy merchants were the great men of the earth; for by thy sorceries were all nations deceived. 24 And in her was found the blood of prophets, and of saints, and of all that were slain upon the earth.*

At the outset let me state that I do not have a definitive answer to the riddle of Revelation 17 and 18, but I do have some thoughts which will give you something to ponder.

As we have discussed elsewhere, the phrase *"many waters"* is a reference to the people of the whole earth. While this *"Babylon"* is a literal city, she is also the base of a system that encompasses the entire earth. Remember that this book is prophetic, and futuristic. The entities described are not necessarily visible throughout all of history. When it describes a city that *"rules over the nations of the earth"*, it may actually be speaking in the future tense. This city may rule over the kings of the earth only during the last of the last days. Cities which have ruled over large parts of the earth, but not the entire globe, are not qualified.

There are several schools of thought regarding the identity of Babylon the Great, or Babylon the Harlot, in this passage. Some identify her as the World, Jerusalem, a future End Times religious system, Rome, and a future, rebuilt, literal city of Babylon.

If we are to be consistent with our literal/natural hermeneutic we must assume that Babylon is Babylon. Babylon was never destroyed in the manner that Jeremiah 50 and Isaiah 14 describe. Furthermore the king of Babylon is likened to be like Lucifer in Isaiah 14, which is likely a reference to the Antichrist. In fact the entire chapter seems to be another account of the Tribulation period. Verse 7 indicates a period of world peace, the millennium, which occurs after the events it describes.

This leaves us with several problems, one of which is the absence of seven mountains in this city. Another is the fact that today, Babylon is a mostly-empty city, partly rebuilt and partly still in ruins. The power and prestige of Revelation's Babylon reminds us of the power and prestige possessed by Rome today. I would submit to you that this is the same power and prestige, which will be transferred from Rome, and that one day soon Babylon will occupy the place on the world stage, that Rome occupies today.

Going back to our premise that there will be a pseudo-Tribulation period, shortly before the actual Tribulation begins, we find that there needs to be a surrogate *"Babylon"* destroyed during the "*decoy*" Tribulation period, in order to divert attention away from the real Babylon of these passages, and to make the appearance of fulfilled biblical prophecy.

Might I suggest that Rome fits the bill? Isn't it possible that Rome will be destroyed during one of the wars that precedes the Tribulation period, specifically the war of Gog and Magog? As more and more Muslim nations join the nuclear club, the possibility that one of them might use their nuclear capability against Rome becomes more likely. The bitterness over the Crusades of the Roman Catholic Church, during the period from 1095 to 1291, still resides in the hearts of many Muslims, not to mention many other religious and even secular groups. I would also suggest that it may be possible for the Vatican to be destroyed, while the Catholic Church herself would not. The surviving Bishops and Cardinals would be forced to relocate their headquarters, and I would speculate that they might chose Babylon.

When Rome is destroyed during a false Tribulation period, this will give many Protestants, and nominal Christians, the idea that this is the fulfillment of Revelation 17 and 18. This will likely occur before the true Tribulation and the Post-Tribbers will be saying *"I told you so, the rapture hasn't happened yet and here we are in the middle of the Tribulation"*. With Rome out of the way and the surviving Catholics so humbled, there will be nothing to stand in the way of world religious unity. Nothing except those pesky Christian literalists! The wars of Psalm 83, Isaiah 17:1, and Ezekiel 38 & 39 will be so bad it will be difficult to believe that things could actually get worse!

The religious system of the Roman Church actually has its roots in Babylon, so to relocate there would be a coming-home of sorts. This scenario is not possible today because of the Muslim presence in Iraq, but after two major military losses I would expect that many Muslims will be reevaluating their faith. Furthermore the Assyrian population of northern Iraq has a large number of Catholics among them. The current ecumenicism permeating much of the World would make the Iraqis receptive to the establishment of the headquarters of the World Church in their nation, plus the possibility of jobs and international prestige would also make them eager for such a move.

Having lost a large territory to Israel, with the accompanying loss of face, the relocation of the world-wide religious system to Babylon would give Iraq/Assyria a means of regaining the prestige it has lost.

This relocation of Rome to Babylon would also give Babylon a connection to seven "mountains", i.e. "The Seven Hills of Rome". It may be, however, that the seven mountains mentioned actually refer to the seven kingdoms that support the Antichrist and put him in power. They will also support the city of Babylon for a time, and perhaps name it as one of the capital cities of the Antichrist. The destruction of Rome would level the playing field, and encourage those religions who are reluctant to join the ecumenical movement, to participate. Such a scenario would encourage many Reformed Churches to think that Revelation 17 and 18 have been fulfilled, the Harlot has truly been done away with, and thus it is OK for them to join! Thinking the Harlot is defeated, they will actually be joining her. In the wake of a major nuclear war there will be tremendous pressure to form a world government.

At this point a word needs to be said about the use of the word "mountain". While it is very often used to denote land-forms, there is scriptural precedent for its use in denoting kingdoms. In Ezekiel 34:5 & 6 the sheep are scattered upon the mountains, which in this instance indicate the kingdoms of the earth. We see the same typology in Micah 4:1, 6:2, Nahum 3:18, and Habakkuk 3:6. In Daniel 2:35 the stone cut out without hands becomes the kingdom of God which crushes the kingdoms of the earth, and then becomes a mountain that fills the whole earth. It is thus a legitimate biblical interpretation to understand the mountains of Revelation 17:9 to be seven world kingdoms. This may refer to the seven of the ten kingdoms that resolutely support the Beast to the end.

On May 1, 2010 the *"Tea Party"* movement in the United States held a May Day rally at the Lincoln memorial in Washington DC. In attendance were several prominent *"Apostles"* of the New Apostolic Reformation movement including Dutch Sheets, Cindy Jacobs and Stacy Campbell. Of particular interest is the use of Seven Mountains terminology in this event. These people are telling us that Jesus can't return until they take over the *"Seven Mountains"* of society. One wonders if there is a connection of this group with the seven mountains of Revelation 17? At this point all I can say is that this movement is certainly worth watching. Don't listen to what they say without having your bible open in front of you. Their theology and eschatology are not biblically correct, but heavily based on subjective experiences, and lying signs and wonders.

If this movement gains steam, I would not be surprised to see them eventually set up their headquarters in Babylon, Iraq. I cannot say they will for certain, but this movement certainly bears careful scrutiny.

The word Babel (בבל) in Hebrew, actually means *"the gates of God"*, and is the word the Old Testament uses for both Babel and Babylon. The Question is, *"Which God"*? Today the ancient city of Babylon resides in Babil province in Iraq. The world-wide system of paganism had its origin in Babel and even today its practitioners would argue that their various religions are variations of the true faith. They claim *"there are many paths to God"*, in opposition to Jesus Christ who said *"I am **the way, the truth,** and **the life: no man cometh unto the Father, but by me"*** (John 14:6). Any Christian who claims that Jesus is *"A way to God"* has stepped off the narrow way, and is apostate. After the flood, man's rebellion against God began at Babel, and it looks like it may well wrap up there as well.

The reason I believe it will be a nuclear attack which will level Rome, and result in the move to Babylon, is because a chemical or biological attack would leave the city intact and allow it to be inhabited again after a short period of time. Since both Hiroshima and Nagasaki have been rebuilt and are inhabited today, it appears the extent of the disaster to Rome will be much greater than that which happened to these cities during World War 2. The move may also be initially viewed as temporary, to wait until the nuclear radiation dissipates to an acceptable level for human habitation once again in Rome. The bible, however, indicates that this move will be final.

The other possibility regarding Rome is that it could be destroyed in a meteor shower, or fire and brimstone from the sky, during the Gog and Magog war. When the armies of Gog and Magog are destroyed in a celestial bombardment, Ezekiel says that this same shower will affect "them that dwell carelessly in the isles", which could include Rome. (Eze. 39:6)

Why are there two chapters, Revelation 17 and 18, that appear to say much the same thing? Is it possible that there are actually two cities being described here? The similarity of the terminology appears to point to the same entity. Both are destroyed by God, since it is God who uses the ten kings to destroy her in 17, and in 18, God personally destroys Babylon. And the method of destruction in both chapters is fire. The name of the city in both chapters is the same "*Babylon the Great*".

On the other hand, Revelation 18 begins with the phrase "*After these things*", which seems to indicate another city is in view. Think about it! In chapter 17 Babylon is destroyed and chapter 18 says "After Babylon is destroyed, Babylon will be destroyed".

It occurs to me that if Babylon is the capital of the Beast's kingdom he will have to have a back-up city in mind to replace her. Could it be that chapter 18 is referring to his back-up capital city? Could the one city be a reference to the seven mountains of the ecumenical world church, led by the New Apostolic Reformation (in Babylon), and the other a reference to the seven mountains, or jabals, of Amman Jordan? Amman was originally built on seven mountains and was a Rome wannabe. If the Antichrist comes from Jordan why wouldn't he name his home town as a back-up capital? It is too early to say for certain, but this is a scenario that deserves further study.

In our scenario of a decoy Tribulation period we must expect a decoy Antichrist. Actually there will be three major false Antichrists, but the world, especially the Christian world, is expecting the one Antichrist to come from Rome, or at least one of the nations from the Roman Empire. What better way for the real Antichrist to deflect suspicion from himself, than for him to expose and defeat three Antichrists, including one from Rome? By defeating the enemies of God he will "*prove*" himself a "*friend*" of God and the

"Church". Christian Eschatologists have actually assisted the Antichrist by concentrating on the Beast himself while ignoring the three kings he will defeat. These three rulers are very significant, and are one way of identifying the real Antichrist.

The attack on Rome will likely be aimed at both the leader of the European Union, and the Roman Catholic Church. I think that prior to this disaster the European leader will have brokered some sort of peace agreement with Israel, and will have initiated some sort of bio-chip identity system. In short he will appear to fulfil many of the prophecies of the Antichrist. He may even be gay, as many prophecy teachers speculate, based on a misinterpretation of Daniel 11:37.

Regarding bio-chip identity systems, it is important to observe everything the Bible says about the mark of the Beast. In order for any bio-chip, or tattoo, to be identified as *"The mark of the Beast"* it will have to incorporate the logo (mark) of the Beast, or the name of the Beast, or his number, which is 666. If a government forces its citizens to take a tattoo or bio-chip which doesn't contain at least one of these items, it is not the mark of the Beast. I would still not agree to take such a mark, however, my body belongs to the Lord Jesus Christ, not to any man-made system, and as such only He can mark it.

> *And that no man might buy or sell, save he that had the mark, **or** the name of the beast, **or** the number of his name. (Revelation 13:17)*

A few years ago I noticed that both my wife's and my credit cards, though different accounts, had the same four digit number at the beginning of the account number. This seems to be part of an identity system that first identifies the type of card, then the rest of the number is your own personal number. I suspect that one, or perhaps all three, of the world rulers who the Antichrist defeats will have similar systems that will ultimately fail due to security breaches in the system.

The Antichrist, by prefixing your number with his own personal number, will be claiming to guarantee your own personal security, something he can't do in reality. It also appears, by the wording of Revelation 13:17, that he will give several different choices in the way the mark is administered. The more choice he can give the recipient the less chance there will be of opposition. Scanners can be designed to identify either a tattooed logo, a number, or an invisible bio-chip.

I do not know where the other two candidates for Antichrist's throne will be from, but I would suspect one will come from North America. Washington has been in the forefront in the race to build the *"New World Order"* for many years, and the world knows this. If a world leader were to defeat a North American *"Antichrist"*, it would certainly calm the fears of many.

I would suspect either Syria or Iraq is the place of origin of the third defeated king. I say this because of the current controversy over the idea of a Syrian/Assyrian Antichrist. As we have seen elsewhere, Assyria is Iraq, and Syria is Aram, in Syria. The two names are not synonymous, though they do have much in common. The following verse really sounds like the Antichrist, and it could be a reference to him, especially if he sets up his throne in Babylon. Is it possible that he will escape to Assyria, in northern Iraq, as his nation is destroyed in Asaph's war? Could he begin his reign as the king/president over the Muslim world from some place in Iraq?

> *And the LORD shall cause his glorious voice to be heard, and shall shew the lighting down of his arm, with the indignation of his anger, and with the flame of a devouring fire, with scattering, and tempest, and hailstones.* **For through the voice of the LORD shall the Assyrian be beaten down, which smote with a rod.** *(Isaiah 30:30, 31)*

As I read through the passage several times, it became apparent that this is indeed an End Times passage. As you will find elsewhere in this document, I do not believe the Antichrist will have Assyrian ancestry. I believe, though, that the city of Babylon will be one of his primary capital cities. Babylon was originally Chaldean and not Assyrian, but the Assyrians were the ones who came in and gave Babylon its prominence in the world. If one of the titles of the Antichrist is "*King of Babylon*", could he then be referred to as "*the Assyrian*", especially if Iraq is broken up before that time, and the remnant north of the Euphrates, is renamed Assyria?

> **Behold the land of the Chaldeans; this people was not, till the Assyrian founded it for them that dwell in the wilderness:** *they set up the towers thereof, they raised up the palaces thereof; and he brought it to ruin. (Isaiah 23:13)*

Adolf Hitler was actually born in Austria, yet he became the

German Chancellor. No one would question that he was German. I am Czech on my father's side, yet English on my mother's side, but I call myself a Canadian. It is possible to be an Israeli and an Arab at the same time. Jesus was the son of David on His mother's side, and the Son of God on his Father's side. Therefore it is equally possible for the Antichrist to claim more than one nationality at the same time. For instance, he could be an Edomite on his mother's side, and Assyrian on his father's side. He could be Arab on his father's side, Edomite on his mother's side, and be raised in Assyria, and thus an Assyrian by nationality. He could be born and raised somewhere else, and immigrate to Iraq, and thus be Assyrian by choice. The pool of nations from whence could come the Antichrist is rather broad, yet I think that as we continue we will be able to narrow it down considerably.

The Russian leader, who is killed during the war of Gog and Magog, could be one of the three kings, subdued at the hands of the Antichrist, or there may be another one of the ten from somewhere else. These are things that will have to wait until the appointed time for the world to know for sure. We do not know everything and so we'd best keep on watching, and comparing current events with the Scriptures.

Some have suggested that the woman and the beast are one and the same. This cannot be so because the destruction of the woman, Babylon, occurs prior to the destruction of the Beast. In chapter 17 it is the ten kings who destroy Babylon, and no doubt it will be with the Beast's permission. In chapter 18 the destruction of Babylon is at the hands of God Himself, and in chapter 19 the Beast is picked up bodily and thrown alive into the Lake of Fire. Again, the best explanation is that these are separate entities.

How can Babylon ride on Babylon? The implication of this passage is that the woman, Babylon, rides along with the Beast and gains power as he gains power. The two work together as a team, but once the Beast is done using the woman he will destroy her. She represents a threat to his power, much as Ernst Roehm was a threat to Hitler's power.

There is more evidence that God is not done with Babylon just yet. Zechariah speaks of an End Times event where something very evil, in the form of a woman, is moved to the land of Shinar, where Babylon is located. (Genesis 10:10, 11:2, Daniel 1:2) ;

And, behold, there was lifted up a talent of lead: and this is a woman that sitteth in the midst of the ephah. And he said, **This is wickedness.** *And he cast it into the midst of the ephah; and he cast the weight of lead upon the mouth thereof. Then lifted I up mine eyes, and looked, and, behold,* **there came out two women, and the wind was in their wings; for they had wings like the wings of a stork: and they lifted up the ephah between the earth and the heaven.** *Then said I to the angel that talked with me, Whither do these bear the ephah? And he said unto me,* **To build it an house in the land of Shinar: and it shall be established, and set there upon her own base.** *(Zechariah 5:7-11)*

The nature of prophecy is that it describes events that are in the future at the time of writing. It is impossible to understand these things without insight from God. That being said I think this passage is describing a movement back to Babylon. The thing that is being set *"upon her own base"*, the woman, is something that came from Babylon in the first place. Her base belongs to her and is already in Shinar, but her house has yet to be built there. She exists somewhere else and will be moved back to Babylon at the appropriate time. The fact that this woman is made of lead should show us that she is some sort of idol, or idolatrous system. I do not yet understand the significance, but the two women with wings are the only female angels mentioned in the Word of God.

Notice that in verse 7 of chapter 18 Babylon considers herself to be a Queen. Now, if she is a Queen, who does she consider to be her King? No doubt she considers herself to be the Queen, on earth, to God in Heaven. This relates to John's astonishment in verse 6 of chapter 17. Why would he be so astonished at the look of this woman? Simply, it is because she looks like the Church. This religious woman looks like the Church yet she is drunk with the blood of the saints, and martyrs, for Jesus. There will be many in her who claim to be Christians! When she preaches *"love"*, however, it is the *"love"* of a harlot. The true Church is a chaste virgin, made up of saved, repentant sinners, while this woman is a spiritual harlot who has prostituted herself throughout the earth, for money and power.

And he cried mightily with a strong voice, saying, Babylon the great is fallen, is fallen, and is become the habitation of devils, and the hold of every foul spirit, and a cage of every unclean and hateful bird. (Revelation 18:2)

In 18:2 we are told of the fate of the demons who assist the devil, and the Beast, to deceive the nations: they will be held prisoner in the city of Babylon during the millennial reign of Christ. Just as God has held captive a certain group of angels at the headwaters of the Euphrates river from the distant past until the Tribulation period itself. He is also able to lock away any number of fallen angels in any location He desires. That city will serve as a witness to God's judgment for those who inhabit the earth during the millennium.

Isaiah provides more insight regarding what is being said here. The term "*satyr*" is an ancient mythical animal and appears to be a reference to demons in both Isaiah 13:21 and 34:14. Both of these passages are describing the condition of an earthly place during the millennial reign of Christ. The first refers to Babylon, and the second refers to Edom. Either this Babylon is in Edom, or there are two Babylons in view here:

> (of Babylon*) But wild beasts of the desert shall lie there; and their houses shall be full of doleful creatures; and owls shall dwell there, and satyrs shall dance there. (Isaiah 13:21)*

> (of Edom*) The wild beasts of the desert shall also meet with the wild beasts of the island, and the satyr shall cry to his fellow; the screech owl also shall rest there, and find for herself a place of rest. (Isaiah 34:14)*

It is no coincidence then, that the marriage supper of the Lamb waits for the destruction of this woman in the early part of chapter 19. Heaven will rejoice at the destruction of this city, and whereas the earth rejoiced at the death of the two witnesses in 11:10, now it is time for Heaven to have a feast and rejoice because God has destroyed Babylon the Harlot!

In the middle of the chapter is a scene in Heaven where the bride is readied for the marriage supper. She is given clean linen to wear, which is the righteousness of saints, and comes from God, the Lord Jesus Christ. (Isaiah 64:6, Romans 3:10)

We are not given any details of the marriage supper, for the next thing we see is the armies of the Lord mounting horses and following Jesus back to earth to wrap up the Tribulation. Verses 11-

21 describe the final battle where Jesus will be victorious over the Beast, the false Prophet and their armies. A key detail in this passage regarding these two men is that they will not die a natural death on the earth. God is so angry with them that they are raptured, or snatched, and thrown bodily into the Lake of Fire. They do not receive a day of Judgment, or sentencing, nor do they spend time in Hell, but are immediately tossed physically into the Lake of Fire. One hundred percent of their armies are killed, and are not resurrected immediately, but wait one thousand years in Hell before they join their leaders in the Lake of Fire. This passage shows us that Hell and the Lake of Fire are not yet synonymous, although all those who go to Hell ultimately will end up in the Lake of Fire. Hell itself will be thrown into the Lake of Fire, so at that time Hell will be synonymous with the Lake of fire.

Notice that the armies of the Lord do not do the fighting in this battle. Jesus will subdue the earth by Himself, by the sword of His mouth (Isaiah 11:4, Rev. 19:15), and His armies will be witness to the power that He commands. I believe that Paul was referring to this power when he spoke of the End Times in 2 Timothy 3:5, *"Having a form of godliness, but denying the power thereof: from such turn away."* This is a reference to those who believe they are commissioned to create the kingdom of God on earth, through fleshly means. These ultimately will be those who populate Babylon, thinking they are serving God, yet in reality they will be creating the kingdom of the Antichrist. Their statement of faith may seem orthodox, but in reality they have abandoned the true God.

The Devil, at this point in chapter 20, will be locked up in the bottomless pit, where Appolyon and the demonic locusts had been, and there he waits until he is released for a short time at the end of the Millennium. The bottomless pit is neither Hell, nor the Lake of Fire, but some other spiritual prison. This incarceration will not change the Devil, for when he is released he will once again deceive the nations as before. The human race will not have changed either. After a thousand years of perfect rule by the Lord Jesus Christ, when they are given the opportunity to rebel they will do it again! The sinful nature is so ingrained in our flesh that even personal knowledge and experience of God will not stop our rebellion. When I say *"us"* I mean natural humanity, not those who have submitted to the Lordship of Jesus Christ, and to the salvation He offers.

As we have already seen, the first resurrection began with the resurrection of Christ, then continued with many Old Testament saints, and shall proceed at the Rapture of the Church. Now we see it again with the resurrection of the Tribulation saints in verses 4 and 5 of chapter 20. This is not a one-time-only event.

This chapter is the one part of the Bible that defines the length of the reign of Christ on earth. Six times the length of a thousand years is stated in this chapter. When God wants to emphasize something he usually repeats it once. When He really wants to emphasize something he repeats it twice, so what does this say about his repeating the same thing six times in this chapter? Do you think that He wants to emphasize that the reign of Christ on earth will be for one thousand literal years? If so how could he have done it better?

The thousand year reign does not mean that Christ's reign will end, but that at the end of the thousand years everything changes. This is the time of the final rebellion on earth, which leads to the end of this world, and the beginning of the eternal state. This is also the time of the resurrection of the lost, and Judgment day.

These last three chapters do not specifically state whether the saved, who come through the millennial reign will be transformed into supernatural bodies as are the Old and New Testament saints, or whether they will enter the eternal state with their fleshly bodies. Paul, however, does state that flesh and blood cannot inherit the kingdom of God, and I take this to mean that all the surviving saints will be transformed at this time in the same way as the Church at the Rapture:

> Now this I say, brethren, that flesh and blood cannot inherit the kingdom of God; neither doth corruption inherit incorruption. (1 Corinthians 15:50)

Following this is the description of the New Jerusalem that comes out of Heaven and settles on the New Earth. The size of the city is given as twelve thousand furlongs each, times length, width, and height. A furlong is defined as 220 yards or 201.168 meters. This equals 2,414.016 kilometres or exactly 1,500 miles. Now since this measurement is given as the height of that city, and outer space begins approximately 100 miles above the surface of the earth, we have the description of a city that will jut out into outer space by some 1,400 miles! Yes indeed, the Bible is a Space-Age book, make no mistake about it!

> For since the beginning of the world men have not heard,

nor perceived by the ear, neither hath the eye seen, O God, beside thee, what he hath prepared for him that waiteth for him. (Isaiah 64:4)

*But as it is written, **Eye hath not seen, nor ear heard, neither have entered into the heart of man, the things which God hath prepared for them that love him.** (1 Corinthians 2:9)*

Man has conceived of some pretty amazing things: airplanes, computers, Star Wars, Star Trek, Independence Day, the Apollo rockets, the Space Shuttle, etc. But man still has no idea of the good and amazing things God has planned for those who wait for Him, for those who receive His only begotten Son Jesus Christ!

While the description of that city is breathtaking, I think it would become boring, over long periods of time, if it were not for the God who resides there. Jesus Christ, and God the Father, are the center of that city and they provide light and life for all of its inhabitants. God, who is infinite, will never reveal everything of Himself to us, but there will always be some mystery to Him. Eternity with Him will be one constant pursuit of love, one eternal adventure the likes of which we cannot imagine today!

This book ends with a warning which is actually a quote from Moses:

For I testify unto every man that heareth the words of the prophecy of this book, If any man shall add unto these things, God shall add unto him the plagues that are written in this book: And if any man shall take away from the words of the book of this prophecy, God shall take away his part out of the book of life, and out of the holy city, and from the things which are written in this book. (Revelation 22:18-19)

Ye shall not add unto the word which I command you, neither shall ye diminish ought from it, that ye may keep the commandments of the LORD your God which I command you. (Deuteronomy 4:2)

Very clearly God did not mean that no books would be added to His word, when He spoke these words to Moses. What He was speaking of is the purity of the Word of God. We are not allowed to change the meaning of His word by either adding to or taking away from it. In recent years many changes have taken place in the new bible versions to the point that many of them are not bibles at all, but New-Age reinterpretations, much like the Talmud. This is precisely what God was talking about in these verses.

The bible is currently sixty six books, an unusual number for God to leave His word standing at. For God, the number of completion has always been seven, or multiples thereof. During the period between the testaments there was a period of over four hundred years where there was not a Word from the Lord, but that did not mean He was finished. Now there has been a period of almost two thousand years without a divinely inspired book. The plan of salvation is complete, and there is no need for any other book for the Church-age saints.

With such a massive destruction of the world-wide communications infrastructure during the last part of the Great Tribulation period, and the amazing exploits of the one hundred and forty four thousand Jewish witnesses, I would not be surprised to see some of those men write accounts of that time which will survive as warnings for the children born during the reign of Christ.

Please do not get me wrong. God is sovereign, and if He wishes His book to end at sixty six books, He is able to keep it at that number. I am just saying that with the frequent emphasis on the number seven throughout Scripture, it seems out of character for Him to leave it with a number indivisible by seven.

With prophecies in Daniel and Revelation telling us that God's servants will do *"exploits"* during the Tribulation it seems odd that the only record of these events would be verbal. With these people actually physically on the earth and reigning with Christ, perhaps a verbal warning from them in person, is all that is needed. It seems to me, however, that it is likely that God has planned for some of those men to write eye witness accounts which will be incorporated into Scripture.

We can add to this the evidence that the book of Genesis has eleven different sections which appear to have been written by eleven different authors. Each section ends with the words *"These are the generations of..."* These sections were likely originally written on clay tablets in some early form of writing, probably some form of pictograph characters, like Chinese. It appears that Moses was instrumental in developing the phonetic Hebrew alphabet and thus it is likely that he amalgamated those tablets into one book. Had each section been left as a book on its own, the Bible today would actually contain seventy six books, leaving only one space for an End Times book. (Assuming that the ultimate number of books will be seventy seven) It appears to me, therefore, that by amalgamating those eleven tablets into one book, God was making room for several books to be written at a much later date.

I am not adamant on this idea, it is merely speculation and a point of interest.

Please do not get me wrong. The standard for inclusion in the Bible is the same as always. The Holy Spirit is responsible for which books are included in the Bible, and ever shall be. It is not up to man but up to God. If the apostate End Times Church decides to add books that do not belong, God is able to destroy those versions, and authors! The book of Mormon will never be a part of the canon of Scripture, nor will any other book of "*Human Wisdom*".

References:

"Dispensational View of Theological Order: Why It Offends Covenant Theologians", Clough, Mr. Charles, The Pre-Trib Research Centre, accessed 10/06/2010, http://www.pre-trib.org/articles/view/dispensational-view-of-theological-order-why-it-offends-covenant-theologians

"Preliminary Critique of Contemporary Amillennialism", Craigen, Dr. Trevor, The Pre-Trib Research Centre, accessed 10/12/2009, http://www.pre-trib.org/articles/view/preliminary-critique-of-contemporary-amillennialism

"On the Last Times, the Antichrist, and the End of the World (English)", Ephraem, Mr. Pseudo, The Pre-Trib Research Center, accesssed 06/05/2010, http://www.pre-trib.org/articles/view/on-last-times-antichrist-and-end-of-world-english

"Hal Lindsey, Dominion Theology, and Anti-Semitism", Ice, Dr. Thomas, The Pre-Trib Research Center, accessed 03/05/2010, http://www.pre-trib.org/articles/view/hal-lindsey-dominion-theology-and-anti-semitism

"Historical Implications Of Allegorical Interpretation", Ice, Dr. Thomas, The Pre-Trib Research Center, accessed 12/05/2010,

http://www.pre-trib.org/articles/view/historical-implications-of-
allegorical-interpretation

"Literal vs. Allegorical Interpretation", Ice, Dr. Thomas, The Pre-Trib
Research Center, accessed 12/05/2010, http://www.pre-
trib.org/articles/view/literal-vs-allegorical-interpretation

"The Rapture in Pseudo-Ephraem", Ice, Dr. Thomas, The Pre-Trib
Research Center, accesssed 06/05/2010, http://www.pre-
trib.org/articles/view/rapture-in-pseudo-ephraem

"The Unscriptural Theologies Of Amillennialism And
Postmillennialism", Ice, Dr. Thomas, The Pre-Trib Research Center,
accesssed 29/04/2010, http://www.pre-
trib.org/articles/view/unscriptural-theologies-of-amillennialism-and-
postmillennialism

"What is the Identity of Babylon In Revelation 17-18?" Woods, Mr.
Andy, The Pre-Trib Research Center, accesssed 11/04/2010,
http://www.pre-trib.org/articles/view/what-is-identity-of-babylon-
in-revelation-17-18

All these and more can be found at: http://www.pre-
trib.org/articles, The Pre-Trib Research Center website, Special
thanks to Liberty University for making this resource available free
of charge.

"Is the way being prepared for the "kings of the east"?" Even at the
Doors Blog, March 26, 2009, Accessed 18/09/2010, from
http://www.evenatthedoors.com/blog/2009/04/01/is-the-way-
being-prepared-for-the-kings-of-the-east/

Six

Why A Millennium?

When they therefore were come together, they asked of him, saying, Lord, wilt thou at this time restore again the kingdom to Israel? And he said unto them, It is not for you to know the times or the seasons, which the Father hath put in his own power. (Acts 1:6-7)

When Jesus was raised from the dead the disciples asked Him if He was going to restore Israel at that time. I think they had in mind Daniel's seventy weeks, but did not understand that the gap of the Church age was next. The Church age was a mystery that had not been fully revealed in the Old Testament. His answer shows that He will one day restore Israel but that wasn't the concern of the early believers. He did not say that Israel was permanently cast away, but only that the time was not right for her restoration.

When a prophet speaketh in the name of the LORD, if the thing follow not, nor come to pass, that is the thing which the LORD hath not spoken, but the prophet hath spoken it presumptuously: thou shalt not be afraid of him. (Deuteronomy 18:22)

If prophecies in Scripture do not come to pass exactly as written we have evidence that either that particular part of Scripture was not written by God, the interpretation is incorrect, or the time is not right for its fulfillment. I am not holding Scripture up to an impossibly high standard, but am only proclaiming the standard that God Himself holds it up to. Those who say that prophecies are generally true are not really honouring God. For example, the Bible speaks of a time when the Lord Jesus Christ will reign with a "*rod of iron*" (Psalm 110:2, Isaiah 11:4, Jeremiah 10:16, Revelation 2:27,

219

12:5, 19:15). Amillennialists tell us that this speaks of today, and certainly it is true that God has the ultimate say as to where history is going, but if Jesus is reigning today He is rather permissive. Today many people get away with a lot of evil. When Jesus actually reigns, sin will be dealt with swiftly and harshly.

This is not all that Scripture says about prophets:

> *If there arise among you a prophet, or a dreamer of dreams, and giveth thee a sign or a wonder, And the sign or the wonder come to pass, whereof he spake unto thee, saying, Let us go after other gods, which thou hast not known, and let us serve them; Thou shalt not hearken unto the words of that prophet, or that dreamer of dreams: for the LORD your God proveth you, to know whether ye love the LORD your God with all your heart and with all your soul. (Deuteronomy 13:1-3)*

A prophet can actually be correct in a prediction of a future event and still be a false prophet. If that prophet leads people to another God besides the God of Scripture, he is a false prophet. The Bible itself actually predicts that there will be miracles performed in the last days that are deceptive. It thus follows that the resurrection of the Antichrist may actually be a genuine miracle!

What we are concerned with in this chapter is whether or not the bible actually predicts a one-thousand year reign of Christ. Are these prophecies just allegories, or must they stand the test that God Himself has laid out for us? The truth is that the Bible has been put together by the Holy Spirit, and He has the power to ensure that every prophecy will be ultimately fulfilled exactly as written.

The Hebrew prophets were not Greek in their outlook, and their prophecies, unless they state that something is *"like"* something else, are meant to be literally understood. Even if the man who wrote Scripture did not entirely understand what was meant, the ultimate author, God, had something specific to say. When the Bible says *"one thousand years"* it must mean one thousand years. If it were to mean *"a long period of time"* it would say *"many days"*, or *"many years"*. Indeed we see such language in other parts of Scripture, so if it is absent here it is because God is saying something specific. When we look at d.n.a. we see that the author is a God of infinite and meticulous precision. This is about the character of God.

So what of the prophecies of the millennium? Where are they found and what do they say? There are actually more prophecies of

Christ's second coming than there were for His first. Isaiah is full of prophecies of Christ's return. Lets look at a few of them:

> *1 And there shall come forth a rod out of the stem of Jesse, and a Branch shall grow out of his roots: 2 And the spirit of the LORD shall rest upon him, the spirit of wisdom and understanding, the spirit of counsel and might, the spirit of knowledge and of the fear of the LORD; 3 And shall make him of quick understanding in the fear of the LORD: and he shall not judge after the sight of his eyes, neither reprove after the hearing of his ears: 4 But with righteousness shall he judge the poor, and reprove with equity for the meek of the earth: and he shall smite the earth with the rod of his mouth, and with the breath of his lips shall he slay the wicked. 5 And righteousness shall be the girdle of his loins, and faithfulness the girdle of his reins. 6 The wolf also shall dwell with the lamb, and the leopard shall lie down with the kid; and the calf and the young lion and the fatling together; and a little child shall lead them.7 And the cow and the bear shall feed; their young ones shall lie down together: and the lion shall eat straw like the ox. 8 And the sucking child shall play on the hole of the asp, and the weaned child shall put his hand on the cockatrice' den. 9 They shall not hurt nor destroy in all my holy mountain: for the earth shall be full of the knowledge of the LORD, as the waters cover the sea. (Isaiah 11:1-9)*

This whole passage is about the return and reign of Christ. Jesus is the Branch of Jesse. Amillennialists try to tell us that Christ is reigning today. If He is, he is not doing a very good job, for we see evil growing around the globe, and seemingly in charge. Today we see nothing happening from this passage at all. The disparate animals we see listed here do not live in harmony. Nothing has changed from the day of Isaiah until today, except that a few more species of animals have become extinct. The term cockatrice in verse 8 appears to be some type of animal, or bird, which has gone extinct. This gives us evidence that Jesus will restore the world to its pre-flood conditions including some extinct species of animals.

Some might say that *"a cockatrice is a mythological animal so this passage must be spiritual, and not literal"*. The other animals are literal, however: wolves, lambs, leopards, cows, bears and asps are all actual animals, just as children are really people. I think a cockatrice was literal at one time, but has since become extinct.

This passage is describing a return to garden of Eden conditions for this planet. God has several purposes in doing this, one of which is to show His faithfulness. Isaiah chapter 11 demands an earthly reign of Christ, and so does chapter 19.

> *In that day shall there be a highway out of Egypt to Assyria, and the Assyrian shall come into Egypt, and the Egyptian into Assyria, and the Egyptians shall serve with the Assyrians. In that day shall Israel be the third with Egypt and with Assyria, even a blessing in the midst of the land: Whom the LORD of hosts shall bless, saying, Blessed be Egypt my people, and Assyria the work of my hands, and Israel mine inheritance. (Isaiah 19:23 - 25)*

This passage is not a symbolic-only passage. It speaks of a spiritual awakening in Egypt, Syria and Israel which has not yet happened. Yes there are a small number of Christians in each country, but this passage speaks of the entire population coming to Christ. In verse 20 we are told that God *"will send them a Saviour, and a great one, and he shall deliver them"*. Then we are told that after this they will build a road from Egypt through Israel to Assyria and there will be an Altar to the Lord in the midst of the land of Egypt. If there is no millennial reign this passage can't come true. If Jesus, the Saviour, returns, takes the Church to Heaven and immediately destroys the world, this passage can't be true! It would be a lie and doesn't belong in the Word of God! Isaiah 19 demands a literal, earthly reign of Christ!

> *But I had pity for mine holy name, which the house of Israel had profaned among the heathen, whither they went. Therefore say unto the house of Israel, Thus saith the Lord GOD; I do not this for your sakes, O house of Israel, but for mine holy name's sake, which ye have profaned among the heathen, whither ye went. And I will sanctify my great name, which was profaned among the heathen, which ye have profaned in the midst of them; and the heathen shall know that I am the LORD, saith the Lord GOD, when I shall be sanctified in you before their eyes. For I will take you from among the heathen, and gather you out of all countries, and will bring you into your own land. (Isaiah 36:21-24)*

Here in Isaiah 36:22 the Lord lays it out in no uncertain terms, that Israel can do nothing about the Lords plans. It is not about them but about Him! He will bring them out of the nations where they were scattered, for His own sake! This passage is not referring to the Church for the true Church of Jesus Christ never did profane His name among the Heathen! There is a false Church that does profane His name, but that is not in view here either, this is natural Israel.

3 For thou shalt break forth on the right hand and on the left; and thy seed shall inherit the Gentiles, and make the desolate cities to be inhabited. 4 Fear not; for thou shalt not be ashamed: neither be thou confounded; for thou shalt not be put to shame: for thou shalt forget the shame of thy youth, and shalt not remember the reproach of thy widowhood any more. 5 For thy Maker is thine husband; the LORD of hosts is his name; and thy Redeemer the Holy One of Israel; The God of the whole earth shall he be called. 6 For the LORD hath called thee as a woman forsaken and grieved in spirit, and a wife of youth, when thou wast refused, saith thy God. 7 For a small moment have I forsaken thee; but with great mercies will I gather thee. 8 In a little wrath I hid my face from thee for a moment; but with everlasting kindness will I have mercy on thee, saith the LORD thy Redeemer. 9 For this is as the waters of Noah unto me: for as I have sworn that the waters of Noah should no more go over the earth; so have I sworn that I would not be wroth with thee, nor rebuke thee. 10 For the mountains shall depart, and the hills be removed; but my kindness shall not depart from thee, neither shall the covenant of my peace be removed, saith the LORD that hath mercy on thee. 11 O thou afflicted, tossed with tempest, and not comforted, behold, I will lay thy stones with fair colours, and lay thy foundations with sapphires. 12 And I will make thy windows of agates, and thy gates of carbuncles, and all thy borders of pleasant stones. 13 And all thy children shall be taught of the LORD; and great shall be the peace of thy children. 14 In righteousness shalt thou be established: thou shalt be far from oppression; for thou shalt not fear: and from terror; for it shall not come near thee. 15 Behold, they shall surely gather together, but not by me: whosoever shall gather together against thee shall fall for thy sake. 16 Behold, I have created the smith that bloweth the coals in the fire, and that bringeth forth an instrument for his work; and I have created the waster to destroy. 17 No weapon that is formed against thee shall prosper; and every tongue that shall rise against thee in judgment thou shalt condemn. This is the heritage of the servants of the LORD, and their righteousness is of me, saith the LORD. (Isaiah 54:3-17)

In Isaiah 54 we have another prophetic passage pertaining to the earthly reign of Christ. In verse 4 we see that Israel shall inherit the Gentiles. The Church of Jesus Christ is largely Gentile. It would be nonsense to say the Gentiles shall inherit the Gentiles. The subject here is therefore the believing remnant of physical Israel, the descendants of Abraham through Jacob.

Verses 7 and 8 leave us with no doubt who is in view here. This is natural Israel, for the Lord never did forsake his Church! He hid his face from Israel, not the Church. The 2700 years they were dispersed will seem like a little moment in the light of eternity.

The reproach of her widowhood is a reference to the present day, when the Lord has set aside Israel until the fullness of the Gentiles shall come in. The 2700 years of Israel's banishment shall be a distant memory. Verses 9-12 seem to be a reference to the eternal state, but he returns to the millennium in verse 13.

Verse 15 can't be a reference to the eternal state, for enemies shall gather against Israel, yet in the eternal state there will be no war. This is a reference to the war of Revelation 20:7, at the end of the millennium, when Satan is released for a short time. Note the phrase *"but not by me"* in verse 15, indicating that this gathering is not the Judgment of God against Israel, during the Tribulation, but something else. Many passages, concerning the Great Tribulation period, specifically state that God is the one who will bring the nations against Israel, so this cannot be a reference to that event. Clearly then Isaiah 54 demands a literal reign of Christ on earth.

Also the sons of the stranger, that join themselves to the LORD, to serve him, and to love the name of the LORD, to be his servants, every one that keepeth the sabbath from polluting it, and taketh hold of my covenant; Even them will I bring to my holy mountain, and make them joyful in my house of prayer: their burnt offerings and their sacrifices shall be accepted upon mine altar; for mine house shall be called an

house of prayer for all people. The Lord GOD which gathereth
the outcasts of Israel saith, Yet will I gather others to him,
beside those that are gathered unto him. (Isaiah 56:6-8)

In Isaiah 56 we have another prophecy about the reign of Christ
on earth. Many today say that the Church is the *"Israel of God"*, but
if that is the case who are the *"sons of the stranger, that join*
themselves to the LORD"? Clearly these people are gentile believers
during Christ's reign on earth. In verse 7 we see that they will make
sacrifices and offerings upon the altar in the Temple, which shall be
accepted. This is not the earth in its eternal state for sacrifices will
not be made at that time. These sacrifices will be made during
Christ's reign on earth.

It is clear that the blood of bulls and goats cannot take away sin,
and never could (Hebrews 10:4). The Old Testament sacrifices were
prefigures of the one true sacrifice that was to come, the sacrifice of
Jesus Christ on the cross. With Jesus reigning on the earth, the
conditions of the garden of Eden will be restored and many people
will live as natural men throughout the entire millennium. Death
will be almost unheard of. No one will die of snake bites, and
animal attacks will be a distant memory. Sacrifices will be
reinstated to show people of that time what it was that Jesus did for
them on the cross.

And they shall build the old wastes, they shall raise up the
former desolations, and they shall repair the waste cities, the
desolations of many generations. And strangers shall stand
and feed your flocks, and the sons of the alien shall be your
plowmen and your vinedressers. But ye shall be named the
Priests of the LORD: men shall call you the Ministers of our
God: ye shall eat the riches of the Gentiles, and in their glory
shall ye boast yourselves. For your shame ye shall have
double; and for confusion they shall rejoice in their portion:
therefore in their land they shall possess the double:
everlasting joy shall be unto them. For I the LORD love
judgment, I hate robbery for burnt offering; and I will direct
their work in truth, and I will make an everlasting covenant
with them. And their seed shall be known among the Gentiles,
and their offspring among the people: all that see them shall
acknowledge them, that they are the seed which the LORD
hath blessed. (Isaiah 61:4-9)

In Isaiah 61:2 we have the prophet declaring the day of vengeance of our God, and in verse 4 we have the people of Zion rebuilding desolated cities. While it may initially appear that this is a reference to the early return of Israel, and the desolation is the result of over 2700 years of neglect, I believe these cities will become desolate again during the Great Tribulation and the Antichrist's persecution of Israel. In verses 5 and 6 we see that foreigners will work in Israel and the people of Israel will be called priests of God. This is not a reference to the Church but to national Israel. In the eternal earth everyone there will be a priest of God. Today the people of the earth still largely curse Israel, contrary to verse 9. Once again we see that the conditions portrayed here do not exist today and shall not exist during the eternal state. The only time where these conditions fit is during a time when Jesus reigns on earth. They may appear to fit, to an extent, during the peaceful interval between Asaph's war and the War of Gog and Magog, but that is not what is meant here.

In Isaiah 65 we have another prophecy of the earthly reign of Christ. Verse 20 tells us that there will no longer be children that die in their infancy. A person who dies at a hundred years old will be considered to have died as a child. We see that death, though rare, will still exist, so this can't be the eternal state. The book of Revelation tells us that death shall not be a concern in the eternal state

> "And God shall wipe away all tears from their eyes; and there shall be no more death, neither sorrow, nor crying, neither shall there be any more pain: for the former things are passed away." (Rev. 21:4)

In verse 25 we see other conditions that can't be said to have happened in our day. Wolves are a scourge to lambs today and lions do not eat straw. So we see conditions in this passage that do not currently exist and also that will not exist during the eternal state, thus Isaiah 65:20-25 demands an earthly reign of Christ. To say that these passages are allegorical is to mock the Word of God!

> There shall be no more thence an infant of days, nor an old man that hath not filled his days: for the child shall die an hundred years old; but the sinner being an hundred years old shall be accursed. And it shall come to pass, that before they call, I will answer; and while they are yet speaking, I will hear.

The wolf and the lamb shall feed together, and the lion shall eat straw like the bullock: and dust shall be the serpent's meat. They shall not hurt nor destroy in all my holy mountain, saith the LORD. (Isaiah 65:20-25)

Micah chapter 4 also speaks of the reign of Christ on earth...

1 But in the last days it shall come to pass, that the mountain of the house of the LORD shall be established in the top of the mountains, and it shall be exalted above the hills; and people shall flow unto it. 2 And many nations shall come, and say, Come, and let us go up to the mountain of the LORD, and to the house of the God of Jacob; and he will teach us of his ways, and we will walk in his paths: for the law shall go forth of Zion, and the word of the LORD from Jerusalem. 3 And he shall judge among many people, and rebuke strong nations afar off; and they shall beat their swords into plowshares, and their spears into pruninghooks: nation shall not lift up a sword against nation, neither shall they learn war any more. 4 But they shall sit every man under his vine and under his fig tree; and none shall make them afraid: for the mouth of the LORD of hosts hath spoken it. 5 For all people will walk every one in the name of his god, and we will walk in the name of the LORD our God for ever and ever. 6 In that day, saith the LORD, will I assemble her that halteth, and I will gather her that is driven out, and her that I have afflicted; 7 And I will make her that halted a remnant, and her that was cast far off a strong nation: and the LORD shall reign over them in mount Zion from henceforth, even for ever. (Micah 4:1-7)

First, note that the time frame of this passage is *"in the last days"*. The eternal state will have no *"last days"* so it can't be in view here. Jesus Himself is the one doing the teaching in verse 2. This passage is also contrasted with the eternal state by the fact that Jesus shall judge between nations. When we are all like Christ there will not be any need for the Lord to settle disputes between us. We also see that the first earth will not yet have been destroyed, for the people will use their weapons to make farm implements. There are references to the return of the Lord being accompanied by fire (Psalm 50:3), but I take it that it shall not be a complete destruction for the weapons will still exist. They can't beat swords into plowshares if they are blobs of melted metal. The fire referred to in Psalm 50 is judgment and destruction, a clean-up of the modern infrastructure, but not complete and absolute destruction of everything on earth. After the earth is destroyed by fire there will be nothing recognizable left of the old earth. Micah 4 demands a literal reign of Christ on the earth sometime before the eternal kingdom is established.

As we have discussed before, Amillennialists claim that Jesus Christ is reigning on the earth today. If this were the case it doesn't make any sense for God, the Father, to tell His son, "*The LORD said unto my Lord, Sit thou at my right hand, until I make thine enemies thy footstool.*" (Psalms 110:1) If the enemies of Jesus Christ are now His footstool, how come they appear to be running this planet?

The Bible states very plainly that Jesus is today sitting at the right hand of God the Father in Heaven. (Hebrews 10:12 & 13, Romans 8:34, Ephesians 1:20, Colossians 3:1, 1 Peter 3:22) Now it is true that God is able to confound the plans of His enemies and carry out His desired outcome, but it cannot be said that Christ is reigning with a rod of iron today. If He is reigning at all, it is in a rather permissive manner.   Once again we see the error of Augustinianism, and the allegorical method of Bible interpretation. The earth is under the sway of the evil one and the majority of humanity is following him. 2 Corinthians 4:4 states emphatically that Satan is the god of this world. He was defeated at the cross, but he has not been locked away just yet.

The Dominionist heresy today says that in order for Jesus Christ to reign on earth, the Church has to set up an earthly kingdom. That God depends on the Church to do His work. This is heresy, for Jesus Christ himself, the Holy Spirit, and God the Father will set up the kingdom on earth. Those who think they are setting up the kingdom of God on earth will actually be setting up the kingdom of the Antichrist! The armies of God who return with Him will not have to fight His battles, for He has the power to destroy every enemy Himself! He does not have to lift a finger, for one word will slay them! This is not allegorical language, it is the literal truth!

Jesus makes a statement in Matthew that would be a lie if there is no literal reign of Christ on earth:

> *Blessed are the meek: for they shall inherit the earth.* (Matthew 5:5)

Think about it. If the meek simply live and die, and then go to Heaven for all eternity, this statement of Jesus would be a lie! Jesus is making a promise here that His followers will indeed inherit the EARTH. We know that many of His followers lived in poverty and died as paupers and martyrs, throughout the entire Church age. Today many of His followers do not even make it into adulthood as Christians, and Christian children are put to death regularly in the Muslim and pagan world.

Jesus has made a promise to his followers that He fully intends to keep, exactly as promised! The meek of all the ages will indeed return to earth with Christ, and will reign here with Him! He will honour those who honour Him. You can bet your life that He will keep His promises!

> *Only let your conversation be as it becometh the gospel of Christ: that whether I come and see you, or else be absent, I may hear of your affairs, that ye stand fast in one spirit, with one mind striving together for the faith of the gospel; And in nothing terrified by your adversaries: which is to them an evident token of perdition, but to you of salvation, and that of God. (Philippians 1:27 & 28)*

Divine Mathematics

Peter, when speaking of the end-times and the return of Christ plainly stated that the return of Christ is directly related to Psalm 90 and the statement that a day with God is a thousand years.

> *3 Knowing this first, that there shall come in the last days scoffers, walking after their own lusts, 4 And saying, Where is the promise of his coming? for since the fathers fell asleep, all things continue as they were from the beginning of the creation. 8 But, beloved, be not ignorant of this one thing, that one day is with the Lord as a thousand years, and a thousand years as one day. (2 Peter 3:3,4,8)*

If a day with the Lord is as a thousand years, then it stands to reason that the seventh thousand years will be the Lord's Sabbath. Jesus claimed to be the Lord of the Sabbath. No doubt He meant literally the Sabbath day of the work week, but this was intended to be a picture of God's week of millennia. James when speaking of the Lord's return called Him the "*Lord of the Sabaoth*" (Sabbath).

> *3 Your gold and silver is cankered; and the rust of them shall be a witness against you, and shall eat your flesh as it were fire. Ye have heaped treasure together for the last days. 4 Behold, the hire of the labourers who have reaped down your fields, which is of you kept back by fraud, crieth: and the cries of them which have reaped are entered into the ears of the Lord of sabaoth. (James 5:3 & 4)*

Some have objected to me that the bible doesn't specifically say that the history of the earth will be one Holy week, or seven thousand years. Well, actually it does:

> *1 Let us therefore fear, lest a promise being left [us] of <u>entering into his rest</u>, any of you should seem to come short of it. 2 For to us was the gospel preached, as well as to them: but the word which they heard did not profit them, not being mixed with faith in them that heard [it]. 3 For we who have believed do enter into rest, as he said, As I have sworn in my wrath, if they shall enter into my rest: although the works were finished from the foundation of the world. 4 **<u>For he spoke in a certain place of the seventh [day] on this wise, And God rested the seventh day from all his works.</u>** 5 And in this [place] again, If they shall enter into my rest. 6 Seeing therefore it remaineth that some must enter into it, and they to whom it was first preached entered not because of unbelief: 7 (Again,<u> he limiteth a certain day</u>, saying in David, To-day, after so long a time; as it is said, To-day, if ye will hear his voice, harden not your hearts. 8 For if Jesus (Joshua) had given them rest, then he would not afterward have spoken of another day. 9 There remaineth therefore a rest to the people of God. 10 For he that hath entered into his rest, he also hath ceased from his own works, as God [did] from his.) (Hebrews 4:1-9)*

Very clearly, this passage is speaking of the millennial reign of Christ as being the seventh, or sabbath day. This is the Christian's day of rest! This passage has further implications for Christians who continue to gather on Sunday. Most Christian teachers tell us that we don't need to keep Old Testament laws unless they are repeated in the New. Here we have a clear New Testament repetition of

Moses' teaching on the Sabbath day, as found in Exodus 20:11. The setting aside of Sunday came from the pagan worship of the Sun god. There is no evidence of its use by the early Church until Constantine and the Council of Laodicea, some three hundred years after the resurrection of Christ! By keeping the first day of the week, instead of the seventh, we have destroyed the picture of earth's timeline, given to us by God in the garden of Eden!

> For the Son of man is <u>Lord</u> even <u>of the sabbath</u>. (Mat. 12:8, see also Mark 2:28 & Luke 6:5)

While Jesus is Lord of the whole week, the only day He ever specifically singled out as His day is the Sabbath!

James Ussher figured out part of the puzzle. He calculated that Jesus was born during the year 4000 of the earth's history. Was he exactly 100% correct? I do not know, but I think he is close to the truth. Jesus' birth was too close to the 4000 year point of earth's history to be mere coincidence. Whether Mr. Ussher may have been out a year or two, one way or the other, is immaterial. Perhaps he began His ministry at the 4,000 year mark, or perhaps the cross was at that point. We don't know for sure, but it's close.

What did Hosea say about the return of Messiah?

> 15 I will go and return to my place, till they acknowledge their offence, and seek my face: in their affliction they will seek me early.

> Chapter 6:1 Come, and let us return unto the LORD: for he hath torn, and he will heal us; he hath smitten, and he will bind us up. 2 After two days will he revive us: in the third day he will raise us up, and we shall live in his sight. 3 Then shall we know, if we follow on to know the LORD: his going forth is prepared as the morning; and he shall come unto us as the rain, as the latter and former rain unto the earth. (Hosea 5:15-6:3)

Here we have the Lord leaving Israel until they acknowledge their offense, and this acknowledgement will take place during their "affliction", or the Time of Jacob's Trouble. He left Israel forty days after the resurrection. They will seek Him early in the Tribulation after the Church is raptured. It is stated in 6:2 that He will revive them after two days. I think this *"two days"* is a reference to Psalm 90 again. Peter said so didn't he?(2 Peter 3:8) So we now have a total of six thousand years, plus the one thousand years of Revelation 20 makes a total of seven thousand years for fleshly man on earth.

Some might object that there is a gap approximately the length of the earthly lifetime of Jesus Christ in this calculation. For us human beings, one thousand and thirty three-or-so years, is good enough. I would say, however, that God is a God of precision. He gave very precise timelines for His first coming in the book of Daniel, and lays out some very specific time periods throughout the book of Revelation. It is uncharacteristic of Him to go from specific timelines to vague generalizations.

I cannot see this scenario being true unless God does something with the extra time of Christ's first coming. Could He count it as being a part of the Millennial reign? Jesus did not reign officially during His first coming, but he was in control of the situation. He did present Himself as king in Jerusalem, and Son of God. The Roman government proclaimed Him *"King of the Jews"* as they crucified Him. Jesus truly had every right to rule the earth from his birth until his death. Today he has even more right, but that's beside my point.

Could it be that God the Father will count Jesus' first coming as the first part of the Millennium? I do not know, but it fits.

It also fits with the scenario at the end of the book of Revelation. (Rev. 20:7-10) At that time Satan will be released and will deceive the nations once more. They will rebel against Jesus Christ, and His government, and come against Israel one last time. This time the battle will be over very quickly and will culminate with the destruction of this present earth.

Why would the people of earth rebel when they have seen a thousand years of perfect government? I think they will have the Bible, and will know that the earth is scheduled to be destroyed at the end of the millennial reign of Christ. They will love this planet just like their ancestors did, and will not want to see the end of it. They will look at a thousand years of work they have done, and the amazing cities, and technology, they have built, and long to save it. I think Satan will convince them that they can save the planet if they take over its government before the thousand years are up. I also think it's possible that by the time they do rebel, the thousand years will already be over, it just will not appear so to them, because it will be something like 967 years since the end of the Tribulation.

As I see it, this is the best scenario that allows for exactly a seven thousand year earth time-line, given that we are already beyond the six thousand year point of earth's history.

As I was telling my twelve year old son about this theory, he pointed out to me that Revelation 20:1 says that Satan will be bound for a thousand years. Now we know that Satan was not bound during Christ's first coming, and therefore he must be bound a thousand years from the time of Christ's return. It appears that I may have been wrong, unless the binding of Satan is simply generally for the extent of the reign of Christ, approximately 1,000 years. We must be willing to allow Scripture to correct us. For this reason you need to check out everything I have said in this work, by the Scriptures.

Another possibility is that God may ignore the time consumed by the first coming and not count it as part of the earth's total time line, or more likely, our calendars are so inaccurate that we are further along than we thought. The truth is that we really do not know for sure. Again, I am merely speculating here for interest's sake, and am not adamant either way.

Another thing we have not gotten into is the fact that biblical years are not exactly the same as the modern western calendar. Hebrew years have only 360 days as opposed to our 365 days. They do add a *"leap month"* periodically, and so over time I believe the difference is negligible. Nevertheless, it is impossible to calculate the exact day that Jesus will return, until the signs given in the books of Daniel and Revelation are observed, and that will not happen until after the born-again Church is removed. (The Jewish Calendar - Structure)

We have covered it before, but it bears repeating in this chapter, that when God wants to emphasize something He repeats it. Jesus often used *"verily, verily"* or *"truly, truly"* when emphasizing a point. The one attribute that God emphasizes the most is His Holiness, which is repeated three times (Isaiah 6:3, Rev. 4:8). So how do we understand it then when in one chapter of the Bible, Revelation 20, God states SIX TIMES that the reign of Christ will be for a thousand year period? I would say that it looks to me like He is emphasizing the time period will be literally one thousand years.

Is it possible that God could wait longer than a full six thousand years? God is sovereign, and I believe He has written His book in such a way that if the human race were to repent, He could delay judgment for a generation or so, as He did with Nineveh. I do not believe this will happen, however, as the world seems to be rapidly heading for a show-down. The time is rapidly approaching that if there is no direct intervention by God, the human race will destroy itself.

Shortly before His ascension Jesus spoke about the End Times and stated that the time has been determined by the Father. (Acts 1:7) I believe that the Lord has given us clues in His word, but no direct statement about the timing of His return, and just like the early disciples who did not understand the first coming, many today do not study, or care about, His second coming.

Is it possible that I may be wrong? Perhaps. All the Lord has to do to prove me wrong is to delay His second coming a lifetime beyond two thousand years after the ascension. If it was He who has led me to the conclusions found in this book then I do not think He would do that. It is up to Him. Now Hosea said the Lord would return *"AFTER two days"*, not *"IN two days"*, nevertheless since His coming in that context is for Israel, his coming for the Church, at the rapture, could still occur shortly before the two days are over, but must occur at least seven years before the second coming.

References

"*The Jewish Calendar - Structure*", Jewish Heritage Online Magazine, Accessed   25/08/2010, http://www.jhorn.com/calendar/structure.html

Seven

The Case Against Jordan

*For my sword shall be bathed in heaven: behold, it shall come down upon **Idumea**, and upon **the people of my curse**, to Judgment. (Isaiah 34:5)*

Most prophecy scholars, when asked, *"Where will the Antichrist come from?"* will reply *"Rome"*, or at least one of the countries occupied by Rome during the days of the Roman Empire. Tim LaHaye believes he will come from Romania, as he shows in his movie series *"Left Behind"*. There is some logic to his reasoning, since the Romanian language is considered to be the modern development of the original Latin language of Rome. Others, such as Grant Jeffrey, believe he will be Jewish. (Prince of Darkness, p. 217)

The idea that the Antichrist will come from a Jewish family, comes from Jesus' statement; *"I am come in my Father's name, and ye receive me not: if another shall come in his own name, him ye will receive."* (John 5:43). The reasoning is that Israel will only accept a Jewish Messiah, and since they accept the Antichrist as Messiah he must be Jewish. This is a wrong interpretation, which has resulted in much suffering of the Jewish people throughout history, and is also related to the subject of this chapter. Many have pointed out that Scripture does not say that Israel will accept the Antichrist as messiah, but only that they sign a covenant with him. Considering that two thirds of Israel will die during the Tribulation period, it may be that this two thirds will accept the Antichrist as messiah, although some may die at his hands for preaching Christ.

*And it shall come to pass, that in all the land, saith the LORD, **two parts therein shall be cut off and die; but the third shall be left therein.** (Zechariah 13:8)*

Jeffrey also notes that the term "*God of his fathers*" (Dan.11:37) is usually a reference to Jewish people. I respectfully disagree: If his family served one monotheistic god for many centuries, even a pagan god, then it could be said of their god that he was "*the God of his fathers*". This chapter will discuss how it might be possible for some of Israel to accept a gentile messiah.

The reasoning for the Roman answers is based on one verse found in the book of Daniel:

> *And after threescore and two weeks shall Messiah be cut off, but not for himself:* **and the people of the prince that shall come shall destroy the city and the sanctuary;** *and the end thereof shall be with a flood, and unto the end of the war desolations are determined.* (*Daniel 9:26*)

Since "*the prince that shall come*" is the Antichrist, and since Rome destroyed Jerusalem in 70 AD it is simple really, doesn't it mean that a descendant of the Romans will become the Antichrist? Well, hold on a minute. It is true that the armies of Rome did destroy the buildings and inhabitants of Jerusalem in 70 AD, and again in 135 AD, but is this what God was referring to? Could he have been referring to another, somewhat obscure yet related, event?

It is a well known fact that Rome had more than merely ethnic Romans, or even Italians, in her army (see Acts 22:28). Italy did not have enough manpower to subjugate the entire Empire without help. The question is, who was present when Jerusalem was destroyed? Which nationalities participated in the destruction of Jerusalem? Which people group was Daniel referring to? Is this the only clue that Scripture gives us as to the nationality of the Antichrist?

Since the destruction of Jerusalem is not contained within Scripture we need to look at other documents. The most important is the writings of a first century Jewish historian by the name of Flavius Josephus. Josephus was in Jerusalem before the fall, and was captured by the Romans in 67 AD. Subsequently released, it appears that he played a role in negotiations between the Jews and Romans. As an eyewitness of the destruction of Jerusalem, his account carries special weight.

I began searching through Josephus' "*The Jewish War*", initially attempting to find out which armies had accompanied the Romans in their attack on Jerusalem. First I found that when Nero sent General Vespasian to subdue Jerusalem, he first went to Syria to collect armies there and sent his son Titus to Egypt to collect two divisions there:

"So Vespasian sent his son Titus from Achaia, where he had been with Nero, to Alexandria, to bring back with him from thence the fifth and the tenth legions, while he himself, when he had passed over the Hellespont, came by land into **Syria**, where he gathered together the Roman forces, **with a considerable number of auxiliaries from the kings in that neighbourhood.**" (Josephus, Book 3, chapter 1)

So we see that there were a considerable number of soldiers with various backgrounds at the siege of Jerusalem. We are not told who the auxiliaries of the local kings were. But we can surmise that kings in the area of Syria would be first Syrians, and then Assyrians and Chaldeans (Iraqis), Lebanese, and possibly Medes, (Kurds) and Persians (Iranians). Titus picked up two legions from Alexandria Egypt, which likely contained Egyptians, Amalekites, and perhaps some Ishmaelite Arabs.

This gives us a wide pool of nations, from whence could come the Antichrist, but is this the entire story? As I searched through Josephus' account I found a rather interesting event occurred shortly before the Romans arrived in Israel. I say *"interesting"* but the account is also very tragic. In Josephus' *"The Jewish War"* Book 4 chapters 4, 5 and 6, we find an account of a confrontation between the Idumeans and the men of Jerusalem.

The story reaches a climax with the Idumeans being let into the city at night, by collaborators among the Zealots, and a massacre ensuing. First the Idumeans killed eight thousand five hundred men in the Temple itself, and then they left the Temple and went throughout the city killing another twelve thousand people (Josephus, book 4, chapter 5, sections 1 & 2).

Josephus makes special mention of the fate of the High Priest Ananus and his deputy Jesus. The Idumeans set up a special court to try these two men, and when the jury failed to convict them, they went ahead and killed them anyway.

Josephus' analysis of this event is that the killing of Ananus, and his deputy Jesus, was the beginning of the destruction of Jerusalem, for these men had the skills to negotiate a surrender with Rome, and the wisdom to know that Rome couldn't be defeated. The deaths of these two men left the Zealots in charge of Jerusalem, who were so full of hate towards the Romans that they were willing to sacrifice the entire city, and its inhabitants, in defiance of Rome.

"I should not mistake if I said that **the death of Ananus was the beginning of the destruction of the city, and that from this very day may be dated the overthrow of her wall, and the ruin of her affairs,** whereon they saw their high priest, and the procurer of their preservation, slain in the midst of their city. He was on other accounts also a venerable, and a very just man; and besides the grandeur of that nobility, and dignity, and honor of which he was possessed, he had been a lover of a kind of parity, even with regard to the meanest of the people; he was a prodigious lover of liberty, and an admirer of a democracy in government; and did ever prefer the public welfare before his own advantage, and preferred peace above all things; for **he was thoroughly sensible that the Romans were not to be conquered. He also foresaw that of necessity a war would follow, and that unless the Jews made up matters with them very dexterously, they would be destroyed;** to say all in a word, if Ananus had survived, they had certainly compounded matters; for he was a shrewd man in speaking and persuading the people, and had already gotten the mastery of those that opposed his designs, or were for the war. And the Jews had then put abundance of delays in the way of the Romans, if they had had such a general as he was. **Jesus was also joined with him; and although he was inferior to him upon the comparison, he was superior to the rest;** and I cannot but think that it was because God had doomed this city to destruction, as a polluted city, and was resolved to purge his sanctuary by fire, that he cut off these their great defenders and well-wishers, while those that a little before had worn the sacred garments, and had presided over the public worship; and had been esteemed venerable by those that dwelt on the whole habitable earth when they came into our city, were cast out naked, and seen to be the food of dogs and wild beasts. And I cannot but imagine that virtue itself groaned at these men's case, and lamented that she was here so terribly conquered by wickedness. And this at last was the end of Ananus and Jesus." (Josephus, The Jewish War, Book 4, chapter 5, Section 2)

So, according to Josephus, the Idumeans began, or were responsible for, the destruction of Jerusalem. I am amazed that I have rarely heard this passage quoted by prophecy scholars, or preachers. Surely such a significant event shouldn't be ignored? As Christians we do not accept Josephus' writings as inspired by God, nevertheless this is eye-witness history. Did God, in Daniel 9:26, intend to point to the people who finished the destruction of Jerusalem, or to those who began it? Wasn't the Temple defiled by the murder of 8,500 men within, and considered already destroyed by God, even before the Romans arrived? Did He simply intend to hint that one of the groups represented would ultimately bring forth the Antichrist? Did He say anything else to give us clues as to the identity of this enigmatic person? Who were the Idumeans?

The Idumeans were the descendants of Jacob's twin brother Esau. Originally Esau's descendants were known as the nation of Edom. Idumea is simply the Greek form of Edom. Esau was hairy and a red colour when he was born and so his name means "hairy" and Edom means "red". Red actually stood for the bowl of red stew that he bought from his brother Jacob, in exchange for his birthright. Since Esau was a child of promise, and the older brother, older by a few seconds, he was the natural heir of His father's possessions, and God's promises to Abraham.

Because Esau was an earthly, carnal man, God intended from the beginning, to pass the inheritance on to Jacob (Genesis 25:23). Ultimately Jacob tricked his father into giving him the greater blessing, the one reserved for the older son. Initially angry with his brother, Esau eventually forgave him, however it appears that there was a small seed of resentment left over, which was passed on to his descendants. This small seed eventually grew into the full-blown hatred which exists today between the Palestinians/Arabs and Israel.

After Israel was taken into captivity the Edomites moved into their territory. The area of Idumea during the time of Christ took in a large part of southern Israelite territory of Judah. Later, after the second Roman destruction of Jerusalem in 135 AD the Idumeans moved into large areas of Israel, where they mixed in with the other inhabitants of the area. (Israelestine, p. 99)(Kinsella, Obadiah's Indictment) Today Esau's descendants can be found primarily in Jordan and among the Palestinians, though like everyone else, some have moved as far as Europe and North America.

In the Bible, the descendants of Esau are referred to with different terms: Sometimes it is with reference to a place, like Bozrah, which is a region in the area of mount Seir, or mount Seir itself, the major mountain in the land of Edom . Sometimes it is referred to as Teman, as in *"Eliphaz the Temanite"* of the book of Job. Teman was a grandson of Esau, and became one of the patriarchs of Edom.

The book of Job appears to have been written by, and has as its subject, a descendant of Esau. This book is about a righteous Edomite, who is in Heaven today. This is important, for it shows God's love for all people. According to Revelation 5:9, God intends to save people out of *"every kindred, and tongue, and people, and nation;"* This would naturally include the family, and nation, of the Antichrist himself!

As we have seen above, God loves all individuals and died for the entire human race, yet there is one nation that God states he hates. It is not Rome, nor Germany, nor France, England or China, as evil as those nations have been. It is the nation that is most closely related to Israel. The nation founded by Jacob's brother Esau.

> *"I have loved you, saith the LORD. Yet ye say, Wherein hast thou loved us? Was not Esau Jacob's brother? saith the LORD: yet I loved Jacob, **And I hated Esau**, and laid his mountains and his heritage waste for the dragons of the wilderness."* (Malachi 1:2 & 3)

As you read this passage you will see that he is not referring to the individuals Jacob and Esau, but to the nations they founded. It does not refer to all the individuals of each nation either, for some of Jacob's descendants will end up in the Lake of Fire, and some of Esau's descendants will end up in Heaven.

This is not all that God has to say against the nation founded by Esau. As you go through this passage you will see that while God had already laid Esau's mountains waste, He states that Esau will one day rebuild and He (God) will destroy them again. Look at what He says next; *"Whereas Edom saith, We are impoverished, but we will return and build the desolate places; thus saith the LORD of hosts, **They shall build, but I will throw down; and they shall call them**, The border of wickedness, and, **The people against whom the***

LORD hath indignation for ever."

Ask yourself, *"Is this the way the world remembers the nation of Edom today?"* No, I don't think so. Today most people, if they even know who Edom is, really probably do not have any opinion one way or the other, though some actually sympathize with them. But let me ask you: Why would God be indignant against this one nation for ever? Germany has, so far, killed more Jews than any other nation, yet Germany does not suffer the indignation of God forever.

Could it be because the nation of Edom will ultimately produce the man known as the Antichrist? I think so, and I think God, who sees all history at once, knew it when He rejected Esau, and alluded to it when Malachi wrote his book. At that time there will be the largest persecution against the Hebrew people the world has ever seen, dwarfing the German holocaust of the Jews, and Edom will be at its lead!

> *Rejoice and be glad, O daughter of Edom, that dwellest in the land of Uz; the cup also shall pass through unto thee: thou shalt be drunken, and shalt make thyself naked.* **The punishment of thine iniquity is accomplished, O daughter of Zion; he will no more carry thee away into captivity: he will visit thine iniquity, O daughter of Edom; he will discover thy sins.** *(Lamentations 4:21 & 22)*

In this passage from the book of Lamentations notice that the ending of the punishment of Israel, coincides with the beginning of punishment for Edom. Israel's punishment has not ended yet. It will end during the second three and one half years of the Tribulation period. This fact places the fulfilment of this prophecy at the end of the Great Tribulation. Backing up to the beginning of the passage, the "cup" mentioned is a reference to God's wrath, but if the Tribulation period is God's wrath against the whole human race, why does He single out Edom for special treatment?

A Small People

Concerning the Little Horn (the Antichrist), the angel told Daniel...

And after the league made with him he shall work

*deceitfully: for he shall come up, and **shall become strong with a small people**. (Daniel 11:23)*

Some might be tempted to think that Israel is referred to here, since Israel is a relatively small nation. If we look for the answer in Scripture we might be surprised that another nation is being pointed to. Please notice the similarity of terminology with the following:

*The vision of Obadiah. Thus saith the Lord GOD **concerning Edom;** We have heard a rumour from the LORD, and an ambassador is sent among the heathen, Arise ye, and let us rise up against her in battle. **Behold, I have made thee small among the heathen**: thou art greatly despised. (Obadiah 1:1 & 2)*

*But **I have made Esau bare**, I have uncovered his secret places, and he shall not be able to hide himself: his seed is spoiled, and his brethren, and his neighbours, and he is not. Leave thy fatherless children, I will preserve them alive; and let thy widows trust in me. For thus saith the LORD; Behold, **they whose judgment was not to drink of the cup have assuredly drunken; and art thou he that shall altogether go unpunished? thou shalt not go unpunished, but thou shalt surely drink of it.** For I have sworn by myself, saith the LORD, that **Bozrah shall become a desolation, a reproach, a waste, and a curse; and all the cities thereof shall be perpetual wastes.** I have heard a rumour from the LORD, and an ambassador is sent unto the heathen, saying, Gather ye together, and come against her, and rise up to the battle. **For, lo, I will make thee small among the heathen,** and despised among men. (Jeremiah 49:10-15)*

It appears then, that Antichrist will use the nation of Edom as his power base. Edom is the nation that is "*small among the heathen*". It is highly likely that he will actually come from there, or at least from the Jordanian diaspora. They will know him as one of their own, though it may be possible that he could be born in Palestine, Europe or even America. At least part of his family will be Edomite, and it will be known. Note though that today it is Israel that is despised among the nations. Edom's day has not yet arrived.

The only other place I have found a nation spoken of as having been made small by the Lord, is the following:

> *But now the LORD hath spoken, saying, Within three years, as the years of an hireling, and the glory of <u>Moab</u> shall be contemned, with all that great multitude; and* **the remnant shall be very small and feeble** *(Isaiah 16:14)*

Interestingly, Moab, one of the two nations that came from the incestuous relationship of Lot with his daughters, has allied itself with Edom for a long time. So has the other one, Ammon, by the way. These three nations occupied the territory of modern day Jordan, and are spoken of together several times in Scripture. A very pertinent prophecy of the End Times concerns these nations and the Antichrist:

> *He shall enter also into the glorious land, and many countries shall be overthrown:* **but these shall escape out of his hand, even Edom, and Moab, and the chief of the children of Ammon.** *(Daniel 11:41)*

This prophecy concerns the actions of the Little Horn, or the Antichrist, during the time he goes to conquer the world. I have read several studies on the End Times that say essentially that *"Israel has nothing to fear from the nation of Jordan"*, because of this verse. (Fruchtenbaum, p.14) Does Daniel actually mean that Jordan will be victorious against the Antichrist? Is there another way to understand this passage that makes more sense, in the light of all of Scripture? Would it make sense that the Antichrist would ignore a small, relatively weak nation right next door to his quarry, Israel?

Let me answer with a series of questions: Did Hitler defeat Germany? Did Stalin defeat Russia? Did Napoleon Bonaparte defeat France? Did Caesar defeat Rome?

In each case the nation in question actually gave support and power to their respective leader. Thus if Edom, Moab, and Ammon, give their support and power to the Antichrist they will escape his hand. So we get back to our earlier verse, from Daniel 11:23. The Antichrist will *"grow strong with a small people"*, thus the small people are Edom, Moab and Ammon, mainly Edom, and known as Jordan today. Going back to Josephus, we see that the people who began the destruction of Jerusalem, the Idumeans, are the people of the Antichrist. Don't think Rome will be let off lightly, however, but we have already discussed that city in chapter 5.

Let's look at some other End Time prophecies concerning Edom:

*1 Come near, ye nations, to hear; and hearken, ye people: let the earth hear, and all that is therein; the world, and all things that come forth of it. 2 For the **indignation of the LORD is upon all nations**, and his fury upon all their armies: he hath utterly destroyed them, he hath delivered them to the slaughter. 3 Their slain also shall be cast out, and their stink shall come up out of their carcases, and the mountains shall be melted with their blood. 4 And all the host of heaven shall be dissolved, and **the heavens shall be rolled together as a scroll**: and all their host shall fall down, as the leaf falleth off from the vine, and as a falling fig from the fig tree. 5 **For my sword shall be bathed in heaven: behold, it shall come down upon Idumea, and upon the people of my curse, to judgment.** 6 The sword of the LORD is filled with blood, it is made fat with fatness, and with the blood of lambs and goats, with the fat of the kidneys of rams: for the LORD hath a sacrifice in Bozrah, and a great slaughter in the land of Idumea. 7 And the unicorns shall come down with them, and the bullocks with the bulls; and their land shall be soaked with blood, and their dust made fat with fatness. 8 For it is the day of the LORD'S vengeance, and the year of recompences **for the controversy of Zion.** 9 And the streams thereof shall be turned into pitch, and the dust thereof into brimstone, and the land thereof shall become burning pitch. 10 It shall not be quenched night nor day; the smoke thereof shall go up for ever: from generation to generation it shall lie waste; none shall pass through it for ever and ever. 11 But the cormorant and the bittern shall possess it; the owl also and the raven shall dwell in it: and he shall stretch out upon it the line of confusion, and the stones of emptiness. 12 **They shall call the nobles thereof to the kingdom, but none shall be there, and all her princes shall be nothing.** 13 And thorns shall come up in her palaces, nettles and brambles in the fortresses thereof: and it shall be an habitation of dragons, and a court for owls. 14 The wild beasts of the desert shall also meet with the wild beasts of the island, and the satyr shall cry to his fellow; the screech owl also shall rest there, and find for herself a place of rest. (Isaiah 34:1-14)*

So how can we date these prophecies? Maybe they've already been fulfilled?

Look at verse 2. Note that the Lord's anger is against the whole earth. The whole earth has yet to taste the wrath of God, thus indicating an End Times fulfillment. The language is the same as is found in the book of Revelation, chapter 19. Verse 4 is a reference to the same event found in Revelation 6:14, an event yet future. Verses 5 through 8 emphasize that while the whole world will suffer the Lord's Judgment, Idumea seems to be at the centre of His displeasure. Notice in verse 5 that Idumea is *"the people of my curse"*. No other nation on earth suffers this distinction, not even Germany. The rest of the passage uses colourful language to describe in detail the carnage coming to this planet. The phrase *"the controversy of Zion"* sounds like it came from a modern newspaper it is so current. (See also Jeremiah 25:29-31) Could verse 12 be a reference to a Palestinian state within the borders of Israel?

Verses 9 and 10 indicate that this judgment will result in the land of Idumea becoming desolate for ever. Today the capital city Amman is a bustling metropolis of some two million people, and there are still inhabitants in the old areas of Edom. Clearly then, the desolation spoken of has not happened yet.

Don't let the mention of *"unicorns"* and *"satyrs"* put you off the clear meaning of this passage. A unicorn may be a rhinoceros, or it could be a supernatural creature that is associated with the people of Edom, in other words a demon. Certainly *"satyr"* appears to be a reference to the demons, or fallen angels, who will be locked away in the territory of Edom, in Jordan, during the millennial reign of Christ, like Babylon. This passage appears to have some parallels with Isaiah 34, and Revelation 17 and 18.

> *1 Moreover the word of the LORD came unto me, saying, 2 Son of man, set thy face **against mount Seir,** and prophesy against it, 3 And say unto it, Thus saith the Lord GOD; Behold, O mount Seir, I am against thee, and I will stretch out mine hand against thee, and I will make thee most desolate. 4 **I will lay thy cities waste,** and thou shalt be desolate, and thou shalt know that I am the LORD. 5 Because thou hast had a perpetual hatred, and hast shed the blood of the children of Israel by the force of the sword in the time of their calamity, **in the time that their iniquity had an end**: 6 Therefore, as I live, saith the Lord GOD, I will prepare thee unto blood, and*

blood shall pursue thee: **sith (since) thou hast not hated blood, even blood shall pursue thee.** *7 Thus will I make mount Seir most desolate, and cut off from it him that passeth out and him that returneth. 8 And I will fill his mountains with his slain men: in thy hills, and in thy valleys, and in all thy rivers, shall they fall that are slain with the sword. 9 I will make thee perpetual desolations, and thy cities shall not return: and ye shall know that I am the LORD. 10 Because thou hast said, These two nations and these two countries shall be mine, and we will possess it; whereas the LORD was there: 11 Therefore, as I live, saith the Lord GOD, I will even do according to thine anger, and according to thine envy which thou hast used out of thy hatred against them; and I will make myself known among them, when I have judged thee. 12 And thou shalt know that I am the LORD, and that I have heard all thy blasphemies which thou hast spoken against the mountains of Israel, saying, They are laid desolate, they are given us to consume. 13 Thus with your mouth ye have boasted against me, and have multiplied your words against me: I have heard them. 14 Thus saith the Lord GOD;* **When the whole earth rejoiceth, I will make thee desolate.** *15 As thou didst rejoice at the inheritance of the house of Israel, because it was desolate, so will I do unto thee: thou shalt be desolate, O mount Seir, and all Idumea, even all of it: and they shall know that I am the LORD. (Ezekiel 35: 1-15)*

What if we ask the same questions about this passage as the last? Look at verse 5: When did the iniquity of Israel have an end? It hasn't happened yet. That day is yet future. It will occur during the last half of Daniel's seventieth week. At that time they will cry out to the Lord and he will hear them and personally come to their rescue.

In verse 6 He states that Edom has not hated blood. In other words, these people have welcomed bloodshed and violence. Who are the people of Hamas and Fatah? Who are those who send suicide bombers, and rockets, into Israel on a regular basis? There is a contingent of Edomites among them. ("Israelestine, p. 88)(Kinsella, How do you Spell Violence)

In verse 9 He states that their cities *"shall not return"*. Today the people of Jordan might look at that prophecy and laugh! They have rebuilt their cities, and have returned. But God said they would return and rebuild, in Malachi 1:4, so it is clear that this prophecy is about a later time, the time of the end of the age. Don't boast against the Lord. He is all powerful and all knowing. He is quite capable of keeping all His promises, both to Israel and to all the nations of the world.

The two nations referred to in verse 10 are Israel and Judah. Just because they were taken away in captivity does not mean that they lost their ownership of the land. They have a divine deed, the Word of God. The big problem with Idumea in verse 13 is boasting. This is the same problem that the Antichrist has. (Daniel 7:8, 11:36, Revelation 13:5)

In verse 14 it states that at the time of Edom's judgment the whole earth will be rejoicing. This is a reference to the time after the return of the Lord Jesus Christ, when Armageddon is over and He has begun His millennial reign. We can thus date the fulfillment of this prophecy to the end of the Tribulation, or Armageddon.

Edom is conspicuous by its absence in the Ezekiel 38 and 39 war. In fact Edom may be mentioned in the passage rather obliquely, as Dedan. Dedan is often identified as either a descendant of Ham through Cush, or a descendant of Abraham through Keturah, and thus Arabs of Saudi Arabia. There are, however, at least two passages that link Dedan with Edom. It could be that the descendants of Esau intermarried with the descendants of Dedan, and thus their territories overlap.

> _Concerning Edom,_ thus saith the LORD of hosts; Is wisdom no more in Teman? is counsel perished from the prudent? is their wisdom vanished? **Flee ye, turn back, dwell deep, O inhabitants of Dedan; for I will bring the calamity of Esau upon him,** the time that I will visit him. (Jeremiah 49:7 & 8)

> Thus saith the Lord GOD; Because that Edom hath dealt against the house of Judah by taking vengeance, and hath greatly offended, and revenged himself upon them; Therefore thus saith the Lord GOD; **I will also stretch out mine hand upon Edom, and will cut off man and beast from it; and I will make it desolate from Teman; and they of Dedan shall fall by the sword. And I will lay my vengeance upon Edom by the hand of my people Israel: and they shall do in Edom according to mine anger and according to my**

*fury; and they shall know my vengeance, saith the Lord GOD.
(Ezekiel 25:12 - 14)*

Edom is clearly a part of Armageddon, which occurs several years after the Gog and Magog war, so it is apparent that this nation will not receive the same consequences of Asaph's war as the other combatants. Here is where I disagree with Salus. He is correct that Edom will receive two judgments, but he says that Edom will be devoid of people by the time the second judgment strikes during Armageddon (Isralestine, p. 186). It doesn't make sense for God to judge an empty body of land. The only way to make sense of all the prophecies against Edom is that some of them will survive on their own land, and will actively support the Antichrist until the judgment of Armageddon.

As the nations gather together to attack Israel, Dedan lodges a diplomatic protest along with Sheba and Tarshish.

Sheba, and Dedan, and the merchants of Tarshish, with all the young lions thereof, shall say unto thee, Art thou come to take a spoil? hast thou gathered thy company to take a prey? to carry away silver and gold, to take away cattle and goods, to take a great spoil? (Ezekiel 38:13)

Is it not possible then, that Israel may take this protest as a sign of friendship? When the war is done will they look to these people to help them rebuild? If Asaph's war ends early, with a treaty between Jordan and Israel, would Jordan be spared the firebombing that is predicted against Lebanon, Syria, and Egypt, in Zechariah 10:11 and 11:1? Today Jordan already has a treaty with Israel, as does Egypt. These nations will have to break their treaties to be involved in Asaph's war.

If this scenario plays out with Jordan suing for peace early in Asaph's war, and signing a treaty, it could give us a new understanding to the treaty that the Antichrist confirms with Israel. Could the peace treaty that these two nations sign to end this war, be the basis for the treaty that Israel signs with "*many*"? (Daniel 9:27) If Israel considers Edom's lack of aggression in Ezekiel's war to be a positive move toward peace, will this give her the motivation to accept the same agreement as the basis for a comprehensive peace with the rest of the Arab world? Will a European leader be involved in negotiating this deal? Will this be the time when Jordan surrenders its control of the Temple mount?

Notice in Joel 3:19 & 20 the contrast between Edom and Judah.

Egypt shall be a desolation, and Edom shall be a desolate wilderness, for the violence against the children of Judah, because they have shed innocent blood in their land. But Judah shall dwell for ever, and Jerusalem from generation to generation. (Joel 3:19 & 20)

We have seen already that Edom will exist during the war of Ezekiel 38 and 39. Here is a prophecy of the End Times that specifically names Edom as being a part of God's End Times Judgment, at Armageddon.

*17 Then took I the cup at the LORD'S hand, and made **all the nations** to drink, unto whom the LORD had sent me: 18 To wit, Jerusalem, and the cities of Judah, and the kings thereof, and the princes thereof, to make them a desolation, an astonishment, an hissing, and a curse; as it is this day; 19 Pharaoh king of Egypt, and his servants, and his princes, and all his people; 20 And all the mingled people, and all the kings of the land of Uz, and all the kings of the land of the Philistines, and Ashkelon, and Azzah, and Ekron, and the remnant of Ashdod, 21 **Edom, and Moab, and the children of Ammon,** (Jordan) 22 And all the kings of Tyrus, and all the kings of Zidon, and the kings of the isles which are beyond the sea, 23 Dedan, and Tema, and Buz, and all that are in the utmost corners, 24 And all the kings of Arabia, and all the kings of the mingled people that dwell in the desert, 25 And all the kings of Zimri, and all the kings of Elam, and all the kings of the Medes, 26 And all the kings of the north, far and near, one with another, and **all the kingdoms of the world, which are upon the face of the earth:** and the king of Sheshach shall drink after them. 27 Therefore thou shalt say unto them, Thus saith the LORD of hosts, the God of Israel; Drink ye, and be drunken, and spue, and fall, and rise no more, because of the sword which I will send among you. 28 And it shall be, if they refuse to take the cup at thine hand to drink, then shalt thou say unto them, Thus saith the LORD of hosts; Ye shall certainly drink. 29 For, lo, **I begin to bring evil on the city which is called by my name, and should ye be utterly unpunished?** Ye shall not be unpunished: for I will call for a sword upon all the inhabitants of the earth, saith the LORD of* *hosts. 30 Therefore prophesy thou against them all these words, and say unto them, The LORD shall roar from on high, and utter his voice from his holy habitation; he shall mightily roar upon his habitation; he shall give a shout, as they that tread the grapes, against all the inhabitants of the earth. 31 A noise shall come even to the ends of the earth;* **for the LORD hath a controversy with the nations, he will plead with all flesh;** *he will give them that are wicked to the sword, saith the LORD. (Jeremiah 25:17-31)*

This is not the war of Psalm 83, for there are too many nations involved, nor is it the battle of Ezekiel 38 and 39 for the same reason. This is the battle of Armageddon, because it involves the whole earth. I find it interesting that Jeremiah is told to give this cup to all the nations of the earth to drink. Jeremiah was not able to carry out that command during his lifetime, but in time God has seen to it that this book, and this warning, has travelled to all the nations of the earth.

As God says, if He brings judgment on the nation called by His name, Israel, surely the whole earth will receive the same judgment, especially those who support the Antichrist. Since Edom is specifically mentioned in this passage we can safely surmise that some of Edom will still be alive when the Antichrist arises.

There is a parallel between God's judgment against Babylon in the book of Revelation and his Judgment against Edom throughout the Old Testament. He says that no man will live there, that it will be like Sodom and Gomorrah. While Edom did suffer destruction in the past, they have returned and rebuilt their cities, as predicted in Malachi. The inhabitants of the land today worship a god named Allah. They think this god can protect them from the God of Israel, but he cannot. Whatever accomplishments they can attain through human effort, God can still destroy them.

16 Thy terribleness hath deceived thee, and the pride of thine heart, **O thou that dwellest in the clefts of the rock,** *that holdest the height of the hill: though thou shouldest make thy nest as high as the eagle, I will bring thee down from thence, saith the LORD. 17 Also* **Edom shall be a desolation:** *every one that goeth by it shall be astonished, and shall hiss at all the plagues thereof. 18* **As in the overthrow of Sodom and Gomorrah and the neighbour cities thereof, saith the**

*LORD, no man shall abide there, neither shall a son of man dwell in it. 19 Behold, he shall come up like a lion from the swelling of Jordan against the habitation of the strong: but I will suddenly make him run away from her: and who is a chosen man, that I may appoint over her? for **who is like me**? and who will appoint me the time? and **who is that shepherd that will stand before me**? 20 Therefore hear the counsel of the LORD, that he hath taken against Edom; and his purposes, that he hath purposed against the inhabitants of Teman: Surely the least of the flock shall draw them out: surely he shall make their habitations desolate with them. 21 The earth is moved at the noise of their fall, at the cry the noise thereof was heard in the Red sea. 22 Behold, he shall come up and fly as the eagle, and spread his wings over Bozrah: and **at that day shall the heart of the mighty men of Edom be as the heart of a woman in her pangs**. (Jeremiah 49:16-22)*

The capital city of ancient Edom was the place known as Petra. This city is extremely inaccessible, being only accessed by a small passageway that would only allow people on foot or on horseback to enter. This could certainly be described as a *"cleft in the rock"*. While Petra is in ruins today, there are people still living in the area and it is a major tourist draw. When God says no man will abide there he means no one! That day is still future, but it is approaching rather quickly.

In verse 19 the shepherd referred to is none other than the Idol Shepherd, the Antichrist. He is the one who will claim to be equal with God. In verse 22 the comparison with a woman in labour pains is used again to indicate the time of the Great Tribulation.

The Judgment of Edom coinciding with the restoration of Israel, as we have seen, is a common theme in the Old Testament:

*Rejoice and be glad, O daughter of Edom, that dwellest in the land of Uz; the cup also shall pass through unto thee: thou shalt be drunken, and shalt make thyself naked. **The punishment of thine iniquity is accomplished, O daughter of Zion; he will no more carry thee away into captivity: he will visit thine iniquity, O daughter of Edom; he will discover thy sins**. (Lamentations 4:21 & 22)*

God is a merciful God, slow to anger and quick to bring mercy and compassion. Why then is there so much judgment against this one nation? I think it is because Edom, as a nation, never forgave his brother and held on to the old hatred. That hatred will ultimately be embodied in one man, God's greatest human enemy, the Antichrist:

> *Thus saith the LORD; For three transgressions of Edom, and for four, I will not turn away the punishment thereof; because he did pursue his brother with the sword, and did cast off all pity, and his anger did tear perpetually, and he kept his wrath for ever: (Amos 1:11)*

Balaam the prophet was one of the few gentile prophets in the Bible, and actually worked for the kings of Jordan. Balaam was a true prophet of God, although his love of money got the better of him, and he was ultimately killed in a war with Israel as an act of judgment. One of the oldest prophecies concerning Edom was spoken by this man, and since it pertains to our subject we need to take a look at what he had to say.

> *15 And he took up his parable, and said, Balaam the son of Beor hath said, and the man whose eyes are open hath said: 16 He hath said, which heard the words of God, and knew the knowledge of the most High, which saw the vision of the Almighty, falling into a trance, but having his eyes open: 17 I shall see him, but not now: I shall behold him, but not nigh:* **there shall come a Star out of Jacob, and a Sceptre shall rise out of Israel, and shall smite the corners of Moab, and destroy all the children of Sheth. 18 And Edom shall be a possession, Seir also shall be a possession for his enemies; and Israel shall do valiantly.** *19 Out of Jacob shall come he that shall have dominion, and shall destroy him that remaineth of the city. (Numbers 24:15-19)*

Verse 17 is a messianic prophecy about Jesus, the Star of Jacob. The Sceptre is a sign of royalty. This verse indicates that Jesus shall be the one who smites Moab and Edom, when He returns.

The next verse indicates the victory of Israel over Edom, in relation to the return of Christ. I wonder, if Jordan sues for peace during Asaph's war, will Israel think that this is a fulfilment of this prophecy? If so they are set-up for destruction.

What is in store for Edom? What will happen to this nation? As we have seen above, Edom will be a possession, and will lose all sovereignty to Israel. The men of Edom will die in the war of Armageddon, and not before. (Ezekiel 35:8, Jeremiah 49:10-11, & 22) What if Jordan becomes a protectorate, or province, of Israel? Could Israel accept a Messiah from within her own borders, though not of Jewish descent?

> But upon mount Zion shall be deliverance, and there shall be holiness; and the house of Jacob shall possess their possessions. And the house of Jacob shall be a fire, and the house of Joseph a flame, and the house of Esau for stubble, and they shall kindle in them, and devour them; and *there shall not be any remaining of the house of Esau;* for the LORD hath spoken it. (Obadiah 1:17-18)

This seems to conflict with Jeremiah 49:11, but there is an explanation that fits both passages...

> "(speaking of Edom) Leave thy fatherless children, *I will preserve them alive; and let thy widows trust in me.*" (Jeremiah 49:11)

> That they (Israel) *may possess the remnant of Edom,* and of all the heathen, which are called by my name, saith the LORD that doeth this. (Amos 9:12)

This shows the amazing mercy of God. If it was up to the human race, those people would bear the shame of their fathers and husbands for ever. The people of the Antichrist's family and nation, who accept Jesus Christ as Lord and Saviour, will be absorbed into Israel. The widows of the Antichrist's soldiers, who trust in Jesus, will leave their land and marry Jewish men in Israel. They shall raise their children as Jews, and the children of the Antichrist's Edomite soldiers will also be raised as Jews, so there will literally be none remaining who would call themselves Edomites.

For the survivors of the nation that brings forth the Antichrist, there will be so much shame in being identified with that man and that nation, that they will desire to become a part of Israel, and forget the shame of the past. God, in His mercy, will grant them their desire. If you ask one of those women, or their children, *"Aren't you an Edomite?"* they will answer *"I am a Jew"*. Being adopted into Israel it will not be a lie. Thus it is possible for there to be none of the house of Esau left, and yet for Israel to still possess the remnant of Edom, women and children who worship Jesus Christ as Lord and Saviour!

Amman Jordan

The capital city of Jordan, Amman, is one of the oldest continuously occupied cities in the world. In the Old Testament it was known as Rabat Ammon, Rabbah, or Rabath Ammon. During the New Testament era Amman was actually known as **Philadelphia**, having been given that name by Ptolemy II Philadelphus, the Helenic king of Egypt, in his own honour. In the third century AD Philadelphia was renamed Amman.

I am not certain exactly how the Antichrist will use this fact, but I think he will likely point to the Philadelphia of Revelation 3:7-13 and claim this is a prophecy for his city. He will likely use God's promises to that church and apply them to himself and his followers. Is it possible that Amman could actually change its name back to Philadelphia? Stranger things have happened!

If you search the Bible for prophecies against Amman you will not find any, but if you look for its old name you will find something rather interesting.

> *Concerning the Ammonites, thus saith the LORD; Hath Israel no sons? hath he no heir? why then doth their king inherit Gad, and his people dwell in his cities? Therefore, behold, **the days come, saith the LORD, that I will cause an alarm of war to be heard in Rabbah of the Ammonites;** and **it shall be a desolate heap, and her daughters shall be burned with fire: then shall Israel be heir unto them that were his heirs,** saith the LORD. Howl, O Heshbon, for Ai is spoiled: cry, ye daughters of Rabbah, gird you with sackcloth; lament, and run to and fro by the hedges; for their king shall go into captivity, and his priests and his princes together. (Jeremiah 49:1-3)*

The people of Ammon are living on Israelite soil to this day, on the east side of the Jordan river in Gilead, as well as in Samaria, commonly referred to as the *"West Bank"*. Now, this passage does not say that the Antichrist will come from Ammon, but it does say that this city, the combined capital of Edom, Moab, and Ammon, will be a desolate heap. The events described in Jeremiah 49:1-6 have not happened to this city. It may have suffered defeats in battle from time to time, but it has never been a desolate heap. The best explanation for this destruction is because this city will be intimately aquainted with the Antichrist.

Verse six shows the Lord's mercy to these people. Though their main city will be a desolate heap, God will cause the remnant of Ammon to return and inhabit their land again during the millennial reign of Jesus Christ. The next verse addresses Edom and, as you go through the section you will find no such hint of mercy aimed at the Edomites.

Amos also has a message against the city of Amman (Rabbah):

> *Thus saith the LORD; For three transgressions of the children of Ammon, and for four, I will not turn away the punishment thereof; because they have ripped up the women with child of Gilead, that they might enlarge their border: But* **I will kindle a fire in the wall of Rabbah,** *and it shall devour the palaces thereof, with shouting in the day of battle, with a tempest in the day of the whirlwind: And their king shall go into captivity, he and his princes together, saith the LORD. (Amos 1:13-15)*

Again we see a judgment against Amman that includes fire. A judgment that hasn't happened as of this writing. This may be describing a nuclear attack, or an attack by God from the heavens, during the battle of Armageddon, but it is certain that this destruction will occur in the last days. As we have already seen, Amman has never seen the destruction which is described here. It remained occupied, and continued to exist as a small village until the late nineteenth century. When it was chosen as the capital of the nation of Jordan, it began to flourish and is today the major metropolis of that nation.

Of particular interest is the fact that Amman was originally built on seven "*jabals*", or mountains, though today it actually covers nineteen. Since we have seen definite prophecies about the End Times destruction of Amman, the question arises: Is Amman, Jordan, the Harlot spoken of in Revelation 17, or 18? Since we have discovered that the Antichrist most likely comes from Jordan, and likely from its major population centre, I think it is unlikely that he will consent to its destruction. Therefore, the prophecies of its judgment will take place during Christ's return and not before. She is likely the Harlot of Revelation 18, but not of chapter 17.

Of course the passage in question speaks of this city as one that trades with the merchants of the earth through shipping. Amman is not a port, however the passage does not say that this city is a port, but only that the merchants sit in their ship afar off and watch her burn. The nearest port to Amman is actually Tel-Aviv/Jaffa, only 60 miles away. It would be very possible for ships to sit outside of the port of Jaffa, and watch the smoke of Amman's burning, rising from behind the hills of Israel!

It may be possible that it will be destroyed during Asaph's war, with its Royal family escaping to Iraq, to set up camp in Babylon. I think this is unlikely because Jordan has consistently shown itself to be a moderate Arab nation. I think this fact, plus the fact that Jordan's founding people are brothers of Israel, will predispose Israel to show more restraint towards Jordan than they will to the other invading nations.

Though Amman is prophesied to be destroyed during the End Times, and though the Antichrist will most likely come from Jordan, I think it is more likely that the Harlot of Revelation 17 will be literally Babylon, Iraq. There are too many prophecies linking the destruction of Edom to the return of Christ, for its major population centre to be destroyed at some time prior to that event.

I'm not sure what to make of the symbolism between Amman and Jerusalem. It appears that Jerusalem and Amman are some sort of twin cities, with the Jordan river serving as a border between them. Crossing the Jordan has often been portrayed as crossing from death unto life. Many have attempted to destroy Jerusalem, yet it appears that it will be Jerusalem's twin, Amman, that God Himself will ultimately destroy.

These observations lead to more questions that I do not as yet have an answer for: Will Jordan be defeated in Asaph's war, yet retain some sort of limited autonomy? Will Jordan recover from Asaph's war to the extent that it will be in a position to provide a leader for the Arab super-state, after the war of Gog and Magog? Is it possible that Jordan could become a province of Israel, so that the Antichrist could actually arise from within the borders of a Greater Israel? Could the Antichrist be a gentile Israelite descended from Jacob's older brother?

Lies and Scripture Manipulation

I hesitate to even write this section, considering that it actually could give the false prophet, and the Antichrist, some ideas. I want you to know, however, that God has deliberately written parts of His Word in ways that an unbeliever could twist to make it appear that the Christ could come from somewhere other than from the physical descendants of Israel. This is a judgment against those who trust themselves and not God, who allegorize the plain text of Scripture without the leadership of the Holy Spirit.

A true reading of the messianic prophecies indicates that the Messiah will come from Israel, from the tribe of Judah, and will be a direct descendant of Jesse, and his son David. No one who cannot trace his genealogy to David could be the messiah. As we have also seen the time frame for the messiah's revealing, and death, was 483 years from the decree to rebuild Jerusalem. This limits his coming to the early years of the first century AD, no later than about the year 33. There are principles and statements in Scripture, however, that could be twisted to make it seem that the Messiah could come from somewhere else.

One of the first things one notices is that biblically the older son always receives the major blessing from his father.

> *If a man have two wives, one beloved, and another hated, and they have born him children, both the beloved and the hated; and if the firstborn son be hers that was hated: Then it shall be,* **when he maketh his sons to inherit that which he hath, that he may not make the son of the beloved firstborn before the son of the hated, which is indeed the firstborn**: *But he shall acknowledge the son of the hated for the firstborn, by giving him a double portion of all that he hath: for he is the beginning of his strength;* **the right of the firstborn is his.** *(Deuteronomy 21:15-17)*

Naming the firstborn as the major heir was always the practise, even before this law was written. Moses was not really writing something new, he was codifying that which was already practised in most of the world. It is important to note that God has the right to override the Law. It is also safe to say that in certain circumstances even a father has the right to do so. If the older son does not have the character, or the father deems him unfit to inherit his business, while the business is his, it is in his power to give it to whom he will.

This passage and its principle is used by the Muslims and Arabs to make the claim that since Ishmael was Abraham's firstborn son, the inheritance should go to him and his descendants. God, however, has the right to override the principle and did so in this case. Ishmael was the child of the flesh and not the child of promise. (The royal family of Jordan, traces its ancestry in a direct line from the Muslim prophet Mohammed, who was an Ishmaelite.)

In the case of Esau we have a slightly different situation. Esau was himself a child of promise. The inheritance should have gone to him naturally.   Esau, being a man of low character, sold his inheritance to his brother Jacob for a bowl of red stew. He sold an eternal inheritance for a benefit that was gone in twenty-four hours! I am sure that some of his descendants are angry over that purchase to this day. It doesn't seem fair or logical. In fact it wasn't fair for Esau to sell his children's birthright from under them, but he did do it, and it was a legal transaction which was agreed to by both sides! If the Edomites are angry with anyone it should be against their father, Esau, not their cousins the Jews.

The truth is that it was God who was behind the transaction. God saw something in Esau that He did not like, even before the twins were born. (Genesis 25:23)   What I think He saw, was something which will ultimately lead to the birth, nurturing, and rise of the Antichrist.

One day, as I was walking my dog, I had been thinking about some of these things and I thought to myself; *"How in the world is it possible that Israel could ever accept a gentile Antichrist?"* It was almost as if God was listening to, or perhaps directing my thoughts, for the very next morning as I was reading through Isaiah and I came upon the following...

> *Who is this that cometh from Edom, with dyed garments from Bozrah? this that is glorious in his apparel, travelling in the greatness of his strength? I that speak in righteousness, mighty to save. (Isaiah 63:1)*

I was shocked when I read this verse. No doubt this is a reference to the return of Jesus Christ when he comes to save the Israelites who will likely be hidden in the hills of Edom, in the area around Bozrah, or, He will first bring judgment to Edom before going out against the rest of the world. It could be, however, very easily twisted to mean that this verse indicates that the Messiah, God Himself will come from Edom, from the nation founded by Jacob's brother!

There is no verse, that I am aware of, that could be taken to mean, even out of context, that the Messiah would come from Rome. This verse, however, very plainly says that God will come from Edom, and if taken out of context could lead many to believe that the Christ will be from Jordan or the Edomites! I have no doubt that this verse will be a key verse that the false prophet will use to claim that the Antichrist is the Messiah of Israel!

> *And he said, The **LORD came from Sinai, and rose up from Seir** unto them; he shined forth from mount Paran, and he came with ten thousands of saints: from his right hand went a fiery law for them. (Deuteronomy 33:2)*

> *LORD, when thou wentest out of Seir, when thou marchedst out of the field of Edom, the earth trembled, and the heavens dropped, the clouds also dropped water. (Judges 5:4)*

Both Seir and Paran are regions in Edom. The Antichrist will use these verses to claim that God, the Messiah, comes from Edom, or is an Edomite. They would have to be taken out of context and twisted to make it say that, but such is the way of allegorical interpretation. Though these are written in past-tense, much of prophecy is also written in past-tense, from a future point of view. In order to understand what is being said here you have to read the context. No doubt the false prophet will be careful to avoid the context. These passages are speaking about the time when the Lord met Israel on their flight from Egypt, in both the Sinai desert and in Edom.

> *And Jacob sent messengers before him to Esau his brother unto the land of Seir, the country of Edom. And he commanded them, saying, Thus shall ye speak unto **my lord Esau**; Thy servant Jacob saith thus, I have sojourned with Laban, and stayed there until now: (Genesis 32:3 & 4)*

Here we have the account of Jacob's return to Canaan with his

wives and children. At this point he sends servants ahead to warn
Esau of his return. Note the use of the terms *"my lord Esau"* and
"Thy servant Jacob". Though Jacob was being polite, and following
the customs of his time, I have no doubt that the false prophet will
exploit this passage to say that Jacob was acknowledging Esau's
superiority in the covenant.

> And he (Esau) said, What meanest thou by all this drove
> which I met? And he (Jacob) said, These are **to find grace in
> the sight of my lord**. And Esau said, I have enough, my
> brother; keep that thou hast unto thyself. And Jacob said,
> Nay, I pray thee, if now I have found grace in thy sight, then
> receive my present at my hand: **for therefore I have seen thy
> face, as though I had seen the face of God**, and thou wast
> pleased with me. (Genesis 33:8-10)

Here is another passage which can be twisted to say that Jacob
acknowledged his brother as Lord, even as God! The word for Lord
in the Hebrew in verse 8 is אדני which is transliterated as Adonai,
and is used as a name for God. It can also be transliterated as
"*Adoni*", which means "*master*" and still denotes one who is superior.
The false prophet will use this to say that God, the messiah, will
come from Jacob's older brother, Edom, or that Edom is superior to
Israel. The truth is that Jacob was only being polite, and he never
gave back the birthright. The birthright belongs to Israel and his
descendants forever! **They could not give it back even if they
wanted to, for God was behind the transaction!**
Verse 10 is another statement that Jacob made which will be
twisted. Here he very clearly equates the face of his brother with
the face of God. No doubt the false prophet will use this to say that
the Antichrist, as "*Christ*", was foreshadowed in his ancestor Esau.
With the world-wide biblical illiteracy that is occurring today, there
is no doubt that the false prophet and Antichrist will be able to get
away with such Scripture twisting.
The bible tells us that Jesus is the second Adam. Adam brought
sin into the world and with sin came death. Since we are all
descendants of Adam we all die. Jesus, the last Adam, is a life
giving, or quickening, spirit. Since the Antichrist is going to try to
impersonate the true Christ he will claim that he is the second
Adam. The names Edom and Adam are so similar that it is obvious
there is a relationship between them. The name Adam can mean

"ruddy" as in "having a reddish complexion", and it appears that Edom is a variant of this same name.

אדם = Adam (note: read Hebrew from right to left)

אדם = Adom or red

אדום = Edom

It appears that there can be a play on words with these two names, which the Antichrist will exploit to his own benefit.

> And Esau said to Jacob, Feed me, I pray thee, with that same red pottage; for I am faint: therefore was his name called Edom. (Genesis 25:30)

In Israel, if you make a reservation at a restaurant or hotel, when you enquire at the desk they will ask you in Hebrew: *"Ma hashem, bevakasha?"* which means, "What's the name, please". Notice that the word *"ha"* is the word *"the"*, and *"shem"* is *"name"*. What is the official name of the nation directly to the east of Israel? *"The **Hashemite** Kingdom of Jordan"*. Mohammed, the prophet of Islam, was a member of the Hashemite tribe, and the kings of Jordan trace their ancestry to him. Did you notice the Hebrew words *"ha shem"* in that title?

The bible tells us that apart from the name of Jesus Christ, there is no other name under Heaven whereby we must be saved. (Acts 4:12) Since the Antichrist is a false Christ, you can bet he will also claim to save, especially after his resurrection. I believe that the false prophet will look at the name Hashemite, and will see the same thing I am seeing, and he will claim that this man is *"The Name"* (hashem) that saves. He will likely claim that the name Hashemite is prophetic in its significance, pointing to the messiah.

For many years Israel has refused to use the name of God that He gave them in the bible. His name is often referred to as the tetragrammaton, YHWH. It has been so long that Israel has used this name that there is a debate as to whether it is pronounced Yahweh or Yehovah. Instead of using His name as He instructed, they have taken to referring to God as "hashem". I do not know for certain, but I believe it would be in character for God to send an Antichrist with the name of Hashem.

I did not want to include these passages in this book. It pains me to do so, yet I believe I need to warn as many as possible. This is not a comprehensive list of all the lies that the Antichrist, and false prophet will spew. These are only some of the types of lies

they will propagate. Remember that God cannot contradict Himself.
The bible is a unit from Genesis to Revelation, and speaks with a
clear and consistent voice. Only an allegorical interpretation of
Scripture would allow one to conclude that the Messiah is someone
other than a direct descendant of David, who lived and died in the
early years of the first century AD.

The Messiah came from Israel, from the tribe of Judah, from the
clan of Jesse, and David. The time of His coming, Daniel's sixty nine
weeks, ended between 18-33 AD. His name is Jesus, and He will
return the same way he left, from the sky. He has fire in His eyes,
and can destroy His enemies with a word!

Truly born-again Christians will never accept an Edomite, or
anyone other than Jesus Christ, as messiah. This fact alone gives us
another reason to expect a pre-tribulation Rapture of the Church.
The world must be plunged into darkness for these lies to work, but
that day is not far off.

At this point I can't claim that any particular member of the
Hashemite family is the Antichrist. Daniel tells us that the most
obvious person is not the one we are looking for...

> *And in his estate shall stand up a vile person,* **to whom**
> **they shall not give the honour of the kingdom: but he**
> **shall come in peaceably, and obtain the kingdom by**
> **flatteries.** *(Daniel 11:21)*

It seems to me that this verse indicates that the man in question
will not be the world's first choice as ruler. In other words he is
likely to come from the royal family of Jordan, but probably is not
the oldest son of the King. The oldest son is always the first choice
to succeed his father, especially in Muslim lands. I take it then, that
he is more likely to be a younger brother, brother-in-law, uncle, or
cousin than the oldest son. Also tending to confirm this diagnosis is
the fact that the *"Little Horn"* is often spoken of as being a *"prince"*,
as opposed to a king. He becomes a king only after taking world
power.

After having written the above I discovered that the youngest
son of king Abdullah II of Jordan, is named Hashem. As of this
writing I do not know if Prince Hashem bin Al Abdullah will become
the Antichrist, or if it will be someone else in this family. It looks to
me like he is being set up for that role, except that he is too young,
in my estimation. As of this writing Hashem is only five years old.

He is a little boy who deserves to hear that Jesus Christ died for his sins, just like any other little boy in the world. If anyone were to kill him they would just be a murderer, and someone else would be the Antichrist.

King Abdullah has four brothers who are all in line for the throne, including one named Hashim, a variation of Hashem. In addition there are a total of twenty-two people in line for the throne of Jordan. I can say, with certainty, that at least twenty-one of them are NOT the Antichrist. While many of them will support the Antichrist in his rise to power, God wants to save some in that family, and I want to see Him do it!

Really, we do not even know for sure if the Antichrist will come from the Hashemites at all. It still could be someone else from Jordan, or even the Palestinians. I am only saying that this family is one to watch.

It is God's will that the Beast, the Antichrist, or The Man of Sin, will rule the world, just as it was God's will that Judas would betray Jesus Christ. As we have seen in Zechariah 11:16, it is the Lord Himself who will raise up the Idol Shepherd. If you fight him with physical arms, you will be fighting God's will, and are guaranteed to lose. As you read the book of Revelation you will discover that God's people attain victory over the Antichrist by laying down their lives for Jesus. True Christians do not pick up weapons and attempt to force their way on anyone. The Crusaders were not biblical Christians, but pagans in disguise.

The People of the Antichrist

Throughout history, as some churches mistakenly taught that the Antichrist would ultimately come from Israel, the result has been that many professing Christians practised antisemitism, and persecuted the Chosen People. As we have seen the Antichrist will not come from Israel, but from his brother, Esau.

The book of Revelation tells us that Heaven will be populated by people from every family of the earth. Remember that the word "kindred" is an old word for family.

> After this I beheld, and, lo, a great multitude, which no man could number, of **all nations, and kindreds, and people, and tongues**, stood before the throne, and before the Lamb, clothed with white robes, and palms in their hands;

(Revelation 7:9)

What should our response be to the family of the Antichrist? The bible tells us that God wants representation of that family in Heaven, with Him. Now, I do not know who the Antichrist is, and if you do know, one thing you can, and should do, is to pray for his family. Pray that someone in his immediate family will get saved. Pray for them by name. Do you know the language they speak? Probably Arabic. If so, could you go and give them the gospel? To reach a close relative of the Antichrist with the gospel of Jesus Christ, would be like snatching a lamb from the mouth of a lion! Can you imagine what it would be like to lead his son or daughter, sister, brother, father, or mother, to saving faith in the Lord Jesus Christ? What an honour that would be! It would be well worth doing, though your own personal safety would be in doubt. Revelation 7:9, among other verses, certainly tells us that it is God's will that they hear the Gospel.

According to Daniel, the man of sin will come from a long line of men who worshipped a god other than the God of the Bible.

> *And the king shall do according to his will; and he shall exalt himself, and magnify himself above every god, and **shall speak marvellous things against the God of gods**, and shall prosper till the indignation be accomplished: for that that is determined shall be done. **Neither shall he regard the God of his fathers**, nor the desire of women, nor regard any god: for he shall magnify himself above all. (Daniel 11:37)*

Since his fathers worshipped a false god, then we can conclude that they are all lost, for there is salvation in no other name, than the name of Jesus Christ. It is God's will that someone in that family gets saved, preferrably more than one.

> *Neither is there salvation in any other: for there is none other name under heaven given among men, whereby we must be saved. (Acts 4:12)*

If we are to show the love of God to this family we need to send missionaries into the dragon's mouth! They need to hear that Jesus died for them! If you can't go yourself, could you send someone?

This should have been the response of the church in the past, toward both Jews and Arabs. Preach the gospel to the enemies of

God, and if they reject it, keep on preaching. Don't react in anger. Don't pick up a sword, unless it is the Sword of the Spirit, the Bible. Love your enemies and pray for those who persecute you.

Resources:

"Josephus: The Complete Works", Sword module version 1.1, Josephus: The Complete Works, translated by William Whiston, public domain

"Isralestine, the Ancient Blueprints of the Future Middle East", Salus, Bill, HighWay a division of Anomalous Publishing House, Crane 65633, USA (July 7, 2008)

"Obadiah's Indictment", Jack Kinsella, The Omega Letter, Saturday, November 25, 2006, Accessed 11/08/2010, from http://www.omegaletter.com/articles/articles.asp?ArticleID=6001& SearchFor=esau_-_hamas_-_and_-_the_-_last_-_days

"How Do You Spell 'Violence'? In the Middle East, it's Spelled H-A-M-A-S", The Omega Letter, Jack Kinsella, Friday, June 24, 2005, accessed 11/08/2010,   from http://www.omegaletter.com/articles/articles.asp?ArticleID=5567& SearchFor=How_-_do_-_you_-_spell_-_violence_-_H-A-M-A-S

"Prince of Darkness, Antichrist and the New World Order", Grant Jeffrey, Frontier Research Publications, Toronto, Ontario, Canada, 1994

"The Use of the Old Testament in the Book of Revelation", Fruchtenbaum, Dr. Arnold, The Pre-Trib Research Center, Mon 03 Dec 2007, Accessed 15/03/2009, http://www.pre-trib.org/articles/view/use-of-old-testament-in-book-revelation

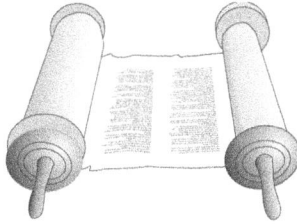

Eight

Homosexuality, Polygamy, Marriage, and the Antichrist

Many have noted that the bible does not specifically condemn polygamy. In fact God is not done with this form of family relationship. A time is coming when it will be practised around the world! Sounds like heresy? Let's examine a prophecy regarding Armageddon, and the return of Christ...

> *24 And it shall come to pass, that instead of sweet smell there shall be stink; and instead of a girdle a rent; and instead of well set hair baldness; and instead of stomacher a girding of sackcloth; and burning instead of beauty. 25 **Thy men shall fall by the sword, and thy mighty in the war.** 26 And her gates shall lament and mourn; and she being desolate shall sit upon the ground. **4:1 And in that day seven women shall take hold of one man, saying, We will eat our own bread, and wear our own apparel: only let us be called by thy name, to take away our reproach.** 2 In that day shall the branch of the LORD be beautiful and glorious, and the fruit of the earth shall be excellent and comely for them that are escaped of Israel. 3 And it shall come to pass, that he that is left in Zion, and he that remaineth in Jerusalem, shall be called holy, even every one that is written among the living in Jerusalem: (Isaiah 3:24-4:3)*

In Isaiah chapter three verses 9 to 12 we see Israel blatantly flaunting their sin. I do not believe we are currently seeing such depravity in Israel, to the extent described here. I think that what this passage is describing is the large number of Israelite women who have been shackled under Islam's heel for over a thousand years. After the Psalm 83 war they are released from the oppression of Islam and return to Israel. I think they will react to their new-found freedom by going wild! Their return to the God of Israel will only be lip service, until after He deals with them.

At this point we see God's judgment coming against them during the Tribulation, and Armageddon, at the end of chapter 3, and the result is that the men are killed in this war. While there may have been partial fulfilments of this prophecy in the past, the final, complete fulfilment is yet to come. In every war there are more men killed than women, but this prophecy gives us a ratio, seven to one, which will verify that this prophecy will be fulfilled to the letter!

The phrase "*in that day*" has two possible meanings. It can mean "*at the same time*" or it can mean "*one event logically follows another as a consequence of it, within a very short period of time*". In any event, it always means a very close context to the prior events. Clearly the seven women of Isaiah 4:1 are from the same generation that were flaunting their sexuality in 3:16. We see an amazing change of attitude of these women from 3:16 to 4:1. At first they are strutting around with jewellery and sensual clothing, not caring what their actions do to men. After Armageddon they will beg to be a part of a harem! They will no longer strut around but will be modest and hard working. What has happened is that they have been saved by Jesus Christ in the mean time, both spiritually and physically. They have been brought to Christ by the horrors of the Tribulation, and the preaching of the 144,000 Jewish evangelists.

The men that they come to for marriage, in Isaiah 4:1, are the same men who are declared holy in verse 3. In 4:2 we see that the phrase "*for them that are escaped of Israel.*" is a reference to the judgments spoken of in chapter 3. While these things may have had a partial fulfilment in the Babylonian captivity, the final complete fulfilment is still future. Today Jerusalem has annual gay pride marches. The inhabitants of that city have never been called holy. This is a future event which will take place only when Jesus returns. Those men will be holy polygamists! As we have seen in the last chapter some of these women will be Edomites. (Jeremiah 49:11 & Amos 9:12)

How can we date this prophecy? There is a cause and effect relationship between the events of chapter three and four. So many men die in the war that it is only after peace is established, that the women go and ask for marriage. No one will be looking for marriage during Armageddon! At that time they will only be looking for survival! Look at verse 2. Who is "*the Branch*"? Jesus Christ and none other! When was the branch "*beautiful and glorious*"? It was not at his first coming, for Isaiah says in chapter 53 that He had "*no beauty that we should desire him*". Jesus has always been beautiful and glorious in Heaven, but this is something we can't see. This is a reference to His second coming, and this event will be verifiable on earth.

When we go back to the passages that speak about the Great Tribulation period in Matthew 24:31 and Mark 13:27 we see that the women spoken of in Isaiah 4:1 are the very same people Jesus spoke of in these two passages. They will be the ones rescued by angels, as Jesus brings judgment on the Antichrist and his armies. They will have seen their neighbours, who took the mark of the Beast, killed with the sword of the mouth of Jesus! These seven women will not be coming to one man to ask for his hand in marriage, without the prior permission of Jesus Christ himself! Having seen the destruction and horrors of the Tribulation and Armageddon, there is no way they would be so presumptuous!

I expect that some of them will visit Him in Jerusalem, and will ask something like this of Him: "*Lord, you have killed our men in Armageddon. Now who are we to marry so that we may have children? Will you create husbands for us?*" I expect that His answer to them will be something like this: "*You are free to marry men in groups of up to seven women. I am not going to create new men for you. You will have to make do with the men who survived Armageddon with you. You were there for the events of Isaiah 3, now go and read chapter 4.*"

In verse 3 we see that everyone who survives the Tribulation will be called holy. This includes both men and women!

Notice that these women are not asking for illicit affairs. They want his name and a legal marriage, because with Jesus, the Branch, ruling there will be no illicit affairs allowed anywhere on earth! In order for them to have children they must be married! Notice also that they are not asking for any thing that is considered normal in marriage. The world has suffered such carnage, and chaos, during the Great Tribulation that all they want is the legitimate name of a husband, and children. They are willing to support themselves. Though it does not say so, I am sure these men will be good fathers and will teach their children about the things they have seen, and about their Saviour, Jesus Christ.

These families will be an anomaly in the history of the world. They themselves will have children with a 50/50, male/female ratio. As Jesus reigns in peace, the world will experience a population boom like it has never seen before. The generations following will not know war and most marriages will be one man/one woman for life, but most of this batch of polygamous marriages will live throughout the entire millennium! God has done this deliberately. The fact of these polygamous marriages will be seen as evidence of the power of God throughout the millennium!

Five hundred years into the millennium, a 20th generation child will be able to go to his twenty times great grandfather and say "*Twenty times Great Grandpa, why do you have seven wives when everyone else I know has only one?*" The 20X Great Grandpa will be able to tell his descendant "*When I was young, the people of the world thought they could fight against the Lord and they sent their armies against Him at the great battle of Armageddon. As a result almost every man of that generation died bearing arms against our great King Jesus. This left us with so many extra women that we had to marry seven per man, so that they all could have children. Jesus is loving as a ruler, but if you rebel against him you will end up as those armies did.*"

As the world is rebuilt during the millennium there will be few signs of the Tribulation left over, but these families will serve as proof to their descendants, that the story of the Tribulation is true, and that Jesus is invincible. Those who do rebel against Him at the end will have no excuse.

Isaiah echoes the thought, that men will be rare, again in 13:12, another reference to the aftermath of Armageddon.

I will make a man more precious than fine gold; even a man than the golden wedge of Ophir.

He is not saying that He will make men good, or pure, though we have already seen that they will be, but that so many more men will die in judgment than women, that men will be rare the way gold is rare in comparison to iron. Have you ever seen the golden wedge of Ophir? Neither have I, but if it still exists there is only one. That is very rare.

Men have much more of a pride problem than women. The attitude of "*I'll do it my way*" is so very common that it is clearly a part of our nature. Women are far more likely to ask directions than a man, and most are far more likely to seek the Lord than men. When the men of the world come against Jesus at Armageddon, some of their wives will be at home seeking the Lord.

Though this passage specifically refers to Israel, if we compare it to Revelation 19 we see that the slaughter of the men of war is not limited to Israel but will be worldwide.

> *17 And I saw an angel standing in the sun; and he cried with a loud voice, saying to all the fowls that fly in the midst of heaven, Come and gather yourselves together unto the supper of the great God; 18 That ye may eat the flesh of kings, and the flesh of captains, and the flesh of mighty men, and the flesh of horses, and of them that sit on them, and the flesh of all men, both free and bond, both small and great. 19 **And I saw the beast, and the kings of the earth, and their armies, gathered together to make war against him that sat on the horse, and against his army.** 20 And the beast was taken, and with him the false prophet that wrought miracles before him, with which he deceived them that had received the mark of the beast, and them that worshipped his image. These both were cast alive into a lake of fire burning with brimstone. 21 And the remnant were slain with the sword of him that sat upon the horse, which sword proceeded out of his mouth: and all the fowls were filled with their flesh. (Revelation 19:17-21)*

While the passage in Isaiah 3 and 4 specifically deals with Israel, its implications are general for the whole world! Every man who picks up arms to fight Jesus Christ, at his return shall be killed, and thus the majority of people who survive the Great Tribulation will be women. Of course many women will die in that war as well. Revelation 13 tells us that any person who has the mark of the Beast will die. It doesn't matter what that person's status is, taking the mark is a declaration of war against God.

An interesting little aside in this passage is the rapture of the Antichrist and the false prophet. God is so angry with these two men that they do not even wait for the day of judgment, but are picked up physically and tossed immediately into the Lake of Fire! Obviously their rapture will be similar to the rapture of the Church, their bodies will be changed instantly into indestructible bodies, so they can enter the Lake of Fire without being consumed. They will be the first two inhabitants of that place and will be all alone there until Judgment day at the end of the millennial reign of Christ.

At the end of World War 2 Adolf Hitler, in desperation, conscripted all men from the age of sixteen to sixty years into his army (Volkssturm or Peoples Army). The Beast will be at least as desperate. You know that he will not accept any man without the Mark of the Beast into the army, thus the slaughter will be complete. Not one soldier will survive! (Rev. 14:9-11) The carnage will be world-wide and only those without the mark, who have received Jesus as Lord and Saviour, will survive.   Still, the Scriptures indicate that of the survivors many more will be female than male.

The Antichrist and Marriage

H ow does the Antichrist himself compare in his policies to those of Jesus on marriage? Let's take a look at what Daniel has to say about it.

> *Neither shall he regard the God of his fathers, **nor the desire of women**, nor regard any god: for he shall magnify himself above all. (Daniel 11:37)*

Many commentators believe the phrase "*nor the desire of women*" indicates that this man will be a homosexual. While he will inherit the Roman Empire, and the majority of Caesars were sexually deviant, I do not think this is a reference to his personal life. I would not deny that, like the Caesars, he could be a closet homosexual, however, this is not referring to something secret, but will be a major sign visible to the whole world. This reference is in regard to the way he governs the nations under his control, to his public policy as a lawmaker.

If the desire of women is to be married and have children then we see that the Antichrist will be a man who will formulate a policy to forbid polygamy in his area of jurisdiction. This would effectivelly eliminate the possibility of a European or North American Antichrist, but would indicate that he will most likely come from an area where polygamy has been practised for a long time. Many scholars believe that the Antichrist will arise after the war of Gog and Magog spoken of in Ezekiel 38 and 39. As we have seen most of those nations are Muslim today. That passage states that one in six soldiers, who come against Israel, will survive.

Modern translations paraphrase this statement to say something like; *"he shall not pay any attention to the god desired by women"* or *"he shall not desire women"*. This is incorrect, and the result of translators inserting their own interpretation into Scripture, rather than simply translating word-for-word what God has placed there. Lets look at verses 36 and 37 together and see if we can make some sense of them.

> *And the king shall do according to his will; and he shall exalt himself, and magnify himself above every god, and **shall speak marvellous things against the God of gods**, and shall prosper till the indignation be accomplished: for that that is determined shall be done. **Neither shall he regard the God of his fathers**, nor the desire of women, nor regard any god: for he shall magnify himself above all. (Daniel 11:36-37)*

Here *"the God of gods"* and the *"God of his fathers"* are separated by the word *"Neither"*. The author is continuing with the same thought throughout. We can surmise then that the Antichrist shall not be from a Jewish, Christian or Catholic family, for these all worship, to some extent, the God of gods. The god of his fathers is another god. Another monotheistic God, thus ruling out a Hindu family as well. Given that the people of Edom have mostly converted to Islam, the God of his fathers must be the one named Allah.

We see in this passage, however, that he himself does not regard, or respect, even the god of his fathers.

Notice the link between the "*God of his fathers*" and the "*desire of women*". This is no accident. The link is this: Islam, from the very beginning, has allowed men to have up to four wives, and unlimited concubines. It is written in the Qur'an, though it was really an old practise that was simply continued. This is one of the predominant characteristics of Islam throughout the world.

I am NOT saying women desire to be a part of a harem, but in a society where the majority of men are killed in war, women generally would prefer life in a harem to a life without children. It's the famous "*Last man in the world*" scenario.

The Desire of Women

What did Daniel mean by the "*desire of women*"? We can ask women we know, and we might get an idea, but that could be wrong. Our modern culture has changed the interpretation of this passage! In the western media today, young women are constantly told that in order to make a positive contribution to society they must find a job. Jobs that deal with children are downplayed, and motherhood is despised. Children are viewed as a burden. Abortion is portrayed as a right, rather than the state-sanctioned murder that it is.

Today we live at a time when the words of Jesus have come to pass: "*For, behold, the days are coming, in the which they shall say, Blessed are the barren, and the wombs that never bare, and the paps which never gave suck.*" (Luke 23:29) I submit to you that this situation has been orchestrated by the devil himself. Looking at western society today one would never understand what Daniel is referring to. The question comes down to: What does Scripture say about the "*desire of women*"?

The first time the phrase is used in Genesis 3 where it links a husband with children:

> 16 Unto the woman he said, I will greatly multiply thy
> sorrow and thy conception; in sorrow thou shalt bring forth
> children; and thy desire shall be to thy husband, and he shall

rule over thee.

While the phrase is not used often in Scripture we can look at several biblical women and see what their desire was;

Sarah was so desperate to have a child that she was willing to let her husband marry a second wife, Hagar, so she could call the resulting child her own (Genesis 16:1-4). Things did not work out as she had planned, however, and the result is the turmoil in the middle East that still exists today.

Rebekah had the same desire for children as Sarah:

> *And Isaac intreated the LORD for his wife, because she was barren: and the LORD was intreated of him, and Rebekah his wife conceived. (Genesis 25:21)*

Jacob's wives had the same desire, and competed with each other to have children in order to be favoured by their husband. They even went so far as to give him their maids, as concubines, so they could have children by them, like Sarah,

> *And when Rachel saw that she bare Jacob no children, Rachel envied her sister; and said unto Jacob, Give me children, or else I die. And Jacob's anger was kindled against Rachel: and he said, Am I in God's stead, who hath withheld from thee the fruit of the womb? And she said, Behold my maid Bilhah, go in unto her; and she shall bear upon my knees, that I may also have children by her. (Genesis 30:1-3)*

Rachel, the woman Jacob loved, was the last to have children.

> *And God remembered Rachel, and God hearkened to her, and opened her womb. And she conceived, and bare a son; and said, **God hath taken away my reproach:** (Genesis 30:22 & 23)*

Here the term *"reproach"* is used to describe the condition of barrenness, or sterility. In our modern, backward society, many have themselves rendered sterile, thinking that this is preferrable to having a family. This is actually an attack on God, for many feel that if God is going to throw the majority of humanity into Hell, then they do not want to add to that number, but God is glorified even by those in Hell!

Abraham's nephew Lot's daughters are another study of this same phenomenon. These two women had been married, or at least betrothed, but their husbands had stayed in Sodom and been destroyed with that city. In Genesis 19:30-38 we see the story where Lot and his two daughters lived alone in a remote area. With no other man around, his two daughters devised a plan to seduce their father. They got him drunk, and slept with him, and thus were both pregnant by him. We are justly horrified by this story, but I want you to notice the motivation of these two women. They knew that if they did not have children there would be no one to care for them in their old age. This same motivation is revealed over and over again in Scripture. I am not justifying what they did, I am just saying that this is the biblical definition for "*the desire of women*".

Tamar, Judah's daughter-in-law, was another woman desperate for children. She had been married to Er, Judah's oldest son, and when he died she married his brother Onan. Onan did not want to do his duty to her, but practised the withdrawal method of birth control, so God slew him. She was then promised the third son Shelah, who was much younger. As Shelah grew up she saw that Judah was not going to keep his word and give her to Shelah. At this point Tamar went out, disguised herself, dressed as a prostitute, and seduced her father-in-law. When it was found out that she was pregnant, Judah was going to have her put to death, until he found out that he was the father. The story is found in Genesis 38:11-30.

Why would a woman act the way Tamar acted? It was because she had the same deep desire that most women have had since creation; To have children. Her actions were that of a desperate woman, not those of a habitual prostitute. In the end she was included in the line of the messiah! I think it is interesting that though Judah had sex with her one time, he never did so again. It is improper for a man to marry his daughter-in-law, and he knew it even though the law had not yet been written.

Hannah, one of two wives of a man named Elkanah, was a godly woman, yet was vexed by the other wife, for Peninah had several children and held it against her.

> *But unto Hannah he gave a worthy portion; for he loved Hannah: but the LORD had shut up her womb. And her adversary also provoked her sore, for to make her fret, because the LORD had shut up her womb. And as he did so year by year, when she went up to the house of the LORD, so she provoked her; therefore she wept, and did not eat. Then said Elkanah her husband to her, Hannah, why weepest thou? and why eatest thou not? and why is thy heart grieved? am not I better to thee than ten sons? (1 Samuel 1:5-8)*

We see in the following passage that Elkanah's words, though true, did not comfort his wife. Hannah knew that as soon as Elkanah died, she would be destitute. His estate would have to be divided up among his children, all of whom came from Peninah. Children were the old-age-security plan in those days. We see her desperation in the passage where she went up to the tabernacle to pray...

> *And she was in bitterness of soul, and prayed unto the LORD, and wept sore. And she vowed a vow, and said, O LORD of hosts, if thou wilt indeed look on the affliction of thine handmaid, and remember me, and not forget thine handmaid, but wilt give unto thine handmaid a man child, then I will give him unto the LORD all the days of his life, and there shall no razor come upon his head. And it came to pass, as she continued praying before the LORD, that Eli marked her mouth. Now Hannah, she spake in her heart; only her lips moved, but her voice was not heard: therefore Eli thought she had been drunken. And Eli said unto her, How long wilt thou be drunken? put away thy wine from thee. (1 Samuel 1:10-14)*

Hannah was desperate to have a son, so desperate that she did some things that some might consider strange. The priest of God thought her actions were those of a drunken woman. Though the word *"reproach"* is not contained in this passage the concept is central to it. Her barrenness was a reproach to her, and was the cause of her desperation. Ultimately Hannah's prayers were answered and she ended up with a total of six children including Samuel. It was the Lord Himself who opened up Hannah's womb, and gave her children.

Elisha the prophet stayed with a couple from Shunem when he was in their area. At the wife's request they built a room for him to stay in when he was there. Elisha wanted to do a kindness to pay her back for her kindness to him, and asked his servant what would be appropriate...

> *And he said, What then is to be done for her? And Gehazi answered, Verily she hath no child, and her husband is old. And he said, Call her. And when he had called her, she stood in the door. And he said, About this season, according to the time of life, thou shalt embrace a son. And she said, Nay, my lord, thou man of God, do not lie unto thine handmaid. And the woman conceived, and bare a son at that season that Elisha had said unto her, according to the time of life. (2 Kings 4:14-17)*

Later on her son died in her arms and the following ensued.

> *And when she came to the man of God to the hill, she caught him by the feet: but Gehazi came near to thrust her away. And the man of God said, Let her alone; for her soul is vexed within her: and the LORD hath hid it from me, and hath not told me. Then she said, Did I desire a son of my lord? did I not say, Do not deceive me? (2 Kings 4:27-28)*

This woman had a deep desire to have a child. When she said to Elisha "*do not deceive me*" she was saying, in effect, "*do not give me a false hope*". When the child died she reminded him of this fact. The child was raised from the dead as a result of her prayer, for while she was talking to Elisha, God heard her. God doesn't give anyone false hope.

Elizabeth, the wife of Zacharias the priest, was barren and at an advanced age. While working in the Temple he had a vision in which Gabriel the angel told him that his wife would have a son. Zacharias did not believe the angel so he was made dumb (silent) until the day he named his son John (Jochanan). It is instructive what Elisabeth said when she conceived.

> *And after those days his wife Elisabeth conceived, and hid herself five months, saying, Thus hath the Lord dealt with me*

*in the days wherein he looked on me, to **take away my
reproach among men.** (Luke 1:24 & 25)*

We see then that Elisabeth's reproach is the same as
Rachel's, and the reproach mentioned in Isaiah 4:1. Her
desire was to have a son, thus pregnancy took away her
reproach. It was the same for Sarah, Rebekah, Rachel, Lot's
daughters, Tamar, Hannah, the Shunamite woman and many
others. Thus, generally speaking, the desire of women is to
have children, preferably by her husband. This is what Daniel
is referring to in Daniel 11:37. God requires that a woman
who has a child also has a husband. He wants fathers to be
involved in the raising of their children, and supportive of
their wives.

As we have seen, the Antichrist will arise after the war of
Ezekiel 38 and 39, the war of Gog and Magog. In that war
one out of six soldiers who come against Israel shall return to
their homeland.

*Therefore, thou son of man, prophesy against Gog, and
say, Thus saith the Lord GOD; Behold, I am against thee, O
Gog, the chief prince of Meshech and Tubal: And I will turn
thee back, and **leave but the sixth part of thee,** and will
cause thee to come up from the north parts, and will bring
thee upon the mountains of Israel: (Ezekiel 39:1-2)*

In the returning army only one sixth shall survive, and the
dead will leave behind their women. Since the natural birth
rate is roughly 50/50, male/female there will be many women
without a man. If you look at the nationalities of the armies
involved you see that most nations mentioned are Muslim
today, with the exception of Russia. In those countries
polygamy has always been practised from long before
Mohammed until now. With very few men available, it will
be natural and normal for several women to request marriage
to one man. Polygamy has always been considered normal in
that society, since pre-islamic times.

The Antichrist shall not respect the desire of those women,
but shall make laws to prohibit the practice of polygamy. As
a result, women who want children, will have to have them
through illicit affairs. As a result they will become harlots,
prostitutes and mensteaders. Thus sin will increase because of

this man, but many "*Christians*" will think he is a Christian or a "*Man of God*", precisely because of this policy! They will think this is a positive step forward! This is because so many Christians rely on the traditions of men, and the interpretations of their pastor, rather than to read the Bible for themselves! Consequently, the Christian Church is preparing the way for the Antichrist!

Now consider 1 Timothy 4:3 and let's ask the question; What does he mean by "*forbidding men to marry?*" Is this only a reference to the Catholic practise of forbidding priests to marry, or does it actually include the prohibition of polygamy? I think the answer is clear.

Where did this idea of "*one man/one woman for life*" come from, if not from the Bible? Rome, actually. Israel was the only part of the Roman Empire where polygamy was legal. The Roman Caesars and Senators were not more moral people than the leaders of Israel. If anything they were more depraved. The Caesars were well known for their affairs, and even homosexuality.

Of the first twelve Caesars only one, Claudius, would have been considered sexually normal by today's standards. (The Twelve Caesars, Suetonius) No doubt the Antichrist will follow in the footsteps of the Caesars, but I think that if he is a homosexual, it will be a "*closet*" type of homosexuality, at least in the early stages of his reign. The "*desire of women*" spoken of in Daniel 11:37 has nothing to do with his personal life, or homosexuality, but with the laws he enacts as a ruler. This is a direct reference to Christ's reign in Isaiah 4:1.

Very obviously the reason that polygamy was prohibited in Rome was because if a man had multiple wives, he would have had multiple children with a claim against his property. We see this in the book of Ruth regarding Boaz's cousin. By prohibiting polygamy, Rome protected the sexual infidels from living up to their responsibilities. By labelling their children as "*Bastards*" they did not have to provide support for them, or their mothers! This is called "*Blaming the victim*"! As Paul said, it was all about money! (1 Tim. 6:10) Morality was just a smoke-screen for their real reasons.

When taking Czech language lessons I was rather surprised to find that the Czech word for a novel is "*román*". I asked why and the answer was because it is a "*Roman story"*. This is where we get the word *"romance"*. Romance has its history in Rome and not in the Bible. The biblical marriage relationship is practical, moral, based on love, and not based on romance. Romance, in comparison is winning a person by flattery, or trickery, and using them for your own pleasure.

When Constantine formed the Roman Catholic Church he simply adopted the morality of Rome as if it were Christian, and when Luther and the reformers left that church, they clung to Roman morality still thinking it was Christian! Like Laban's daughters, sometimes believers hang on to things that don't belong to them, and ultimately bring destruction! During the many wars throughout the last two thousand years the *"Christian Church"* has been a party to turning countless young women into harlots for the very reasons outlined in this chapter.

Please let me say that what I am teaching is not something I have invented. It is there in plain language in the Word of God, and has been there for thousands of years! Christians have misinterpreted what was said, because of their preconceived ideas about God's character, and morality. Once you have a system of biblical interpretation it is very difficult to break-free and see what it really says.

It is not wrong for a man to have only one wife. The majority of men have always had only one wife, even in David's day. This observation leads to another question: Why did God not choose some monogamist to write the Psalms, and be the most notable ancestor of Jesus Christ? I think the answer lies in the fact that David, like Moses, knew the Lord in a way that few Christians, or Jews, have known Him before or since. You may be saved and on your way to Heaven, but how well do you know your God? The Lord is so wild, and untamable, and Holy, that He frightens us, as well He should, yet if we draw close to Him we find He is so attractive, we are drawn like a moth to a flame. Unlike the flame, however, He is able to preserve us and cleanse us.

During World War 1 there were approximately 19 million people killed, the vast majority of whom were men. Each of them left behind a woman, some of whom already had children, though many were childless. The *"Christian"* policy of allowing a man only one wife led to huge amounts of suffering, and sin! Those bereaved women still had the same desires as all women throughout the ages, only they were forbidden to marry. I personally believe God sent the flu epidemic of 1919 to even out the numbers.

The same thing occured after the second World War. Did all of those women spend their lives without children? Of course not! They did what women throughout history have done; they stole men and had affairs. This led directly to the common idea that French and German women are *"loose women"*.

In the 1980s there was a war between Iran and Iraq in which approximately one million men were killed. Those countries do not have the same problem as the West, since they have always allowed polygamy. The result has been that the women left without a man simply had to become the second, or third, wife of a man who had survived the conflict. While we in the West do not like this solution, these women at least have a chance to have a family. Their nations have given them the chance to be respected in their community. Muhammed was correct to allow polygamy to continue, although it appears that his motivation was simply because of his own lusts. We can see this in the way women are treated in the Qur'an, and the Muslim world. God does not allow polygamy because men are superior, or more favored, but because of His love for women. Men are more likely to rebel against God, and are more likely to be killed for their rebellion!

Today, in the west, we tend to think we are more advanced than those of the past. The widespread teaching of evolution has made westerners think that they are more *"evolved"* than those *"primitive"* ancient people. The truth is that those men, like David, and Jacob were morally more advanced than western society today. They understood the problems faced by women without children. We have a tendency to think that our government programs will care for our aged parents, but the truth is that our system is about to fall apart, and where will the money come from then? God had a program for war-ravaged nations so the widows would have someone to care for them in their old age: polygamy.

These laws against polygamy which are considered *"progressive"* in Western society are actually regressive, and responsible for much of the moral depravity we see around us. They turn women into harlots, yet Christians who support them think they are following God! This tragedy has played itself out time and time again throughout the last two millennia, and very soon it shall play its role again during the reign of the Antichrist.

The Moral High Ground

As we study the personality of Lucifer in Scripture, who became the devil, we find that his goal is to become like the most High God. As he said; "*I will ascend above the heights of the clouds; I will be like the most High.*" (Isaiah 14:14) While he is evil, in order to deceive many people he has to appear to be "good". Accordingly he has been searching for an area of morality where he can appear to hold "*the Moral High Ground*".

The area of marriage in general, and polygamy in particular, is the one area where he has found this appearance of "*Moral High Ground*" in the eyes of many. Remember that the Devil is able to transform himself into the appearance of an angel of light. (2 Corinthians 11:13-15) As this subject is very contentious, I want to remind you to read every passage I have quoted in its entirety, make sure that what you believe is what God says and not what I, or anyone else says.

> *Now the Spirit speaketh expressly, that in the latter times some shall depart from the faith, giving heed to seducing spirits, and doctrines of devils; Speaking lies in hypocrisy; having their conscience seared with a hot iron; Forbidding to marry, and commanding to abstain from meats, which God hath created to be received with thanksgiving of them which believe and know the truth. (1 Timothy 4:1-3)*

As you read through the Old Testament you will see descriptions of one war after another. In the descriptive passage you will also notice that the count of the dead from that particular conflict is usually in the thousands, and at one point is actually a half million men. (2 Chronicles 13:17) Given a birth rate of roughly 50/50 male/female children born in Israel, as in any nation, this condition of constant warfare left a shortage of men for many generations.

God's response to the disparity between the numbers of men

and women was to allow men to marry more than one wife. His reason was that women need an old age security plan. Another reason for His allowing polygamy/polygyny was for the survival of the nation. How was a nation of old women to protect itself from its hostile neighbours?   Those women needed to have sons and daughters who would care for their mothers in their old age, and also be willing to join the army to fight off the nation's many enemies.

The bible states that God does not change, that He is the same yesterday, today and forever. If this is the truth then why does it seem that there are contradictions between the Old and New Testaments?   The truth is that there are no contradictions in the bible. Neither Jesus, nor the apostles, ever contradicted the writings of the Old Testament. This is not about me, it is about God and His relationship with His creation. It ultimately is about His love for people, and His provision for the weaker.

In the book "The Twelve Caesars" by the first century historian Gaius Suetonius, one is struck by the fact that of these twelve men, eleven were accused of sexual perversion. Caesar Augustus, the ruler at the time of Jesus' birth had adopted his nephews, Mark Anthony and his brother as children, and was later accused by them of demanding sexual favours in exchange for this adoption. Similar accusations are leveled against all of the Caesars except Claudius. Nero seems to have descended to the deepest depravity, and actually married a man who had been castrated. Given the stand against perversion that Christians have always taken, it is no mystery the hostility that men like Nero have held against the Christian Church.

All the Caesars married women at one time or another, some of them marrying more than one wife, but only one at a time. It seems that they married in order to have successors, and were essentially "closet" homosexuals, playing sexual games with little boys. This practice was carried over from Greece and the "Platonic" ideal. In the nineteen thirties and forties this same practice was carried on by many Nazi's in Germany. The excellent book "The Pink Swastika" by Scott Lively and Kevin Abrams, gives substantial documentation to this fact.

Simultaneously, while such perversion and depravity was taking place at the upper echelons of Roman society, polygamy, the practice of marrying more than one wife at a time, was banned throughout the Roman empire, with the one exception being Israel.

As a young Christian I made the mistake that many young

Christians make. Contrary to the Word of God, my parent's, and pastor's advice, I dated and married a non-Christian. This relationship only lasted a couple of years and produced one child. My son is a wonderful person, but I am not talking about him, but only of the morality and wisdom of my own actions. Strangely enough, we do not often hear preachers speak against being "unequally yoked" as often as we did thirty or more years ago.

God used my marriage break-up to bring me back to Himself. No matter how hard and often I prayed to restore the marriage, it was not to be. The Lord had other plans for me. Ultimately he used that tragedy to bring me closer to himself, and the curiosity aroused has resulted in this book.

A few years later, I was engaged to the young woman who ultimately became my second wife. During counselling our pastor stated to me that, if I were to remarry, I would lose the right to work as a pastor or deacon in a Christian church. His reasoning was based on 1 Timothy 3:2, 12 and Titus 1:6 which state that a bishop/pastor, or a deacon, must be the "*husband of one wife*". He stated that this was a reference to divorce, and perhaps also polygamy. Since that time it has become apparent to me that it is likely only a reference to polygamy. As we go on I think you will agree with me.

I am sorry to say that as I have read articles about polygamy on the Internet, I have found that most who are in favour of this practise have questionable motives. Some men say that polygamy is acceptable because they like sex and thus want to marry many wives. They should remember that a man with two wives is disqualified from Christian ministry as either a pastor/bishop or deacon. They should also remember that God intended marriage for life, and if you marry more than one woman you have dependants for the rest of your life.

In the same vein many of my Christian brothers take the opposite stand and contradict themselves on this subject, doing harm to their own cause in the process! Much of Christianity has absorbed a view of morality that came from Rome rather than the Bible!

A few years after my second marriage a missionary came to our church, speaking about his ministry in Africa. In his message he stated that when polygamists came to Christ they were told to leave all but their first wife. He told them that only the first marriage was legitimate, and to live with more than one wife is to live in sin. I have since heard this same teaching in other churches and denominations, so it appears to be common among professing Christians today.

At the time I accepted what they said, after all they were the *"experts"*, and who was I to question them? There were, however, some nagging questions that kept coming up as I read the Scriptures. When I read *"But to the rest speak I, not the Lord: If any brother hath a wife that believeth not, and she be pleased to dwell with him, let him not put her away."* (1 Corinthians 7:12) I could not help but ask *"does this verse apply in this situation?"* If a Muslim man marries four Muslim women, and then he gets saved, he will have four wives who *"believeth not"*. Ultimately I realized that it does apply, and it seems that these missionaries are the cause of the wives of these men committing adultery!

In the same chapter Paul goes on to state *"Let every man abide in the same calling wherein he was called."* And *"Brethren, let every man, wherein he is called, therein abide with God."* (1 Corinthians 7:20 and 24) Immediately afterwards he goes on to talk about marriage again. Using the rule of context we see that Paul is speaking of marriage throughout the entire chapter. Many translators, and bible publishers, try to separate the middle part of the chapter from the beginning and the end, but those divisions were not there in the original. Thus if a man is a polygamist before he is saved he must not leave any of his wives! This is according to Scripture, the Holy Word of God!

Weren't David, Moses, Abraham, Jacob, Gideon, Solomon and others polygamists? If it was wrong, why is God silent about it in His dealings with them? Abraham was called a *"Friend of God"*. Many times in Scripture God calls Himself the *"God of Jacob"* without even mentioning Abraham or Isaac. Jacob was the man of four wives! Today many churches would not allow a man like Jacob to become a member. David the polygamist, is the only person in both the Old and New Testaments, who is called a *"man after God's own heart"*! (1 Samuel 13:14, Acts 13:22) We sing songs based on David's psalms, but David himself would not be welcome in our midst! Today *"the Gideons"* would not allow Gideon to be a member of their organization, and certainly not a leader!

This contradiction does not come from the Bible. It is a product of human reasoning, for God never contradicts Himself!

I have heard pastors call polygamy *"an attack on the family"*. These same pastors also say that *"homosexuality is an attack on the family*". (Name witheld to protect the guilty)   Are they therefore saying that polygamy is equal to homosexuality?   They are, and in fact many of these men would consider it even more depraved, than allowing Gay marriage, for our governments to allow polygamy. If this is the case the logical questions arise: Why didn't God destroy Abraham at the same time He destroyed Sodom and Gomorrah? Why didn't he destroy Jacob, or at least confront him over his polygamy? Why didn't God destroy David instead of rewarding him with being a "*Father of the Messiah*"? Where there no monogamists in Israel at the time of David?

Our pastors point to Jesus' words in Matthew 19:6-9 especially the phrase "*from the beginning it was not so*", to imply that marriage is only for two people, and it has always been thus "*from the beginning*". The truth is that even polygamous marriages are always between two people. The women do not marry each other!

> *Wherefore they are no more twain, but one flesh. What therefore God hath joined together, let not man put asunder. They say unto him, Why did Moses then command to give a writing of divorcement, and to put her away? He saith unto them, Moses because of the hardness of your hearts suffered you to put away your wives: but from the beginning it was not so. And I say unto you, Whosoever shall put away his wife, except it be for fornication, and shall marry another, committeth adultery: and whoso marrieth her which is put away doth commit adultery. (Matthew 19:6-9)*

Remember that every word is important, not just general thoughts.

What was the subject that Jesus was addressing? If it is God who puts the couple together, does this automatically exclude any other relationship?   First, we must understand that Jesus was specifically speaking of divorce or "*putting away*" of one's wife, and taking away your support from her. The passage says nothing about a man marrying more than one woman at the same time. Marriage is a permanent relationship between a man and woman. Divorce is adultery because the first wife is abandoned in order for the husband to use her support money for the second wife.   The husband is breaking his vow to support her. If he marries two women, and supports, and continues the relationship with both at the same time, it is not adultery according to the Bible! Jesus was not contradicting Exodus 21:10, He was explaining it!

> *If he take him another wife; her food, her raiment, and her duty of marriage, shall he not diminish. (Exodus 21:10)*

What did Moses mean by "*duty of marriage*"? It includes the entire relationship of a wife with her husband, from cooking meals and cleaning, to communication and sexual intimacy. If the husband withdraws himself from his first wife, he is the cause of her committing adultery!

God is concerned with how we treat each other. He wants to form us into the image of His Son. He never broke a promise, ever! Each person has the same value to God, therefore to cease supporting one wife in favour of another is to devalue the first wife, and to devalue your own word. God can love and support many people at the same time, and He always honours His word.

To whom is Jesus referring to in verse eight? Who is it with a hard heart? Was it Moses, or the people he was governing? What does it say? Moses didn't have a hard heart. He understood the love of God. Jesus was not referring to David either, for David had a heart after God's own heart! (1 Samuel 13:14, Acts 13:22)

Why would God create only one wife for Adam? Was He setting up an example for us or could there be another explanation? Did the Bible ever say that the example in the garden of Eden was to be the only legitimate pattern of marriage in all of human history? What does the Bible say?

> *Therefore shall a man leave his father and his mother, and shall cleave unto his wife: and they shall be one flesh. (Genesis 2:24)*

Notice that in the original the word "*two*" is not in the text. A man is one flesh with his wife. The word "*two*" is inserted in our English translations, in the new testament references to this passage, but it is not in the original. It thus follows that a man is "*one flesh*" with his first, and each subsequent wife. His relationship with each wife is on a one-to-one basis, and is permanent. It is this permanence that Jesus was referring to in his discourse on divorce.

Please don't forget that there were other things not done in the garden of Eden that most people do every day. Adam was a vegetarian. It was not until after the flood, some fifteen hundred years later, that Noah was told he could eat meat. The eating of animal flesh is the result of sin, but it is not a sin in itself. The sin of mankind has caused some of the original plants to become extinct, or to be degraded to such an extent that complete vegetarian nutrition is not possible, or at best very difficult. In time it became necessary, or at least desirable, for people to eat meat.

Adam was created naked, and it was not until he sinned that he began to wear clothing. If you go about naked today you are considered strange and will be arrested, given enough time.

No doubt it was not God's plan for men to have multiple wives in the original perfect world. What happened, however, is that sin entered the picture, and men started killing each other off, or dying early in crazy stunts. Polygamy is thus an indirect result of sin, as is the eating of meat, or the wearing of clothes.

Adam was created with only one wife. It was later, as a result of war, and death, that men were allowed to marry more than one wife. It is not a sin per-se for a man to marry a second or third wife, but it is always the result of sin, though not necessarily the sin of that couple. It could be the result of the sin of one nation attacking a neighbouring nation, and killing large numbers of its men. In the same way the largest sin of this type, that the world will ever witness, Armageddon, will result in the largest number of practising polygamists the world has ever seen, and they will be holy men of God!

Do not forget that David, **the** "*Man After God's Own Heart*", had access to the books of Moses, and did not understand Genesis 2:24 to mean that polygamy was forbidden. Very clearly he understood this passage to mean that marriage was for life. It is obvious from the life of David that he took his vows seriously. The only time he fell in this regard, was in his relationship with Bathsheba, a married woman. Notice though, that even in this situation David did not break his own vows, rather he disregarded the vows Uriah had made to Bathsheba. Technically it was Uriah's vows that David disrespected, since the woman does not make vows in a Jewish wedding.

Imagine the Garden of Eden where Adam has been created with two wives, Eve and Evelyn, both equally beautiful and perfect. Now Eve is approached by the serpent and eats the fruit. Evelyn, like Adam, wasn't there when the fruit was eaten, but discovers Eve's sin at the same time as Adam. Now Adam has a predicament. One wife has sinned and the other hasn't. If he eats the fruit it will leave Evelyn alone in fellowship with God. If he doesn't, it leaves Eve alone to suffer the wrath of God. As the Bible says, Adam wasn't deceived. He would have to chose Evelyn and leave Eve to suffer God's wrath. He would still have one perfect wife. The Lake of Fire would only have one occupant besides the fallen angels.

This scenario sounds good to us, except for a huge problem from God's perspective. God never intended that Heaven's occupants would be there by their own righteousness. Had this scenario taken place, all of human history would have been different. Eve would have been alone as the only human sinner, and Christ would have had to die for her alone. There could have been two strains of humanity, one perfect and the other fallen.

Would God want heaven filled with people boasting of their own righteousness? Anyone who has read through the book of Romans would know that He would never allow such a situation. In order for the plan of salvation to go ahead God needed the entire human race to fall, not just one person. God needed the entire human race to be descendants of only two sinners. In order for God to be our kinsman-redeemer He needed us all to be one family into which He could be born. In order for the plan of Salvation to advance, God could not create two wives for Adam. The fact that He only created one wife does not mean that this is the only legitimate form of marriage for all time. We only need to read the rest of the Old Testament to see this.

I say that God *needed* sin to enter the world. I do not say however, that God wanted sin, or is the author of sin. God treats sin the way a farmer treats manure. As a teenager I worked for local farmers, and one of my tasks was to drive a manure spreader around in the fields and spread that stinking muck all over the place. At the end of the day, I was expected to use the shower stall at the door of the house, before I came in for dinner. In the same way God does not create sin, but directs sin and uses it to create character in His people. He will not allow us to enter into His house with our sin still on us. That is why Jesus died on the Cross. His crimson blood washes us white as snow, and takes away our sin.

God allows us to sin, even though He hates it, because of the principle found in Luke 7:47, "*Wherefore I say unto thee, Her sins, which are many, are forgiven; for she loved much: but to whom little is forgiven, the same loveth little.*" We only learn to love God when we discover just how horrible our own sins are in reality, and in His sight. Only then can we begin to understand the love of Christ on the Cross.

David, Gideon and Solomon certainly had access to Moses' writings. The modern "*Christian*" teaching is that "*These men were hard hearted men for marrying more than one woman*". This is gross error. Since David had a heart like God's own heart, it follows that God Himself is hard hearted! (1 Samuel 13:14, Acts 13:22)

The key here is to differentiate between what Moses wrote, and how he allowed Israel to interpret his writings. The word "*suffered*" in verse 8 explains what went on. While Moses wrote all that God had commanded him, he suffered, or allowed Israel under protest, to interpret it to mean any reason was acceptable for a divorce. He was tired of arguing with them so he let them have their way. (Exodus 24:4, 40:16, Numbers 29:40)

Mercy in the Law of Divorce

In order to move forward we must now go back and see what Moses actually wrote. It is also important to note that nothing that God allowed in the Law is sinful in and of itself. Sometimes there is a better way, but nothing God allows in the Law is truly sinful. For instance, it is not wrong for a man to be circumcised. If you think circumcision will save you, you are wrong, but the practise itself is not wrong. It is not wrong to abstain from pork. If you do not like bacon you do not have to eat it, but do not think there is any spiritual merit in abstinence.

If a man be found lying with a woman married to an husband, then they shall both of them die, both the man that lay with the woman, and the woman: so shalt thou put away evil from Israel. (These verses define adultery according to God) If a damsel that is a virgin be betrothed unto an husband, and a man find her in the city, and lie with her; Then ye shall bring them both out unto the gate of that city, and ye shall stone them with stones that they die; the damsel, because she cried not, being in the city; and the man, because he hath humbled his neighbour's wife: so thou shalt put away evil from among you. But if a man find a betrothed damsel in the field, and the man force her, and lie with her: then the man only that lay with her shall die: But unto the damsel thou shalt do nothing; there is in the damsel no sin worthy of death: for as when a man riseth against his neighbour, and slayeth him, even so is this matter: (adultery is akin to* stabbing another man in the back) *For he found her in the field, and the betrothed damsel cried, and there was none to save her. If a man find a damsel that is a virgin, which is not betrothed, and lay hold on her, and lie with her, and they be found; Then the man that lay with her shall give unto the damsel's father fifty shekels of silver, and she shall be his wife; because he hath humbled her, he may not put her away all his days. (Deuteronomy 22:22-29)*

After this Moses digresses and talks about a few different sins and the subject of personal uncleanness, then he returns to the subject of marital sin...

When a man hath taken a wife, and married her, and it come to pass that she find no favour in his eyes, because he hath found some uncleanness in her: then let him write her a bill of divorcement, and give it in her hand, and send her out of his house. And when she is departed out of his house, she may go and be another man's wife. (Deuteronomy 24:1)

Very clearly Moses is referring back to chapter 22 on the subject of "*uncleanness*". The digression is to point out that there are many things that can make a person unclean to God, not merely the items listed in chapter 22.

What Moses is essentially saying is "*if you find that your wife is cheating on you, you have a choice: You can do the things listed in chapter 22 and insist on justice, or, if you understand that you yourself might one day need God's mercy, you might consider showing mercy yourself, by quietly giving her a bill of divorce.*" Thus she may go and be married to the one she has been fooling around with. Look at how he uses the word "*may*" in verse 2. It sounds like divorce is already her desire.

To sum it up then - Justice is correct, but mercy is better. Divorce was given as a gift of mercy to the guilty. This was Joseph's understanding when Mary was found to be pregnant with the Lord Jesus, "*Then Joseph her husband, **being a just man**, and not willing to make her a publick example, was minded to put her away privily.*" (Matthew 1:19) Joseph, as a just man, knew that he himself was a sinner and under the judgment of God, thus to put her away privately was to show mercy on the one he perceived to be guilty.

Jesus, therefore, was clarifying what Moses had written and not condemning him for the same. After all "*All scripture is given by inspiration of God"* (2 Tim. 3:16). If Jesus was actually criticizing Moses for what he wrote, we could justifiably throw out the Torah (Pentateuch) as being garbage! Many *"Christians"* do effectively throw it out, but Jesus Christ Himself challenges us to search the Old Testament Scriptures, *"Search the scriptures; for in them ye think ye have eternal life: and they are they which testify of me."* (John 5:39) Jesus is appealing to Moses for support! How could He condemn Moses and then appeal to Moses' writings? That would be confusion and a contradiction.

> *Do not think that I will accuse you to the Father: there is one that accuseth you, even Moses, in whom ye trust. For had ye believed Moses, ye would have believed me: for he wrote of me. (John 5:45 & 46)*

The Jews from the writing of the law, and onward, were attempting to use it for that which it was not intended. They were looking for an excuse to divorce because they did not want to have to support more than one woman at a time! It came down to money. Moses was simply tired of fighting with them, and gave in to their demands. Israel was not alone in this, however, and as we look at the Roman solution we see that what they did was no better.

In fact Moses, whom Jesus was quoting, had at least two wives, Zipporah, the daughter of the priest of Midian, and an Ethiopian woman. Though Aaron and Miriam were angry with Moses over the second marriage, God was not! (Numbers 12:1)

This passage seems to indicate that the debate over polygamy has existed for a long time among the people of God. Read the passage carefully and you will see that Aaron and Miriam thought that since Moses had married a second wife, he should step down as Israel's prophet. God spoke to the three of them and said that Moses was His choice for Israel. Notice that though Aaron and Miriam were in the wrong, they did not lose their status as prophet/priest and prophetess. A Christian, then, can be wrong on some (minor) points and still be a minister, though he should repent when biblically corrected.

Aaron had a history of compromise. Though he was a priest and blessed of God; though at times he actually spoke with God, and even saw Him, yet there was something of weakness in his character. When Moses was up on the mountain conversing with God, Aaron was down in the valley making a golden calf. He thought that it was acceptable to portray God in the form of an animal. God was angry with Aaron yet he did not lose his status as a priest. In both of these incidents we see Aaron did not understand the character of God in the same way that his brother did. Today we have many men who make up their own laws, or teach man-made traditions about how we should live, yet they do not understand the character of God either.

> *And if a man entice a maid that is not betrothed, and lie with her, he shall surely endow her to be his wife. (The word "endow" means "to provide support for") (Exodus 22:16) (See also Deuteronomy 22:28 & 29 above)*

Please note that a man who seduced an unattached woman was required to marry her. Notice that the phrase "*a man*" is not modified by any qualifiers, such as "*single*" or "*unmarried*". Nothing is said about the man's marital status, whether he is married or single. It did not matter. He was required to take her as his wife. Going back to Deuteronomy 22:26, we see that adultery was defined as having sex with a woman who is married to another man. Thus, though it may be fornication for a man to seduce an unmarried woman, it is not adultery, a sin that deserves the death penalty. The essential thing is the covenant between the man and his wife. Jesus adds to the definition by stating that divorcing your wife so you can remarry is the same thing. Please note that He did NOT say that marrying a second woman, while remaining married to the first, is adultery! God has reasons for not saying things, and the bible warns us in many places, not to add to His Word. (Deuteronomy 4:2, Proverbs 30:6, Revelation 22:18)

The one exception, in this case, was if the young woman's father objected to the union, then the man was to pay a substantial sum (support) to the father who would then look after her. This was obviously to allow the father to keep her from being involved in a situation that was dangerous for her. Perhaps the man is already known for this sort of thing and already has a number of wives he can't support, or has problems such as drinking or gambling. It was left to the judgment of the young woman's father.

We see therefore, that in this case polygamy was the consequence of sin. It was not, however, a punishment for sin. Sometimes it was done for the survival of the nation of Israel, and even commanded by God...

If brethren dwell together, and one of them die, and have no child, the wife of the dead shall not marry without unto a stranger: <u>her husband's brother shall go in unto her, and take her to him to wife</u>, and perform the duty of an husband's brother unto her. And it shall be, that the firstborn which she beareth shall succeed in the name of his brother which is dead, that his name be not put out of Israel. And if the man like not to take his brother's wife, then let his brother's wife go up to the gate unto the elders, and say, My husband's brother refuseth to raise up unto his brother a name in Israel, he will not perform the duty of my husband's brother. Then the elders of his city shall call him, and speak unto him: and if he stand to it, and say, I like not to take her; <u>Then shall his brother's wife come unto him in the presence of the elders, and loose his shoe from off his foot, and spit in his face, and shall answer and say, So shall it be done unto that man that will not build up his brother's house. And his name shall be called in Israel, The house of him that hath his shoe loosed</u>. (Deuteronomy 25:5-10)

Invariably the living brother would already be married, for men married early in those days. It would be unusual for that man to be single. Having a family and heirs was very important. This is not about the marital status of the living brother, nor is it about his libido; it is about the survival of the nation of Israel.

Since the dead brother would have inherited land from his father it would now go to his widow. She would otherwise be free to marry whom she would, and could conceivably marry a person from outside Israel. Thus the land of Israel would be owned by outsiders.

An example of this principle is very apparent when you read the account of Ruth. Ruth was a Moabitess who had married a Jewish boy. When he died she inherited his land. If she had married someone from her own country they could have raised their children as Moabites on Israel's land. As it was she married a relative of her husband's and joined Israel herself. The other relative would not marry her, because he was afraid that if he and Ruth had children, those children would have a claim against his own inheritance. He therefore lost his chance to be in the line of the messiah!

Please understand that this man's refusal to marry Ruth in no way indicates polygamy is wrong, but only shows one man's preference. The story actually shows that he knew he had a right to marry Ruth, but chose not to for his own reasons. It seems he was prejudiced against Moabites, and did not want children who were half Moabite having a claim against his own ancestral land, along with the children he already had. If he only had one son from his first wife and had two or three from a second, the larger number of children from the second wife would have a claim against the property of the other son, so his ancestral property would end up being divided.

So we see that there were at least two places in the Law of Moses where polygamy was commanded; In the case of fornication and in the case where a married brother, or close relative, dies without children. There is, however, another circumstance where it is allowed...

> *When thou goest forth to war against thine enemies, and the LORD thy God hath delivered them into thine hands, and thou hast taken them captive, And seest among the captives a beautiful woman, and hast a desire unto her, that thou wouldest have her to thy wife; Then thou shalt bring her home to thine house; and she shall shave her head, and pare her nails; And she shall put the raiment of her captivity from off her, and shall remain in thine house, and bewail her father and her mother a full month: and after that thou shalt go in unto her, and be her husband, and she shall be thy wife. And it shall be, if thou have no delight in her, then thou shalt let her go whither she will; but thou shalt not sell her at all for money, thou shalt not make merchandise of her, because thou hast humbled her. If a man have two wives, one beloved, and another hated, and they have born him children, both the beloved and the hated; and if the firstborn son be hers that was hated: Then it shall be, when he maketh his sons to inherit that which he hath, that he may not make the son of the beloved firstborn before the son of the hated, which is indeed the firstborn: But he shall acknowledge the son of the hated for the firstborn, by giving him a double portion of all that he hath: for he is the beginning of his strength; the right of the firstborn is his. (Deuteronomy 21:10-17)*

In verses 10 through 14 Moses provides instructions for men who would like to marry a woman who is taken captive in war.

Read it slowly and carefully. They were commanded to live together for a month without having sex. She was to trim her nails and cut her hair, the things that likely first attracted him to her. After the month was up he could go in and have sex with her and she would be his wife. No ceremony is prescribed, nor is his prior status as a married or single man even mentioned. It was not important. People who call themselves "*Christians*" and yet are offended at this passage, really do not believe the whole Word of God, and this applies to those who say that there are "*moral problems with the Word of God*".

Please note that verse 15, about a man with two wives, immediately follows the passage about marrying a woman who is taken captive in war. This is no accident, but is actually continuing with the same thought. It is likely that a man who marries a captive woman will find that she will become more attached to him than his first wife. She is living in a land of strangers and finds kindness from this one man. She does not know anyone in the neighbourhood and will probably find herself very dependant on her new husband. He, on the other hand, will find her attractive because of her foreignness and beauty. She would present a challenge to him and thus would receive more of his attention. It would be very natural for her to become his favourite wife.

His first wife would most likely be a Jewish girl from the same neighbourhood, who he has known most of his life. Their marriage would most likely be an arranged one, whereas the second wife is one of his choice. She would most likely be older than the new wife and perhaps also showing a few wrinkles. This woman would have a network of friends and relatives in the neighbourhood and would not be as dependant on him for companionship. The old axiom "*familiarity breeds contempt*" would certainly apply here.

In this passage, then, the Lord is protecting the firstborn child from favouritism of the father. It does not matter which wife actually has the first son, that son is to receive a double portion of the inheritance from his father. It was common for a man to have more than one wife at that time, not only in Israel but around the world.

The idea that marriage is a "*sacrament*" does not come from the Bible but from Roman Catholic church tradition. There is nothing in marriage that is required for salvation. God simply wants us to keep our vows, and care for dependants, but I can assure you that David's vows were different from your own.

The oldest son was to receive a double portion of the inheritance because he was the one who was to take care of his parents during their declining years. Being the oldest he would have the most time on his own, to establish himself, before having to take on the responsibility of caring for aged parents. This just shows the foresight and mercy of God. Had it been the youngest child he would have no time to establish himself before having to care for his aging parents. Of course the other children also had a responsibility to care for their parents, but the bulk of the burden would naturally go to the oldest.

If you go back to chapter 20 you see a list of those in Israel who should not go to war. In verse 7 we see that a man who is betrothed but not yet married is excused from going to battle.

> *And what man is there that hath betrothed a wife, and hath not taken her? let him go and return unto his house, lest he die in the battle, and another man take her. (Deut. 20:7)*

> *When a man hath taken a new wife, he shall not go out to war, neither shall he be charged with any business: but he shall be free at home one year, and shall cheer up his wife which he hath taken. (Deut. 24:5)*

The Hebrew honeymoon lasted a whole year, so we see that an engaged young man and a newlywed were excused from going to battle.

What is the implication of this principle, and how does it relate to our subject? It follows then, that most of the men who went to battle were already married and likely had children from at least one wife. Deuteronomy 21:10-13 thus gives married men permission to marry captive women from among their enemies, and then to be excused from the next war. Notice also the word "new" in Deuteronomy 24:5, very clearly the implication is that it is the status of his having a new wife that gives him this privilege and not his "old" wife!

This exact scenario is played out in the book of Numbers:

> *9 And the children of Israel took all the women of Midian captives, and their little ones, and took the spoil of all their cattle, and all their flocks, and all their goods. 14 And Moses was wroth with the officers of the host, with the captains over*

thousands, and captains over hundreds, which came from the battle. 15 And Moses said unto them, Have ye saved all the women alive? 16 Behold, these caused the children of Israel, through the counsel of Balaam, to commit trespass against the LORD in the matter of Peor, and there was a plague among the congregation of the LORD. 17 Now therefore kill every male among the little ones, and kill every woman that hath known man by lying with him. 18 But all the women children, that have not known a man by lying with him, keep alive for yourselves.32 And the booty, being the rest of the prey which the men of war had caught, was six hundred thousand and seventy thousand and five thousand sheep,35 And thirty and two thousand persons in all, of women that had not known man by lying with him. (Numbers 31:9, 14-18, 32, 35)

Here we see that there were thirty two thousand Midianite women who were absorbed into Israel. This is not a trifling number. These women ultimately became the mothers of Israel! It is very likely that every single Hebrew today is a descendant of at least one of these women!

No doubt many modern westerners would view this passage as being somewhat barbaric. Please try to imagine what life would be like for one of those boys had they been allowed to live. No doubt they would be told, at some point, their history. Being boys there would be the tendency for them to want to get revenge against the people who had raised them, Israel. It would not happen over night but several years later when the boys were teenagers. No doubt some of them would have become Jews, but Israel would never know when some of them would snap and kill someone. It may seem heartless, but it was the best way for Israel to protect themselves in that situation.

It is the nature of women to be more forgiving than men. Thus by keeping the girls alive, Israel was showing mercy to the Midianites, as much as the situation would allow. The women who had lost their virginity had already been corrupted by Balaam's advice and would pose a threat to Israel's stability and relationship with God.

A Logical Solution

The passage doesn't state in so many words, but it is likely that some Israelite men had died in this battle, and we know that during other battles around the same time, there were Israelite casualties in the thousands. Given a birth rate of approximately 50/50 male/female we can see that with the dead of battle plus a new influx of thirty two thousand young Midianite women the ratio of men to women in Israel would have tipped the scales heavily in favour of the fairer sex. It appears then that polygamy was common in that day for a very practical reason.

Had God insisted on one man/one woman for life, there would have been a large number of women who would grow old without having children. This would have been a huge demographic problem for the leaders of Israel. Who was to care for these women in their old age? It is natural for women to want children, so would they not leave to find men in neighbouring countries if they could not find a husband in Israel? Considering that the neighbouring nations were constantly at war with each other isn't it likely that these women would find the same situation if they went abroad?

These women had the same desires as the other women in Israel and indeed women throughout the world, even today. They would want a family. Not only is it natural for a woman to want a family, it is still God's command for the human race to "*be fruitful and multiply*". If something wasn't done about this situation it would lead to moral disaster for Israel.

With large numbers of unattached women about there would be the tendency for them to try to snag men who were already married. There would also be the tendency for some of them to act as prostitutes. The solution is simple if you keep an open mind. In a nation with substantially more women than men, it is natural to allow men to marry more than one wife! This is the solution Moses employed and it allowed women to have their desire for children and yet not to act as prostitutes. It gave them the standing as married women, who would be respected in their community, and it gave them children who would care for them in their declining years. It also gave the nation a pool of young men who were needed to populate its army.

Those who insist that the only legitimate rule is "*one-man-one-woman-for-life*" are actually the cause of prostitution, and sexual immorality in their society! This is especially true in war-ravaged nations.

This same scenario repeated itself many times throughout the history of Israel. One of the most striking examples occurred during the time that Israel split into two nations. During the fighting between Jeroboam and Rehoboam there was a battle where five hundred thousand men of Israel died in battle. (2 Chronicles 13:17) This would have been a fatal blow to the nation were it not for polygamy, for that number of dead would have been close to an entire generation of men. What was to happen to the half million women who had no man to marry? Because the practise of polygamy was so widespread there was no need to make mention of it as the reason Israel survived.

When did God rescind the command to be fruitful and multiply? If the neighbouring nations practised polygamy, and Israel did not, they would rebuild at a much faster rate than Israel, and thus be in a position to attack before Israel was ready to defend. We see then that God used polygamy as a way to rebuild the nation. Polygamy was necessary for Israel's national defence!

Don't forget that God loves people and wants to see the earth full of them.

> For thus saith the LORD that created the heavens; **God himself that formed the earth and made it;** he hath established it, he created it not in vain, **he formed it to be inhabited**: I am the LORD; and there is none else. (Isaiah 45:18)

Looking at Moses' history in Exodus 2, we see that he was uniquely prepared to understand the situation. Being one of a handful of survivors of the Egyptian genocide of Hebrew baby boys, Moses would have grown up with large numbers of girls around him but few, if any, boys his own age. There was a problem that those girls faced as they grew up. With most of their corresponding neighbourhood boys having been killed by the Egyptians, they would find there was no one for them to marry.

Though Pharaoh obviously had intended for them to become wives, or concubines, of Egyptians, it is extremely unlikely that their parents would allow this to occur. The parents had been witness to the slaughter of their sons, years before, by this same Egyptian nation. Very likely many of those Hebrew girls ended up marrying older Hebrew men rather than becoming concubines to the murderous Egyptians.

It seems then that God had been in control of the situation and had inspired Moses' mother to make the basket and hide it in the Nile. God had arranged protection for one Hebrew child in the house of Pharaoh, his great enemy! God was preparing a future leader for Israel with the unique understanding required for a national political and spiritual leader.

A careful study will reveal that slavery in the Old Testament, in Israel, was not the same as was practised in the United States in the nineteenth century. Slaves in Israel had rights and were treated as persons. Slavery was usually only temporary. One passage relates to the subject of marriage...

> And *if a man sell his daughter to be a maidservant,* she *shall not go out as the menservants do. If she please not her master, who hath betrothed her to himself, then shall he let her be redeemed: to sell her unto a strange nation he shall have no power, seeing he hath dealt deceitfully with her. And if he have betrothed her unto his son, he shall deal with her after the manner of daughters.* **If he take him another wife; her food, her raiment, and her duty of marriage, shall he not diminish.** *And if he do not these three unto her, then shall she go out free without money. (Exodus 21:7-11)*

Very clearly then this passage relates closely with the absorption of the thirty two thousand Midianite women into Israel. No doubt many of the young women started off as being maid servants to families in Israel, but ended up becoming a wife of their master. Note in Numbers 31:18 his use of the phrase *"for yourselves"* in relation to the Midianite women, shows that he knew and allowed this to occur.

Power has been called *"the ultimate aphrodisiac"* and do doubt there is some truth to the rumour. Men who have power over women often take advantage of that fact. God placed provision in the law to protect women who find themselves in this situation. When it happens, she goes from being a servant to being a wife with all the rights, privileges and obligations that any wife has. It is not about the man but the woman, and the love of God.

What is the *"duty of marriage"* in verse 9? Doesn't it include cooking and washing, cleaning and child care? Do not forget, it also includes friendship, fellowship, sex and intimate contact! God is saying that you must not neglect your first wife in any way, **when you marry a second!**

Before you think that it was just Moses who wrote in favour of polygamy I want to point out something Moses said about Jesus in Deuteronomy 18:15. *"For Moses truly said unto the fathers, A prophet shall the Lord your God raise up unto you of your brethren, like unto me; him shall ye hear in all things whatsoever he shall say unto you."* (Acts 3:22) Yes Jesus is like Moses in many ways, one of which is that He views marriage the same way as Moses. When Jesus reigns on earth, His reign shall be similar to Moses, and David. After all He is a Jew, and King of the Jews!

But God did not just allow polygamy, He actually identifies with the man of the house! In Jeremiah chapter 3 we see that God identifies himself as a polygamist, and Israel and Judah are like the man's two wives! Historically, Israel had split into two nations and the relationship between them and their God is compared to that of a man with two wives...

*1 They say, **If a man put away his wife, and she go from him, and become another man's, shall he return unto her again?** shall not that land be greatly polluted? **but thou hast played the harlot with many lovers; yet return again to me,** saith the LORD. 2 Lift up thine eyes unto the high places, and see where thou hast not been lien with. In the ways hast thou sat for them, as the Arabian in the wilderness; and thou hast polluted the land with thy whoredoms and with thy wickedness. 6 The LORD said also unto me in the days of Josiah the king, Hast thou seen that which backsliding Israel hath done? she is gone up upon every high mountain and under every green tree, and there hath played the harlot. 7 And I said after she had done all these things, Turn thou unto me. But she returned not. And her treacherous sister Judah saw it. 8 And I saw, when for all the causes whereby backsliding Israel committed adultery I had put her away, and given her a bill of divorce; yet **her treacherous sister Judah feared not, but went and played the harlot also.** 9 And it came to pass through the lightness of her whoredom, that she defiled the land, and committed adultery with stones and with stocks. 10 And yet for all this her treacherous sister Judah hath not turned unto me with her whole heart, but feignedly, saith the LORD. 11 And the LORD said unto me, The*

backsliding Israel hath justified herself more than treacherous
Judah. 12 Go and proclaim these words toward the north,
and say, Return, thou backsliding Israel, saith the LORD; and I
will not cause mine anger to fall upon you: for I am merciful,
saith the LORD, and I will not keep anger for ever. 13 Only
acknowledge thine iniquity, that thou hast transgressed
against the LORD thy God, and hast scattered thy ways to the
strangers under every green tree, and ye have not obeyed my
voice, saith the LORD. 14 Turn, O backsliding children, saith
the LORD; for I am married unto you: and I will take you one
of a city, and two of a family, and I will bring you to Zion: 15
And I will give you pastors according to mine heart, which
shall feed you with knowledge and understanding. (Jeremiah
3:1-15)

God uses the situation as an analogy of an **innocent man** who
has been wronged by both of his wives. One wife leaves and takes
up with another man, but the one who stays with him is secretly
committing adultery. Ultimately God prefers open abandonment to
hypocrisy, though in the end his desire is that both would return to
Him! Though he gave them a certificate of divorce, He is really still
married to both of them! So we see that God himself identifies with
polygamous men. It is hard to imagine God identifying with these
men if they were living a life of perpetual adultery. Obviously God
does not see it this way.

Later on in the New Testament the Christian Church is called
"*the bride of Christ*" (Mark 2:19, Luke 5:34, Rev. 21:9). She would
then be the third wife of God spoken of in Scripture! The Old
Testament believers of Israel are a separate group of believers from
the New Testament Church. Jesus Himself stated that the position of
New Testament believers is a higher position than Old Testament
saints. (Matthew 11:11) There are indeed divisions among the
people of God, for the Old Testament saints, unlike the Church, did
not have the gift of the Holy Spirit, and neither will the Tribulation
saints, though they will indeed be saved.

We see here also a similar way of speaking about the Law to the
way Jesus referred to it. "*The Law says, but I say*". This does not
mean that the Law is wrong, but that while the Law is correct, there
is a higher standard. I believe that the section of law referred to
here is addressing the situation where a woman who is divorced and
remarries, should her second husband die, she must not go back to

the first husband. The reasoning is that she likely would have had children by the second man and were she to return to her original husband, the children would suffer abuse at his hands. They would remind him of his humiliation. The same is not true spiritually speaking. God desires that all sinners would return to Him, for only He can save them, and He does not abuse anyone.

Why would God use polygamy as an analogy? Like many Calvinists, Israel thought they were God's favourite people, chosen and predestined for salvation, and thus spent very little time in missionary efforts. They may have thought that if the Sovereign God really wanted to save gentiles, He could do it without them sending missionaries! God created all mankind for fellowship with Himself. He truly desires to save all of mankind. He is the one who created the Lake of Fire and knows just how truly horrible it is.

For a sinner to spend eternity in that place would truly satisfy justice, because God is eternal, and our sins have eternal consequences. Had God planned to satisfy justice this way he would have been alone with his angels in Heaven. He thus designed to save as many as possible by satisfying His law by Himself, through the sacrifice of His only begotten Son. His love for mankind is like the love of a lover, and husband.

This was His plan from the beginning and He planned to use Israel as his missionary family to the world. Israel was a stiff-necked and hard-hearted people, so he had to bring them to a place where he could use them. The time for Israel was interrupted by the Church Age, but she has seven years to go (Daniel 9:25 & 26). At the rapture of the Church, Israel will be jealous like the first wife when a man marries his second, and leaves her at home to mind the children! (Deuteronomy 32:21) At that time Israel will realize she needs to be faithful to her husband. This will be the time of the Great Tribulation.

The Judges of Israel

Let's go back to the book of Judges for a moment. While reading through this book I found a rather unusual situation kept repeating. I'll let you read it for yourself...

*And **Gideon had threescore and ten sons of his body begotten: for he had many wives.** And Gideon the son of Joash died in a good old age, and was buried in the sepulchre* *of Joash his father, in Ophrah of the Abiezrites. And it came to pass, **as soon as Gideon was dead, that the children of Israel turned again, and went a whoring after Baalim, and made Baalberith their god.** And the children of Israel remembered not the LORD their God, who had delivered them out of the hands of all their enemies on every side: (Judges 8:30-34)*

Again:

*And after him arose <u>Jair,</u> a Gileadite, and judged Israel twenty and two years. And **he had thirty sons that rode on thirty ass colts,** and they had thirty cities, which are called Havothjair unto this day, which are in the land of Gilead. And <u>Jair died,</u> and was buried in Camon. **And the children of Israel did evil again in the sight of the LORD, and served Baalim, and Ashtaroth, and the gods of Syria, and the gods of Zidon, and the gods of Moab, and the gods of the children of Ammon, and the gods of the Philistines, and forsook the LORD, and served not him.** And the anger of the LORD was hot against Israel, and he sold them into the hands of the Philistines, and into the hands of the children of Ammon. (Judges 10:3-7)*

And again:

*And after him Abdon the son of Hillel, a Pirathonite, judged Israel. And he had forty sons and thirty nephews, that rode on threescore and ten ass colts: and he judged Israel eight years. And **Abdon the son of Hillel the Pirathonite died,** and was buried in Pirathon in the land of Ephraim, in the mount of the Amalekites. **And the children of Israel did evil again in the sight of the LORD;** and the LORD delivered them into the hand of the Philistines forty years. (Judges 12:13 & 13:1)*

Do you see the pattern? Here we have a series of godly men who had multiple wives, and when the godly man dies, Israel turns against God! No man has thirty sons from one woman. A man's status as a man of God, is not determined by the number of wives he has, but by the state of that man's heart! These men by their leadership kept Israel close to the Lord God! This gives us scriptural evidence that a man can have multiple wives and still be close to God. No doubt these stories have been included for our edification, and education.

In the past I had been told that a polygamist "has a character flaw", and this is the reason that Paul excludes him from ministry. It appears to me now, that the number of wives a man has is morally neutral, it's neither-here-nor-there, but a man with many wives has to learn how to love more than one person at a time. He has to learn how to juggle the interests of competing parties, and act as a mediator in disputes between them. In this sense a polygamist begins to learn to love his family in the same way that God loves His people. He actually begins to develop the character of God! We see this concept being played out in the lives of Jacob, Gideon, Jair, Abdon and David.

David

What about David? A study on prophecy, or on polygamy, cannot be complete without a look at this intriguing man.

Try, for a moment, to imagine David as he was growing up. The books of Moses, Joshua, Judges and Job were the only parts of God's Word that had been written up to that time. He no doubt had some knowledge of Adam and of Jacob. No doubt he knew that the monogamist Adam's first son was the first murderer in the world. Cain himself was also a monogamist. As he read of Jacob's family he would see the parallels. While the brothers of Joseph had a murderous anger against him, it was the oldest brother, from another mother, who saved Joseph's life, and planned to restore him to his father unharmed. (Gen. 37:22) No doubt it would appear that polygamy was the equal, if not superior to monogamy.

Who did David have as an example but godly men like Jacob, Moses, Gideon, Jair, and Abdon? It is true that the first polygamist mentioned in the Bible was a murderer, but the majority were men of God. I put no stock in the "*Law of first mention*", it has no biblical support and no validity for in-depth bible study. You have to read every passage in the light of all Scripture, and on its own merits.

Reading through 1 Samuel, 1 Kings, and 1 Chronicles you will be able to piece together the life of David. David also wrote the majority of the Psalms. David had more than one wife before he was made king. If this type of relationship were considered adultery he would have been stoned, not made king.

Ultimately David did commit adultery with Bathsheba.   The prophet Nathan confronted him over the situation. God would have sent Nathan to David before he even became king, if He considered polygamy to be adultery. We must allow God to define the words He uses and not impose twenty-first century definitions on Him. After all, God is the creator of language. As I read through these passages I found that I cannot name a single person in the bible whose character is as close to Christ's, as David. He was kind, loving and forgiving of his enemies, yet still took a strong stand against God's enemies.   He had a passion for God that exceeded all the other issues in his life, which were many.

What about the affair with Bath-Sheba?   Let's take a look at Nathan's confrontation with David:

> *1 And the LORD sent Nathan unto David. And he came unto him, and said unto him, There were two men in one city; the one rich, and the other poor. 2 The rich man had exceeding many flocks and herds: 3 But the poor man had nothing, save one little ewe lamb, which he had bought and nourished up: and it grew up together with him, and with his children; it did eat of his own meat, and drank of his own cup, and lay in his bosom, and was unto him as a daughter. 4 And there came a traveller unto the rich man, and he spared to take of his own flock and of his own herd, to dress for the wayfaring man that was come unto him; but took the poor man's lamb, and dressed it for the man that was come to him. 5 And David's anger was greatly kindled against the man; and he said to Nathan, As the LORD liveth, the man that hath done this thing shall surely die: 6 And he shall restore the lamb fourfold, because he did this thing, and because he had no pity. 7 And Nathan said to David, Thou art the man. **Thus saith the LORD God of Israel, I anointed thee king over Israel, and I delivered thee out of the hand of Saul; 8 And I gave thee thy master's house, and thy master's wives into thy bosom**, and gave thee the house of Israel and of Judah; and if that had been too little, I would moreover have given unto thee such and such things. 9 Wherefore hast thou despised the commandment of the LORD, to do evil in his sight? thou hast killed Uriah the Hittite with the sword, and hast taken his wife to be thy wife, and hast slain him with the sword of the*

*children of Ammon. 10 Now therefore the sword shall never depart from thine house; because thou hast despised me, and hast taken the wife of Uriah the Hittite to be thy wife. 11 Thus saith the LORD, Behold, I will raise up evil against thee out of thine own house, and **I will take thy wives before thine eyes, and give them unto thy neighbour,** and he shall lie with thy wives in the sight of this sun. 12 For thou didst it secretly: but I will do this thing before all Israel, and before the sun. 13 And David said unto Nathan, I have sinned against the LORD. And Nathan said unto David, The LORD also hath put away thy sin; thou shalt not die. 14 Howbeit, because by this deed thou hast given great occasion to the enemies of the LORD to blaspheme, the child also that is born unto thee shall surely die. (2 Samuel 12:1-14)*

Notice how Nathan compares wives with sheep. One man had many sheep and the other had only one. In verse 8 God takes credit for giving David his many wives. Remember, Jesus said *"What God hath put together, let not man put asunder"*. Some have suggested that it means that David was only given Saul's wives to care for, and not actually to marry. That explanation seems more like a curse than a gift, a burden rather than a blessing. Given the sheep illustration this is highly unlikely. No doubt this is metaphorical, and not literal. It simply means that David was in the place of Saul, and had the same right, or power, to marry several women.

Considering that David was Saul's son-in-law it would be against the law for him to marry Saul's wife. Saul only had one wife, plus one concubine, so the use of the plural *"wives"* is clearly not literal. The use of the word *"bosom"* is telling, however. This word means *"breast"* or *"chest"* and implies intimacy. This type of intimacy speaks of a wife, but not a normal house guest.

Nathan tells David *"thou shalt not die"*, because at this point David deserved to die. The penalty of adultery was death, as was the penalty for murder. David had committed both in the affair with Bathsheba, and deserved the just penalty of the Law. God desires that we repent from our sins more than that we should die for them. *"For I desired mercy, and not sacrifice; and the knowledge of God more than burnt offerings."* (Hosea 6:6) David did indeed repent from this sin. He did not excuse it or belittle it, but took responsibility for his actions.

How many men would name a child after the man who

confronted him about major sins like adultery, and murder? We see then, that David truly was a man of extraordinary character. He was truly humble enough to repent when confronted with his sin. Psalm 51 is David's Psalm of repentance which he wrote at that time. It is important to note that repentance for David did not mean abandoning Bathsheba, that would have added sin upon sin!

In the genealogies of Christ given in Matthew and Luke, one finds that the Lord Jesus Christ traced his ancestry through the wife acquired in adultery. Jesus traced his legal right to the throne as an adopted son of Joseph, a descendant of Solomon (Matthew 1:1-17) . His true ancestry is traced through Mary, his mother, who was a descendant of Nathan (Luke 3:23-38). Both Solomon and Nathan were sons of David and Bath-Sheba! (1 Chronicles 3:5) I take it from this fact that had David waited, he probably would have been given Bath-Sheba ultimately anyway. It seems that God actually wanted the union, though not in the manner in which it occurred. Likely it would have happened after Uriah was killed in battle as a hero, and not as a victim of a murder conspiracy. As in Abraham's case, David's impatience was the cause of much suffering, both to himself, and to his family.

Later, after David fled from Absalom, and Absalom slept with ten of his father's concubines, we see David's understanding of divorce to be laced with mercy. Notice in verse 11 that God calls David's concubines "wives", this shouls settle the status of cocubines for us. Once David was back on the throne he refused to have relations with those women, though he continued to feed, clothe and shelter them for the rest of their lives. This shows that David knew that since he had received mercy himself, over the affair with Bath-Sheba, he could do no less toward those ten wives who had been unfaithful to him. (2 Samuel 16:21-22, 20:3) I suspect that had Absalom lived, David would have likely insisted that they would become Absalom's wives, and would have divorced them so they could do so.

What is the Lord's testimony concerning King David of Jerusalem? There was no significant sin in David's life except for the matter of Uriah and his wife. These verses tell us that polygamy is not a significant sin, if it is a sin at all.

> Because **David did that which was right in the eyes of the LORD, and turned not aside from any thing that he commanded him** all the days of his life, **save only in the**

matter of Uriah the Hittite. (1 Kings 15:5)

> *For it came to pass, when Solomon was old, that his wives turned away his heart after other gods: and his heart was not perfect with the LORD his God, as was the heart of David his father. (1 Kings 11:4)*

Because these verses do not condemn David for his multiple wives before the case of Uriah and Bathsheba, our pastors tell us that we can't trust the plain sense reading of these, and many other verses of scripture.

Not only is the practise of polygamy common throughout the Old Testament, but we see that even in the New Testament it is never condemned, nor contradicted. As we have seen already, Jesus, when speaking of the Law, actually confirmed what it says about marriage and divorce. The apostles, while condemning adultery and fornication, never actually identify polygamy as either.

If God was really against polygamy, as a form of adultery, how easy would it have been to simply define it so? When writing Romans 7:3, how easy would it have been to just change the word order to say that a man with two wives is an adulterer?

> *So then if, while her husband liveth, she be married to another man, she shall be called an adulteress: but if her husband be dead, she is free from that law; so that she is no adulteress, though she be married to another man. (Romans 7:3)*

Why didn't Paul say: "*if, while his wife liveth, he be married to another woman, he shall be called an adulterer*"? As stated elsewhere, Israel was the only nation in the Roman empire where polygamy was legal. Therefore to make the opposite statement would actually have been a lie, and men who make it today are adding lies to Scripture. It truly was not unlawful for a man to have two wives.

Paul, when stating the qualifications of a deacon or a bishop/pastor, stated that holders of these offices in the Church should be the husband of one wife. The fact that such a statement was made is an indication that there were people in the Church who were not qualified for these offices. Thus we know that there was no general rule against polygamy in the early Church. As Jesus stated, to divorce your wife and marry another is adultery, but to marry another while remaining married to the first is not considered so. (Exodus 21:10, Mathew 19:6)

> *A bishop then must be blameless, the husband of one wife, vigilant, sober, of good behaviour, given to hospitality, apt to teach; (1 Timothy 3:2)*

> *Let the deacons be the husbands of one wife, ruling their children and their own houses well. (1 Timothy 3:12)*

> *For this cause left I thee in Crete, that thou shouldest set in order the things that are wanting, and ordain elders in every city, as I had appointed thee: If any be blameless, the husband of one wife, having faithful children not accused of riot or unruly. (Titus 1: 5)*

Jesus never contradicted the teachings of the Old Testament. There were times when He spoke of a higher Law, but he never stated that Moses was wrong. Even when clarifying the situation regarding divorce, He stuck to the O.T. Definitions.

> *And if a woman shall put away her husband, and be married to another, she committeth adultery. (Mark 10:12)*

If He was defining marriage the same as modern western societies do, Jesus could have easily stated that *"if a woman shall put away her husband, she causes him to commit adultery"*. The truth is that such a statement would be a contradiction of the Law. If she divorces her husband and marries another she is guilty of adultery, but if he marries another (virgin), though she divorces him, he is not. You see, if she divorces him, she still belongs to him in God's eyes. To our western way of thinking this seems unfair. You need to discard your western world view, and I do not mean take up an eastern way of thinking. A biblical way of thinking is the only one that God approves of.

What of the statement that the *"two shall be one flesh"*? Does this mean that men must marry only once? How does Scripture treat this concept? *"What? know ye not that he which is joined to an harlot is one body? for two, saith he, shall be one flesh."* (1 Corinthians 6:16)

Consider the case before us here: A married man has relations with a harlot and God says he is one flesh with her. Does this mean that he is no longer one flesh with his legitimate, married wife? Of course not. There is no place in Scripture where a woman is allowed to divorce her husband just because he has another woman. Therefore we can biblically say that a man can be "*one flesh*" with more than one woman at a time. It logically follows that if he is legitimately married to two women, he is legitimately "*one flesh*" with each at the same time.

Marriage is a picture of Christ and the Church, and it is also a picture of His relationship with Israel. God can have both the Church and Israel at the same time. He cares for both, and is faithful to both even though they may be unfaithful to Him. He will not divorce either, but will woo both to Himself.

In the same way the relationship from husband to wife is different than wife to husband. The man is commanded to **love** his wife, but she is to **reverence** him. It may seem unfair, but as Christians we are to accept the Word of God even if we do not like what it says.

> *Nevertheless let every one of you in particular so love his wife even as himself; and the wife see that she reverence her husband. (Ephesians 5:33)*

There has been much speculation about the following passage due to its peculiar language. Regardless, I think some parts of it are abundantly clear. Note that the passage is addressed to "*any man*", similar to the language in passages we have seen in Exodus and Deuteronomy. It literally means "***Any Man***". It matters not whether the man in question is already married, or not, if he marries a virgin he has not sinned.

> *But if any man think that he behaveth himself uncomely toward his virgin, if she pass the flower of her age, and need so require, let him do what he will, he sinneth not: let them marry. (1 Corinthians 7:36)*

Why would any single, unmarried man, think it would be a sin to marry a virgin? Such a thought is ludicrous and contrary to everything written in the Bible about marriage! This passage is addressing another situation altogether.

I think that this passage is specifically directed towards married men. Perhaps the virgin in question has been promised to him, but he has married someone else. Maybe he was Jewish and promised to a Jewish girl, but is now Christian, and has married a Christian woman in the mean time. Now he has the problem of keeping his word, and becoming a polygamist, or breaking his word. I think the situation is one where there is a hope that another single man may come along to marry the virgin in question. Do not forget that the early Church was made up largely of converted Jews, who had a Jewish mentality, which is what we have been discussing throughout this chapter.

As she gets older and no Christian man comes along she has the option of becoming a second wife to the one she has been promised to, or remaining single. When she is in her early thirties she has to make a decision to marry, or not have children at all. Paul is simply stating that she may become the second wife of a believer, rather than marry an unbeliever. Christians are commanded not to be unequally yoked. (2 Corinthians 6:14) We ought to take such commands seriously.

If you have believed the Roman lie that second marriages are prohibited in the Church, you will not understand this passage as God intended it. God does not spell out everything in plain, simple terms. He gave us brains and He wants us to use them. He wants us to study all of the Scriptures, not just our favourite books and passages. Scripture is a unit from Genesis to Revelation.

Going back in the same chapter we have some more instructions about marriage:

> *And unto the married I command, yet not I, but the Lord, Let not the wife depart from her husband: But and if she depart, let her remain unmarried, or be reconciled to her husband: and let not the husband put away his wife. (1 Corinthians 7:10 & 11)*

Please note that it doesn't say she is free to remarry if her husband marries another. Her vows are between him and her. His relationship with another has no bearing on her relationship with him. The bible is consistent all the way through. Marriage is for life.

In Matthew 25:1-13 we have a rapture passage which also relates to the subject at hand. Most pastors in the western world claim that the ten virgins in this passage are bridesmaids. This gives us the unlikely scenario of a wedding with bridesmaids and a bridegroom, but no bride! This explanation does not fit the context. All ten of the virgins are looking forward to more than a meal with the married couple! Very clearly the virgins are representative of the Christian Church, and are looking forward to Eternity with Jesus. He is using the analogy of a king marrying ten brides at once, as a picture of Him and his Church.

The bridegroom represents the Lord Jesus Christ and the bride, the Church is looking forward to unending intimacy with Him. This is a picture of marriage. The five virgins without oil represent Church members who do not have the Holy Spirit. They want very much to be taken to Heaven, but have neglected their relationship with the Lord. They may have said a prayer, but they have not been born-again.

> *1 Then shall the kingdom of heaven be likened unto ten virgins, which took their lamps, and went forth to meet the bridegroom. 2 And five of them were wise, and five were foolish. 3 They that were foolish took their lamps, and took no oil with them: 4 But the wise took oil in their vessels with their lamps. 5 While the bridegroom tarried, they all slumbered and slept. 6 And at midnight there was a cry made, Behold, the bridegroom cometh; go ye out to meet him. 7 Then all those virgins arose, and trimmed their lamps. 8 And the foolish said unto the wise, Give us of your oil; for our lamps are gone out. 9 But the wise answered, saying, Not so; lest there be not enough for us and you: but go ye rather to them that sell, and buy for yourselves. 10 And while they went to buy, the bridegroom came; and they that were ready went in with him to the marriage: and the door was shut. 11 Afterward came also the other virgins, saying, Lord, Lord, open to us. 12 But he answered and said, Verily I say unto you, I know you not. 13 Watch therefore, for ye know neither the day nor the hour wherein the Son of man cometh. (Matthew 25:1-13)*

In a land where polygamy was legal, and men were commanded to marry virgins, the plain understanding of this passage is somewhat different than what is understood in modern western Christendom. If these women were bridesmaids would it not be the bride herself who would tell them "*I know you not*"? As we noticed, though, they ARE the brides. The ones who had respect to the bridegroom's instructions are the ones who will go into the marriage. The others, who had lamps but never had any oil, will be left out and will go through the Great Tribulation period.

There is no place in the entire bible where God says that polygamy is adultery. He never even implies it, but rather gives ample indication that He accepts it. He has had ample opportunity to condemn the practise, but He never did. There must be a reason for this omission. There are no accidents in the Word of God.

Practical Implications for Today

Does all this mean that it is OK for you to marry a second wife? How should churches treat converts to Christianity, who come into the Church with multiple wives?

As I said before, all Scripture is a unit. We can't take one part and pit it against the rest. In Romans 13:1-7 Paul stated that Christians should obey the laws of the nation they live in. Thus we should obey our national law, unless the law commands us to sin. It is not wrong for a man to only have one wife, though **it is a sin to abandon your wife, even if you have three**!

Jesus spoke about keeping one's word, saying *"Let your yea be yea and your nay be nay"* (Mat. 5:37). Did you promise your wife that there would be no one else? By doing so you have removed yourself from the *"pool"* of potential polygamists. He expects you to keep your word. Don't forget your promise was made before God. Sometimes, however, once one's word has been broken it is impossible to go back to the way it was. At that point you need to follow the Scriptures, and make the best of a bad situation. Have you, as a married man, had an affair with another woman? Exodus 22:16 is still God's will for fornicators, and 21:10 still applies to those who marry again. Jesus is the one who said the Law is still valid (Mat. 5:18). Doing the right thing will not save you, but it is still the right thing to do.

We have discussed some of the pertinent Scriptures above, but Christians should act in love toward their brothers. If a polygamist gets saved he has a built-in mission field. God's command is clear *"Let every man abide in the same calling wherein he was called."* (1 Cor. 7:20) If you were saved as a polygamist you need to stay that way to show the love of God to your wives and children. But what if one wife gets saved and two do not?

> *But to the rest speak I, not the Lord: If any brother hath a wife that believeth not, and she be pleased to dwell with him, let him not put her away. And the woman which hath an husband that believeth not, and if he be pleased to dwell with her, let her not leave him. For the unbelieving husband is sanctified by the wife, and the unbelieving wife is sanctified by the husband: else were your children unclean; but now are they holy. But if the unbelieving depart, let him depart. A brother or a sister is not under bondage in such cases: but God hath called us to peace. (1 Corinthians 7:12-15)*

What could the word "*bondage*" possibly mean but the bonds of marriage? If the unbeliever leaves, you are under no obligation. If one of your wives is a Jihadist and wants to stay with you only to kill you. What should you do? I can't give a rule for every possible situation that might arise. You need to seek the Lord on this and every issue. In the mean-time her husband and saved family members should pray for her salvation.

For those living in nations where this practise is allowed, pay attention to what Paul said later in the same chapter:

> *But if any man think that he behaveth himself uncomely toward his virgin, if she pass the flower of her age, and need so require, let him do what he will, he sinneth not: let them marry. (I Corinthians 7:36)*

As a westerner I am predisposed to dislike the practise of polygamy, but I cannot say it is wrong. The Word of God never says it is wrong, only that certain offices in the Church are prohibited for such a man, but God will find other areas of ministry for him.

In Western countries today there are many Muslim polygamists living among us. Because polygamy is illegal in the West, these men divorce their wives yet still live with them. These women then apply for welfare as single mothers, and the taxpayer is stuck footing the bill for raising their children. (Usama Dakdok video) As Jesus said in Matthew 5:32, God does not respect any divorce unless it is given for the cause of fornication. Just because you have a piece of paper saying you are divorced does not mean you are actually divorced in God's eyes! If the woman has not been unfaithful she is not actually divorced, but still married to her husband, even if he has married another! In God's eyes, then, we have a multitude of polygamists living in our midst already! Our governments need to recognize this reality.

Western governments are living in a state of denial. Really, what business is it of the government how many wives a man has? They cannot, and are not interested in, stopping a man from having illicit affairs. They allow gay marriage, which is definitely contrary to the Scriptures. (Lev. 18:22 & 20:13, Deut. 23:17, 1 Kings 14:24, 15:12, 22:46, 2 Kings 23:7, Rom. 1:24-27, 1 Cor. 6:9) The only business the government has in this case is to ensure that men care for their dependants. If men are required to support all their dependants it would provide incentive for them to minimize the number of wives they have, and at the same time it would relieve the taxpayer of an unnecessary burden.

What should churches do if a Muslim polygamist gets saved and wants to join the church? Should the church insist that the man abandon all but his first wife, as many churches have done? As we have seen such advice is contrary to Scripture, and is actually promoting sin! In God's eyes those women are married to that man and deserve his protection and provision. If he gets saved, they and their children, become his mission field. He needs to deal with them in love as a husband, and exercise all due benevolence towards them (1 Cor. 7:3). We need to see things as God does, by reading His Word, and not view the world through our cultural traditions.

If a polygamist professes salvation by faith alone, through the shed blood of Jesus Christ alone, he should be welcomed in the Church as a brother in Christ. He is barred from being a pastor, elder, or deacon, but I cannot see any place in Scripture where he would be prohibited from serving the church in other ways. There are many ways such a brother could serve the Church, but he must remember not to neglect his family. If he is exercising due benevolence toward his family he will truly have very little time to work for the church. His Christian brothers should keep this in mind, and not put too great a burden on him. This is why such a man is not allowed the office of a pastor, elder, or deacon. God does not want His men neglecting their families, regardless of the number of wives he has. That would be a situation that would reflect badly on the Church. And yet it does happen, even to men with only one wife.

If you live in one of the nations spoken of in Ezekiel 38 and 39, where one out of six soldiers return from war, what will the following passage mean in that context? You are likely to see the rise of the Antichrist. Most will not recognize him because most

Christians have rejected the biblical teaching on this subject.

> *Now the Spirit speaketh expressly, that in the latter times some shall depart from the faith, giving heed to seducing spirits, and doctrines of devils; Speaking lies in hypocrisy; having their conscience seared with a hot iron; Forbidding to marry, and commanding to abstain from meats, which God hath created to be received with thanksgiving of them which believe and know the truth. (1 Timothy 4:1-3)*

Look to Jesus. Read and Follow His teachings in the Bible. Love even your enemies.

The truth is that many man-made laws are unjust and unbiblical. Jesus will make all things right when He returns. In the mean time what should a man do if he finds himself in the situation described in Deuteronomy 22:28 & 29? First of all, he shouldn't find himself in that situation, but realistically, it does happen. This is why God wrote it! God is the one who says to marry the second woman without divorcing the first! (Deut. 22:28 & 29 & Ex. 21:10) Ultimately you will have to answer to Him, not to me, your pastor, your president, or prime minister.

Isaiah 4:1 indicates that the government of Jesus Christ will view marriage very differently than the governments that rule the world today. He will overturn all their unjust laws, including laws against polygamy! His rule will be just and perfect!

God had a reason, from the very beginning, to allow polygamy. He did it so women would have support in their declining years, especially women in war-ravaged nations. He also allowed this practice so that nations could replenish their army, so that they would be secure from attack, especially the nation of Israel. Knowing the nature and desires of women He allowed it so every woman could have a husband during times when men were scarce, so they would not have to act as prostitutes and harlots.

These reasons converge in the End Times wars of Gog and Magog, and Armageddon, and show the difference between the reigns of Jesus Christ and the Antichrist. The desire of women, is shown consistently throughout the bible to be the desire to have children by their husband, even at a time when there are not enough men to go around. Jesus will regard, or respect, the desire of women, and the Antichrist will not, something that is opposite to the teaching of most Christian churches. As a consequence these churches are preparing their congregations to accept the Antichrist, when he shows up, as a "man of God"!

I will leave this subject with one final thought; Will there be some polygamists caught up in the rapture of the Church? I think so, and what will those left behind say about them? Is it possible they might say *"They were taken in judgment for their wicked lifestyle"*?

It is enough for the disciple that he be as his master, and the servant as his lord. If they have called the master of the house Beelzebub, how much more shall they call them of his household? (Matthew 10:25)

References

"The Project Gutenberg EBook of The Lives Of The Twelve Caesars, Complete", Tranquillus, C. Suetonius, Release Date: October 22, 2006 [EBook #6400], Accessed 02/20/2010, found at http://www.gutenberg.org/files/6400/6400-h/6400-h.htm

"The Pink Swastika, Homosexuality in the Nazi Party", by Lively, Scott and Abrams, Kevin E., Published by Veritas Aeterna Press, January, 2002

The Truth about Barack Hussein Obama, Video series by Usama Dakdok, 2008, accessed 29/09/2010, http://www.thestraightway.org/revealingtruthab.php

Nine

The Strong Delusion

And for this cause God shall send them strong delusion, that they should believe a lie: (2 Thessalonians 2:11)

I also will choose their delusions, and will bring their fears upon them; because when I called, none did answer; when I spake, they did not hear: but they did evil before mine eyes, and chose that in which I delighted not. (Isaiah 66:4)

For there shall arise false Christs, and false prophets, and shall shew great signs and wonders; insomuch that, if it were possible, they shall deceive the very elect. (Matthew 24:24)

For false Christs and false prophets shall rise, and shall shew signs and wonders, to seduce, if it were possible, even the elect. (Mark 13:22)

The attack on the Bible began even before it was finished being written. When Jesus spoke about deception in the latter days, He was not referring to only one deception, but to many lies that fall under the umbrella of deception. We have discussed some of them in every chapter of this book. In this chapter I want to address an attack against the Church and against potential Christians that has gone on for well over a century now. I am referring to a process of conditioning that the world has been undergoing. Like a frog in a frying pan, this process has been so slow and subtle that few have noticed it.

The What-If Game

Have you ever thought about the difference between Pre-millennial versus A-millennial Eschatology? I know Christians who don't think it's all that important what you believe regarding the End Times. I have heard Christians say that all the different understandings have come from God Himself! Is it possible that interpretations which are mutually exclusive could come from the same God?

> *For God is not the author of confusion, but of peace, as in all churches of the saints. (1 Corinthians 14:33)*

Have you ever played the *"What If"* game with these two interpretations, or the multitude of variations within them?

What if A-millennialism is correct? Basically, there will be no warning, or maybe the Tribulation, and all of a sudden Jesus will return, the Church will be raptured, the dead will be raised, and it will be Judgment day with the saved going to Heaven and the lost going to the Lake of Fire. If this scenario were correct it wouldn't matter what you believe about the return of Christ. It will just happen and then earth's history will be over.

Now what about the other side of the coin? What if Pre-Millennial, or Dispensational Eschatology is correct?

All of a sudden, after some warnings, many of which we are seeing today, the Church will be raptured and God's Judgment on earth, the Tribulation period, will begin. From the standpoint of the saved the results are much the same either way. This time, however, there will be people left on earth. What will they be saying about those who have disappeared?

Considering that the majority viewpoint in the professing Church is A-millennial, and thus those left behind will, for the most part, be familiar with that idea, won't they be saying something like this? *"Those crazy Christians! They said Jesus was going to come and judge us, and instead they are the ones who have been judged as unworthy, by Space Aliens, and have been removed from our beloved planet! Now we have inherited the earth! That just shows how wrong they were!"* Others, like Emergents and New Apostolic Reformers, will be saying *"The evil people who stood against the Church have been removed and now it is time for the kingdom of God on Earth to be ushered in by us, the true Church!"* (the difference between these viewpoints is slight)

Please understand, this is not merely speculation. New-Agers have been saying this very thing for decades! The devil is preparing our society for the rapture, and as time goes on he is intensifying his efforts. Look at the popularity of science-fiction in the media. Star Trek gave the world an explanation for the rapture that doesn't include the Lord Jesus Christ, or if it does, lowers Him to the status of an alien being! *"Beam me up, Scotty!"* is a phrase so common that it has entered the modern English vernacular, and is an integral part of the End Times delusion. New movies and TV shows are continuing the theme at breakneck pace.

Many preachers ignore the idea of aliens, or pass them off as being ludicrous. I'm afraid this is a serious mistake. Just because we have not seen certain things, it does not mean they do not exist. No one has ever seen electricity, or gravity, yet no one seriously doubts their existence. God Himself has never been seen, yet Christianity and most other religions have as their foundation the existence of a God or gods.

The Bible does indeed make mention of beings who would pass themselves off as aliens, if they could get away with it. Indeed those beings are predisposed to say or do anything to make their audience doubt, or belittle, God Himself. They would like nothing better than for mankind to worship them rather than God. What is their motivation? They are fallen angels who have no hope, unless they can prove that God is a liar. Since God says that He always reserves a remnant who worship Him, they appear to think that if everyone worships Lucifer and the Antichrist instead of Jehovah, this would prove Jehovah/Jesus is a liar. They will not succeed, but they will come close to it.

The Days of Noah

Jesus said it would be like it was in the days of Noah, just prior to his second coming. Have you ever wondered what it was like in the days of Noah? Many Christians have read Genesis, probably many times, but did you ever wonder who were the *"sons of God"* mentioned in chapter 6? The very last thing mentioned before the flood is the marriage of the *"Sons of God"* to the daughters of men. The phrase *"Sons of God"* never refers to humans until the New Testament. In the Old Testament it always refers to angelic beings. In the New Testament it is revealed that human beings can become sons of God, with the power and status that angels now possess. (John 1:12, Matt. 22:30)

> *1 And it came to pass, when men began to multiply on the face of the earth, and daughters were born unto them, 2 That the **sons of God** saw the daughters of men that they were fair; and **they took them wives of all which they chose**. 3 And the LORD said, My spirit shall not always strive with man, for that he also is flesh: yet his days shall be an hundred and twenty years. 4 There were giants in the earth in those days; and also after that, when the sons of God came in unto the daughters of men, and they bare children to them, the same became mighty men which were of old, men of renown. (Could the story of Hercules have its basis in this event?) 5 And GOD saw that the wickedness of man was great in the earth, and that every imagination of the thoughts of his heart was only evil continually. (Genesis 6:1-5)*

I have heard pastors say that the *"Sons of God"* in this passage were believers, and the daughters of men were unbelievers. Such an explanation really does not fit the context of the passage. Since when are the children of mixed marriages between believers and unbelievers, giants, or more exceptional people than children of two unbelievers or two believers? The best explanation of this passage is that the *"sons of God"* are angelic beings. This explanation fits the old pagan stories of women marrying "gods" and producing exceptional children, like the story of Hercules, who's father was a god and who's mother was a woman.

This story is written into the biblical account as the last significant event before the flood, as if it was the *"last straw"*. There was much sin and violence in the world, but this was the event that angered God so much that the flood became inevitable. I think the phrase *"and also after that"* is a reference to the flood, and is saying that even after the destruction of the flood, there were angels who did it again.

Could it be that Goliath and his family were descendants of these unions, and this was why God had determined to erase them from off of the face of the earth? Jude seems to allude to this event in Jude 1:6 with his reference to the angels who *"kept not their first estate"*. Could this mean that their *"first estate"* was that they were created as spiritual beings, but left that condition to live as physical beings, among men? Their habitation, or home, was the spiritual realm.

> *And the angels which kept not their first estate, but left their own habitation, he hath reserved in everlasting chains under darkness unto the judgment of the great day. (Jude 1:6)*

Peter also seems to be alluding to this same event in 2 Peter 2:4. We know that many angels have sinned, and are not in Hell today, but wandering the earth, creating chaos. This is a reference to a specific group of angels, and not just any sin but to a specific sin:

> *For if God spared not the **angels that sinned**, but cast them down to hell, and delivered them into **chains of darkness**, to be reserved unto judgment; (2 Peter 2:4)*

The devil and his angels today are not locked up in *"chains of darkness"* but have access to the throne room of Heaven, as well as to the earth (Job 1:6 & 7). Job is a post-flood book which means the events in question occurred after Noah's flood. We can surmise then, that the group of angels locked up in II Peter 2:4, and Jude 1, are not the same angels referred to as *"Sons of God"* in Job 1.

Could the term *"perfect in his generations"* be a reference to Noah's ancestry, and not to his lifestyle? Once we harmonize all of scripture it becomes clear that the word *"generations"* must be a reference to his ancestry. Noah did not have any angelic blood in his ancestry, as well as being a man who walked with God. If a man, though a sinner, walks humbly with his God, and is all that God can expect of him, the bible sometimes does refer to him as perfect, but this is not the context here. The word perfect is connected to the plural *"generations"*, which indicates his ancestry.

If angels had a physical presence on the earth before the flood, and used it to deceive people at that time, then why wouldn't they attempt to do the same again in the last days? Given that they know their time is extremely short, isn't it more likely than ever that they will pull out all the stops in their quest to deceive the inhabitants of earth?   Isn't it possible that they may attempt even more tricks than ever, because they know the next stop for them is the Lake of Fire?

Could Daniel 2:43 actually be a reference to an attempt on the part of some fallen angels to do the same thing that other fallen angels did in the pre-flood, and early post-flood world? He is speaking of the ten toes of the image in Nebuchadnezzar's dream. Given the fact that Paul speaks of our adversaries the fallen angels, as being principalities, and powers, and Jesus' prophecy that the End Times would be like it was before the flood, it appears as if those angel's, in their desperation will once again try the same thing they saw others do before. This verse seems to indicate that they will try, but it will be to no avail. I think that over the last four thousand years, or so, that God has modified human DNA so that it is no longer compatible with angelic DNA.

> *And whereas thou sawest iron mixed with miry clay, they shall mingle themselves with the seed of men: but they shall not cleave one to another, even as iron is not mixed with clay. (Daniel 2:43)*

Most comentators believe this passage refers to the last days human government being disunited, but I think it refers to an attempt of fallen angels, the governing principalities, to do the same thing as was done in Genesis 6. If you read through Daniel chapter 10, you will see that human governments have angelic princes, assigned to them, some are God's angels and many are Satan's. Paul also refers to our spiritual adversaries as "principalities" in Ephesians 6:12. It thus follows that the governments of the world are controlled by angelic beings, and it is they who are in view in this passage from Daniel.

In order for them to attempt this deception they will have to have a story to explain their presence on the earth. Saying that they are fallen angels working against God will be the last thing they would say! For a generation schooled in evolutionary thought, and who carry cell phones, and iPads, and laptop computers, the alien explanation will be the more believable one.

Remember that Jesus spoke about deception being something characteristic of the last days. (Mat. 24:24) What could be more deceptive than angelic beings staging an alien landing, and pretending to be from another planet, or dimension? Remember the author of Hebrews said that some have *"entertained angels unawares"*? (Heb. 13:2) In Genesis chapter 18 the Lord God Himself took on a physical form and visited Abraham along with two angels. During that visit they were able to appear as men, and even ate food that Abraham had provided for them. If God's angels can take on a physical form, then why can't the devil's angels do the same thing? After all, the devil's angels started off as God's angels. Personally, I do not think God will allow them to go too far while the Church is on earth, but after the rapture all bets are off!

For the mystery of iniquity doth already work: only he who now letteth will let, until he be taken out of the way (2 Thessalonians 2:7)

Please note that the word *"let"* in old English has the exact opposite meaning to the modern English. *"Let"* used to mean to hinder or oppose, now it means *"to allow"*.

Many have speculated about the meaning of this passage, especially the subject of the word *"he"*. Could *"he"* be the Holy Spirit? Isn't the Holy Spirit removed along with the Church at the rapture? The problem with this interpretation is that it is apparent that the Holy Spirit will be very active on earth throughout the Tribulation period.

Many have claimed that the *"he"* cannot be the Christian Church because the Church is referred to as the bride of Christ, in the feminine. The Church, like God Himself, is actually sexless. God refers to Himself in the masculine because His attributes are closest to the masculine, but the Church changes its role with regard to the persons it interacts with.

The Church has a feminine role in its relationship to God, because it is submissive to Him, as His bride, but in relation to this world, and the devil, the Church takes on a masculine role. The Church is often pictured in Scripture in the role of a soldier. (Phil. 2:25, 2 Tim. 2:3 & 4, Philemon 1:2, Eph. 6, 1 Thes. 5:8, Mat. 16:18). Thus the "he" in 2 Thes. 2:7 is the Church. Note the context is the antagonistic relationship of the person referred to as "he" to the spirit of Antichrist, as opposed to "his" relationship to God. The role of the Holy Spirit in the Church is unique, and though He will remain on the earth after the rapture, His role will not be exactly the same as it is in the Church today. Yes, He will still save, but those saved will not have the same status as Church-age saints in Heaven, they will not be indwelt with the Holy Spirit. They will have faith mixed with sight, today we have only faith.

So we see then that the presence of the Church of Jesus Christ, and its special relationship with the Holy Spirit, is what is keeping the devil and his angels from exercising all of the deceptive power they have at their disposal. It is the rapture of the Church which will change this global dynamic.

Aliens and UFOs

"In 1900, the French Academy of Science offered a prize of 100,000 francs for the first person to make contact with an alien civilisation — so long as the alien was not from Mars, because the Academy was convinced that Martian civilisation was an established fact!" (Gitt, God and the Extraterrestrials)

The widespread belief in evolution is largely responsible for the belief in extraterrestrial life, after all *"if life evolved on earth it must have evolved elsewhere"*. This belief is defined as *"religious"* because it is based on one's desires, and not actually on any scientific fact.

In my grade twelve high school biology class, I did a project based on the question *"Could there be life in outer space?"* My answer, from a *"Christian"* perspective was *"The Universe is so vast it seems incredible that this is the only place that God would have made life. Therefore He must have created life somewhere else."*

Though He did create life somewhere else, there was a flaw in my reasoning. First, besides creating life on earth, He created life in Heaven. Second, while the Bible doesn't directly deal with the question of life in the universe, it states that at the end of the millennium the universe will be destroyed along with the earth. (Isa. 65:17, 66:22, Rev. 21:1)

"But the day of the Lord will come as a thief in the night; in the which the heavens shall pass away with a great noise, and the elements shall melt with fervent heat, the earth also and the works that are therein shall be burned up." (2 Peter 3:10)

The Day of the Lord begins with the Great Tribulation period, and ends one thousand years later, with an earthly rebellion and the destruction of the earth and universe. If there was spiritual or intelligent life in the universe, who had not sinned, it would not be fair, or just, for them to be destroyed when the earth is destroyed.

Since God is Just we can conclude that there is no life anywhere else in the universe. The Bible is clear that only descendants of Adam can be saved. Christ is our kinsman redeemer. He is a part of the human family. God came to earth and lived as a man, a descendant of Adam. He did not come to aliens, nor did He die for aliens.

The Search for Extra Terrestrial Intelligence, or SETI, has been searching for signs of life from outer space for many years. The first attempt was made in 1960 by Cornell University astronomer Frank Drake, with repeated attempts made regularly since then.(Wikipedia, SETI) What has been the result? A great amount of tax-payer money and donated funds has been expended with nothing resembling an intelligent broadcast of any sort, over a period approaching fifty years, has ever been received.

While UFOs have been seen on radar screens, they have never been seen entering the earth's atmosphere from outer-space. Nevertheless UFO reports continue to be made

The UFO phenomenon has several explanations that fit the known facts: they may be experimental craft produced by the US and other governments, sometimes they are natural phenomena such as birds, meteorites or the planet Venus, they may be hoaxes, or they may be physical manifestations of spiritual/angelic beings. Many of the reports describe phenomena that are not possible with physical craft, such as sudden direction changes at very high rates of speed, or craft that change shape in mid-flight. (Alien Intrusion, p. 146)

There have been many hoaxes regarding the UFO phenomena. Some people want to see them so badly that they are willing to create them. Because of a few hoaxes, some people discount all reports of UFOs as being more of the same. I think this is a mistake. There are so many reports of UFO sightings, that discounting the hoaxes and the natural phenomena there are still a great many reports that do appear to be legitimate. Something is going on.

These reports are not new, either, for ancient Romans and Greeks left reports of *"flying globes"* or *"flying shields"*. North American Indians had legends of *"flying canoes"* and *"great silvery airships"*. Similar sightings have been reported in a great many cultures for many years. (Alien Intrusion, p.152-154)

In the fall 2002 edition of the International UFO Reporter, an article entitled *"We Know Where You Live"*, gave some interesting insights into many of the UFO sightings. The article documented that many observers have watched as UFOs flew geometric patterns in relation to celestial objects such as stars and the moon. Sometimes the UFO flies a complete circle around the object with the appearance of keeping an exact distance from it. Since these flights are not observed by observatories actually circling the star, and if they were they would have to be traveling at many times the speed of light, it appears that the UFO is in rather close proximity to the observers.

Sometimes they are seen by small groups of people but not by others in the same geographical area. This would indicate that the UFO is very close to the observers, perhaps as close as a few hundred to a few thousand feet away. The UFO must be aware that they are being observed for just a slight change in position would destroy the geometric effect. The conclusion of the article is that the UFOs are putting on a *"display"* or are *"performing"* for the observer. (Swords, We Know Where You Live)

In the mean time there have been thousands of people claiming to have been contacted by alien beings.

It has become very clear that where there is contact with Alien beings, this phenomenon is not physical, but spiritual. One common factor in these alien *"contactees"* is their prior experience with the occult: Séances, Ouija boards, drug use, and hypnotism, etc. In fact the way persons contact these so-called *"aliens"* is identical to the way witches and occultists have contacted the spirit world for centuries.

Aliens are really fallen angels masquerading as life from outer-space. They know what you want to hear and will tell it to you. Do you believe in aliens from other planets? They will say *"I'm an alien"*! What if you believe in Leprechauns? They will say *"I'm a Leprechaun"*. If you believe the earth is alive they will say *"I'm a tree spirit"*. In the Old Testament they are also called *"familiar spirits"* because they are very familiar with everything about you, and we are commanded not to contact them. (Leviticus 20:27)

A great many contactees claim they have been abducted by aliens. The abduction stories have a great many things in common even though they can occur in different cultures on opposite sides of the globe. There is no doubt that the abductees have had a very real experience. Many of the things they speak of, however, cannot happen in the physical world, such as passing through walls, or going out into the stars in space ships. It is apparent that many of these experiences are spiritual and not truly physical. There is a sexual aspect to many of these encounters, where contactees speak of having eggs or sperm extracted for experimental purposes. These people are told that they are specially chosen for a mission and it appears that this experience is designed to make them feel special, i.e. to produce loyalty toward the "*aliens*". (Alien Intrusion, p. 304, 329)

Alien contactees have been given messages like *"Jesus is an alien and is going to return in his starship"*, and *"Sodom and Gomorrah were destroyed by an alien attack from outer space"*. Another message has been *"We aliens planted life on the earth millions of years ago and have been guiding evolution since then"*! (Bates, Aliens)

At first blush these sound crazy, but I believe there is something deliberate, and very sinister going on. What will the armies of the world do when Jesus returns? How will they interpret God's attack on the Russian and Iranian armies who attack Israel, during the war of Isaiah 38 and 39? If they believe it was really the creator God they will repent and worship Him, but if they believe He's just another alien they will ready themselves to fight Him! Which interpretation would Satan prefer?

> *And I saw the beast, and the kings of the earth, and their armies, gathered together to make war against him that sat on the horse, and against his army. (Revelation 19:19)*

Why would normal intelligent people pick up arms to fight against the Lord Jesus Christ? What kind of delusion would they have to believe, to think they could defeat the King of Kings? If they think He's an alien, like the one's they have seen, it would make the most sense. Does it seem like a contradiction when you compare Revelation 19:19 with Matthew 24:30?

> *"And then shall appear the sign of the Son of man in heaven: and then shall all the tribes of the earth mourn, and they shall see the Son of man coming in the clouds of heaven with power and great glory." (Matthew 24:30)*

This is not actually a contradiction. The timing may be different, or different people are in view in each passage. The armies of the world in Revelation 19:19 are unbelievers. The tribes of the earth who mourn are either believers, or they people who believe they are under alien attack, perhaps some of each. The armies of the world will think they are seeing an alien starship and will ready themselves to fight! Given what we've just covered, it is likely that they will know that it is Jesus Christ they are fighting but they will deny that he is the Creator and owner of the world. They will think he is *"just another alien"* and thus can be beaten.

In Chuck Swindol's audio series on Revelation, in the section on Revelation 16, he says he doesn't know why the unclean spirits are characterized as frogs. (Insight for Living, April 12-16, 2007)   I think I know why. John was not accustomed to 20th, and 21st, century popular depictions of aliens as *"little green men"*. To him they looked like frogs!

> And I saw **three unclean spirits like frogs** come out of the mouth of the dragon, and out of the mouth of the beast, and out of the mouth of the false prophet. For they are the **spirits of devils**, working miracles, which go forth unto the kings of the earth and of the whole world, to gather them to the battle of that great day of God Almighty. (Revelation 16:13-14)

Given the events of Genesis 6, I expect these evil spirits will take on a physical form, and lead the armies of the world openly against the Lord! As it says, they will be working miracles. Many will take any miracle as authentication, rather than believe the truth. The miracles will make the armies of the world think they are supporting *"good aliens"* against a hostile alien bent on destroying the earth! The miracles will make them think their aliens are equal to the other *"alien"*, the Lord Jesus Christ!

God has told them the truth in His Word, but they refuse to believe it, so He will send them a delusion. Thus it appears the End Times delusion includes a belief in aliens and UFOs. The devil has enough tricks up his sleeve to make people believe it! During the End Times God will purposely allow Satan to deceive his own people with miracles and smooth words. What could be more deceptive than something appearing high-tech and space-age?

> I also will choose their delusions, and will bring their fears upon them; because when I called, none did answer; when I spake, they did not hear: but they did evil before mine eyes, and chose that in which I delighted not. (Isaiah 66:4)

The movie *"Star Wars"* came out while I was in high school, and was a huge success! It was not the first science-fiction movie but it set a new standard for production and realism. Of course before that there was Star Trek in the 1960s, which has become a very popular syndicated TV show, has been translated into many languages, and viewed around the world! Star Trek led to a series of eleven spin-off movies and five TV spin-off series. The eleventh Star Trek movie was released during the summer of 2009.

The recent Indiana Jones movie *"the Crystal Skull"* features some skulls carved out of some sort of crystal. At the end of the movie the skulls come together and form a live alien. As the alien ship is flying away Indiana states that these aliens are *"inter-dimensional beings"*. Now this is closer to the truth! The other dimension is the spirit world, and these beings are spiritual, or angelic, with the ability to take on a physical form.

While these shows are extremely popular they also are serving to create a mindset, or new paradigm, that accepts aliens as real. In doing so they also increase the fear of the unknown, and ready the world for the End Times.

The world we live in has been subject to a great many deceptions for a long time. As far back as the Garden of Eden, actually.

The Devil, or Satan, is desperate to prove that God is a liar. He knows that his time is very short and he appears to think that if he could prove God to be a liar he would be spared the Lake of Fire. This explains why he has persecuted Israel from the beginning. God has made promises to Israel and if Satan can rid the world of Israelites then God could not keep his promises. If there was even one promise God did not keep it would make Him a liar. As a liar caught in a lie, how could He throw anyone into eternal fire? This seems to be the devil's reasoning, but he has forgotten one thing: God has the power to keep all his promises, and is always many steps ahead of all His enemies.

The same applies to the Christian Church. If Satan can get the world to reject Jesus Christ, then God would not be able to save anyone. Consequently the Christian Church has had as many attacks as Israel, though the attacks on the church often take a different form than the attacks on the Jews. Satan has learned that frontal attacks don't always work against the church, so these attacks are often more subtle, and very often come from within the

"Christian" ranks themselves. While he wants to destroy Christians, the best way for him to do that is to get them to worship him rather than their Saviour, Jesus Christ!

The Grand Illusion

S atan's End Times conditioning is not limited to the visual media of TV and Movies. Music is at least as effective as the other two. We often listen to radio stations without thinking about what we are hearing. We often find ourselves singing along without even thinking about what we are saying. The music, and the tune, is used to get the words into our head. This is a very effective form of conditioning.

As a teen-ager I purchased an album by the rock group Styx and listened to it many times over a few years. The music is catchy, polished, and I would say there is an element of quality in the sound. Years later, I had not listened to this type of music for a long time, some fellow employees were listening to a popular music station playing *"Come Sail Away"*, and I found myself singing along. I still knew the words even though I had not listened to that music for some twenty years!

Let's examine *"Come Sail Away"*, written by Dennis DeYoung of Styx. This is a song that ranks in anyone's list of the top Rock Ballads of all time. At the outset please let me say that I do not believe the group is deliberately Satanic in any way. Satan is very good at impersonating an angel of light, and has a lot of people fooled. He actually wants people to think of him as Lucifer, an angel of light rather than Satan, the adversary. The members of Styx are a group of very talented musicians, and are not any greater sinners than this author. As the chief of sinners, I have received the forgiveness Jesus offers, and I hope the members of Styx avail themselves of this same forgiveness before it is too late.

Some Christians have claimed that this song contains backward masking. Frankly, it's irrelevant if it does. Its New Age message is very straight forward in the plain English lyrics, if we care to read them.

In the first verse, he invites you aboard and introduces himself as the captain. I think he is implying that he is the captain of his own soul for he says he needs to *"be free to face the life that's coming to him"*. Since the singer calls someone else *"Lord"*, however, then he can't be the one in charge, can he? His reference to a *"Lord"* is not the Lord God of the Bible, but to another Lord. There is more than one being who claims to be Lord, for Baal, or Baalim, also means Lord, but he is not the Lord God of the Bible, and calling God Baalim, or Baali, is an insult to Him.

> *And it shall be at that day, saith the LORD, that thou shalt call me Ishi; and **shalt call me no more Baali**. (Hosea 2:16)*

Later the song gets more interesting. In the third verse he sees a group of angels singing a song of "hope" that he can somehow sail away with them. *"A group of Angels appeared above my head, They sang a song of hope and here is what they said, They said, "Come sail away..."*

So far so good, but who are these angels? Mr. De Young tells us:

"I originally thought they were Angels, but to my astonishment, We climbed on board their spaceship, we headed for the heavens" (my paraphrase)

So what is his message? Isn't he saying that *"the beings we once thought were angels are actually aliens from somewhere else in the universe, and they can save us."* Has he ever asked "If these beings once stated they were gods, or angels and now claim to be aliens, when were, or are, they lying?"

The chorus repeats the message *"Come sail away"*, initially being spoken by angels, and later by aliens, inviting him to come away with them among the stars!

This message reminds me of an End Times prophecy in the Bible. Obadiah 1:4 says, *"Though thou exalt thyself as the eagle, and **though thou set thy nest among the stars**, thence will I bring thee down, saith the LORD."* Note to whom this prophecy is aimed...Edom. He is not saying that they really can go to the stars, but that if they could He could still find them. This takes on great significance as we study Edom in the End Times. I suspect that the "aliens" the Antichrist is in contact with, will promise him that they will be able to hide him from Jesus Christ, among the stars. To my surprise, the little book of Obadiah is more up-to-date than modern rock musicians!

This song is from the album entitled *"The Grand Illusion"*! Now, something that is *"Grand"* is *"Large"* or *"Big"* or *"Strong"*. When I looked up the word *"Illusion"* in the Oxford dictionary, it used the word *"Delusion"* in the definition! The devil likes to play games with his own people and I believe this is one of them. I think he is signaling what he is planning to use to deceive people with for the End Times "*strong delusion*".   Ultimately he will mock those who believe him: "*didn't you pay any attention to the words of the songs I inspired?*"

The cover art of the album consists of an optical illusion of the silhouette of a man on a horse in the woods, with a female face overlying the silhouette. It is interesting that he is using the biblical symbolism of a man on a horse, since this same imagery is used in the book of Revelation in reference to the Antichrist. (Rev. 6:2) If you look closely at the rider's head you will see that either he has really *"poofy"* hair, or a crown on his head.

Led Zeppelin and Biblical Prophecy?

f I were to ask you which is the most popular rock ballad of all time? What would you say? Would you guess *"Stairway to Heaven"*, by Led Zeppelin?   If so you would be right, or at least very close. Every survey has the songs in a slightly different order, but *"Stairway"* is always near the top. I think that this song will be hailed as prophetic during the Tribulation period. The music itself is brilliant, but it is the words that I take issue with.   The music is catchy, and is used as a medium whereby the words lodge themselves in your brain.

In the second verse the singer gives us a *"heads up"* when he states: *"Because you are aware that occasionally words have two meanings."* We should take it from this that the song will be full of doublespeak. If they tell you it means something, it probably means something else.   This is something that the Occult is famous for; teaching one interpretation to the public, and something quite opposite to the adepts, to those who have been initiated into the *"Mysteries"*. Sometimes they bury many meanings, so that if you have found two you are just scratching the surface. If you guess correctly they will just say that you are wrong and give you another supposed explanation.   It is impossible to pin them down on anything, so let's just say that this is my analysis of their lyrics.

The fourth verse begins to tell us the benefits of unity: *"And it's reported that soon if we all exercise authority, Then the piper will lead us to sanity."* Note that the original line *"Call the tune"* means to exercise authority, or be in charge, but I think the context in which it is used here actually implies that we all have to get in line, and obey. In other words the doublespeak meaning is exactly the opposite of the plain sense meaning. Another example of doublespeak is the reference to a piper: is the *"piper"* a reference to the pied piper of nursery rhyme fame, or is it a reference to Lucifer, the first piper?

> *Thou hast been in Eden the garden of God; every precious stone was thy covering, the sardius, topaz, and the diamond, the beryl, the onyx, and the jasper, the sapphire, the emerald, and the carbuncle, and gold: the workmanship of thy tabrets <u>and of thy pipes</u> was prepared in thee in the day that thou wast created. (Ezekiel 28:13)*

In the fifth verse he says *"If there's a commotion in your hedgerow, Don't be dismayed now, Its just a spring-cleaning going on for the May queen."*

I was musing on what this might mean one day, and it occurred to me that hedgerows in England are very common dividers between properties. In other words, your hedgerow is someplace close to you... at the edge of your yard. If a bustle, or commotion, in your hedgerow would alarm you, then it is something uncomfortably close. Could he be referring to the Rapture of the Church? When people all around the world disappear in one day, many will find this alarming. Some will have heard some of these Christians speaking of the rapture of the Church by the Lord Jesus Christ, so the Antichrist and his people will have to do some damage control. I think he is trying to anticipate the rapture with a bogus explanation long before it actually happens. I actually doubt that the author of this song ever heard of the Rapture, I think it is the spirit who inspired him who gave him these words.

What do you do when you are doing a spring-cleaning? You throw out the trash that has built up over a long winter...correct? So is he saying that *"if someone close to you disappears in the Rapture of the Church, don't be alarmed. It's just a spring-cleaning, throwing out the trash for the arrival of the "May Queen"." "Winter is over and now it's time for spring...peace and safety".* (1 Thes. 5:3)

> "The May Queen is a girl (usually a teenage girl from a specific school year) who is selected to ride or walk at the front of a parade for May Day celebrations. She wears a white gown to symbolize purity and usually a tiara or crown. Her duty is to begin the May Day celebrations. She is

generally crowned by flowers and makes a speech before the dancing begins. Certain age groups dance round a Maypole celebrating youth and the spring time." (May Queen, Answers.com)

The May Pole dance, practiced throughout Europe since pre-Christian times, is based on a phallus symbol. A pagan symbol of fertility. May-Day itself is also a hold-over from pagan times, and is still celebrated by practitioners of Wicca today.

The specific *"May Queen"* referred to here is the name of a poem by Aleister Crowley, a leading Occultist from England in the early twentieth century. In the poem Crowley talks of making love with *"God's daughter"*, the May Queen, and of rescuing her from a *"Beast that lurks down by the Water"*. I cannot help but wonder if this is a veiled reference to the Beast from the Sea, of Revelation 13:1. As is usual in occultism, things are upside down, so the *"Beast"* he is referring to could well be Jesus Christ! Jimmy Page, the lead guitarist and really the leader of Led Zeppelin, was an open and devout follower of Crowley, so devout in fact that he bought Crowley's *"Boleskine"* mansion on the shores of Loch Ness.

Who is the Lady who is the subject of the song, and apparently we all know? The Lady who *"beams bright light and wants to demonstrate that all that glitters turns to gold"*? The language is somewhat negative, and I suspect she is the Catholic Church, and/or perhaps the Harlot of Revelation 17. She will be an object of hatred to the Antichrist, though he will tolerate her for a time and will use her to gain power before disposing of her.

The song ends by encouraging you: *"And if you listen very diligently the song will come to you in the end. When all are one and one are all, yeah, to be a stone and not to turn."* What is he referring to when he says this? Isn't he talking about the End Times when the whole world, with one mind, gives themselves to the Beast? When he says *"Yes, there are two roads you can go on but in the long term, You've still got time to change the way you're going."* he is not referring to repentance toward Jesus Christ, but a turn toward another Christ, the Antichrist. He does not name his Christ, only because he does not know who the Antichrist is just yet. (lyrics are my paraphrases, any similarity to the actual lyrics is purely unintentional, but is nevertheless covered under "fair use" legislation)

I do not think the author actually believes his *"Christ"* is really the Antichrist. He really believes that once the world unites as one, that the man who arises to lead it will be the true *"Christ"*, and will bring peace to the world. They really believe that what they are doing is good. This is the nature of delusion. Satan, who wishes to be known as Lucifer, is very good at impersonating an angel of light. It is impossible to see his deception unless you compare what he says to the Word of God, and trust God rather than your own understanding.

The album within which *"The Stairway to Heaven"* was included, is a rather enigmatic album. It has no name, and no text on the cover. It has been variously known as Led Zeppelin IV, the ZOSO album, the fourth album, and the four symbols album. (wikipedia, Led Zeppelin IV) This album is absolutely full of occult symbolism, including each of the four aforementioned symbols. The cover features a picture hanging on a wall covered in old, peeling wallpaper. The framed picture is that of an old man, bent over with the weight of a large bundle of sticks. The picture wraps around to the back of the album where the wall is broken down revealing a modern city in the background. I would suggest you search the Internet to find a good scan of the album cover, or borrow one from a friend or a local library.

I suspect that the peeling wallpaper represents what they think of Christianity, that it is old, broken down, and needs to be replaced, but it is the bundle of sticks upon which I would like to focus for a moment. In ancient Rome one of the symbols of the state was a bundle of sticks. Sometimes this bundle, called a fasces, had an axe blade protruding from between the sticks, and at other times it did not. Either way it was a symbol of the Roman Empire, or state.

The Italian fascist party of the 1920's and 30's used this symbol on its flag, and various military insignia.

Of particular interest is the fact that the United States of America has frequently used this same symbol as an emblem of government. The *"Mercury"* dime, minted from 1916 to 1945, used a fasces symbol. The United States National Guard Bureau uses the symbol of an eagle overlaid with two fasces on its official seal. The official seal of the United States Senate also contains a pair of fasces. There are many other branches of the United States government that also use fasces, but I will not itemize them here. (Fasces, Wikipedia)

Why would a rebellious rock group like Led Zeppelin use a symbol of fascism, and the United States government, on the cover

Occult/Symbolic Elements of Led Zeppelin IV (Untitled) Album Cover

Bundle of sticks; Fasces, or Faggot: Symbol of Rome, and Fascism. Used by Krampus to beat bad children and women.

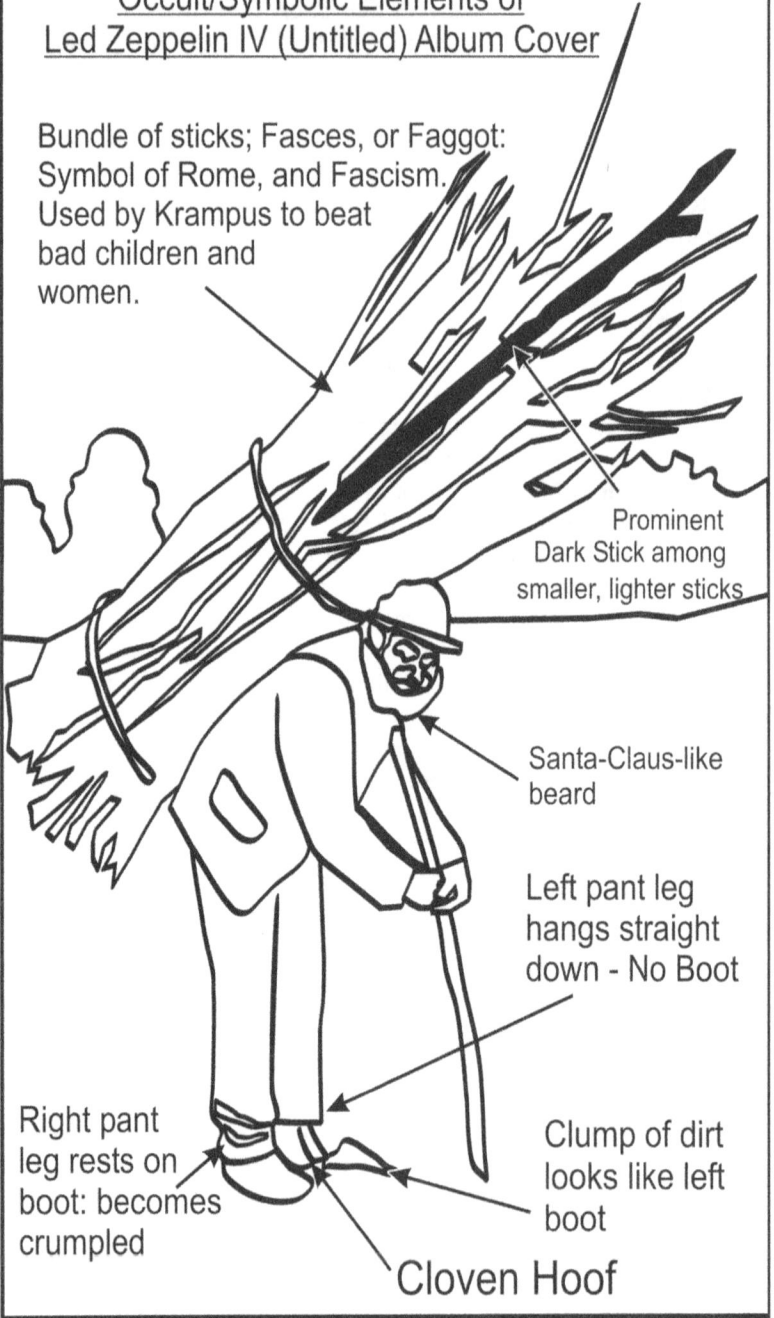

Prominent Dark Stick among smaller, lighter sticks

Santa-Claus-like beard

Left pant leg hangs straight down - No Boot

Right pant leg rests on boot: becomes crumpled

Clump of dirt looks like left boot

Cloven Hoof

of its album? I think the answer lies in the root symbolism of the fasces, and also in the Luciferianism of Crowley, and the upper levels of Freemasonry. Both governments are, or were, controlled by occultists.

The fasces, or fagot, is a symbol of strength in unity. It appears to go back to Aesop's fable, where a father calls his argumentative and disunited, sons to him, and asks them to break a bundle of sticks. None of the sons can do it, so then he unties the bundle and hands each one an individual stick. The sons are able to break the individual sticks with ease. The lesson being taught is that there is strength in unity.

Unfortunately for the New Age movement, should the whole world unite against the God of the bible, He could still destroy us all with a word from His lips! Nevertheless they will never succeed in obtaining a 100% complete earthly unity, even when enforced by the death penalty, for God always reserves a remnant for Himself!

Fascists are really Socialists with a capitalist veneer. In both cases the state is god, and all citizens *"owe"* their existence, and allegiance, to the state. In over one hundred years of experimenting with both styles of the socialist system, the human race has shown repeatedly that statism is an abject failure, and yet there is a movement today to build a One World government based on these same failed principles!

Over and over again we are taught of the strength of unity. Unity is preached in our churches to the point where truth is sacrificed on its altar. Led Zeppelin speaks of this same unity in *"Stairway to Heaven"* when they speak of *"all being one, and one being all"*.

Can two walk together, except they be agreed? (Amos 3:3)

As you look at the fasces in the cover art, note that most of the sticks look pretty much the same. They all have roughly the same length and diameter, except that there is one stick that is darker, thicker, and longer than the rest. I believe this stick is representative of the Antichrist, or, if each stick represents world religions, then the prominent stick would represent the Antichrist's new religion.

Look at the picture of the old man. You will need a magnifying glass or a good quality scan that you can zoom-in on. Now have a look at the man's left foot. The pile of dirt just ahead of his foot almost blends in to make it look like a normal foot from a distance, but on closer examination you can see the background between his real foot and the clump of earth, thus revealing that his left foot is a short little cloven hoof!

In parts of Eastern Europe the story of Saint Nicholas has him accompanied by a being, known as Krampus, closely resembling the pagan depictions of the devil. It was this character who would give children lumps of coal or even beat bad children with birch switches. So now we see a double meaning of the bundle of sticks on his back. Does the big stick represent a particularly powerful weapon with which to force uncooperative nations into line?

Of particular note, Krampus is often depicted with a human foot and a cloven hoof. (Krampustime, Andrew Hammel) Often there was sexual innuendo attached to this figure in the form of an impossibly long tongue. According to pagans he could also be portrayed as an old bearded wild-man, just like the one depicted on Led Zeppelin's album cover:

> "Known by many names across the continent, such as Knecht Ruprecht, Klaubauf, Pelzebock, Schmutzli and Krampus, this figure is unmistakably evil; **he often appears as a traditional red devil with cloven hoof and goatish horns**, though he can also be spotted as an **old bearded wild-man** or a huge hairy beast." (Pagan Space, Who in Hell is Krampus?)

This same web page lists several other names for Krampus, among which is Bellzebub, a variation of the biblical Beelzebub, the chief of the devils. Having read several accounts of the story of Krampus, it is apparent that he is sometimes made out to be the alter-ego of Saint Nicholas. In other words the story has elements of the Eastern yin/yang idea of God being both good and evil in one. (Yes, Santa Claus is a false god) While many pagans and New Agers claim this idea, it is quite apparent that they have a tendency to focus on the evil *"side"* of *(their)* *"God"*. The bible, however, stands squarely opposed to the idea that God could be both good and evil. This should be an indication to us that they are speaking of another god.

> *This then is the message which we have heard of him, and declare unto you, that God is light, and in him is no darkness at all. (1 John 1:5)*

Even the western version of Santa Claus has God-like qualities. For instance the popular song says that Santa knows when all the children are asleep or awake, and whether they have been bad or good. This is omniscience, which is a characteristic of God alone.

Given the fact that alien contactees often report sexual contact with aliens, as do New Agers, with their spirit being contacts, it is really quite easy to see the connection between the End Times delusion and musical groups like Led Zeppelin and Styx. While Led Zeppelin did not specifically mention aliens in *"The Stairway to Heaven"*, it is the same delusion. When the rapture of the Church occurs, the New Age leadership will be able to point to these albums, and others, and say *"See, we told you it would happen"*.

The only reason I chose these two groups to highlight some of their music was simply because of the prominent place they have achieved in the music industry. There are many other groups with similar symbolism and philosophy. It is virtually impossible for a music group to reach top ten status without knowingly, or unknowingly, being a contributor to the End Times delusion.

Even in the Contemporary Christian music scene one can find similar symbolism. Michael W. Smith has used a New Age runic font on one of his album covers, and has recently endorsed mystical/Emergent author Brendan Manning. The very successful CCM group *"the Newsboys"* in 1996, produced an album entitled *"Take Me To Your Leader"*, featuring a vehicle on the cover that looks much like a UFO. Maybe they think it's funny, but it still plays into the hands of the End Times delusion.

At first the following may not seem relevant to our topic, but I can assure you it is...

> *But when the Pharisees heard it, they said, This fellow doth not cast out devils, but by Beelzebub the prince of the devils. And Jesus knew their thoughts, and said unto them, Every kingdom divided against itself is brought to desolation; and every city or house divided against itself shall not stand: And if Satan cast out Satan, he is divided against himself; how shall then his kingdom stand? And if I by Beelzebub cast out devils, by whom do your children cast them out? therefore they shall be your judges. But if I cast out devils by the Spirit of God, then the kingdom of God is come unto you. Or else how can one enter into a strong man's house, and spoil his goods, except he first bind the strong man? and then he will spoil his*

*house. He that is not with me is against me; and he that
gathereth not with me scattereth abroad. Wherefore I say unto
you, All manner of sin and blasphemy shall be forgiven unto
men: but the blasphemy against the Holy Ghost shall not be
forgiven unto men. (Matthew 12:24-31)*

Someone, at some point in time, put a divider between verse 30
and 31, but it doesn't belong there. The whole passage is about the
unforgivable sin. Jesus had been casting out demons by the power
of the Holy Spirit, and the Pharisees accused Him of casting them
out by the power of the devil. They were blaspheming against the
Holy Spirit! Essentially then, Jesus is saying that to attribute an act
of the Holy Spirit to the devil is the unforgivable sin. God did not
destroy those men immediately, but the Holy Spirit stopped
prodding them at that time. Without the prodding of the Holy Spirit
no one can be saved, for it is He who convicts us of sin and leads us
to repentance toward Jesus Christ.

This is totally relevant to our subject, for anyone who attributes
the Rapture of the Church to be the work of Alien beings, is
attributing the work of the Holy Spirit to be the work of devils! So
we see then that the End Times delusion will result in those who
believe the rapture was the work of aliens being lost forever, for the
Holy Spirit will stop convicting them of sin and they will remain
deluded until the coming of Christ Himself. These will be the men
who pick up arms to fight Jesus at his return! A more pitiful army
this world has never seen! They will be slaughtered by a mere Word
from His lips! This is made all the more tragic by the fact that His
shed blood on the cross was sufficient for all men of all time,
including them!

A Strong Delusion

As I said before, there are many facets to the one great
delusion. I can't say that aliens are all there is to it. In fact I
believe the devil has a deception for everyone, no matter
what your background or beliefs. For the Muslim, the Antichrist will
appear as the Imam Mahdi, and the false prophet will appear as the
returned Jesus, or Isa. For the Jew, the Antichrist will pass himself
off as the Messiah, and the false prophet will appear to be Elijah.
For the New Ager, the Buddhist, and the Hindu, the Antichrist will
appear as the embodiment of the Christ Consciousness. For the

Liberal Christian, the Catholic, the Emergent Church, and New Apostolic Reformers, he will appear to be a man of God, and perhaps the returned Christ. Some Christians are so close to the New Age movement, that if he appears as the *"Embodiment of the Christ Consciousness"* many of them will not even bat an eye!

I think it is safe to say that to many secular people and evolutionists, the Antichrist will have to pass himself off as an evolved super-human leader in contact with super-evolved alien beings. To all those that he has deceived he will explain that in order for the human race to evolve to the next level they have to unite as one.

I do not think the Antichrist will necessarily deny the existence of Jesus Christ, but will demote Him to the status of being *"just another alien"*. He will explain that Jesus is actually a hostile alien being, bent on taking over *"Your world"* and enslaving you. When the sign of the Son of Man appears in the heavens (Matthew 24:30), many will be conditioned to believe it is a space ship bringing this *"alien"* back, and that they must unite to fight him! Believers who trust in the shed blood of Jesus Christ to save them will be considered enemies of humanity, and will die in the millions, but be of good cheer! He knows His own and will make it worthwhile for you!

> *Precious in the sight of the LORD is the death of his saints.*
> *(Psalms 116:15)*

So many people have a vague idea of what the Bible teaches about the Tribulation period, that in order to deceive, the devil has to provide a time period so close in many respects, that most will not suspect that it actually hasn't even begun yet. The people the devil is working the hardest to deceive are those with some biblical knowledge. Asaph's war will be considered to have been a Tribulation event, and the battle of Gog and Magog will be perceived as having been Armageddon. Many other events in between these wars will fit in with a general Tribulation scenario, including the destruction of the Harlot church.

Don't be alarmed if the European Union sheds some nations, and ultimately ends up with only ten members. This is not the kingdom of the Antichrist, but a clever decoy. The actual Antichrist's ten nation confederacy will include the entire world, made up of ten regions, or *"super nations"*, not merely Europe. The E.U. may end up with a gay leader from Italy, who insists that everyone in the E.U. must take a biochip in order to buy or sell. If it doesn't include his name or number, and if that number is not 666, it is not the mark of the Beast. If it is limited to Europe, it is not the mark of the beast. If Rome is destroyed in a nuclear blast it will be a tragedy, but it will not be the destruction of Babylon the Harlot of Revelation 17 and/or 18, rather it is preliminary to the creation of that same entity. We have seen that the real Antichrist will come from an area much closer to the holy land, and from a family much closer to the Jewish people, though his background is Arab Muslim, not Jewish.

The left-wing liberals like their prototype, Neville Chamberlain, appear to be about to get us into a World-War with Islam, likely two! I expect there will be a strong right-wing backlash to the left-wing insanity, and it may appear that "*Christians*" are taking over the world! If so, watch-out! You are witnessing the creation of the Antichrist's kingdom!   Using the allegorical method of Bible interpretation, many false teachers will be able to *"prove"* that "*since the Tribulation is past, now is the time to usher in the kingdom of God on earth!*"

> *For when they shall say, Peace and safety; then sudden destruction cometh upon them, as travail upon a woman with child; and they shall not escape.*
>
> *1 Thessalonians 5:3*

References

"Alien Intrusion,UFOs and the Evolution Connection", Bates, Gary,copyright 2004 by Gary Bates, Creation Book Publishers, P.O. Box 350, Powder Springs, GA, 30127 (May 2010)

"UFOs and aliens — is there something going on?" Bates, Gary, Creation Ministries International, CMI–Australia 2003, Accessed 07/05/2010, from http://creation.com/ufos-and-aliensis-there-something-going-on,

"SETI — coming in from the cold of space; Fantasy fuels funding", Bates, Gary, Creation Ministries International, June 2004, Accessed

12/06/2010, from http://creation.com/seticoming-in-from-the-cold-of-space

"SETI—religion or science?", by Catchpoole, David , Creation Ministries International, 18 August 2006, Accessed 25/08/2010, http://creation.com/seti-religion-or-science

"SETI", From Wikipedia, the free encyclopedia, 25 August 2010, Accessed 25/08/2010, http://en.wikipedia.org/wiki/SETI

"Shock and Awe Revisited", Insight for Living broadcast, Apr 12-16, 2007,   Accessed   10/05/2010,   from http://www.insight.org/broadcast/library.html

"May Queen", Answers.com, the world's leading Q & A site, Accessed 02/08/2010, from http://www.answers.com/topic/may-queen-1

"Led Zeppelin IV", From Wikipedia, the free encyclopedia, 24 August 2010,   accessed   27/08/2010,   from http://en.wikipedia.org/wiki/Led_Zeppelin_IV

"The Pentagram and Ram's Head", by Stewart, David J., Accessed 30/08/2010,   http://www.jesus-is-savior.com/False%20Religions/Wicca%20&%20Witchcraft/pentagram.htm

"Who in hell is Krampus?" Pagan Space.net The Meeting Space For The Occult Community, by SIN (pen name), December 10, 2009, accessed   31/08/2010,   from http://www.paganspace.net/forum/topics/who-in-hell-is-krampus?page=2&commentId=1342861%3AComment%3A6531037&x=1#1342861Comment6531037

"Krampustime is Coming", by Hammel, Andrew, German Joys, Nov. 06,   2009,   accessed   31/08/2010, http://andrewhammel.typepad.com/german_joys/2009/11/krampustime-approaches.html

"The May Queen", from *"AMBERGRIS, A SELECTION FROM THE POEMS OF ALEISTER CROWLEY"*, LONDON, ELKIN MATHEWS, VIGO STREEM, MCMX, Copyright (c) Ordo Templi Orientis, JAF Box 7666, New York NY 10116 USA, www.oto.org

"The UFO phenomenon—growing and not going away! Is it the next great challenge for the church?" Bates, Garry, Creation Ministries International, Published: 15 August 2009, Accessed 06/09/2010, http://creation.com/ufo-phenomenon-growing

"Deceiving the Elect - Why Study UFOs?" Alien Resistance Ministries, Accessed   06/09/2010,   from http://alienresistance.com/DeceivingtheElect.htm

"God and the extraterrestrials, Are we alone, or is there life elsewhere in the universe?", by Gitt, Werner, Creation Magazine, Sept. 1997, accessed 06/09/2010, from http://creation.com/god-and-the-extraterrestrials

"WE KNOW WHERE YOU LIVE", Swords, Michael D., Center for UFO Studies, The International UFO Reporter, fall 2002 edition, Accessed 07/09/2010, from http://www.cufos.org/swords2.pdf

"The Present Day UFO-ALIEN ABDUCTION PHENOMENON as interpreted from a Biblical Precedent", by Unruh, J. Timothy, 1996, Accessed 07/09/2010, from http://www.ldolphin.org/unruh/alien/

"The J. Allen Hynek Center For UFO Studies", Accessed 08/09/2010, http://www.cufos.org/"A PRETRIBULATION RAPTURE OF THE CHURCH – DOES THE BIBLE TEACH IT?", Rapture Ready, Accessed 28/09/2010, from http://www.raptureready.com/soap/pretrib.htm

7000 Year Earth Time Allotment (1 Week)

2 Tribulations - 1 False and 1 Real - 14+ years

- Psalm 83; Asaph's War
- Nukes used
- Arabs Defeated;
- Israel Expands
- Someone Signs a Treaty With Israel
- Time of Peace
- Persecution of Christians
- Rest of Israel Returns and Becomes Prosperous
- Temple Construction Begins (Sponsored by E.U.?)
- Natural Disasters and Earthquakes
- Cashless Economy -
- Implantable Bio-Chip
- Push for Unity of Religion Under Rome
- Destruction of Rome; a Decoy Harlot, Probably Using Nukes, during, or shortly before, War of Gog and Magog; A Decoy Armageddon
- Antichrist Confirms the Covenant/Treaty from Asaph's War;
- Bans Polygamy in Arab World & Declared a "Man of God" by Harlot Church
- World Religions United
- Help Antichrist build his Empire
- Apparent Triumph of Christianity
- 2 Witnesses in Jerusalem
- Judgments of God Begin

- Antichrist Dies and is Resurrected
- 2 Witnesses Killed and Resurrected
- Mark of the Beast instituted
- Rapture of Ark of the Covenant
- Abomination of Desolation in Temple
- Rapture of 144,000 Witnesses
- Destruction of Babylon the Harlot
- Appearance of "Alien Beings" in Public
- War of Armageddon
- Removal of Elect in Physical Bodies By God's Angels
- Return of Christ with OT, NT, & Tribulation Saints
- Destruction of Antichrist and World's Armies
- Beginning of Millennial Reign of Christ

Wars & Rumours of War
Approximate 7 Year
False Tribulation Period

Destruction of 3 Antichrists

Rapture of
The Church

Bowl and Trumpet Judgments

The Great Tribulation Period
Seven Years

Creation and the Garden of Eden

The Flood
1500 Years Approx.

Age of Israel

First Coming
of Christ -
4000 - 4033 Years

Church Age Approx 2000 Years
Saints Receive Holy Spirit

False Tribulation
Great Tribulation
2nd Coming of Christ

Millennial Reign
of Christ and
His Saints

Final Rebellion
Destruction of Earth
and Universe
Judgment Day - Lost
Cast into Lake of Fire
**Creation of the
New Earth**

Note: All time placements are approximate. Only God knows the exact time. Only major events are covered.

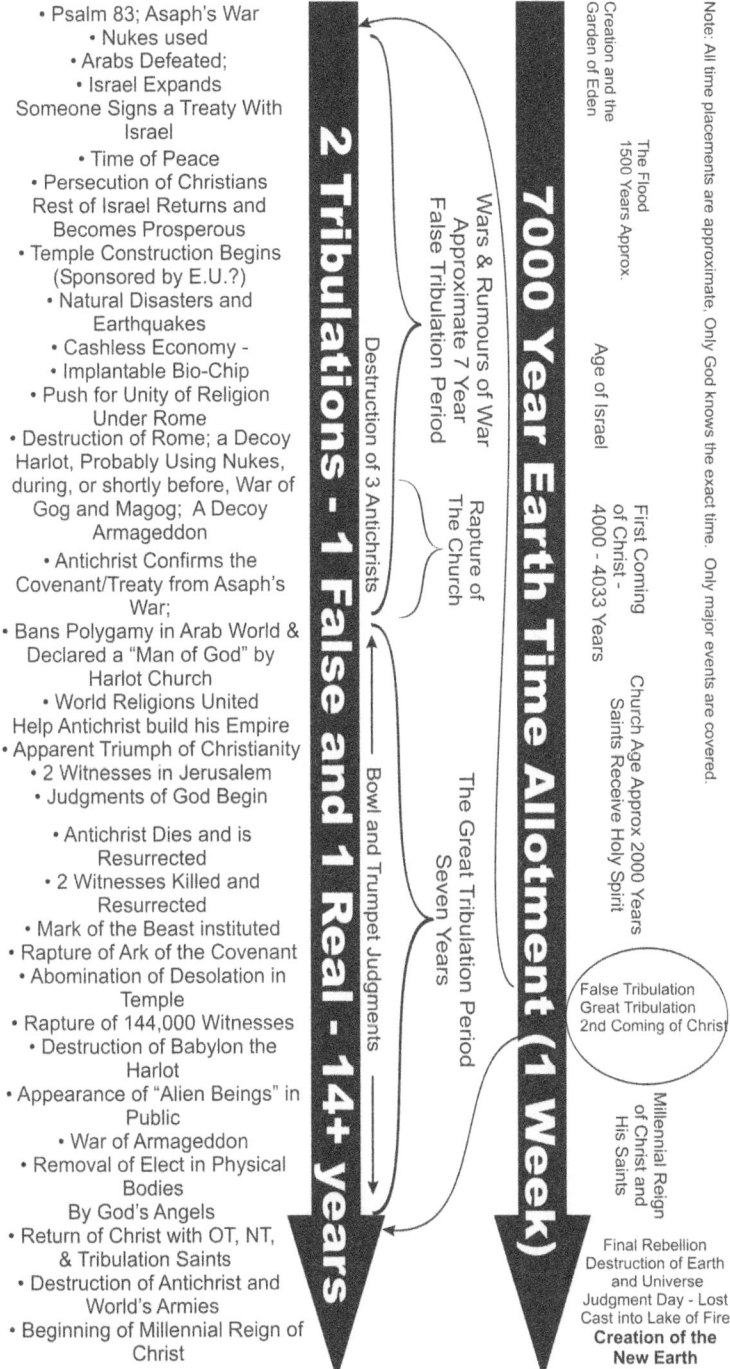

Resources

"A STRONG DELUSION - The New Apostolic Reformation", by McCumber, Mishel, Deception Bytes, Accessed 29/09/2010, from http://www.deceptionbytes.com/content/strong-delusion-new-apostolic-reformation

"A Tale Of Two Cities -TORONTO", Richardson, Neil, Christian Witness Ministries, Accessed 08/08/2010, http://www.christian-witness.org/archives/van1998/alpha2_98.html

"Alpha USA: What Church Leaders Say", Alpha North America website, accessed 08/08/2010, from http://www.alphana.org/Groups/1000047512/What_Church_Leaders.aspx

"Alpha: The Unofficial Guide – Overview", McDonald, Elizabeth and Peterson, Dusty, published by St. Matthew Publishing Ltd., Cambridge, UK (2004)

"Antiochus Epiphanes", George Burnside, Thursday 06, 2007, Accessed 20/11/2009, from www.whitehorsemedia.com/docs/ANTIOCHUS_EPIPHANES.pdf

"Concerned Nazarenes exposing the infiltration of the Emergent Church movement into the Nazarene denomination", accessed 07/08/2010, www.concernednazarenes.org

"Cross + Word", an archive of articles from Banner Ministries by Trish Tillin, Accessed 07/08/2010, www.intotruth.org/misc/alpha.html, Cross + Word, an archive of articles from Banner Ministries by Trish Tillin, Accessed 07/08/2010

"Deceiving the Elect - Why Study UFOs?" Alien Resistance Ministries, Accessed 06/09/2010, from http://alienresistance.com/DeceivingtheElect.htm

"Dispensational View of Theological Order: Why It Offends Covenant Theologians", Clough, Mr. Charles, The Pre-Trib Research Centre, accessed 10/06/2010, http://www.pre-trib.org/articles/view/dispensational-view-of-theological-order-why-it-offends-covenant-theologians

"Do I Interpret the Bible Literally? Seven Tests to See If I Truly Do", Middletown Bible Church, Middletown CT, accessed 05/08/2010, from www.middletownBiblechurch.org/dispen/literal.htm

"Hal Lindsey, Dominion Theology, and Anti-Semitism", Ice, Dr. Thomas, The Pre-Trib Research Center, accessed 03/05/2010, http://www.pre-trib.org/articles/view/hal-lindsey-dominion-theology-and-anti-semitism

"Harpazo: The Scriptural Concept of Rapture", Steward, Tom 27 March 2007, Accessed 28/09/2010, from http://www.raptureready.com/resource/steward/7.htm

"Historical Implications Of Allegorical Interpretation", Ice, Dr. Thomas, The Pre-Trib Research Center, accessed 12/05/2010, http://www.pre-trib.org/articles/view/historical-implications-of-allegorical-interpretation

"How Do You Spell Violence? In the Middle East, its Spelled H-A-M-A-S", The Omega Letter, Jack Kinsella, Friday, June 24, 2005, accessed 11/08/2010, from http://www.omegaletter.com/articles/articles.asp?ArticleID=5567&SearchFor=How_-_do_-_you_-_spell_-_violence_-_H-A-M-A-S

"Important Dates In The Lives Of Jesus And Mary", Conte, Ronald L. Jr., Catholic Planet, Copyright Ronald Conte Jr. 2002-2007, (June 13, 2007), See the book's website at www.BiblicalChronology.com, accessed 19/10/2010

"In The Name of Purpose: Sacrificing Truth on the Altar of Unity", by Tamara Hartzell, 2006, Accessed 25/01/2010, from www.inthenameofpurpose.org/

"Index page of articles about the Alpha Course", Bible Theology Ministries, Accessed 07/08/2010, www.christiandoctrine.net/doctrine/topics/topic_1_web.htm#Alpha%20Course

"Interview with Joel Richardson: The Islamic Antichrist", Larry

Amon, Baltimore Christian Conservative Examiner, Examiner.com, http://www.examiner.com/x-4291-Baltimore-Christian-Conservative-Examiner~y2009m9d21-Interview-with-Joel-Richardson-The-Islamic-Antichrist, accessed 05/08/2010

"Is the way being prepared for the "kings of the east"?" Even at the Doors Blog, March 26, 2009, Accessed 18/09/2010, from http://www.evenatthedoors.com/blog/2009/04/01/is-the-way-being-prepared-for-the-kings-of-the-east/

"Isralestine, the Ancient Blueprints of the Future Middle East", Sallus, Bill, HighWay, A division of Anomalous Publishing House, Crane 65633, 2008

"Land of Israel", Wikipedia, the free encyclopedia, 13 September 2010, accessed 16/09/2010, from http://en.wikipedia.org/wiki/Land_of_Israel

"Literal vs. Allegorical Interpretation", Ice, Dr. Thomas, The Pre-Trib Research Center, accessed 12/05/2010, http://www.pre-trib.org/articles/view/literal-vs-allegorical-interpretation

"Mankind at the Turning Point: The Second Report to the Club of Rome", Mesarovic, Mihajlo, and Pestel, Eduard, Clarke, Irwin and Company, Toronto and Vancouver, 1974

"Nazareth and The Branch, Matthew 2:23 and Interpretation of the Old Testament", CRI/Voice, Institute, by Dennis Bratcher, accessed 02/06/2010, from www.crivoice.org/branch.html

"NET Bible ™ Learning Environment", Gebal", accessed 09/08/2010, from http://net.bible.org/dictionary.php?word=GEBAL

"Noosphere", Wikipedia, the Free Encyclopedia, Accessed 17/08/2010, from http://en.wikipedia.org/wiki/Noosphere

"Norm Geisler Takes "The Shack" to the Wood Shed", Geisler, Norman, Novermer 12, 2008, posted on Christian Wworldview Blog, Accessed 09/10/2010, from http://thechristianworldview.com/tcwblog/archives/934

"Obadiahs Indictment", Jack Kinsella, The Omega Letter, Saturday, November 25, 2006, Accessed 11/08/2010, from

http://www.omegaletter.com/articles/articles.asp?ArticleID=6001&
SearchFor=esau_-_hamas_-_and_-_the_-_last_-_days

"On the Last Times, the Antichrist, and the End of the World
(English)", Ephraem, Mr. Pseudo, The Pre-Trib Research Center,
accesssed 06/05/2010, http://www.pre-trib.org/articles/view/on-
last-times-antichrist-and-end-of-world-english

"Preliminary Critique of Contemporary Amillennialism", Craigen, Dr.
Trevor, The Pre-Trib Research Centre, accessed 10/12/2009,
http://www.pre-trib.org/articles/view/preliminary-critique-of-
contemporary-amillennialism

"Prince of Darkness, Antichrist and the New World Order", Grant
Jeffrey, Frontier Research Publications, Toronto, Ontario, Canada,
1994

"Proposal for Future South Asian Union (SAU)", accessed
17/08/2010, from http://www.southasianunion.net/

"Protection from al-Masih ad-Dajjal", The Dajjal System, accessed
05/08/2010, http://etori.tripod.com/dajjalsystem/protection.html

"Rick Warren Connections, especially to the ecumenical Third Wave
New Apostolic Reformation (NAR) and "Positive Thinking"
Movement" compiled by Sandy Simpson, 1/04 Appologetics
Coordination Team, Accessed 07/08/2010,
www.deceptioninthechurch.com/warrenquotes.html

"The "New Apostolic" Church Movement", Let Us Reason Ministries,
2009, accessed 06/10/2010,
http://www.letusreason.org/Latrain21.htm

"THE "NORMAL LITERAL" METHOD OF THE INTERPRETATION OF
BIBLE PROPHECY", David Cloud, Way of Life Literature, accessed
05/08/2010, from
www.wayoflife.org/files/64cd39027b2e673d1812ef383063e256-
93.html

"The Annals of the World", Ussher, James, Revised and Updated by
Larry and Marion Pierce, copyright 2003 by Larry and Marion
Pierce, sixth printing November 2006, Master Books, Inc. P.O. Box

726, Green Forest, AR 72638

"The Berean Beacon", The website of former Roman Catholic priest Richard Bennet, Accessed 10/02/2010, www.bereanbeacon.org

"The Devil in the Shack", a resource page featuring several articles exposing the errors of "The Shack", accessed 07/08/2010, from http://www.infointersect.com/the_devil_in_the_shack.html,

"The Emerging Church, Revival Or Return To Darkness?" Commentary by Roger Oakland, Roger Oakland, Understand the Times International, Accessed 07/08/2010, from http://www.understandthetimes.org/commentary/c29.shtml

"The Encyclopedia of Creation Science, Gomer", accessed 2/22/2010, http://creationwiki.org/Gomer

"The Encyclopedia of Creation Science, Meshech", accessed 2/22/2010, from http://creationwiki.org/Meshech

"The Israeli Source of the Pathan Tribes", From the book, Lost Tribes from Assyria, by A. Avihail and A. Brin, 1978, in Hebrew, by Issachar Katzir, http://www.dangoor.com/74069.html, Website of the Scribe Magazine, Autumn 2001 Accessed 05/08/2010

"The Jewish Calendar - Structure", Jewish Heritage Online Magazine, Accessed 25/08/2010, http://www.jhorn.com/calendar/structure.html

"The May Queen", from "AMBERGRIS, A SELECTION FROM THE POEMS OF ALEISTER CROWLEY", LONDON, ELKIN MATHEWS, VIGO STREEM, MCMX, Copyright (c) Ordo Templi Orientis, JAF Box 7666, New York NY 10116 USA, www.oto.org

"The Moscow Guide: History", Russian SunSITE, accessed 10/05/2010, from http://redsun.cs.msu.su/moscow/history.html

"The Pink Swastika, Homosexuality in the Nazi Party", by Lively, Scott and Abrams, Kevin E., Published by Veritas Aeterna Press, January, 2002

"The Project Gutenberg EBook of The Lives Of The Twelve Caesars, Complete", Tranquillus, C. Suetonius, Release Date: October 22,

2006 [EBook #6400], Accessed 02/20/2010, found at http://www.gutenberg.org/files/6400/6400-h/6400-h.htm

"The Prophecy That Is Shaping History: New Research on Ezekiels Vision of the End." Ruthven, Jon, PhD, and Griess, Ihab, PhD, Fairfax, VA: Xulon Press, 2003

"The Purpose Driven Life", Warren, Rick, Copyright 2002 by Rick Warren, Zondervan Books, Grand Rapids, Michigan 49530

"The Rapture in Pseudo-Ephraem", Ice, Dr. Thomas, The Pre-Trib Research Center, accesssed 06/05/2010, http://www.pre-trib.org/articles/view/rapture-in-pseudo-ephraem

"The Serious Problems with Rick Warrens Purpose Driven Movement", Lighthouse Trails Research Project, Accessed 07/08/2010, www.lighthousetrailsresearch.com/warren.htm,

"THE SHACK: Exposing The Deception", Spiritual Research Network, a discernment ministry, accessed 07/08/2010, http://www.spiritual-research-network.com/theshack.html

"The Shack, Where Tragedy Confronts Eternity", Young, Wm. Paul, 2007, Windblown Media, 4680 Calle Norte, Newbury Park, CA 91320

"The Toronto Blessing", by Needham, Dr Nick, Orthodox Christian Information Center, Accessed 14/09/2010, from http://www.orthodoxinfo.com/inquirers/toronto.aspx

"The Unscriptural Theologies Of Amillennialism And Postmillennialism", Ice, Dr. Thomas, The Pre-Trib Research Center, accesssed 29/04/2010, http://www.pre-trib.org/articles/view/unscriptural-theologies-of-amillennialism-and-postmillennialism

"UFOs and aliens, is there something going on?" Bates, Gary, Creation Ministries International, CMI–Australia 2003, Accessed 07/05/2010, from http://creation.com/ufos-and-aliensis-there-something-going-on,

"Websters Integrated Dictionary and Thesaurus", Geddes & Grosset, 2006, David Dale House, New Lanark ML11 9DJ, Scotland

"What is a Christian Fundamentalist?, Modified and expanded by Craig Ledbetter from an article by David Cloud". Bible Baptist Church, Ballincollig, Cork, Ireland, www.Biblebc.com/Christian_Helps/what_is_a_christian_fundament ali.htm, accessed 05/08/2010

"What is the Identity of Babylon In Revelation 17-18?" Woods, Mr. Andy, The Pre-Trib Research Center, accesssed 11/04/2010, http://www.pre-trib.org/articles/view/what-is-identity-of-babylon-in-revelation-17-18

"A Time of Departing" by Ray Yungen, STL Distribution North America, 2 edition (April 15 2006)

"A Wonderful Deception: The Further New Age Implications of the Emerging Purpose Driven Movement" by Warren Smith, Published by Lighthouse Trails Publishing, Silverton, Oregon (July 2009)

"Alien Intrusion,UFOs and the Evolution Connection", Bates, Gary,copyright 2004 by Gary Bates, Creation Book Publishers, P.O. Box 350, Powder Springs, GA, 30127 (May 2010)

"Faith Undone: The Emerging Church: A New Reformation Or An End-Time Deception?" by Roger Oakland, Lighthouse Trails Publishing, Silverton, Oregon, (August 2007)

"God and the extraterrestrials, Are we alone, or is there life elsewhere in the universe?", by Gitt, Werner, Creation Magazine, Sept. 1997, accessed 06/09/2010, from http://creation.com/god-and-the-extraterrestrials

"Important Dates In The Lives Of Jesus And Mary", Conte, Ronald L. Jr., Catholic Planet, Copyright Ronald Conte Jr. 2002-2007, (June 13, 2007)

"In Gods Name" by Yallop, David, Carroll and Graff Publishers 245 W 17th, St., 11th floor, New York, New York 10011-5300, Published in the UK by Jonathan Cape Ltd. (1984)

"Krampustime is Coming", by Hammel, Andrew, German Joys, Nov. 06, 2009, accessed 31/08/2010, http://andrewhammel.typepad.com/german_joys/2009/11/krampu

stime-approaches.html

"Led Zeppelin IV", From Wikipedia, the free encyclopedia, 24 August 2010, accessed 27/08/2010, from http://en.wikipedia.org/wiki/Led_Zeppelin_IV

"May Queen", Answers.com, the worlds leading Q & A site, Accessed 02/08/2010, from http://www.answers.com/topic/may-queen-1

"SETI, coming in from the cold of space; Fantasy fuels funding", Bates, Gary, Creation Ministries International, June 2004, Accessed 12/06/2010, from http://creation.com/seticoming-in-from-the-cold-of-space

"SETI; religion or science?", by Catchpoole, David , Creation Ministries International, 18 August 2006, Accessed 25/08/2010, http://creation.com/seti-religion-or-science

"SETI", From Wikipedia, the free encyclopedia, 25 August 2010, Accessed 25/08/2010, http://en.wikipedia.org/wiki/SETI

"Shock and Awe Revisited", Insight for Living broadcast, Apr 12-16, 2007, Accessed 10/05/2010, from http://www.insight.org/broadcast/library.html

"The J. Allen Hynek Center For UFO Studies", Accessed 08/09/2010, http://www.cufos.org/

"The New Age of Alpha", by Dusty Peterson, 2009, Accessed 18/03/2010, from http://www.users.globalnet.co.uk/~emcd/TheNewAgeOfAlpha.pdf

"The Pentagram and Rams Head", by Stewart, David J., Accessed 30/08/2010, http://www.jesus-is-savior.com/False%20Religions/Wicca%20&%20Witchcraft/pentagram.htm

"The Present Day UFO-ALIEN ABDUCTION PHENOMENON as interpreted from a Biblical Precedent", by Unruh, J. Timothy, 1996, Accessed 07/09/2010, from http://www.ldolphin.org/unruh/alien/

"The UFO phenomenon, growing and not going away! Is it the next great challenge for the church?" Bates, Garry, Creation Ministries

International, Published: 15 August 2009, Accessed 06/09/2010, http://creation.com/ufo-phenomenon-growing

"Tithing: Low-Realm, Obsolete & Defunct"   by Matthew E. Narramore, Tekoa Publishing (May 2004)

"WE KNOW WHERE YOU LIVE", Swords, Michael D., Center for UFO Studies, The International UFO Reporter, fall 2002 edition, Accessed 07/09/2010, from http://www.cufos.org/swords2.pdf

"Who in hell is Krampus?" Pagan Space.net The Meeting Space For The Occult Community, by SIN (pen name), December 10, 2009, accessed   31/08/2010,   from http://www.paganspace.net/forum/topics/who-in-hell-is-krampus?page=2&commentId=1342861%3AComment%3A6531037&x=1#1342861Comment6531037

"Whos Driving the Purpose Driven Church?: A Documentary on the Teachings of Rick Warren" by James Sundquist, Bible Belt Publishing, (January 2004)

A Readers Review of The Shack, Challies, Tim, Tue 20 May 2008, Accessed   07/10/2010,   from   http://www.challies.com/book-reviews/a-review-of-the-shack-download-it-here

The Pre-Trib Research Center website, Special thanks to Liberty University for making this resource available free of charge. http://www.pre-trib.org/articles,

Antiochus IV Epiphanes   [ca. 215 -164 BCE], Smith, Mahlon H., Accessed   24/09/2010,   from http://virtualreligion.net/iho/antiochus_4.html

Douma, M., curator. (2008). The Jewish Calendar. In Calendars through   the   Ages.   Retrieved   08/24/2010,   from http://www.webexhibits.org/calendars/calendar-jewish.html, Calendars Through the Ages

Eric Bargers "Take a Stand Ministries", a discernment ministry featuring articles exposing the New Age infiltration into the Christian Church, accessed 07/08/2010, www.ericbarger.com

Jan Markells Olive Tree Ministries website, featuring articles and radio .mp3 downloads on prophecy related topics, Accessed 07/08/2010, www.olivetreeviews.org

Josephus: The Complete Works, Sword module version 1.1, Josephus: The Complete Works, translated by William Whiston, public domain

Movie Documentary: "Quest for the Lost Tribes", Simcha Jacobovici, A&E Home Video, July 29, 2008

Online Book: "HIDDEN SECRETS OF THE ALPHA COURSE ~The dark agenda behind Alpha~" John D. Christian, Published by Underground Press, New Zealand, First published in New Zealand, April 2005, http://www.scribd.com/doc/15118047/Hidden-Secrets-of-the-Alpha-Course

The Truth about Barack Hussein Obama, Video series by Usama Dakdok, 2008, accessed 29/09/2010, http://www.thestraightway.org/revealingtruthab.php

The Use of the Old Testament in the Book of Revelation, Dr. Arnold Fruchtenbaum, The Pre-Trib Research Center, Mon 03 Dec 2007, Accessed 15/03/2009, http://www.pre-trib.org/articles/view/use-of-old-testament-in-book-revelation

The website of Southwest Radio Church Ministries, a discernment resource since 1933, accessed 07/08/2010, http://www.swrc.com

Thirteen Heresies in The Shack", Youssef, Dr. Michael, Accessed 09/10/2010, from http://www.leadingtheway.org/site/PageServer?pagename=sto_Th eShack_13heresies

Xiphos Bible Software, available free of charge, from www.xiphos.org

<u>Scripture References</u>

1 Chronicles
3:5,310
5:10-12,141
5:19,141

1 Corinthians
1:2,121
1:23,126
2:9,212
2:11,20
2:14,11,34
3:11,114
5:6 & 7,101
6:16,312
6:9,318
7:10 & 11,314
7:12,286
7:12-15,317
7:20,316
7:20, 24,286
7:3,318
7:36,313
7:36,317
11:24,17
14:37,101
15:20,67
15:50,211
15:51 & 52,64
16:2,115

1 John
1:5,340
2:18,95
4:1,11,83,97,126
4:8,110

1 Kings
9:26,167
11:4,311

14:24,318
15:12,318
15:5,311
22:46,318

1 Peter
1:16,114
3:22,226

1 Samuel
1:10-14,277
1:5-8,277
13:14,286,288,291
15,143
15:7,142

1 Thessalonians
2:1-12,175
3:13,65
4:16,64
4:16-18,56
4:17,57
5:1-6,40
5:3,170,155,335,344
5:9,56

1 Timothy
3:12,285,312
3:2,285,312
4:1,83
4:1-3,265,283,319
6:10,280
6:12,176

2 Chronicles
13:17,266,283,301
20,143

2 Corinthians

4:4,226
6:14,314
6:2,92,187
10:3-5,176
11:13-15,265,283
14:18-19,98

2 John
1:10,111

2 Kings
4:14-17,278
4:27-28,278
23:7,318

2 Peter
3:3-13,45
3:3, 4, 8,227
3:8,229
3:10,186

2 Samuel
12:1-14,309
16:21-22,310
20:3,310

2 Thessalonians
2:1 & 3,83
2:3,126

2 Timothy
2:15,19,23
2:3,176
3:16,9,19,34, 101,
110,293
3:16 & 17,106
3:5,210
4:3,83,110,126
4:7,176

Acts
1:7,46
1:9,46
1:22,72
1:6-7,217
1:7,231
1:11,47,173
3:22,303
4:10-12,120
4:12,259,262
7:55 & 56,112
13:22,286,288,291
17:11,7,11,19,106
17:2,13,19
17:29,125
17:30,101
22:28,2,234

Amos
1:7-8,144
1:11,250
1:13-15,253
3:3,339
3:7,41
9:12,251,268

Colossians
3:1,226

Daniel
1:2,208
2,3,171
2:31-45,48-49
2:35,203
2:45,31
3:2521
7,179-181
7:23-24,32
7:25,61
7:7-8,31

7:8,245
7:8 & 24,169
7:9-11,29
8,3
8:21-24,30
8:25,31
8:8-9,30
9:24-27,54,84
9:25 & 26,305
9:26,2,234,,237
9:27,153,246
11:21,260
11:23,240,241
11:36,245
11:36-37,273
11:37,2,5,205,234,2
62,272,279,280
11:41,241
12:9,57

Deuteronomy
4:2,213,294
4:27 & 28,79
11:24,76,159,162
13:1-3,218
18:15,303
18:22,152,154,217
18:9-14,49
20:7,298
21:10-13,298
21:10-17,297
21:15-17,255
22:22-29,292
22:26,294
22:28 & 29,294,319
23:17,318
24:1,292
24:5,298
25:5-10,295
28:36,79
28:64,80

32:21,58,305
33:2,257

Ephesians
1:1,121
1:20,226
1:5,21
4:6,117
4:14,110
4:15-16,120
5:33,313
6:12-17,177

Exodus
17,143
20:4,124,127
21:10,288,312,316,
319
21:7-11,302
22:16,294,316
22:18,49
24:4,291
34,108
40:16,291

Ezekiel
4:5,18
9:9,182
11:17,182
13:22,113
14:13,182
25:12 - 14,245
25:13,166
26:3,181
27:13,164
27:9,141
28:13,335
28:13 – 19,29
29:9,159
30,147

30:1-19,145
34:5 & 6,203
35:1-15,244
35:2-7,147
35:8,251
36:22 & 32,86
37:11-12,78
37:16-22,78
38,156-158
38 & 39,156-
158,202
38:13,246
38:20,197
38:20-22,40
38:8 and 11,163
39:1-4,168
39:1-2,279
39:11,169
39:11-12,173
39:2,173
39:6,171
39:9-10,171
47:18,161

Galatians
1:8-9,97
3:24,19
4:5,21
5:9,93
5:9,101,191

Genesis
1:20,70
2:16,15
2:24,288,289
3:16,274
5:24,90
6:2 & 4,21
6:3,43
7:12,108

10:10,208
11:2,208
12:3,150
15:18,64,158
16:1-4,275
19:30-38,276
22:7 & 8,24
25:15,141
25:21,275
25:23,237,256
25:30,258
30:1-3,275
30:22 & 23,275
32:3 & 4,257
33:8-10,258
37:22,307
38:11-30,276
40:12,18

Habakkuk
3:6,203

Hebrews
1:13 & 14,29
1:3, 10:12,112
10:10,112
10:12-13,226
10:4,223
11:5,90

Hosea
2:16,333
3:4-5,77
5:15-6:3,46,229,231

5:15-6:2,64
6:6,309
9:10,42
13:13,63

Isaiah

3-4,271
3:24-4:3,267,268
5:20,122
6:3,231
11:1-9,219
11:12-13,75
11:4,210,218
12:12 & 13,76
13:12,270
13:21,209
13:8,63
14:12,29
14:14,265,285
16:14,241
17,142
17:1,167,202
17:12 & 13,181
19:17-22,146
19:18,158
19:23,152
19:23 - 25,220
21:11-13,167
23:13,207
26:17 - 21,62
26:20,68
27:11,93
27:12-13,64
27:13,65
29:9-10,99
30:30-31,206
34:1-14,242
34:14,209
34:5,233
34:8,137
36:21-24,221
4:1,269,279,280,31
9
45:18,301
46:3-4,110
48:9,86
49:19-20,144